I do hope you e ,
reading this !
        But wishes
            Stephen
    EASTER 2010

DISSENT
IN ALTRINCHAM

RELIGION, POLITICS AND A TOUCH
OF SCANDAL 1870-1905

BY STEPHEN BIRCHALL

AuthorHouse™ UK Ltd.
500 Avebury Boulevard
Central Milton Keynes, MK9 2BE
www.authorhouse.co.uk
Phone: 08001974150

First published by AuthorHouse 18/01/2010

ISBN: 978-1-4490-6950-6 (sc)

This book is printed on acid-free paper.

ABOUT THE AUTHOR

Stephen Birchall read history and then law at Gonville and Caius College, Cambridge. He lives in Altrincham with his wife, Judy, and has three children. He plays keyboards in an amateur rock band and enjoys canal boating and croquet. He has been a governor of a local school and is chair of City Light Trust, a charity working principally in Salford. He is the author of a book which advised churches on compliance with the Disability Discrimination Act.

Stephen has been involved with churches of many different denominations over the years. He had a career choice of being a history lecturer or a lawyer and chose the latter, but his interest in history has continued unabated.

Dedication

To my father Dennis Birchall, who has been an inspiration to me, and who I wish could have lived to read this book.

Note to the reader

I could have written this book primarily as a source book for local and church historians. There is much original material here, which I hope those readers with a specialist interest will find useful. However, I wanted to make the book readable (and enjoyable) for a wider audience, hence the style of some of the chapters and the use of separate inset sections. I also wanted to paint a picture of a group of people in their social, political, cultural and religious context. I hope therefore that this is not just an ordinary history, but an attempt to understand those people and the forces and passions that drove them.

Above all, I want you to feel and understand what it was like to live in Altrincham at the time.

I hope you enjoy reading this book as much as I have enjoyed writing it.

An election cart in Altrincham, promoting Jacob Bowland as a Liberal Party candidate in local elections.

CONTENTS

INTRODUCTION

On a cold, frosty December morning in 1878, a group of people gathered at the edge of an Altrincham field. After a brief ceremony, they hurried down the road to hear speeches in a nearby building.

One of these people was one of the most famous preachers of his time, and his visit showed the importance he attached to the project. For the others, this was both a beginning and the culmination of six years' hard work. They were ordinary men and women of passion, courage and vision, but in their enthusiasm they made mistakes that were to have huge repercussions.

As you follow their story, you will see how closely connected it is with much of culture and life in Altrincham and the wider world. This is a story of heroism and sacrifice mixed with drama. You will see a church split, a church bankruptcy, ministers of Altrincham churches refusing to pay their rates, demonstrations by the clergy and the Victorian equivalent of a modern multi-millionaire giving everything up to live in the slums of Manchester.

This is a work of history of course. Some of the issues which concerned those Victorians and early Edwardians may indeed seem strange to us, but what they did and what they believed continues to affect us all, whatever our beliefs. Some of the cultural problems and issues they faced are just as relevant today as they were then.

We will ask whether William Llewellyn was foolhardy. You will have to decide whether Henry Mowbray was a hero or (as he has been portrayed) a villain, or perhaps just a man doing his best in difficult times. You will visit Jamaica and look at the abolition of slavery and its Altrincham connection. You will look at theology and politics in Altrincham. Was Cowell Lloyd one of the great people of Altrincham whose story has not until now been fully told?

On the way, you will pause to look at other churches and people of influence. The names of McLaren, Spurgeon, Crossley, Smith, MacKennal and Collier will become familiar to you, but this is above all the story of ordinary men and women doing extraordinary things. Local families who have not featured elsewhere in the story of Altrincham will now appear.

These people, many of them so very poor, have all left their imprint on the Altrincham of today. It is by understanding our past that we can look with confidence to the future. We all have a shared heritage, and this is not just a book about one church, but about those around them and the society, culture and politics of that most interesting of towns: Altrincham.

FINDING YOUR WAY AROUND ALTRINCHAM

At the end of this book are some technical notes about such matters as changing names and spellings of churches, roads and people, prices and other matters.

If you are the sort of person who likes to know where things are or were, the map on the facing page shows the location of some of the key places and events covered by the book. It shows the Altrincham of around 1878, but looks both forwards and back from then. It is not to scale.

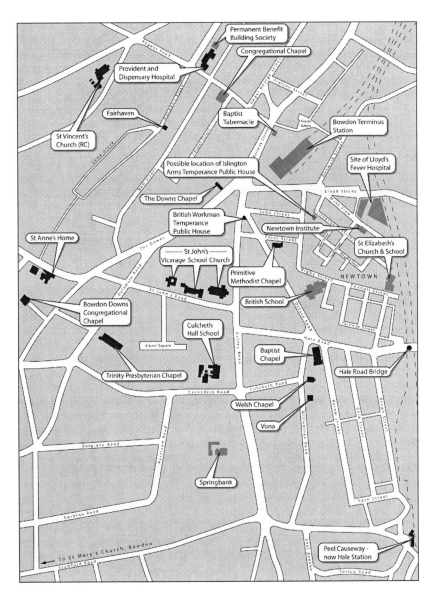

Simplified map based on the 1878 OS Map showing the boundaries of Bowdon, Dunham Massey, Hale and Altrincham.

PERSECUTION

Imagine you live in a country where you can be imprisoned for attending a religious service which is not in a set form laid down by the State. Your minister or priest has been sent to prison because he refused to take a solemn oath binding him to agree never to try and change the government. You yourself are denied higher education because you do not follow the State religion.

That country was once Britain. It is a sobering thought to realise that much of our modern tolerant society (and indeed the toleration found in many countries) comes from the fight for the freedom to worship without interference. So where did this persecution come from?

Much of it began with the restoration of the monarchy in 1662 after the English Civil War. There were high hopes for a new era of co-operation and toleration in a re-united society. This was not to be. Almost immediately, those who would not submit to the new *Book of Common Prayer*, with its novel ways of worship and theology, were often quite literally thrown out of the Church of England. These people became known as 'Dissenters' or 'Nonconformists' because they 'dissented' from, and did not want to 'conform' to, these Church of England rites.

This happened in Bowdon parish in the Altrincham area too. Adam Martindale had to seek asylum at Dunham after he was ejected from Rostherne Chapel. In 1663, the Bishop of Chester increased the pressure and preached fiercely against Nonconformists at Bowdon.

You might think these Nonconformists were some small sectarian group. They were not. They comprised nearly all the Christian denominations in England, except for the Church of England and Roman Catholic Church. They included Baptists, Congregationalists, Huguenots, Presbyterians and Quakers. There is an argument for saying that the Methodists became Nonconformists in 1748. Combined together, these denominations claimed to exceed the Church of England numerically by the beginning of the twentieth century.

When they were forced out of the Church of England, these groups met in what they called 'chapels' and not churches. The word 'chapel' was used deliberately: to them, the church was the people and not any building.[1]

The persecution eventually moderated to discrimination, but by the time the story of this book starts, there was still legal discrimination against Nonconformists. The comparatively tolerant society we now live in is, in historical terms, a recent invention. It owes much of its existence to this fight for freedom by the Nonconformists.

So we now look at the denomination which the Nonconformists left or were forced out of: the Church of England.

---

[1] The word 'ecclesia' in the New Testament always refers to an assembly of people and not to the building in which they meet.

THE CHURCH OF ENGLAND

Even in the reign of Victoria, the Church of England had ambivalent attitudes to the Nonconformists. In 1875 the local newspaper in Altrincham reported legal opinion which said that Anglican clergy should not preach in Nonconformist pulpits, and that the Bishop of Lincoln refused to allow 'Reverend' on the gravestone of a Methodist minister.

Although they had left it, or been evicted from it - what happened in and to the Church of England was of great interest to Nonconformists; indeed, much of their own theological development in the Victorian era can be perceived as a reaction to theological changes in the Church of England.

So let us start with what at first sight appears to be a startling proposition: the Church of England today is substantially a Victorian creation, from its buildings to many of its practices.

At the start of Victoria's reign, the Church of England was what we might call 'low church' or 'broad church' in its style of worship and theological emphasis. This meant that there was little use of ritual or symbolism. The style was in many respects not too far removed from that of some Nonconformists.

What we call the 'Oxford Movement' and the 'Ritualists' began a quest for a different style of worship and theology within the Church of England. The first generation of the Oxford Movement – Newman, Pusey and Keble – would still have felt comparatively 'broad church'. They were more concerned with theological issues. It was the later generation that adopted new customs. Ritualist clergy began to copy Roman Catholic clergy by facing east at the communion table during part of the service, rather than standing at the north end. Some wore coloured outer garments, just as did Roman Catholic priests. They began to light candles. Their parishioners were encouraged to think of them as priests rather than vicars and they wore special collars. They preferred to be called 'Father', an epithet in fact later copied by Roman Catholics. Even in Altrincham in 1874, there was correspondence in the local newspaper about precisely where at the communion table a vicar should stand.

These new rituals, with their sense of theatre, occasion and mystery, were often popular in the poorer parishes. They were controversial too. The introduction of new elements of ritual would bring hissing or walkouts, and in some cases riots. In 1877 the Bishop of Manchester spoke at a meeting for the 'Suppression of Ritualism'. However, much of what the Ritualists introduced in the way of ritual, although not necessarily theology, came in time to be accepted as normal, even in evangelical parishes. Most Church of England churches would now, for example, use candles in some form in their services.

Queen Victoria herself disapproved of the Ritualists. She saw them as a movement to make the Anglican Church become Roman Catholic. When in Balmoral, Victoria appeared comfortable attending the local Presbyterian church. When Alexander MacKennal of Bowdon Downs Congregational Church came in his capacity as President of the Congregational Union to give his loyal address to celebrate Victoria's golden jubilee, she stood up to listen to his speech. This was regarded as significant as she had stayed seated for everyone else before him.

A legislative attempt was even made to control some Ritualist practices by the passing of the Public Worship Regulation Act of 1874. Five clergymen were imprisoned for refusing to obey, the longest sentence being served by Sidney Green of St John's Church, Miles Platting, in Manchester. The Act was eventually repealed, but it gave the Ritualists their martyrs and an increased sense of purpose.

The Ritualists were not, however, just after changing style and symbols; there was an underlying theological agenda. There were increasing tensions between liberals and evangelicals in general and between Ritualists and evangelicals within the Church of England. At the start of the Victorian era, the Church of England's 'Thirty-Nine Articles' of faith at the back of the *Book of Common Prayer* were widely supported, but by the end of Victoria's reign, many found they could not agree with all of them.

Many Nonconformists backed the 1874 Act, even though it concerned a different denomination. In a strange way, perhaps they felt that they were now the real guardians of the true, Bible-based faith in Great Britain: the true church as the Church of England slipped, as they saw it, towards Rome and a denial of the authority of Scripture.

The Church of England still had its solid evangelical section though, the spiritual heirs of Wilberforce. Often they were members of the Church Association and were prepared to work with the Nonconformists, as happened in Altrincham. The Revd A.W. Thorold, the future Bishop of Winchester, is quoted as saying in 1868 that the Church of England evangelicals were engaged in campaigns against such things as 'rationalistic and Romish aggression'.[1]

> In 1882, outside London, nine Church of England churches used incense, 336 used vestments and 1,662 used the eastward position at the altar. By 1901, the number has increased dramatically to 393 using incense, 2,158 vestments and 7,397 the eastward position at the altar.[2]

So having looked briefly at the changes and stresses within the Church of England nationally, we will now look at the Church of England in Altrincham itself.

---

[1] Quoted in James, Lawrence: *The Middle Class: A History*, Little, Brown, 2006.
[2] Quoted in Wilson, A.N.: *The Victorians*, W. W. Norton & Company Limited, 2003

THE CHURCH OF ENGLAND IN ALTRINCHAM

The Church of England expanded rapidly in Victorian England. In Altrincham, new churches were built to cope with immigration following the arrival of the railway in 1849. Altrincham had a population of 2,708 in 1831; but by 1901 it numbered 16,831 – a six-fold increase in seventy years.[1]

Altrincham is, in fact, part of the much larger parish of Bowdon. The parish once extended far beyond its current boundaries.[2] When Victoria came to the throne, there was Bowdon Parish Church and St George's Church in what we would now regard as the Altrincham area. By the time of her death, the number of Church of England churches in Altrincham, Bowdon, Hale and Dunham Massey had at least quadrupled.

Local readers will be familiar with the sight of these churches, but let us look at them briefly in historical terms.

St George's Church was founded in 1799 and mostly rebuilt in 1897. It was what was called a 'chapel of ease'. The idea was that it would 'ease' local residents from having to make the journey to the more distant Bowdon Parish Church to take communion. The Revd Oswald Leicester was the first vicar of St George's and quite a character. He was the son of an Altrincham shopkeeper and much influenced by the Methodists. Reputedly he sent his evening congregation to the local Methodist Chapel.

St John's Church, Altrincham, is only 200 yards from Hale Road Baptist Church. It was consecrated on 14 December 1866 and was a church plant of Bowdon Parish Church. In 1879 it was said to be 'the poor man's church'.[3] In 1877, for example, Sunday evening services were aimed exclusively at issues faced by working men. The vicar, Canon Wainwright, was the most likely to co-operate with the Nonconformists in the area, often appearing on joint platforms.

In 1876 St John's Church set up St John's Infant School on land donated by the Earl of Stamford at Islington Street in the Newtown district of Altrincham.[4] The wealthy William Crossley later funded the purchase of houses on Pownall Street and Islington Street to extend the site. St Elizabeth's Mission Church was then constructed to serve what was one of the poorest areas of Altrincham.

St Luke's in Bowdon Vale was a further part of the general Anglican expansion. It first met in a house in Priory Street in 1871 and the church was built as a mission church in 1880.[5]

In November 1900 St Alban's Church was opened in Broadheath and was also initially a mission church. It succeeded an earlier school church and a canal boat mission.

---

[1] In the same period Bowdon grew from having 458 inhabitants to 2,788, Hale from 942 to 4,562 and Dunham Massey from 1,105 to 2,644.
[2] It included Agden, Ashley, Baguley, Bollington, Carrington, Dunham Massey, Hale, Hale Barns, Oldfield Brow, Partington, Ringway and Timperley. As new churches were planted, so new parishes came into existence, carved out of the original Bowdon parish.
[3] Ingham, Alfred: A History of Altrincham & Bowdon with an account of the Barony and House of Dunham, 1879.
[4] Much of Newtown has been replaced by modern social housing, a supermarket and a car park. It lies between Hale Road and Lloyd Street.
[5] Ridgway, Maurice H.: The Story of Bowdon Vale - St Luke's Church 1880-1980.

St Margaret's Church, Dunham Massey, was completed in 1855 and was built as the parish church for a new area where the housing was still to be constructed. All Saints' Church off Regent Road was in turn a branch of St Margaret's.

This more than quadrupling in numbers in less than forty years still leaves out a number of Church of England mission churches in Dunham Town and Lower Houses (now part of Oldfield Brow), and a Congregational chapel which became St Margaret's.

None of these were empty churches. The Victorian Anglicans fully expected to fill all the new churches they built.

The Ritualist movement certainly affected Altrincham. Even St John's, one of the least Ritualist churches, found itself the subject of a complaint in the local newspapers when it installed a reredos,[6] seen as a manifestation of Ritualism. Letters to newspapers complained about Ritualist forces in Altrincham.

The Church of England in Altrincham today has much of its foundation in its Victorian past, both in its buildings and its worship. What we have to understand is that religion and religious activity pervaded Victorian life much more than they do now. In order therefore to better understand society in late Victorian Altrincham, we also need to understand the other religious groups and how they related (or in some cases didn't relate) together.

Even Bowdon Parish Church is Victorian. There may have been a Saxon church, but the Normans replaced it. Their church was then replaced in the fourteenth century. When that church was in need of repair and extension, it was demolished and reconstructed in 1858-60 as a simulation of an older church. The architect George Gilbert Scott advised in favour of repair but the vicar, the Revd Pollock (probably influenced by some of the richer parishioners), insisted on a new building. The Manchester architect W. H. Brakspear designed the new church.[7] The photograph above shows the church in 1859 before demolition and subsequent reconstruction.

---

[6] A reredos is an ornamental wall or screen at the back of the high altar.
[7] Ridgway, Maurice H.: A Short Guide to The Parish Church of St Mary Virgin, Bowdon.

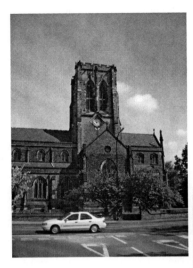

St Margaret's Church, Dunham Massey, as it is today without its spire, and as it was in 1902. The spire was visible for miles around.

St Margaret's has a colourful history. There is a theory that the Earl of Stamford might have financed the church because of disapproval by the congregation of Bowdon Parish Church of his second marriage, although sadly the dates do not quite fit the theory, and the 'distance' between Bowdon Parish Church and the earl probably started with his first marriage. While at Cambridge, the earl enjoyed the company of Elizabeth Billage, the daughter of his servant, and he eloped to Brighton to marry her. She died in 1854 and he then married Kitty Cocks, a lady who had been a horse-riding performer in a circus. This did not endear him to the parishioners of Bowdon Parish Church.

St Margaret's was probably named after the earl's sister, Margaret Henrietta Maria Millbank, who died during the church's construction.[8]

The earl built St Margaret's to serve a wealthy parish which he created by selling off land and placing covenants on the land titles which only allowed expensive houses to be constructed.

[8] See Bamford, Frank: *Mansions and Men of Dunham Massey: From Errant Earl to Red Dean*, 1991

Ringway Chapel, on the edge of the parish of Bowdon, was a source of dispute in the seventeenth and eighteenth centuries. The congregation defected from the Church of England to the Nonconformists, but in 1722 local landowner John Crewe and his followers turned up at a service, dragged the hapless preacher Mr Warburton from the pulpit, and evicted the congregation.[9]

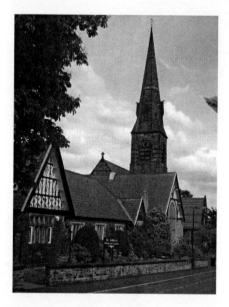

St John's Church, shown above, built to serve the poorer areas of Altrincham. The building was designed by J. Medland Taylor.

Wainwright Road in Altrincham, named after the once famous Canon Wainwright of St John's.

---

[9] It is estimated that the congregation numbered about 400 at the time. For further reading, see Groves, Jill: 'The Fight Over Ringway Chapel 1640-1721: Religion and politics in a Cheshire township', in *Open History Special Conference Edition Religion*, 2007.

The former Pownall Road Day Care Centre now stands on the site of St Elizabeth's Mission Church and the former St John's Infant School.

Left is St Elizabeth's church in 1965

St Peter's Church in Hale has a railway connection. The meeting to establish whether there was interest in a new church in Hale was held in the rather unusual location of the Hale railway station waiting room. The new church first met in a house on 4 July 1889. The building itself was consecrated in 1892 and its foundation stone was from the old Bowdon railway station.

So we turn to a denomination in Altrincham which never originally intended to be one.

THE METHODISTS

The Wesleys and George Whitfield never intended to leave the Church of England. By 1872 however, the Methodists had split into several denominations and were themselves technically Nonconformists. It has been said that Methodism was instrumental in preventing in Britain the sort of revolutions that happened in the rest of Europe, particularly in 1789 and 1848.

The Methodists were controversial and certainly lived up to their reputation in Altrincham. John Wesley first ventured into the town itself in 1761. The meeting was so packed that he could not at first get into the chapel. His last visit to Altrincham was in 1790 when he was eighty-seven. He recorded in his journal that he hoped the people of Altrincham on this visit would be less 'furious' than they had previously been.

In fact Wesley had first visited the area surrounding Altrincham much earlier in 1738 when he preached at Booth Bank Farm in nearby Millington. There he met a Quaker who, he recorded, was 'as I soon found, sufficiently fond of controversy'. In 1745, he took an early morning service under the shade of a pear tree in the orchard of a Mr Priestner at Oldfield Brow. He preached again in 1747 to a much larger congregation at Oldfield Brow.

The farm at Booth Bank soon became a church and then the parent church of the Altrincham Methodist churches. The first Methodist chapel in Altrincham itself was built on Regent Road in 1788. In 1866 it relocated to Bank Street.

In Bowdon, the Methodists first met in houses. In 1856 they built a chapel at Bell Field between Stamford Road and Rose Hill. They held many missions in the area. In Bowdon Vale, they had a mission at Primrose Cottages until 1833, and from this they built a chapel on Vicarage Lane. In 1880 they finished building St Paul's Wesleyan Chapel, a huge building which was also called the 'Dome', on Enville Road in Bowdon.

> According to to Ingham, the first Methodist service held at Regent Road was an Anglican one. This is not surprising as Methodism began as a revival movement within the Church of England.

In Hale the Methodists also held house missions and in 1897 built Hale Chapel.

The Methodists were passionate about their beliefs, and one side effect was a tendency to split. The first to split off from the main denomination in Altrincham was the Methodist New Connexion. The New Connexion in Altrincham first met in a kitchen in a house at Norman's Place. Their first chapel was on George Street in 1821.

The Primitive Methodists were predominantly a working-class movement and will feature much in this book. Their spiritual home is the wonderfully-named Mow Cop, a hill on the border of Cheshire and Staffordshire. It was here in 1807 that Hugh Bourne, a wheelwright, and William Clowes (reputedly a potter and once one of the best dancers in the country) held a fourteen-hour meeting from which sprang the Primitive Methodists. They wanted to get back to what they felt were the true roots of Methodism and were duly expelled from the Methodist Church.

These Primitive Methodists developed a reputation for political involvement on the 'left', coupled with a zeal for evangelism.

In Altrincham, the Primitive Methodists first met in 1835 in a stable loft in Newtown[1] and they then built a chapel in 1875 on Oxford Road. By 1905 they had ninety-four members and 144 Sunday school pupils. They also had a chapel on Devonshire Road in Broadheath.

By 1905 there were an astonishing nine Methodist chapels or missions in Altrincham. The growth of the Church of England was almost outpaced by that of the Methodists.

Hugh Bourne, shown above, wheelwright and founder of the Primitive Methodists. When the Primitive Methodists opened their new chapel in Altrincham in 1875, the local newspaper reports the Primitive Methodists as saying at their inaugural service: 'We have come to help church people, Wesleyans, Independents and Baptists to get people converted. We have not come to steal sheep, but to make goats into sheep.'

The Dome Wesleyan Chapel, reminiscent of St Paul's Cathedral, both by name and design. The grandiose nature of the chapel shows what the Primitive Methodists rebelled against. The architect was the same Brakspear who also designed the new Bowdon Parish Church. The Dome had structural problems and was eventually demolished about 1960. This photograph shows it as it was in 1884.

The Methodist Chapel in George Street in 1966 before it was demolished.

There is, however, one Methodist denomination in Altrincham that we have left out, and they did not even hold their services in English.

---

[1] Newtown was the new development with housing for the poor, mostly between Hale Road and Lloyd Street.

THE WELSH METHODISTS

It may come as a surprise to readers outside the area to know that there is still a Welsh-speaking church in Altrincham.

William Jones and his wife Jane from Beaumaris worked for the local water company and occupied a house owned by the company. William discovered that a number of Welsh servant girls in the area were homesick, and so in 1869 the couple began services in Welsh in their home.

Numbers grew and so at the beginning of 1870, with a membership of twenty-eight, they rented a room in the British School off Oxford Road. Each year they held a rally there and for a time there was an annual eisteddfod in Broadheath. They were supported by Canon Wainwright of St John's Church.

In 1890 this Welsh church decided that it needed to build its own chapel, and in 1899 began to look for a permanent site. The hunt cannot have been easy, but according to local deeds, a piece of land on Willowtree Road was allocated as a future Methodist chapel. In 1902 the Welsh Methodists were then able to secure the site and to build their chapel.[1] The foundation stone was laid on Saturday 25 July 1903. The guests of honour were the minister of Ashley Road Congregational Church, Canon Wainwright of St John's and the then Baptist minister (who had Welsh ancestry), who was the principal speaker. The cost of the chapel was to be £800.

On completion of the chapel building, a tea party was held at the British School after the opening dedication service. David Lloyd George, the future Prime Minister, gave the address. The chapel was formally opened on 19 December 1903.

By 1905 these Welsh Methodists had grown sufficiently numerous to be able to appoint their own minister. In the same year the annual tea party at the British School (where the supportive Baptist minister was on the platform) attracted over 600 people. This was at the time of the famous Welsh Revival, and we will look at the impact of that on Altrincham later in this book.

The Welsh Chapel on Willowtree Road. The church was originally called the Welsh Calvinistic Methodist Church. The denomination is, however, the Presbyterian Church of Wales and combines elements of both Methodism and Presbyterianism. The references to the Welsh church could have been placed in either the chapter on the Presbyterians or the Methodists, but are placed here as, during the period of this book, the church was called the Welsh Calvinistic Methodist Church. Calvinism and Methodism are not at first sight easy to reconcile. We will look at this issue in more detail later.

We now turn to the largest Christian denomination in the world and look at the Roman Catholic Church in Altrincham.

---

[1] In the same year, Miss M Williams transferred to the Welsh Chapel from Bowdon Downs Congregational Church.

THE ROMAN CATHOLIC CHURCH

We have looked at discrimination against Nonconformists. Although this book looks at events and theology principally from a Nonconformist point of view, it is fair to say that the discrimination against Roman Catholics was often much worse and more sustained than that suffered by Nonconformists. Positioned at opposite ends of the religious spectrum, Nonconformists nonetheless had much in common with Roman Catholics. Roman Catholic emancipation was partially achieved in 1829, and yet Roman Catholics suffered practical discrimination long after that.

The Nonconformist reaction against events in the Church of England in the Victorian era was intimately connected with the Roman Catholic Church, and yet on the ground there is little evidence of much tension in Altrincham. Instead, the Nonconformist concern was more at the perceived drift of the Church of England towards Rome and the betrayal of its Protestant heritage. The Nonconformists might fight to keep the country Protestant, but implicitly their concepts of religious freedom meant that most supported, with some lapses, the right of Roman Catholics to worship without hindrance. To do otherwise would be to deny their own views that all should be allowed to practise their religion freely.

Protestant sensibilities were stirred up from time to time, however. Prime Minister Peel wanted to increase state funding to the Maynooth Roman Catholic Seminary, and yet Protestants saw this as unfair state discrimination in favour of one denomination: many Protestant equivalents had no such funding. The issue took the northern Peel by surprise. Another example was the reaction against the Pope's attempt in 1850 to create Roman Catholic bishoprics based on the new cities. Legislation was passed to counter this but was never enforced. Gladstone quietly abolished the legislation in 1871.

In Altrincham itself, the Roman Catholic church began relatively late. It too was partly a product of the arrival of the railways which allowed easy immigration. It consisted mostly of poorer people, many of whom were Irish.

In 1847 the Roman Catholics began meeting in houses in George Street. As we have seen, it was quite usual for a church to start with this sort of meeting. Father O'Reilly was the first priest and was succeeded by Father Berry and then by Father Walton. It was, however, Father Alcock who appears to have been the most dynamic of the priests. In 1858 he bought two cottages on New Street. A small church was built with an equally small presbytery, followed by another church in 1860 on New Street in the cottage grounds. This was named St Vincent de Paul and seated 350.[1] In 1872 St Vincent's School was built on Hale Moss. Father Alcock, meanwhile, busied himself with founding churches in Knutsford, Latchford and Sale Moor.

By 1899 the congregation had outgrown the New Street Church, with 1,300 attending four masses on a Sunday at one point. Land was therefore bought from the Stamford Estate and a new St Vincent's Church was built and then opened in September 1905. The architect was Edmund Kirby of Liverpool, whose firm still continues. The church was opened by Dr Allen, Bishop of Shrewsbury.

---

[1] St Vincent de Paul was born in 1581 in the foothills of the Pyrenees. He founded the 'Congregation of the Mission', known as the Vincentian Fathers, to go all over the earth 'to inflame people's hearts to do what the Son of God did'. He also co-founded the Daughters of Charity.

Late Victorian Roman Catholics in Altrincham perhaps also looked to the influential Bishop Vaughan of Salford even though he was in a different diocese. In 1879 he preached at St Vincent's. He saw a leakage of Roman Catholics through poverty, the bias of the educational system and Protestant missionaries. In Altrincham as in Salford, the drive therefore was to build new schools to educate the children of the faithful and to maintain them in that faith.

St Vincent's Church soon after it was built.

The laying of the foundation stone of the new St Vincent's Church.

We now move in our story from the Roman Catholic Church to one of the more flamboyant characters in the religious life of Victorian England and his impact on Altrincham: Robert Aitken. The story of this extraordinary man and his connection with Altrincham has not really been told before. You will find him rather unusual.

JUMPERS ON THE DOWNS

Robert Wesley Aitken was a larger-than-life character. Even to this day, opinions are sharply divided about him. Was he a genuine revivalist, a charlatan or just eccentric? Whatever the answer, he had an impact on Altrincham, although not quite the one he intended.

Born just outside Jedburgh near the English-Scottish border in 1800, Aitken secretly married the daughter of a wealthy soap manufacturer from Warrington. For her health, they moved to the Isle of Man. There Aitken fasted and prayed for sixteen days, and then announced his conversion to Christianity.

At first, he was part of the Church of England and became vicar of Crosby on the Isle of Man, where he built a church. A sympathetic source says that 'the Spirit of the Lord' came upon him in 1834. 'Being an earnest man', we are told, he believed that 'in Jesus Christ there was perfect salvation which brings perfect satisfaction'. He prayed and 'laid aside the Parson's Gown and left the Established Church with all its forms and ceremonies'.

Aitken then tried to join the Methodists. Crosby Chapel is now indeed a Methodist chapel. This is perhaps not surprising given that Aitken's middle name was Wesley. The Methodists clearly did not know how to take him. Although they allowed him to preach from their pulpits in some areas, he was controversial and they were wary of him.

He moved his ministry from the Isle of Man and preached in Liverpool about what he saw as 'the glorious gospel of Holiness and the New Birth'. He then began open-air preaching in London.

Aitken adopted the style of a travelling revivalist, at the same time enthusiastically advocating total abstinence from alcohol. His followers, according to a less sympathetic source, carried out frenzied revival activities. They would rise up, dance and caper about the room, jump over the forms, tear their hair and clothes and throw themselves on the floor. His followers were known, at least in Liverpool, as 'Jumpers' or 'Ranters', although the official name of the sect was the 'Christian Society'.

Based on an amalgam of Anglicanism and Methodism as well as a bizarre mixture of evangelicalism and Tractarianism, by 1837 the sect he formed claimed 1,500 members spread across seven towns. His followers were mostly working class. Aitken had his largest following in Liverpool, where he built Hope Hall as his headquarters in 1836.[1]

He arrived in Manchester like a whirlwind. His first visit in September 1833 drew mixed reactions from the Wesleyans. Edmund Grindrod, Superintendent of the Irwell Street Circuit, refused to allow him to preach in the Salford Methodist chapels, but elsewhere he was given pulpit space, especially on the Oldham Circuit.

The wife of the Methodist James Wood wrote: 'I thought I could distinguish very perceptibly an effort in the preacher to produce an animal excitement.... I could not divest my mind of the idea of a maniac.'

---

[1] Hope Hall is now part of the Everyman Theatre on Hope Street in Liverpool.

Aitken's influence spread to Altrincham. Two residents heard him speak, possibly in Manchester, and joined his growing sect. John Clarke was a local landowner and owned a field called the 'Longcroft' at the foot of The Downs. It was there that he and John Broom, a local grocer, organised the building of a chapel for a Revd William Essler.[2] In 1841, 71% of those living on The Downs were working class. This was the sort of community where the Aitkenites might flourish.

The chapel they built was officially recorded as an Aitkenite chapel. It is likely that Aitken visited it. We have no record of what went on there, but from the descriptions of what happened at Liverpool, services can hardly have been dull. You can still see the outline of the original chapel to this day on The Downs behind two shops.

The life of the Altrincham Aitkenite chapel was, however, relatively short-lived and the chapel soon closed. As for Aitken himself, when his first wife died, he remarried. His second wife did not like his Isle of Man base and Aitken ended up back in the Church of England as a vicar at Pendeen in Cornwall from 1840. He ran his new, but equally eccentric, Anglican ministry on somewhat unusual Methodist-Catholic lines, mixed with doses of revivalism. At the vicarage, devotional books were read aloud while the housework was done. The angelus was rung at noon daily, and the household duly stopped work and joined in prayer for fifteen minutes. There was even a mini-revival in Cornwall under his influence.

---

[2] See Nickson, C.: *Bygone Altrincham: Traditions and History*, Mackie and Co, 1935. Nickson says 'even the name of the clergyman who established it cannot be found, either in written document or carven marble'. We now know his name.

This photograph shows the house next to the Downs Chapel when the chapel was still in use. On the right you can just see the edge of the chapel itself. This is perhaps the only photograph of the outside of the original chapel.

Crosby Methodist Chapel in the Isle of Man, the first chapel founded and designed by Robert Aitken. He was then an Anglican minister.

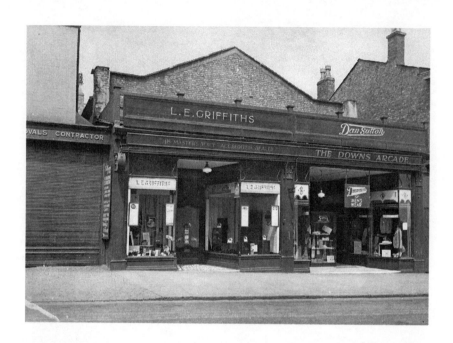

The Downs Chapel in former times after it ceased to be a chapel and was converted into a shop, and the chapel in 2007. You can still make out the outline of the chapel behind the later shop front extension. Inside, the steps to the mezzanine floor are where the original steps at the front of the chapel were located.

Robert Aitken. Aitken was partly responsible for an extraordinary event in 1851 which has passed into Christian folklore. Revd W. Haslam visited Aitken at Pendeen in Cornwall to advise him on the building of his new church. While sitting beside Aitken's fire, Aitken told Haslam that he did not think Haslam, even though he was a vicar, had been 'converted' as a Christian because of Haslam's objections to the new-found faith of his gardener.

The pair carried on the conversation that night and then the next morning. That Sunday, Haslam entered the pulpit in his own church and preached on 'What think you of Christ?'[3] He only intended to say a few words but as he spoke, he became persuaded by what he was saying. 'I felt a wonderful light and joy coming into my own soul, and I was beginning to see what the Pharisees did not.' A local preacher who happened to be in the congregation stood up and shouted, 'The parson is converted. The parson is converted! Hallelujah!'[4]

In his early days in the Isle of Man before his new zeal overtook him, Aitken was more interested in hunting with his gun and dogs than in being a clergyman. He was once late for a funeral and was seen leaping over the back wall of the churchyard with his dogs and gun and scurrying into the vestry to robe. However he was remembered as a kindly man by the Manx.

True to form, even Aitken's death was unusual: he died suddenly on the Great Western Railway platform at Paddington on 11 July 1873. Aitken had a son called Hay who became a well-known evangelist (especially at Cambridge), working with one Francis Caudwell. Robert Aitken's daughter, Robina, married Caudwell in 1857. The couple named their son, born the very next year, Robert.

So we leave the little chapel at the foot of The Downs empty. Were the Aitkenites forerunners of the later charismatics, a throwback to some of the early Puritans like the Shakers, or just simply eccentric? We shall never really know, and even today opinions are divided. What we do know is that the chapel they put up for sale was to play a key part in the future of three denominations in Altrincham. Much more was to come.

---

[3] Matthew 22: 42.
[4] Haslam, Revd W.: *From Death Into Life*, 1894.

THE RICH AND THE FAMOUS

Where the Aitkenite congregation went, we do not know. They probably disbanded to other churches. In any event, the chapel was up for sale. The time of the Congregationalists had arrived. They are to play a key role in the life of Altrincham and of this book.

Victorian Baptists and Congregationalists had almost identical theology and beliefs. They both believed in government of the church by the gathered congregation, which met to pray and discover what they believed was God's will for their church. Both denominations were generally evangelical. They often co-operated closely together. Sometimes they formed 'Union' churches, which were joint Baptist and Congregationalist churches, although usually with a Baptist minister. The one thing they could not agree about was baptism, but that was not usually a serious source of contention between them.

The Congregationalists tried on two occasions to start a church in Altrincham from their base in Knutsford, but with no success. For the third attempt, they decided to forget house meetings and instead to buy a building. The wealthy Ibotson Walker was a merchant and manufacturer who lived at the house at the top of The Downs known by 1871 as 'The Beeches'. This house was later to become St Anne's Home. He and others saw that The Downs chapel was empty and bought it from the Aitkenite trustees on 6 May 1839 for £465.

The Congregational chapel opened on 4 July 1839, and the first service was conducted by Revd D. Raffles of Liverpool, Mr S. Luke of Chester and the Revd James Turner of Knutsford. It was Turner who had first attempted a Congregational church plant from Knutsford in 1803, and it must have pleased him to see his work finally come to fruition.[1]

The church started with only ten members so, but for the wealthy financial backing of Walker, it was on shaky ground. However, demographics were working in their favour. Many wealthy people were moving to Bowdon and desired to worship in a Nonconformist church. By its second year, the Congregational church had grown enough to appoint its first minister. It was initially assisted by a grant of £25 per annum from the Congregational Union, but soon ceased to require that.

Over the next thirteen years there were six ministers but, despite the high turnover (sometimes due to ill health), by 1846 the church had outgrown The Downs chapel. Initially, the church leaders considered trying to add another 200 seats by constructing a gallery, but on 20 February 1846 they abandoned this scheme and resolved to find a new location.

They gave three reasons for wanting to move. The first was that they did not like the idea of being near to the new Bowdon railway station with its noise and smoke. The second was the more obvious difficulty they had in using their current building and the third was the anticipated expansion of Bowdon, an area that they felt needed a Congregational church.[2]

The land for the new chapel was not hard to identify. Adjoining The Beeches was an empty piece of land owned by the estate of the same John Clarke who had

---

[1] Handwritten notes of the history of the church in its Minute Books and also Nickson, op. cit.
[2] Building Committee Minutes, 1846.

founded the Aitkenite chapel. Walker himself was on the building committee and funds were quickly raised to buy the land. The new chapel was ahead of its time in having gas lighting. A ballot was held for pews, with some being left over for Sunday school children and the poor.

Bowdon Downs Congregational Church then grew dramatically in size and in influence. It was in many respects the sort of church that modern church growth theorists might look to. It set up mission stations and new churches. Some of these churches remained part of Bowdon Downs, and others became fully independent.

Let us take a quick look at this phenomenal mission activity. The church helped a struggling Lymm Church, Hey Head Mission and a church at Gatley. In 1864 it planted a mission church in Mobberley. It helped plant a church at Partington, partly financing an extension to the chapel there in 1892. After successful work at Baguley, fourteen members left Bowdon Downs and built a chapel in 1868, which became independent in 1872. For many years, Bowdon Downs had a mission church off Oxford Road. It was led by a minister, with five deacons being appointed by the mission church and five by the mother church.[3] Bowdon Downs Congregational also paid for itinerant evangelists in rural parts of Cheshire.

> Like many churches with an active youth group, the Victorian Bowdon Downs Congregational Church found it difficult to keep some order in services. Volunteers were asked to sit with the young people in the transepts to keep them quiet.

In 1899 some members of Bowdon Downs Congregational left to plant a new church in Ashley Road, and shortly afterwards funds were raised to build a chapel, which is now the United Reformed chapel. The first minister was Alfred James who was later to join forces with others in public protests in Altrincham, as we shall see.

By today's standards, services at Bowdon Downs Congregational were quite traditional, but every first Sunday evening of the month, the church held a more accessible 'People's Service'. By 1865 they had outgrown even their new chapel, and the deacons wanted to move. This time however, the church overruled the deacons and decided to extend the current chapel. In 1875 Alexander MacKennal became minister following the departure of a Professor Griffiths. MacKennal was to become one of the most well-known Congregationalists.

When the Congregationalists relocated to their new chapel on Higher Downs, they could have sold their former chapel at the bottom of The Downs. Instead they decided to keep it for use as their Sunday school.[4] In 1859, however, they decided that the old Aitkenite chapel had outlived its time as a Sunday school and they needed a purpose-built building. They therefore relocated their Sunday school in 1861 to Oxford Road.

---

[3] The deacons are the lay leaders in Baptist and Congregational churches.
[4] The reason for this may be that the deeds for their new building allowed use as a church, but not as a school.

In 1859, Bowdon Downs Congregational Church began its most unusual church plant. The members wished to plant a church in Broadheath. Having some difficulty in finding a suitable meeting place, they hired a canal boat on the Bridgewater Canal. This eventually led to the formation of Broadheath Congregational Church.

Bowdon Downs Congregational Chapel newly built in 1848. The extensions have not been added and the chapel has a rural feel.

The chapel from the front as it used to appear.

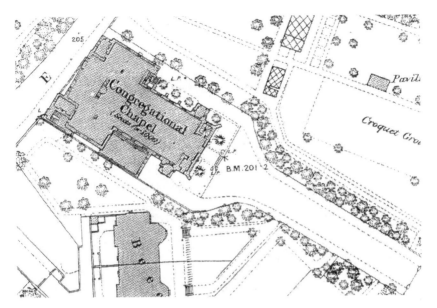

Bowdon Downs Congregational Chapel from an 1876 map. The chapel was extended later.

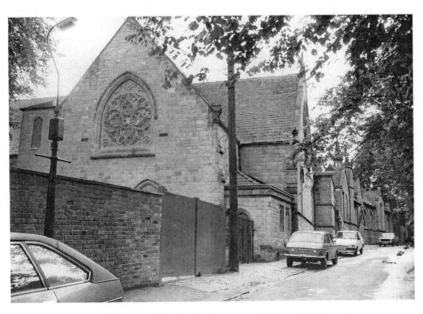

An older view of the rear of the chapel. One can see the size of the later extensions.

The pulpit was designed for St George's Chapel, Windsor. Queen Victoria took one look at it and rejected it. Her loss was Altrincham's gain and it is still in the chapel today.

A detail from the pulpit

The inside of the chapel after a full morning service. It is today home to the Upper Room Christian Fellowship. Part of the interior is made of iron and is still visited by science students to see how well it has lasted.

The departure of the Congregationalists left The Downs chapel empty once more, but eager eyes were already sizing up the opportunities it might offer.

THE SCOTTISH CHURCH

The Welsh had their church in Altrincham (although not yet a permanent home). Now it was the turn of the Scottish. The Presbyterians in Altrincham had long possessed the reputation of being a predominantly Scottish church. Presbyterians are Nonconformists, but with a different concept of congregational government from Congregational churches.

The Presbyterians seized the opportunity and took over the empty Downs chapel. Trinity Bowdon Presbyterian Church was founded on 22 December 1867. The first minister of the new church was the Revd W. T. Johnston who, as one might expect, was a Scot and hailed from Greenock.

The Presbyterians started in The Downs chapel with a congregation of thirty-five. They grew in numbers and in 1870 decided to build a new chapel on Delamer Road in Bowdon. This new building was opened on 22 September 1872. The spire today is truncated, but when built it was a magnificent 120 feet high and rivalled that of nearby St John's.

In 1883 the church commenced a mission in a small room in Victoria Street. A new mission hall was opened on Stamford Street in 1891.[1]

By now, you will have noted the key role of The Downs chapel. It housed the Aitkenites, two Congregational churches and one Presbyterian. Each time it became vacant, it was the catalyst for the formation of a new church in Altrincham. The reason was that it was cheap to rent and was a ready-made base. For little outlay, a denomination could see if it could attract sufficient adherents and then build its own chapel.

> Our look at the churches in Altrincham must also mention that by 1905 when this book ends its story, there were the Christian Brethren on Lower George Street, the Church of Christ on Ashfield Road, services at the Newtown Institute, the Plymouth Brethren at the Old Market Place and the long-established Unitarians on Dunham Road.

Trinity Presbyterian Chapel on Delamer Road in 1919 with its spire.

---

[1] Nickson, op. cit.

Trinity Presbyterian Chapel as it was with its spire and as it is now.

The Altrincham Baptist Church congregation at the former Trinity Presbyterian Chapel on Delamer Road during a morning service in 2009. The Baptists could not fit their morning congregation into the Hale Road church and so rented the building from the United Reformed Church.

Once again The Downs chapel lay empty. A new denomination looked round it. It is their story we now follow and it is through their eyes that we look at events in Altrincham and the wider world.

WHO ARE THESE PEOPLE?

What have John Bunyan, Martin Luther King, six American presidents (including Abraham Lincoln and Jimmy Carter), Al Gore, Billy Graham, Charles Colson and Joe Frazier got in common?

The answer is that they (and many others) have claimed to be Baptists.

We now focus on one denomination. This book uses the story of one poor and sometimes fairly radical church in Altrincham to look at the religious, cultural and political life of the late Victorian and early Edwardian eras. This is not, therefore, a book just about one denomination; it ranges far wider than that. However, it is only fairly recently that the church archives have been uncovered for some crucial years of this story, so we have an excellent opportunity to use this new material to help us understand what went on.

Baptists believe that people should only be baptised when they are old enough to make their own choice about what they believe. However, this is not enough to set them apart. Pentecostals, Brethren, Independent Methodists and many others do likewise, and it is not uncommon to find people of other denominations being baptised as believers, sometimes in Baptist churches, and then happily returning to their own church.

The first Baptist church was founded in Amsterdam in 1609 by John Smith and Thomas Helwys who had fled for refuge to Holland. Helwys then founded the first Baptist church in England in 1612 and it is to him that many Baptists worldwide look back.

In the English Civil War, the Baptists, often known later for their pacifism, actually fought on the side of Parliament to preserve their freedom, but Cromwell later became less tolerant of them. Like other Nonconformists, they were the object of persecution and discrimination for many years.

> The early Baptists at Broadmead Church in Bristol in the seventeenth century had a clever way of preventing their preachers from being arrested. Several strong men would stand around the preacher, and at the first sign of trouble a trap door was opened so that he could quickly disappear from sight.

It is difficult to know when the first Baptists came to the Altrincham area. The problem is that they probably did not want to attract attention to themselves. There were certainly Dissenters in Bowdon parish from an early date. In 1699, Josiah and Timothy Hankinson were recorded as being baptised at Robert Hankinson's house 'by one Dermily…contrary to the law, the house not being licensed. He preaches at Ringey Chappell, a chappell anciently belonging to the Church of England and under Bowdon Church.'[1] However, Ringway Chapel as a centre of Dissent was predominantly Presbyterian or Congregational in its time, and these were almost certainly baptisms of children.

A famous census entry for the Bowdon area of the time records 'Papists nil, no independents, no Anabaptists'. If there were any Baptists, they were lying low in Bowdon parish and not registering themselves as Baptists. This is hardly surprising.

---

[1] Ingham, op. cit.

Like the Roman Catholics, the majority of Baptists probably came to Altrincham after the arrival of the railway in 1849.

One of the first signs of Baptist activity in the north-west was in 1605 when six men and their wives had legal action taken against them for leaving their children unchristened. Two were put in prison.

This photograph shows the entrance to Chetham's College in Manchester, which was the site of the first Baptist church in the north-west of England. It met between about 1649 and 1657 and was founded by John Wigan, a Church of England curate at Gorton in Manchester.

Early Baptists were often referred to disparagingly as 'covenantors of dippers'.

> In 2007 Baptists accounted for 8% of all churchgoers in England and 19% of attenders of Nonconformist churches.

Before their first church was formed however, where did the Baptists worship? The answer to that question takes us into an aspect of Altrincham history that has almost been forgotten.

THE MISSING CHURCH

It may seem strange to lose a church, but that is what once nearly happened in Altrincham.

Clearly the first Baptists in Altrincham did not just spring from nowhere. Where did they worship before 1872?

Sometime after 1862, the Minute Books of Union Chapel, Manchester, start to show transfers to and from an independent church in Bowdon. It is given no name. It is simply called 'The Independent Church at Bowdon'. This cannot have been Bowdon Downs Congregational, because there are also specific named transfers to and from that church at the same time.

Union Chapel was a combined Congregational and Baptist Church and would accept transfers to and from Congregational and Baptist churches on a letter of introduction. It had a more rigorous interview procedure before accepting transfers from other denominations. This means that from 1862, this independent church must have been recognised as a proper Congregational church. It hardly features in any books today however.

It seems that after Bowdon Downs Congregational Church moved its Sunday school from the chapel at the bottom of The Downs to Oxford Road, an independent Congregational church was formed and rented the chapel at the foot of The Downs from Bowdon Downs Congregational. We know the minister in 1868 was A. Dewar. A year later we know that W. B. MacWilliam from Middlewich succeeded him and he was followed by C. Aylard.[1]

At first sight, it might seem as if this church was a breakaway rival to Bowdon Downs. This was not the case, as we see transfers to and from Bowdon Downs Congregational to what they called simply 'The Church at Altrincham', and Bowdon Downs would hardly have rented to a breakaway church. We know that Professor Griffiths, the minister of Bowdon Downs, spoke at this church in 1872 and his successor, MacKennal, preached at an anniversary service in 1877. This was not an insignificant church either. MacWilliam was Secretary of the Congregational Union. The Congregational District Committee met on one occasion at the chapel. According to a brief reference in the *Congregational Year Book* it was 'small but vigorous', paid £50 a year to rent the Downs Chapel and by 1864 no longer needed a grant from the Congregational Union.

It almost seemed as if Bowdon Downs was happy to have an independent alternative to itself. The reason is four-fold. First, Bowdon Downs was becoming a church of the middle and upper classes. The poorer Congregationalists wanted to meet in a freer Altrincham-based church where they did not need to pay expensive pew rents. Second, the chapel on Higher Downs was getting crowded. Third, Bowdon Downs looked to Bowdon, whereas the new church had its natural constituency among the poorer people of Altrincham.

The final reason may have been connected with the trust deeds of Bowdon Downs itself. These prohibited any teaching that agreed with the Baptist understanding of believers' baptism. Although it was not a Union church, was one of the reasons for

---

[1] There is a puzzle about some of these dates, as in 1880 Aylard referred to the fact he had been pastor for twelve years.

the existence of this church to allow Baptist believers to practise their beliefs within a Congregational church in Altrincham?

We may never know but, given the fact that many Baptist churches emerged out of Congregational ones, it is likely that some of the early Baptists would have worshipped in this church. This was also very much a church of the poorer people, and the early Baptists may have felt more at home there than in the more rarefied and academic atmosphere of Bowdon Downs Congregational Church.

The brief reference in the Congregational Year book to this church appears, however, to be wrong in one significant respect. It states that the church stayed at The Downs chapel. That is not true. Other records show that the church relocated by 1867 to Regent Road and took over the Methodist chapel there. It is certainly marked on the Ordnance Survey map of that period as an 'Independent Congregational Church'.

A postcard of The Downs. The old Downs chapel is at the bottom left.

The Independent Congregational Church relocated to this former Methodist chapel on Regent Road after they left The Downs chapel. It is likely some of the early Baptists worshipped with them, first in The Downs chapel and then here.

The location of the former chapel on Regent Road, by The Grapes pub (at the time of writing, an Italian restaurant).

So once more the former Aitkenite chapel at the foot of The Downs was empty. It is now time to introduce John Betts and his simple but daunting mission: to found a new church in Altrincham.

MAN WITH A MISSION

Who was Betts and why was he chosen?

Henry John Betts was the son of an Anglican clergyman from Great Yarmouth. He was well educated. To his father's disappointment no doubt, he became a Baptist by conviction through study of the Bible. Betts was a self-taught academic and became a schoolmaster at a private school in Linton in Cambridgeshire. There he met there a certain Doctor Brock who became his mentor. Brock encouraged the young Betts to write several sermons and then to enter college in order to train to become a Baptist minister. Although Betts wanted to be a minister, he decided instead to study privately and bypass theological college.

His first church was at Romney Street in Westminster. The congregation was so poor that it was unable to pay him, so he had to move to a church at Borough on the south bank of the Thames in London. The church flourished under Betts, although he still found it necessary to supplement his pay. Clearly a man of energy, he did this by getting up at 5am most mornings to write. When he had finished writing, he went on to hold early morning services in a warehouse.

His next move was north to a church in Bradford. Whilst there, he was on the examining committee of Rawdon Bible College (then called Horton). He stayed in Bradford for nine years.

Betts then moved to Manchester and succeeded the famous Arthur Mansell at Grosvenor Street Baptist Church. He became Secretary of the Manchester and Salford Baptist Union and his job seems to have been to assist them with church – planting. He lived in Crescent Park, Heaton Norris. Until the crucial year of 1872, he was also a committee member of the Lancashire and Cheshire Association of Baptist Churches, often opening meetings in prayer. In effect, he became a link between the two Baptist organisations. This link was important for what was to happen in Altrincham.

Betts had an excellent track record and he was clearly highly regarded in Manchester Baptist circles. So in 1872 Betts, now aged fifty-eight, was sent to Altrincham on behalf of the Manchester and Salford Baptist Union.

Betts had no idea that what he was to set in train was to lead to some extraordinary events.

John Betts

THE BEGINNING

When she was writing her brief centenary history of Altrincham Baptist Church 1872-1972,[1] Cynthia Walker had before her the notes of William James Brewer, who was associated with the church from 1876. Those notes, sadly, have been lost. However, in reconstructing the year 1872 from other sources, much more has now emerged about the early history of the Baptists than was previously known. According to Cynthia Walker, there is no record of their first meeting. Brewer apparently stated that a few people in the neighbourhood met together and decided to start a church. Help was promised by the Manchester and Salford Baptist Union.

The truth is more complex than this. There must have been early contact between these Baptists and Betts at the Union. Certainly we know that the Union had long wanted to start a church in Altrincham, but may have been frustrated by the difficulty of finding a building to rent. We also know that one history book refers to Betts calling them together, rather than a group just happening to meet together.[2] If they were worshipping as part of the independent Congregational church at Regent Road, this would be a comparatively easy process for both Betts and the Baptists.

Why did all this happen when it did? Why did they first meet together in September 1872? The answer lies with the Presbyterians. If the Baptists wanted to start a church, they needed somewhere to meet. If they were meeting as part of the independent Congregational church at Regent Road, those with longer memories would recall the chapel at the foot of The Downs where the Congregational church had previously met. It was obvious The Downs chapel was about to become empty as the new Presbyterian chapel on Delamer Road neared completion. Why not rent it to start their new church? If they were to do this, they needed first to leave the Independent Congregationalists at Regent Road, set themselves up as a new church, see if they were viable and then negotiate the lease.

We do not know where these they met for their first services, but it was almost certainly in a house in Altrincham. By the end of 1872, Bowdon Downs Congregational Church recognised them as an official Baptist church, as some members are recorded as transferring to the Baptists from Bowdon Downs. This adds credence to the idea that they came out of the Congregational churches. This was not uncommon, and there appears to have been no animosity at the time with either Congregational church in Altrincham.

In February 1873, the Baptists were able to set up a sub-committee (as churches often do) to survey The Downs chapel and to negotiate terms. The chapel was not in good condition following its intensive use by different denominations, but it was at least available. The rent agreed was £55 a year, a £5 increase on the Presbyterians, but they hoped to sub-let the schoolrooms at a rent of £10 per year. There were fit-out costs and the cost of buying fittings from the Presbyterians. These were quite expensive at £100, but the Union paid for them.

At first Betts was to assist them for just three months, but this was later extended to one year. Clearly this was an experimental period to see if the church was viable. The first Baptist church in Altrincham was more of a mission station than a church

---

[1] Walker, C.M.: Century of Witness: A Short History of the Baptist Cause in Altrincham 1872 to 1972, 1972.
[2] Whitley W.T.: Baptists of North West England 1649-1913, Kingsgate, 1913.

when it started[3] and Betts was more of an evangelist and church-planter than a minister.

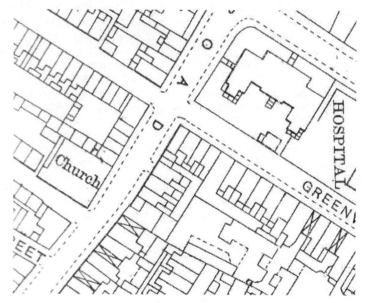

A 1908 map showing the chapel on Regent Road where the Altrincham Congregational Church met. This is also where some of the early Baptists may have worshipped before they formed the church which met in The Downs chapel.

How well would the Baptists do in Altrincham? The answer is not as obvious as you might think.

---

[3] The Lancashire and Cheshire Association of Baptist Churches regularly called the church its 'mission station' until the new Hale Road chapel was built. The church was part-funded by a Home Mission grant.

THE WIDER WORLD IN 1872

Before we look at those tentative beginnings in Altrincham in 1872/3, we now look briefly at the world into which it emerged. This can at best only be a short account, but it is a good idea to look at the wider context beyond Altrincham.

When the Germans fought and beat the French at Sedan in the Franco-Prussian war in 1870, a new epoch began for Europe. At first, there was support for the Germans, as the French were seen as the aggressors. Victoria initially felt proud of the triumphs of her son-in-law, the Prussian Crown Prince, and of the predominantly Lutheran country, but even her sympathies began to shift to the underdog French. When the besieged Paris fell on 28 January 1871, London sent £80,000 to the starving Parisians.

Italian unification came in 1870 and German unity in 1871. Britain began military reforms and the build up of its armed forces to counter the growing threat from the new European powers.

Historians generally recognise the early 1870s as a dividing point in the history of Victorian Britain. Life in Britain in 1872 was, however, almost detached from the dramatic changes on the continent. While in Paris they formed a commune, in London they played the first Football Association Cup. As the Communards were butchered in Paris, the English set up the Local Government Board.

The shift of continental power was to Germany. In Britain, the shift of power was to democracy. The 1832 Reform Act had begun a move in this direction, but it was the Disraeli Government that pushed reform further in 1867. The Ballot Act of 1872 introduced secret voting to the Altrincham electorate. The rural franchise extension of 1884 moved the reform process still further, significantly increasing the voting population. However, this was male suffrage only. Women and the poor were still a long way from having the vote. It was only in 1918 that most adults were able to vote.[1] From 1867 a number of the male Baptists would have been able to vote, but many still could not. Although the tide was moving to full democracy, in 1872 there was a long way to go.

The Civil Service was thrown open to competitive examination in 1870, and as democratic freedoms expanded, the bureaucracy of the State also expanded.

Land ownership however, was still concentrated in relatively few hands. In 1873, half the country was owned by just 4,217 people.

The British were fascinated by the political duel between Gladstone and Disraeli, even if many of them could not vote. In 1872, Gladstone was Prime Minister, to be defeated in 1874 by Disraeli.

The first of a series of Acts to legalise Trades Unions was passed in 1871, and so began the slow climb to power of the organised working class.

1870 also saw the first move to free, national education. In 1870, W E Forster made elementary education compulsory, with some schools being church-run and others not. Religious liberty was given to all schools but specifically denominational

---

[1] It was not until 1928 that all women were allowed to vote. In 1918 it was mostly women over thirty with property or who rented for at least £5 a year or who were married to such a person who could vote.

teaching was prohibited. However, everyone had to pay for their education at the Board schools unless they could establish their poverty. In 1891 elementary education became free, and yet, as we shall see, the Education Acts later raised serious issues for Nonconformists.

1872 was the high point for British agriculture. Soon there was to be a decline in the face of cheap foreign imports, particularly from America. Britain and Belgium were the only western European countries not to introduce import tariffs.

All this was accompanied by a massive increase in population. Between 1871 and 1911 the population of England and Wales increased from 22,712,266 to 36,070,492, an increase of nearly 60 per cent. Cheap imports fed the people, but they had to be traded for industrial goods and services. Between 1871 and 1881, the population grew at a rate of 16.9 per cent, but this was 19.63 per cent in towns and 7.42 per cent in the country. Increasingly Britain was becoming urbanised. Family sizes declined, but families of six to eight children were still quite usual. There was a huge influx of labour into Lancashire: by 1860 there were some 2,650 cotton factories there.

Charles Dickens died in June 1870 and Charles Darwin published his *Descent of Man* in 1871. The early Victorian period is generally regarded as being much more prolific in terms of art and science than the later Victorian period. Parry, Stanford, Mackenzie and Sullivan emerged as leading composers. In the late 1870s, Gilbert and Sullivan teamed up to write light operas. In Manchester, Sir Charles Hallé formed the Hallé Orchestra in 1858, and in the 1870s promoted it by extensive concert tours. Dr Barnardo opened his first home in 1870.

The first England vs Scotland football match took place in 1872. Football grew rapidly in popularity. Many football clubs had their origins in church teams, examples being Aston Villa Wesleyan Chapel (now Aston Villa), Christ Church Bolton (which became Bolton Wanderers) and Altrincham Association Football Club.

The English Rugby Union was founded in 1871. W. G. Grace began his main cricket career in 1870. In 1874, lawn tennis was invented under the bizarre name of 'Sphairistike'. Golf was still not a major sport however, except in Scotland.

Many newspapers were established and flourished in the 1870s. Most were sold for 1d. *The Manchester Guardian* was a leading national newspaper. *The Daily Telegraph* was also a Liberal newspaper but, like others, was to change allegiance over the Irish Home Rule issue.

In 1870 the supremacy of British foreign trade was established, substantially overhauling France and Germany, its nearest international competitors. Britain as a whole was prosperous, and yet the prosperity was unequally shared. It was however in the period from 1870 onwards that British manufacturing began to be seriously challenged by foreign competition. It was also in this period that there began the conversion of firms to limited liability companies, and the age of the nepotistic industrialist gave way to the age of the large company. The merchants and industrialists of the new town of Bowdon would see big changes in the way they operated.

At the same time, the British Empire was in a rapid period of expansion, culminating in the crowning of Victoria as Empress of India. Victoria herself had become increasingly unpopular, and the period marks a shift of power away from the Crown. Her reclusiveness and permanent mourning after the death of her husband did not help. Her son, the Prince of Wales, was not popular either, and was even booed at Epsom Races after a divorce case in which he was named. However, in 1871, public sympathy moved back to Victoria and the Prince of Wales when he became seriously ill with enteric fever. He recovered on the tenth anniversary of his father's death and a thanksgiving service was held in St Paul's Cathedral on 27 February 1872.

Altrincham Football Club has a partial Nonconformist foundation. Bowdon Downs Congregational Church planted a Sunday school in Broadheath. Mr J. Rigby was the founder, and Frank Crossley, who will appear later in this book, was on the fund-raising committee and was probably a substantial donor. The Rigby Memorial School footballers were a precursor of Altrincham Association Football Club.

William Ewart Gladstone, who, together with Disraeli, dominated politics.

Now we look at what Altrincham would have felt like to live in at the time.

THE STREETS OF ALTRINCHAM IN 1872

There are many good books that will tell you what Altrincham might have *looked* like in the past, but how would Altrincham have *felt*, smelt and sounded in 1872-73?

Before the young Victoria came to the throne, major industrialisation was confined to a few towns, and only about 20 per cent of the population lived in urban areas. By her death, about 80 per cent of the population lived in towns. Railways and factories covered much of Britain and were spreading across the rest of the world. The march of technology had become unstoppable. Altrincham was dramatically affected by these changes.

Altrincham is an ancient market town. Its first major transformation in more modern times came with the construction of the Duke of Bridgwater's canal from Manchester, although the canal did not come through the centre of Altrincham, instead swinging to the west at Broadheath. Produce could, however, still be delivered from Altrincham to Manchester, and in return Manchester exported its euphemistically-named 'night soil' to make some of the fields in what are now Timperley and Dunham Massey as fertile as they now are.[1]

It was the railway rather than the canal that really transformed Altrincham from a Cheshire market town into an outer suburb of Manchester. The railway first arrived in Altrincham in 1849. The original Altrincham station was to the north of the present one. Bowdon station became the terminus. This was on Railway Street, very near to the chapel at the foot of The Downs. In 1881, the two stations were amalgamated into the current station.

On 12 May 1862, the Cheshire Midland extended the line through Hale to Knutsford, then in 1863 to Northwich and in 1874 to Chester. By 1862 there were six trains each weekday from Altrincham to Manchester and back. Train times to Manchester were eighteen minutes for the first class express and one hour for the slow train. Quick transport to and from Manchester was available and the age of the commuter had arrived. With the railways came rapid population growth, coupled with the influx of labour from the countryside.

Many of the population were therefore immigrants, brought in with the railways and from the countryside, but the town still had the feel of a smaller town, where many people knew each other. Much of the Altrincham they inhabited would be familiar to you. Many buildings and roads would be recognisable, for it was the Victorians who left us much of our infrastructure, from the sewers under the streets to the roads, the layout of estates, the railways and the numerous churches and chapels. However, the underlying feel of the place was different. The rapid expansion of the town meant that large areas were building sites. Construction roads were laid out; grand schemes were planned; houses were built and occupied; community facilities were developed.

The smells were different: horse dung on the streets, poor hygiene for those who could not afford to wash, halitosis for the many who could not afford even the rudimentary dental care available, the stench of sewage.[2]

---

[1] In 1876 the 'night soil' depot was the subject of successful litigation by local Timperley residents against Manchester City Council because of the foul smell.
[2] See Bayliss, D.: *A Town in Crisis - Altrincham in the Mid-Nineteenth Century*, 2006.

40

The social hierarchy was apparent on the streets and in the houses. Status and deference were accepted. There was a clear divide between different parts of Altrincham. There was an enormous contrast between the slum areas of Altrincham and the merchants' houses on the higher ground of Bowdon, even though the two areas were close together. The further up the hill you lived, the better was the quality of the air you breathed and the water you drank. 'Soapy Town' in Bowdon Vale at the bottom of the hill was the laundry for Bowdon, with many of its houses such as Primrose Cottages built with the yard at the front for ease of receiving the laundry of the rich and sharing a communal drying area.

Children played on the streets and even on main roads with little threat from traffic. Street vendors were common. With many houses occupied during the day, there were door-to-door sales and services. Butchers, milkmen and bakers would deliver daily. Traders would wander the streets. Lamplighters carried their ladders around, tending to the gas-lights.

The post was efficient. The postmen, resplendent in their red coats with gold or blue piping, brought four or five swift deliveries each day to residents. The railways were generally on time, with fast and regular services, the great engines producing plenty of smoke and noise. Shops were local and small: no supermarkets, but usually specialised purveyors of goods and services.

As the town grew, however, so did its public houses and the attendant alcohol problems which the Nonconformists later fought against so strenuously. The local newspaper in the 1870s has regular accounts of drunken and anti-social behaviour in Altrincham. Two gangs from Altrincham and Hale, for example, had an encounter on Hale Road on the evening of Saturday 6 September 1868 which ended in the death of one of their number.

Christian values pervaded much of Altrincham society, or at least Christian values as they were then perceived. Those who did not wish to conform to these still felt obliged to do so on a superficial level. Sunday observance, despite the Prince of Wales and the coming invention of 'the weekend', was almost universal. All this did lead to a superficial hypocrisy. An example of these double standards was the large number of prostitutes in most towns and cities.

Military parades were a common sight, as soldiers and sailors went away to fight for the Empire. Soldiers drilled in the Altrincham parade ground between Market Street and Greenwood Street.

People walked a lot further than they do today. Apart from railway trains, horse-drawn vehicles were still the main means of transport for the wealthy. A passenger arriving at Bowdon railway station would have been greeted by the sight of horse-powered hansom cabs and no doubt the smell of the horses themselves.

Bicycles were just beginning to gain in popularity as an efficient means of transport before the arrival of the car. Bicycles in Altrincham would still have been of the type with a very high front wheel and a low back one. Men's bicycle-wear evolved in this period to allow ease of movement on the bicycle. It was only in the 1880s, however, that safety devices were introduced which allowed ladies, with their cumbersome dresses, to ride bicycles. In the 1870s, they had to ride tricycles. By the late 1890s, there was a Bowdon Cycling Club and regular reports of 'furious cycling' and bicycle crashes in the local newspapers.

Clothing was beginning to change, particularly for men. Gentlemen in full dress wore a black frock coat, top hat and wide tubular trousers. However, they no longer needed to wear frock coats or top hats when walking in the country. For town and Sunday wear, a morning coat with tails was becoming increasingly popular. The Prince of Wales also popularised an early form of lounge coat. Tradespeople began to abandon clothing that showed their actual trade or occupation.

While men were moving to clothing that was easier to wear, the trends in women's clothing seemed far less progressive. The crinoline was beginning to disappear from use and the bustle (more politely termed the 'tournure') was becoming fashionable. Corsets of steel and whalebone restricted the body and produced wasp waists. Skirts trailed on the floor for a yard or so. A lady walking in Altrincham had to hold her skirt up with one hand as she walked. It was only in the 1880s that skirts were shortened so as to be just off the ground.

Paris fashions were followed, but not always copied. The local newspaper carried a regular column, reporting on what the magazine *Le Follet* stated were the latest Parisian fashions.

Entertainment for the working classes principally comprised sport, walking, the public house or the church. Fairs were held, and often brought trouble with them. The upper and middle classes in Altrincham entertained mostly at home. It was entirely normal for them to have servants, and a substantial proportion of the Altrincham population were servants in these houses.

For most Altrincham Victorians, home life was paramount. The song 'Home, Sweet Home' was to achieve almost cult status and reflected the Victorian view of home life.

The Old Market Place Altrincham in 1900. The post office is directly ahead and a gunsmith's shop is to the left.

So having painted a brief picture of Altrincham life in the early 1870s, we now turn to two Victorians from the same denomination who were hugely influential on religious thought throughout the world. One was based in Manchester and the other in London. Both were equally well known in their time, but one has virtually disappeared from history. Why was this, and how did these two men influence not only the Altrincham Baptists but so many others in Altrincham? Their story, and the contrasts between them, is a fascinating one.

THE MAN WE FORGOT

To understand the significance of this man to Altrincham, think of the name of a current world-renowned preacher. People come from all over the world to hear him preach. If you do not attend a church, you will have to use your imagination at this stage. If you do, and if that person is not of your denomination, make him so. His sermons are considered so worth hearing that his previous Sunday morning's sermon is regularly printed in your denominational paper in its entirety. Now put him in a church that is packed each Sunday. Make him leader of your denomination for two two-year periods. Place him on the committee that gives leadership to your denomination in your area. Now put his church about ten miles from your own and you will realise the impact of McLaren on Altrincham, one of the most renowned preachers of his time.

The fact that the name of Alexander McLaren is on the foundation stone of the Hale Road Baptist chapel is an accident. He was not originally intended to lay the stone. However, McLaren has been involved with Altrincham more than anyone has, until now, fully realised.

McLaren's name has however virtually disappeared from the history books. It is time to restore the reputation of this great man who was based in Manchester.

McLaren was born on 11 February 1826, the youngest of six children. While McLaren was still young, his businessman father left the Congregational church for the Baptists.

As a young boy, McLaren enjoyed travelling on the canals and operating locks. He came to faith early in life and was baptised on 17 May 1840 at Hope Street Baptist Church in Glasgow. He had an early sense of a calling to preach. As a Baptist, he was barred from Oxford or Cambridge, so he went instead to the Baptist College at Stepney, which was later to become Regent's Park College. His first church was Portland Church in Southampton.

In April 1858 McLaren was asked to preach at Union Baptist Chapel in Manchester with a view to becoming its minister. At the time he described Manchester as the 'smokey city', but jokingly said there were intelligent 'north men'.

Union Baptist was then opposite Ducie Street. Under McLaren's ministry, Union Baptist grew in numbers and a new chapel was built on the site of what is now St Mary's Hospital on Oxford Road. This new

> McLaren believed that the rise of the church through history was through sudden spurts of revival and then sometimes decline, but overall upwards.

chapel seated 1800 and was called the 'Nonconformist Cathedral of Lancashire'. It was opened in 1869 and was packed from the start. In January 1890, McLaren took on an assistant, J. Edward Roberts a man whose particular connection with Altrincham we will see later.

In January 1911 *The American Review and Expositor* said of the Union Chapel congregations that they 'were as remarkable for their composition as for their size. They contained men of all classes and creeds, rich and prosperous merchants, men distinguished in professional life, and others working their way towards success. Young men from the offices and warehouses of the city sat side by side with artisans. Strangers were attracted in large numbers, and among them clergymen and dignitaries of the Established Church, Non Conformist Ministers, Literary Men, Artists and students from the Theological Colleges'.

McLaren was above all a gifted preacher. He spent much of each week in prayer and in the study of the scriptures in their original Hebrew and Greek, and brought a profound theological understanding to all he spoke about. He read theological texts in German. He always felt his main purpose was expounding the scriptures. He would generally preach through a book of the Bible over a sermon series and draw his conclusions from it. He never wrote out his sermons but used compressed notes only. His words kept people absolutely enthralled.

His first biographer says of him: 'There is little doubt that anyone who knew Dr McLaren well would agree with the statement that the most marked feature in his character was his entire freedom from anything approaching to egotism. His deep vein of shyness, as well as refined taste, made egotism, in the way of speaking of his own doings, an impossibility to him.[1]' It is interesting to note that he regularly felt sick from nerves before he entered the pulpit to preach.

Union Baptist grew mostly through his preaching, but he did not entirely neglect church-planting. In 1874 a new church was built in West Gorton and he set up the Wilmott Street Mission in 1872 in Rusholme. Although Baptist funded, the Wilmott Street 'mission station' was undenominational.

> 'We must carefully divest our evangelistic work of apparent pretensions to superiority, and take our stand by the side of those to whom we speak. We cannot lecture men into the love of Christ. We can but win them to it by showing Christ's love to them'.
>
> Alexander McLaren[2].

McLaren regularly attended the Lancashire and Cheshire Association of Baptist Churches committee meetings and was, as we shall see, clearly influential there.[3] He encouraged new churches through the Association.

In 1871 he became President of the Baptist Union. In 1900, he was appointed by the largest vote then ever registered as Vice President of the Baptist Union and became President in 1901 for a second time.[4] His last address to the Baptist Union was on 'Evangelical Mysticism'.

McLaren received honorary degrees from Glasgow, Edinburgh and Manchester Universities. In 1885 however, he was asked to become Hebrew Professor at Regent's Park College but turned the post down as he wanted to continue to give priority to his preaching. Even when away from Manchester he always read *The Manchester Guardian* to keep abreast of contemporary affairs.

McLaren never visited America, but Americans regularly came to hear him at Union Baptist in Manchester. He wrote in an American magazine and is still quoted in America to this day. In 1888 he went on a preaching tour of Australia, and in 1901 he met the new King Edward VII, although what they made of each other we do not know.

McLaren's portrait was hung in the Manchester City Art Gallery. It was painted by Sir George Reid, President of the Royal Scottish Academy. Reid said of McLaren:

---

[1] McLaren, E.T.: *Dr McLaren of Manchester*, Hodder and Stoughton, 1911.
[2] From MacLaren, A.: *The Secret of Power and Other Sermons*, 1882. McLaren's name was sometimes spelled MacLaren.
[3] The Association Minutes show he rarely missed a meeting.
[4] Being President of the Baptist Union twice is very unusual, even today.

'His conversation was delightful, full of interest and animation, his eager Celtic temperament making itself felt in everything he said, and in his way of looking at people and things. But there was nothing of the Ecclesiastic about him, and he had the saving grace of humour.'

McLaren finally retired from Union Baptist Chapel in 1903. The hymn sung as he left was 'Lord, dismiss us with thy blessing'. His last significant public act was his great speech as elder statesman of the Baptists at the first Baptist World Congress in 1905.

He died on 5 May 1910, five years after the end of the period covered by this book. His ashes were taken to Brooklands Cemetery. The cross over his grave reads: 'In Christo, in Pace, in Spe' (in Christ, in peace, in hope). His story is also part of the story of Altrincham.

> Alexander McLaren married his cousin, Marion, on 27 March 1856 at her family's house, which was customary in Scotland at the time. They later had two daughters and one son, all born in West Gorton, Manchester. Marion died on 21 December 1884 of pleurisy. McLaren and his family went to Ambleside in the Lake District for two weeks to get over the loss. It is said that McLaren never fully recovered from the death of his wife.

> McLaren was a Governor of the John Rylands Library in Manchester. John Rylands was a Nonconformist cotton manufacturer who died in 1888. His widow Enriquetta inherited nearly £3 million and built the library in memory of her husband. She collected archives and old collections from around the world, no doubt sometimes on the advice of McLaren. The library contains what is probably the oldest fragment of the New Testament in the world. Visitors can see a papyrus on which are clearly visible verses 31 to 33, 37 and 38 of chapter 18 of the Gospel of John. These deal with the exchange between Jesus and Pilate before the crucifixion. The text was almost certainly copied onto the papyrus from older sources between AD 100 and AD 150.

McLaren at the age of 30 while at Portland Street, Southampton, two years before he moved to Manchester.

Marion McLaren

McLaren aged 75, by now one of the most famous of Victorian preachers.

Marion McLaren later in life. McLaren never really got over her death.

McLaren's 'rival' from London was Charles Haddon Spurgeon. We look next at Spurgeon to see why the Londoner's name is still much remembered, while that of the Manchester man with the Altrincham connection is largely forgotten.

SPURGEON

Today, many of us think of mega-churches as being a North American invention. However, let us look at a startling fact about Spurgeon: he preached Sunday after Sunday to *over 10,000 people*. He was probably one of the most famous preachers and ministers of all time anywhere in the world.

It would take a substantial book just to write about Spurgeon. This chapter therefore can only be a brief introduction to this giant of the world Christian stage who, as we shall see, had connections with, and indirectly influenced, people and events in Altrincham.

Charles Haddon Spurgeon was born on 19 June 1834 in Kelvedon, Essex. He was brought up in a fairly old-fashioned Puritan way. His father worked in a coal merchant's office but was also an unpaid minister at the local Congregational church. His mother was perhaps the key influence in his spiritual growth.

In January 1850, the young Spurgeon attended a Primitive Methodist church service in Colchester. The Primitive Methodists were known for their direct style of preaching and enthusiasm. To Spurgeon's surprise, the preacher pointed directly at him and challenged him. Spurgeon later wrote in his autobiography, 'I can testify that the joy of that day was utterly undescribable'.

By February, Spurgeon was distributing tracts and in April he became a member of his father's Congregational church. However, he had previously decided that believer's baptism was the correct course in Scripture for a new convert. Spurgeon was therefore baptised at Isleham in Cambridgeshire by the Revd W. W. Cantlow. This event, as we shall see later, has an interesting connection with Altrincham.

Spurgeon decided not to go to the Baptist Regent's Park College to train as a minister, but instead went straight into the ministry. At the time, this was quite common. His first church was at Waterbeach in Cambridgeshire and then at the age of 20 he became minister of New Park Street, Southwark for a trial period of three months. His preaching rapidly drew

> Spurgeon's mother was a convinced Congregationalist and told Spurgeon she had prayed for his conversion, but not for him to become a Baptist. 'Well, dear mother', Spurgeon replied, 'you know that the Lord is so good, that He always gives us more than we can ask or think.'

large numbers and his story then becomes one of moving to larger and larger buildings to accommodate the increasing congregations.

The Metropolitan Tabernacle was built at the Elephant and Castle in London and was Spurgeon's most famous church. After this new chapel was built, he regularly preached to those 10,000 or more each Sunday for the rest of his life.

Spurgeon was an evangelical who also believed in the literal truth of the Bible. His preaching was powerful and stimulating and appealed to people of all classes. He attached great importance to depth and variety of thought and disliked artificial oratory. He struggled, however, throughout his life with Bright's disease, compounded by rheumatic gout.

Spurgeon's influence spread much further than the Metropolitan Tabernacle through his printed sermons. By 1872, 25,000 copies of his sermons were printed each week. By 1879 half a million copies of his sermons had been sold in the United States. They were even more widely printed in American newspapers. A million were even distributed in Russia with the approval of the Orthodox Church.

In 1865, Spurgeon launched his widely read magazine, the *Sword and Trowel.*

Perhaps Spurgeon's two greatest legacies to our times are the number of Baptist churches he was involved in planting (mostly in the south-east), and the theological college he founded and which is now named after him.[1] He pioneered the provision of cheaper, briefer and less academic courses at the college, particularly to make preachers (rather than scholars) out of students of more humble backgrounds.

He personally directed students to their first churches, giving priority to new ones. He and his students tended to keep in touch, and he took pride in the fact that the growth of those churches where his students went was above the average for the denomination.[2] Each year he organised an annual conference to bring past and current students together.

Spurgeon was highly respected by politicians. In 1882, Gladstone and his eldest son attended the Metropolitan Tabernacle and then met privately with Spurgeon after the service.

Spurgeon's funeral in 1892 was on a monumental scale and was attended by Gladstone, the two English Archbishops, the Chief Rabbi and the Prince of Wales. It would perhaps only be surpassed in that period by Queen Victoria's own funeral.

Spurgeon's teachings undoubtedly influenced many in Altrincham. A number of Nonconformist ministers would have read the *Sword and Trowel.* There is a more direct connection with Altrincham, however, as Spurgeon was a good friend of Betts. Betts' church in London was near to the Spurgeon's church, and it was there the two became friends. Betts' church nearly purchased the site of Spurgeon's future Metropolitan Tabernacle before Spurgeon beat them to it! The influence of Spurgeon on the Altrincham Baptists and others was much greater than just through Betts, though, as we shall see.

Spurgeon preaching at the Metropolitan Tabernacle.

Spurgeon is still famous today, but what of McLaren? An internet search against the names of McLaren and Spurgeon reveals a startling fact: McLaren's name is little featured compared to that of Spurgeon. The reason probably lies in the fact that Spurgeon and McLaren were two vastly different personalities with very different talents. Spurgeon was involved in planting many churches and founded a theological college. He was a consummate preacher but yet, although well read, not ultimately a theologian.

[1] This was also founded in 1865 and was initially called the 'Pastor's College'. Several Baptist ministers at Altrincham have been trained there. One former pastor, Dr Nigel Wright, is at the time of writing the college principal and a former pastor, Dr Paul Beasley-Murray, was a previous principal. Books by both of them are quoted in this book.
[2] Clifford, J. (ed): *The English Baptists, Who They Are and What They Have Done*, E. Marlborough & Co.,1881.

By contrast McLaren, equally renowned in his time, was not a church-planter, nor did he found a theological college. He was by nature a shy person who did not court publicity. He was a man of profound learning and theology and an encourager of church-plants, but not usually someone who initiated them. He saw his gifting as primarily a preacher of the word of God and a theologian. His legacy is in churches without any association with his name, and in his preaching and influence on others.

McLaren became increasingly willing to support and work with other denominations, whereas Spurgeon worked much more within, and ultimately on his own and outside, his own Baptist denomination. McLaren believed that the way ahead was for the Nonconformist evangelical churches to work together, and possibly for the Congregationalists and Baptists to unite. The fact that the Methodists were working effectively in Manchester city centre, as we shall see later, was a source of joy to him, and he gave them his full support. This openness to other Christian denominations must in part be explained by his experiences at Union Chapel where he was minister. Union Chapel was a combined Baptist and Congregational church, but also welcomed other Nonconformists. McLaren was prepared to rejoice in the triumphs of others and not stick to an exclusively Baptist line. This perhaps partly explains why the reputation of this self-effacing man has not lasted as well as that of Spurgeon.

McLaren outlived Spurgeon by eighteen years. McLaren was one of the chief mourners recorded at Spurgeon's funeral and the Minute Books of his church record his condolences. He also wrote his own tribute, which was published as part of his weekly sermons in *The Freeman*.[3] Spurgeon in turn had said of McLaren that he was 'the most remarkable minister of Christ now living'. Although rivals in a sense, they respected each other.

> Spurgeon said he could never have coped with a small church, which he likened to a canoe on the Thames. He said he would have sunk it at once, but the Metropolitan Tabernacle was so big that it was like a steamboat on the Thames: 'Whether I walk here or there my weight will not upset it.'

---

[3] The Freeman was the predecessor of The Baptist Times.

The Metropolitan Tabernacle today. The facade is original, but the building behind was bombed in the Second World War and the capacity is now smaller. The sheer size of the original building was extraordinary. It was built in the style of a Greek temple and opened in March 1861. It cost £32,000 to build and seated 5,500 with room for a further 1,000 standing. Two galleries stretched all the way round the building and the whole focus was on the pulpit and the baptistry beneath. It is still a thriving Baptist church.

We shall now look at a third key player – a man who was not a Baptist, but who possibly met McLaren for the first time through the Altrincham Baptists. This man lived in Bowdon and worked closely with McLaren in a major project to re-unite denominations. That man's name is Alexander MacKennal. At the time, this Altrincham-based man was nearly as famous in England as McLaren and Spurgeon. He will play a crucial role in the events that are about to unfold.

MACKENNAL

Alexander MacKennal was a Cornishman but ultimately of Scottish descent. Born at Truro on 14 January 1841, he was the third child of seven. His father Patrick was from Galloway and his mother was English.

When MacKennal was seven, the family moved to London. Patrick worked in a wholesale drapery. The young MacKennal arrived just in time to see the sand-bags being removed from around the Bank of England, near where they lived, at the end of the great Chartist demonstrations.

The young MacKennal was befriended by the five-year old girl, Nellie next door. Tragically, she died of scarlet fever and throughout the rest of his life, MacKennal always carried a lock of her hair with him.

MacKennal attended school at Madras House in Hackney, then in 1851 he went to Glasgow University to study medicine. While at Glasgow, he spent a summer holiday staying with a Baptist family in the Highlands. It was while out walking on his own one day that MacKennal seems to have had some personal encounter with God that changed the direction of his life.

After gaining his degree, he returned to Hackney, but this time to the theological college there.

In 1858 he became pastor at Burton-on-Trent Congregational Church, and then in 1862 he moved to Surbiton, a suburb of London. In 1867, he helped to organise a London conference on why the working classes were attending chapels less than they had been, and what could be done about it.

While he was at Surbiton, two ladies always sat very near the pulpit. One was Mrs Wilson, who was deaf and needed to be near the pulpit to hear the sermon. The other was a young widow and the daughter-in-law of Mrs Wilson. The young lady may have had her own motives for sitting near the pulpit, because she married MacKennal in the summer of 1867. When the chapel-keeper objected to the marriage, MacKennal told him it was his fault for putting an attractive young lady so near the pulpit.

Three years later, the young couple moved to Leicester where MacKennal became pastor of Gallowtree Gate Congregational Chapel.

The MacKennals had two daughters and two sons. The elder son was educated at The Leys School, Cambridge, and the younger at Harrow. In 1897 tragedy struck when Harry, then a junior doctor at Ancoats Hospital, died. MacKennal was, however, able to enjoy being a grandfather through his daughters, Euphemia and Margaret.

MacKennal was a slightly reserved and deeply intellectual man. He travelled abroad frequently (he was especially popular in the United States) and wrote quite extensively. He was an active member of the Literary and Philosophical Society in Leicester. He gave lectures on local flora, Wordsworth, Tennyson and Arthurian Legend and colour in landscape. He was chair of the meteorological society and an amateur poet. In Bowdon he joined the Nature Students' Association, giving a talk after a ramble in 1887 on 'Springtime' and one in 1888 on 'Insects and Flowers'.

When the Haworths, members of Bowdon Downs Congregational Church, visited him in 1876 to discuss a possible move to Bowdon from Leicester, the call must have been attractive to him, given his interests and the intellectual, literary and scientific atmosphere of Bowdon. At his induction service as a minister in 1877 he welcomed advances in scientific thought. He thought that Christians should not be afraid of them, but rather embrace them. In 1883 we find him at the Altrincham Literary Institute giving the vote of thanks after a lecture on Wordsworth.

MacKennal grappled with the scientific and theological thinking of his day, including the theories propounded by Darwin. He was an evangelical but not a creationist, and one suspects he was more liberal in his theology than McLaren and certainly more liberal than Spurgeon. In 1885 he wrote a scholarly book, *The Biblical Schemes of Nature and Man*, which referred to the creation 'legends'.

He was, though, prepared to challenge the Bowdon Downs Congregationalists to mission and to their care of the poor. He felt missions were good for a church with a 'careful intellectual type of religion'.

Such a man was bound to progress his career beyond Bowdon, and eventually he was asked to become Secretary of the Congregational Union. The deacons of Bowdon Downs Congregational Church saw this as an irrelevant desk-job. Although he was later to be President of the Union, MacKennal reluctantly turned down the job of Secretary at their request, but not until after the deacons had seen off a deputation from the Congregational Union at a crisis meeting at the County Bank on King Street in Manchester.

MacKennal's wife died in 1903 after eight years of heart problems and the Haworths took him to the Riviera to recover. However, in 1904, he caught a chill while in Newcastle. He desperately wanted to return to Bowdon, often checking the railway timetables, but after three months he died on 23 June 1904. His death was one of the major stories in the newspapers.

McLaren and MacKennal had much in common: both were intellectual Scots and great preachers. It is no wonder that they came to work together from their different denominations as their respective careers developed. Altrincham residents should be proud that it was Altrincham that brought them together.

MacKennal became a good friend of McLaren's. Both had a sense of humour, although of the two it was McLaren who had more of a twinkle in his eye. On 20 February 1902, McLaren wrote to MacKennal: 'It was good of you to send me your greetings on my birthday, and I would have said so before now, but that I was in Scotland all last week tramping about through cruel, cold and bleak fog, like a Buddhist beggar, for our Century Fund a wise proceeding for a man of seventy-six! The Scottish Baptists were as frozen as the weather, and not a trickle of subscription would run.'

MacKennal in later life.

MacKennal's vestry at Bowdon Downs Congregational Chapel with its own fireplace.

The Board of Directors of the Altrincham Literary Association in front of the British School off Oxford Road in Altrincham. MacKennal was an enthusiastic member of the Association.

So now we will turn to the launch of the Baptist church in Altrincham, a church which was soon to become one of the most controversial in the area in Victorian times.

THE OFFICIAL START

They called themselves Bowdon Baptist Church.[1] Their first meeting was in a house on 29 September 1872 and they had just twenty-six members.[2]

In the next chapters we will follow their story as a case study in the formation of a Victorian Nonconformist church. We will see the stresses and strains of the time. This is a particularly fascinating and surprising story. The impact of what happened goes well beyond just the Baptists in Altrincham.

On 28 February 1873 this new church held its official launch. The press were invited.[3] They needed a star speaker. Betts as minister asked McLaren. McLaren and the Lancashire and Cheshire Association of Baptist Churches had recently approved a yearly mission grant of £30 per annum to this new church. McLaren and Betts were both on the Association Committee. McLaren agreed to speak.

The reason the official launch was delayed was probably to accommodate McLaren, who had been away for three months on sabbatical in Italy, and also to allow the Baptists to move in and clean out their new rented premises. We know that the old Downs Chapel was not in the best of condition, but it was sufficient for the launch service after some further decoration.

McLaren began his address by saying that when he had left home three months earlier, he had thought that Bowdon Baptist Church was a thing of the future, and was surprised and pleased to hear that it was already established. He only hoped that the baby had not been let down to walk too soon, 'because the result of that with real babies at times is to make them bandy'.

He added that he was glad 'that in this growing neighbourhood there has been opened a place of worship where God's truth will be faithfully and lovingly preached'... 'You preach Christ, yet not a person, nor even a name, but Christ in you crucified. In that a doctrine is embedded and becomes the vehicle of the proclamation of the person. I take it that will be the staple truth, the Alpha and Omega of the Truth to be proclaimed here. If it is not so, I do not care if this church's doors are never opened again...The one thing that binds a man to his Redeemer is his personal acceptance of and adhesion to His great work. Without that nothing is of any account'.

Revd D MacGregor (Manchester), Revd Davies of Grosvenor Street Chapel in Manchester and Revd J. P. Chown of Bradford all then spoke. It is likely that Chown was a friend of Betts' from his Bradford days.

Chown remarked that people tended to think that the church would be advanced by organisations, forgetting that it is people who bring activity. 'You can never have a proper church until every individual member feels his responsibility for its

---

[1] This perhaps shows they had initial aspirations of moving to Bowdon in due course, just as had the Congregationalists and Presbyterians before them. Bowdon Downs Congregational Church, however, often called them 'the Baptist church meeting at Altrincham' until 1875, when they finally recognised that Mrs Penny, Miss Young and a Miss M.E. Young were transferring to 'Bowdon Baptist'.

[2] Unfortunately, we do not know their names. On 30 December Mrs Leech, Miss Crook and Joseph Moore joined them from Bowdon Downs Congregational Church, followed by Mr and Mrs Kenworthy on 29 January 1873, Sarah Crookes on 2 April and David Kenworthy of Ashley Road in May 1873. These are the first officially recorded names we have of members of the new church. We know from later records that Mr and Mrs Hewith were early members. Others to join the Baptists from Bowdon Downs Congregational were Mrs Pilling and Miss Smith in March 1876 and Mr and Mrs F.G. Woodcock in 1881. It is almost certain that William Simmons was a founder member.

[3] The main report is in *The Freeman* of 1873.

advancement. Then you should look at the spirit in which you work.' He quoted Spurgeon, who said that a great many were more anxious to live *on* Christ than *for* Christ. 'It is very well to look to a Minister to lead you up to all that is exalted, but you must be ready to live what you hear... Those who only receive are never blessed. It is always far more blessed to give than to receive. A congregation must be prepared to hear as well as their Minister be prepared to preach.'

The next Sunday, the first believers' baptisms of Bowdon Baptist Church took place.[4]

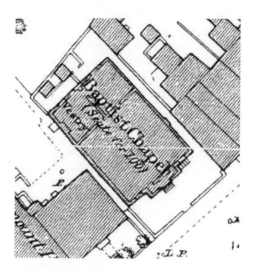

The Downs chapel from a map of 1878. Note that it is stated to seat 100. The chapel had a small platform with a reading desk rather than a pulpit. The two small rooms behind served as classrooms and a minister's vestry. The seats were uncomfortable movable forms.

---

[4] One unanswered question is, who installed the baptistry? Was it the Baptists, or was it there because the independent Congregationalists had installed it as they had Baptists amongst their number?

The junction of The Downs and Railway Street at some time after 1907 when the trams were introduced, and in 2007 before the 2007 roadworks.

McLaren at around the time he spoke at the launch of Bowdon Baptist Church.

Everything looked set for growth. The problem was that Betts was only on short-term secondment as minister. His days were numbered.

WHAT HAPPENED TO BETTS?

It was clear from the start that Bowdon Baptist Church was a mission-minded church; indeed, it had to be in order to survive. Could the fledgling church follow the lead of others and build a new chapel? Its rented building at the foot of The Downs was certainly showing signs of age. It was called an 'antiquated building' by one local author.[1]

Other Baptist churches were springing up in Lancashire and Cheshire. Churches at Hyde Road and Rawtenstall were launched in the same year. This was a time of great Baptist growth.

As Betts was only on loan for a year, he continued to live in Heaton Norris. He did however throw his energies into building the new church.

On the first anniversary of its foundation, the church held a fund-raising tea party. This was to become an annual event. On the Tuesday evening, members and guests assembled and fourteen trays of food and drink were served, donated by members. The building was decorated with evergreens and mottoes. After tea, there was entertainment. The Betts family were a sort of early family von Trapp and, accompanied by a harmonium, the two adults, five daughters and two sons sang to the congregation.

The church secretary then reported that the church was in a flourishing state and the Treasurer even reported a small surplus. They had thirty-nine members, fourteen having joined in the last year.[2]

At the end of his allotted year as church-planter, Betts left for Darlington. We know from the Altrincham newspaper of the time that he settled happily there. After Darlington, he went to Rye Hill Church in Newcastle-upon-Tyne. The church owned a large chapel which could seat 1,200. He was there for six years before he retired to Leicester. Even then, he remained a speaker in the Leicester churches for some time. He died in 1898 aged seventy-four after a highly productive ministry.

The Downs.

The Bowdon Baptists urgently needed a new minister with drive and energy. The search was to prove difficult.

---

[1] Ingham, op. cit.
[2] Astute readers will note that they had also lost one member.

LLEWELLYN

The departure of Betts caused a stall in the growth of the new church. It appears that two lay preachers were recruited to fill the gap and may have continued in post for some time, although we do not know their names.

The deacons began the search for a new minister. It took nine long months to find the right man. However, one of the strengths of Baptist churches is that they believe in the ministry of every member. There is a high degree of lay involvement, and this can help to ameliorate the problems caused by a lengthy period between ministers.

William Samuel Llewellyn was that new man. Born on 24 February 1848, he was the oldest child of Samuel Llewellyn, who was a deacon and church secretary of Cefn Baptist Church, Tydu, in Wales for sixty years. Llewellyn was educated at Stow Hill School in Newport and was baptised in the River Ebbw at the age of twelve. He was Welsh to the core.

The minister of Cefn Church saw potential in the young Llewellyn and encouraged him to consider the ministry. Llewellyn duly entered Spurgeon's College in 1872. From there, he moved to Altrincham and became minister of Bowdon Baptist Church in 1874 at the age of twenty-six. It is quite likely that Spurgeon himself helped to arrange Llewellyn's first post at Altrincham, as Spurgeon liked to see his students settled under his personal supervision.

Llewellyn found an unexpected bonus in coming to Altrincham, because there he met a young girl called Ann (or 'Annie') Barlow. They married in 1877.

According to a contemporary author, Llewellyn was 'distinguished by great earnestness and practical piety'.[1] *The Baptist Union Handbook* says, 'He was enthusiastic, deeply affectionate and sensitive, yet he held his congregations with great tenacity and warmth through his life'. He had a 'fervent religious faith'.

He was the first permanent minister of Bowdon Baptist Church and is indeed referred to in *The Baptist Union Handbook* as being the church's first minister. This reinforces the idea of the temporary church-planter status of Betts.[2]

William Llewellyn

Llewellyn was welcomed to Altrincham by the characteristic holding of a tea party at The Downs chapel on 10 October 1874. The tables were filled with beautiful flowers, paid for by a Mr Lee, and eight ladies prepared and served the food and drink.[3] At the meeting, the choir sang. Mr Kenworthy then told the meeting that it had been a difficult period without a minister, but they had kept well together and had not suffered from changes they had made after the departure of Betts.

---

[1] Ingham, op. cit.
[2] The position was ambiguous however, and probably deliberately so. Accounts in the local newspaper do refer to Llewellyn as being successor as minister to Betts.
[3] It is likely that they were the wives of prominent early members, so for the record they are Mrs Spence (Frank Spence was Treasurer), Mrs Kenworthy (Mr Kenworthy chaired the meeting and was probably Church Secretary), Mrs Sheldon (she was a member until 1895), Mrs Forster (Mr Forster was possibly a deacon and later a trustee), Mrs Leech (mother of Edward Leech who later became Treasurer), Mrs Ormond (Mr Ormond was also probably a deacon and later a trustee), Miss Parker and Miss Smith.

A Mr Nixon from Manchester made a speech, followed by Frank Spence. Spence was the son of the well-known and wealthy manufacturer Peter Spence. Frank Spence recounted how they had all said, when Llewellyn came to preach with a view to becoming minister, 'This man has come here to preach the gospel'. He regretted how some were beginning to move into theological areas that were 'not healthy; it is leaving the old lines'. To applause he recounted how their new minister had 'plighted his troth to the good old gospel, and for that too you are to be congratulated'. Clearly the deacons had made sure that Llewellyn was firmly on the evangelical track. Coming from Spurgeon's College, it was unlikely he would be anything else, but this illustrates some of the emerging theological tensions even within the Baptists, tensions that were later to cause them serious problems.

The Revd Duncan McGregor from Manchester spoke next, and finally it was the new minister's turn. He confessed he felt himself unworthy of the position. He said he came to Bowdon 'with some feelings of dread as I heard it was a suburb of Manchester and the people very wealthy and I am not one of the 'upper ten'.[4] However, when I look to Christ, these fears fade away...I hope by the strength and grace of God that we will leave our mark upon the neighbourhood and upon the community around us'. He sat down to applause, and the meeting finished with a vote of thanks to the choir, seconded by a Mr Gilchrist, a Presbyterian from Delamer Road and there to welcome his new near-neighbour.

Llewellyn worked hard to increase the numbers attending the church.

In the summer months you would have seen the Baptists pour out of The Downs chapel after the Sunday evening service, where they would gather around what was called the 'Big Lamp' outside the chapel and hold an open-air service. There was very little traffic then, and the lamp was in the middle of The Downs at its junction with Railway Street. Horse-cabs waited in a queue at the lamp.

---

[4] i.e. the top 10 per cent of society.

The big lamp at the bottom of The Downs. Although the picture is taken after the Baptists had left the chapel, one can still get a sense of what services around the lamp would have been like. Note the horse-drawn taxicabs.

As Llewellyn began his work at Altrincham to grow this new church, he was unexpectedly aided by two visitors to Manchester from the United States: the names of these two are still remembered today, and their influence can still be seen in mass Christian rallies.

MOODY AND SANKEY

Britain had never seen anything like Dwight Moody and Ira Sankey before. These two Americans toured Britain in 1874 and 1875. The nearest more modern equivalent would be the evangelistic tours of Billy Graham in the twentieth century, but Moody and Sankey were the pioneers of this kind of mass evangelism.

Spurgeon appears to have been unsure of Moody and Sankey. McLaren had a similar struggle. These two Americans had a very 'un-British' and direct way of presenting the gospel. However, when Spurgeon and McLaren saw the large number of people becoming Christians, they both acknowledged that there must be something positive happening. Spurgeon eventually endorsed the pair in an article in the *Sword and Trowel*.

The impact of Moody and Sankey on the country was enormous. In Manchester, the Free Trade Hall was packed. People had not seen anything like this before. Perhaps they were drawn to the spectacle, but once there something strange happened. Moody was the preacher and Sankey sang. Many were moved to tears as they heard his voice.[1] After Sankey's singing, Moody would preach, and he would usually ask for those who wanted to respond to stand. That was a very novel thing at the time.

These revival tours had a profound impact on people. It is highly likely that the Altrincham Nonconformists would have taken their friends to hear Moody preach and Sankey sing at the Manchester Free Trade Hall.

As no one had come across the Moody and Sankey style of evangelism before in Britain, it was not known how successful it would be. The success appears to have caught the Altrincham churches by surprise, but in what seems to have been a spontaneous coming together to capitalise on the mission, many of them united to carry out their own spin-off united local mission.

The first report in the local press was in January 1875, when there were stated to be large attendances and conversions to the Christian faith at a week-long Altrincham mission. The missioner was a Mr Dunn. The meeting to conclude the week's mission was held at the British School off Oxford Road. Each night people who responded would go into an enquiry room at the back. Llewellyn was on the platform, as was Wainwright of St John's Church.

Such was the success of the Altrincham mission that another week was hastily planned. Who could they invite to speak? They (or more likely Llewellyn on behalf of the Altrincham churches) approached McLaren at short notice. McLaren fortunately was available.

> The impact of Moody and Sankey and the Altrincham missions can be seen by the fact that by February 1876, Llewellyn reckoned he had baptised sixty people, no mean feat in fourteen months of ministry.

After a prayer by Llewellyn and announcements by Frank Spence about the arrangements for the second week, McLaren spoke. McLaren was never an evangelist, but his talk was much more direct than his usual style. One can sense the caution in McLaren's opening words in Altrincham, however: 'Whatever people

---

[1] Sankey's song collections were later used by many churches, being similar in impact in their day to the *Mission Praise* songbook of the Billy Graham missions.

might say about Messrs Moody and Sankey, there is at least this in them – that they do not let anyone get away from the intensely personal character of Christ's faith and message.'

The rest of McLaren's message was based on the text, 'If anyone thirsts....' McLaren believed that people in Altrincham were thirsting for God and needed to come to God.

The mission was successful and was extended for a further week, moving to the lecture hall at the back of the Presbyterian Church on Delamer Road. Later in 1875, Dunn returned for a follow-up week's mission. Something was clearly happening in Altrincham.

> There is a hand-written note in the Manchester City Mission archives of the effect on one person of the Moody and Sankey mission. The anonymous author wrote: 'When Moody was in Manchester the first time at a meeting in the Free Trade Hall 49 rose when he gave the appeal. Moody said he was sure there was a 50th man. MS rose. What a change there was in him from then to the end. When Oakfield House was started, Matthew became the laundry man and carter. He was a great soul winner and one of the best 'finders' in the Ambulance Corp'.[2]

> The Manchester Young Men's Christian Mission (the 'YMCA'), a Christian evangelistic organisation, benefited from the Moody and Sankey mission. At one meeting at the Free Trade Hall a large collection was given toward a new building which provided the nucleus of more than £30,000 ultimately raised.[3]

> There were, of course, mockers of Moody and Sankey. An anonymous 'London physician' wrote, 'Alas! Judged by the low standard of an American ranter, Mr Moody is a third-rate star. As for Mr Sankey, the friend who can sing, his voice is decidedly bad, and, like all worn-out singers, he endeavours to conceal this by startling alternations of high and low notes.' This was a minority opinion, however.

---

[2] The first 'preventative home' of the Manchester City Mission, where 'fallen' and 'at risk' young ladies were sent to be rescued. See further in the next chapter. It is not clear who 'MS' was.
[3] The current YMCA is at Castlefield in Manchester.

The hall at the back of the former Presbyterian church on Delamer Road in use in 2006 for coffee after an Altrincham Baptist Church morning service. Part of the Altrincham spin-off Moody and Sankey mission was held here.

Moody and Sankey contemporary souvenirs.

The mission of Moody and Sankey to Manchester was substantially funded by an immensely wealthy man called Frank Crossley. Without him, Moody and Sankey might never have come to the north-west of England.

We will now look at this man who made so much money, and then gave it all away. His story is one of the most remarkable in Altrincham. Not only that, but he may have had a link to our case study church in a way that has remained hidden until now.

THE MAN WHO GAVE IT ALL AWAY

Like McLaren, the name of Frank Crossley has almost disappeared from the collective memory of Altrincham. True, his name can be found in books on engineering, where the name of Crossley Engineering is still a by-word for British manufacturing achievements, but as a philanthropist and devout man, there is very little said of him today. The name of his brother William appears on one of the rear foundation stones of the extension to the Hale Road Baptist Chapel, and yet few in Altrincham today will have heard of the Crossley brothers.

That is a tragedy. The Crossley story is fascinating.

To understand Frank Crossley, you will have to use your imagination again. He is one of the wealthiest men in the United Kingdom. Imagine he lives nearby in a mansion. He is head of a major British company which has an international reputation and which he co-founded with his brother. He supports and funds large-scale Christian and philanthropic projects; indeed he appears to give most of his wealth as a multi-millionaire away.

This is Francis J. Crossley, who lived in Bowdon.

Frank Crossley aged 20. While living in Newcastle at about this age and short of money, Crossley would go to the theatre for entertainment. A friendly usher took pity on him and let him in for free. Years later, Frank paid the theatre £60 in compensation.

Frank Crossley was born in 1839 and his brother William in 1844, both in County Antrim in Ireland. Their mother's family was descended from Huguenot refugees who had fled France in the 1680s. Their father was a retired army major from the East India Company. The family was devoutly Christian.

Crossley was educated at Castletown in the Isle of Man, Tarvin Hall in Cheshire and then Dungannon in Ireland. When he left school, he joined Robert Stephenson's engineering works in Newcastle.

He then re-located to Liverpool to be a draughtsman, before setting up his own engineering works with his brother. Together, they took over Dunlop's rubber business at Great Marlborough Street in Manchester.[1]

In its heyday, Crossley Engineering was a huge Manchester company. The brothers' stroke of fortune was when they bought the patent to the German 'Otto' engine, which they adapted, enhanced and developed. Sales of the engine became the foundation of the company. Production started in the 1870s in Hulme, and they then acquired a new site in Openshaw in order to expand.

When they first moved to Manchester, the brothers (with their sister Emmeline), took lodgings with local builder Martin Stone at 1 Bell Place, 24 Stamford Road in Bowdon. Later Frank moved to Oaklands on Langham Road.

---

[1] This Dunlop is no relation to any Dunlop of Dunlop Tyres, but he did sell machinery for working India rubber. The factory was near Oxford Road railway station in Manchester.

The brothers attended St John's Church. William remained an Anglican throughout his life, becoming a churchwarden of St Margaret's, Dunham Massey, but Frank soon gravitated to a church in Manchester. That church was McLaren's Union Baptist, and Crossley and McLaren became good friends.

When Crossley attended his first service at Union Chapel, he was greeted by McLaren's cousin Alexander, known as 'Alick' to avoid confusion. Crossley's only sister, Emmeline, eventually married Alick. Crossley himself married the Canadian-born Emily Kerr, and as Crossley Engineering prospered, the couple moved in the mid 1870s to a purpose-built mansion they called 'Fairlie' in Bowdon, named after the Kerr family's holiday home on the Clyde.

Crossley then decided to attend a more local church and, while continuing to be involved with Union Chapel, he joined Bowdon Downs Congregational Church. Later, he became friends with MacKennal. For many years he worked with the children in the Sunday school.

The Crossleys had five children: Helen Katherine ('Ella'), Richard ('Richie'), Alan, Erskine Alick and Francis. The Crossleys were deeply affected by the early death of their young son Richie in 1884 aged eleven, who died in Crossley's arms. Richie was buried in Bowdon parish churchyard.

Crossley was much influenced theologically by reading Erskine, St Francis of Assisi and Madame Guyon.[2] In 1887, he delivered an address to Bowdon Downs Congregational Church on 'The Ideal Church'. It would be interesting to know what he said. He later became influenced by the 'holiness' movement, something which took him away from his earlier Calvinism and into the same theology as that held by the Salvation Army, many Methodists and indeed probably MacKennal. In 1888 and 1889 he held his own holiness conventions in a marquee at Fairlie.

Although they were members of Bowdon Downs Congregational, with Crossley being a deacon between 1881 and 1888, it is clear the Crossleys had sympathy with the Baptists on the subject of believers' baptism. They never christened their children, and when the children were old enough to make their own choice, they were baptised as young believers by MacKennal at Fairlie in 1883.

Crossley was involved in the Social Purity Campaign. This has led to subsequent (and perhaps unfair) criticism.[3] He was seriously concerned that young girls were being forced into prostitution in Manchester and he campaigned for tougher laws on brothels. He and others in the Campaign (which was genuinely ecumenical) tried to 'rescue' prostitutes. Later, it was found that the police *Frank Crossley in 1894* were involved in corruption concerning prostitution. Crossley set up a women's rescue home in Cheetham Hill and two in the Altrincham area. Manchester City Mission was at the forefront of giving these young girls an alternative life and the Mission's records for Altrincham show that street girls in Altrincham were referred to the 'Bowdon' refuges.

---

[2] A French Roman Catholic mystic, much persecuted by the authorities for her faith.
[3] For a critique of this aspect of his life, see *Frank Crossley: Saint or Sinner* by Edward Mynott, who judges him with the hindsight of modern liberal thinking.

Sometimes Crossley would arrange to meet prisoners as they left prison and would take them for a meal, talk to them about Christianity and try and help to set them up in a new life.

Crossley became involved in politics as a result of massacres in Armenia, and personally gave support to refugees and orphans.[4]   He also supported the beleaguered islanders of Crete.[5]   He corresponded about these and social issues in the columns of *The Manchester Guardian* and even exchanged letters with Gladstone.

Crossley, however, found his own personal wealth an increasing burden and felt it might corrupt him as a Christian.   He startled a visiting American evangelist by saying: 'We think a great deal about consecration, and talk a great deal about it, but I do not think this house looks consecration'.   He said to MacKennal: 'Don't be afraid of bleeding me. I am the possessor of a patent...While I am making money, I ought to give it away'.

Frank Crossley's signature. A signed Crossley cheque to a deserving organisation was often for a very significant sum.

On 6 February 1888 he held a conference at Bowdon Downs 'on the duty of the church to the poor of Manchester'.   At around the same time he urged the members of the church to get on their knees.   'To some of you this place is sacred for its quiet, refined associations; you love it.   As for me, I hate it all.   Let us leave this respectable neighbourhood and go right down among the poor folks.   That is where a church should be'.[6]

Crossley's fellow members at the affluent Bowdon Downs Congregational Church were taken aback.   Surely he did not expect them to give up all their riches and move from comfortable Bowdon to the slums of Manchester?   Crossley was serious though about moving.   He talked it over with Emily.   He resigned as a deacon, they sold their beloved Fairlie, gave most of their possessions away and moved to Ancoats to work with the poor.[7]

Ancoats at the time was one of the most notorious slums of Manchester.   The police only went about in threes and it was regarded as advisable to carry a gun.

The Crossleys deliberately chose one of the toughest areas of Manchester in which to live, and in the case of Frank, to die.

William Eadson was Crossley's main agent in trying to close brothels in Manchester. A handwritten note by Eadson's daughter records that Eadson found the work so difficult that his only release was to come home and, on a starry night, indulge his passion for astronomy with his telescope.[8]

---

[4] The first massacres by Ottoman Turks were in 1894. The Baptist minister in the late 1890s was a member of the local Armenian support society, along with MacKennal.

[5] Armenians and Greeks were among those paying special respects at his funeral. Armenia was a favourite Liberal Party cause.

[6] The statement is quoted in Harris, J. Rendel (ed): *The life of Francis William Crossley*, James Nisbet and Co, 1899, and also in Crossley, E.K.: *He heard from God*, Salvation Army, 1959, albeit with slight variations.

[7] Both MacKennal and McLaren immediately wrote in support. Emily said later that the plunge 'was a big one', but one that proved to be right. The Crossleys donated their paintings to the Art Gallery in Manchester. Emily gave away her jewellery.

[8] Manchester City Mission archives.

The Crossleys outside Fairlie in 1877. One day, Crossley saw a man admiring the flowers at Fairlie. Characteristically, he went up to him and took him on a tour of the gardens while explaining the gospel to him. The man eventually confessed that he was, in fact, a burglar.

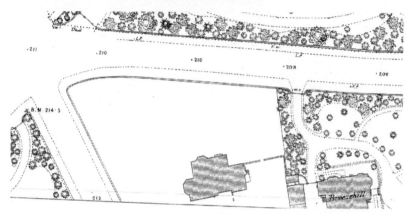

Fairlie from an 1878 map.

Frank Crossley wrote to a friend after a Salvation Army meeting, 'If Jesus says to me, "Frank Crossley, you must sell up Fairlie and go", I will do it, and now I will do it with joy'. Not long afterwards Crossley sold Fairlie.

The main entrance to Fairlie. The house is now part of Altrincham Grammar School for Girls.

The entrance to Crossley Engineering in Manchester, now part of Rolls Royce. Some families worked here for generations.

The remains of the chapel of the old Crossley Engineering on Pottery Lane. There is still a painting of the Last Supper inside. Services were held here every morning before work started.

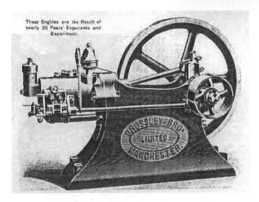

A Crossley engine. The brothers were able to buy the rights to the German Otto engine. You can see Otto and other Crossley engines and a Crossley car in the Museum of Science and Industry in Manchester.

Frank Crossley while living in Ancoats.

Not only did the Crossleys move to Ancoats, they also bought the old Star Music Hall there, demolished it and replaced it at a cost of over £20,000. This artist's impression is of Crossley's new Star Hall. The first meeting was held in the hall on 4 August 1889. The Crossleys worked in the hall and lived in a very modest house adjoining it. Seven hundred workers met there each Sunday evening and there was a thriving youth movement. The hall provided baths and laundry services for

the poor. The Crossleys personally brought the poor in from the streets to look after them. The hall had a coffee tavern on the ground floor and rooms for people to meet in. In the winter, they distributed blankets to those in need.

The Openshaw Club moved to the former mechanics' institute in Pottery Lane in 1896. Before that it was next to Star Hall.

Crossley Youth Centre in Openshaw founded by William Crossley.

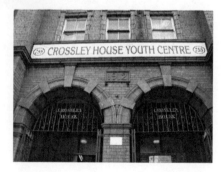

The children's home on Ashley Road which later became Hale Urban District Council (UDC) and is now the site of an hotel. The first photograph shows the children's home and the second is taken in the coronation year of 1953 and shows the building now as Hale UDC. This home and one further along Ashley Road were funded by Frank Crossley. In October 1880, 42 Chapel Street in Altrincham was bought as a refuge 'to give religious, moral and industrial teaching, similar to that which a good mother would bestow, to female children who are unprotected or in circumstances of degradation'. Mrs Crossley, Mrs Geldart (wife of the famous painter) and Mrs Morris were on the committee. A meeting to consider setting up a new refuge was held in 1881 at Townfield House and hosted by the Armitage family. In 1882 the Chapel Street home was transferred to the former Hale UDC site and supervised by Isabella Burns. Crossley paid £2,500 towards the cost of the new home. In 1891, 25 girls were resident, aged six months to sixteen years old.

On 31 May 1883, Crossley also bought land near the junction of Warwick Drive and Ashley Road in Hale from Robert Harrop (239 Ashley Road) and further land at the junction of the two roads. Crossley agreed to construct a girls' home within one year, again at his own cost. In 1891 there were nineteen girls at this second home aged four to fourteen. The wonderfully named Alice Death was matron, later moving to the other orphanage. Much later, after Crossley died, Emily Crossley sold the building at number 239 to John Ferguson, the former head of the British School in Altrincham, who converted the premises into a place for social and political gatherings dedicated to St Baldred. Given the Crossley family's involvement in the Liberal Party, it is ironic that it later became the Conservative Club.[9]

[9] This appears to be the story from looking at title deeds, Alfred Tarbolton's notes and Manchester City Mission archives, although the stories do not entirely coincide. At the time of writing it is no longer the home of the Club.

Although this chapter is about Frank Crossley, his brother William is also connected with the Hale Road Baptist Chapel, partly because his name is on one of the foundation stones for the rear extension in 1908. William was a philanthropist in his own right. He established the Openshaw Boys' Club and was Chair of the Manchester Hospital for Consumption and Diseases of the Throat. He made a substantial contribution towards the accommodation and equipment at St Anne's Home in Altrincham. He was passionate about education and the benefits of electricity. In 1903 he was made a freeman of the City of Manchester. He was elected as the first Liberal MP for Altrincham. He was made a baronet in 1909 and a director and founder of the Manchester Ship Canal. He died in 1911.

The enormous sanatorium at Delamere in Cheshire funded by William Crossley. In 1900 he gave a staggering £70,000 towards the project.

We now look at the Salvation Army, for without the Crossleys there would probably not be a Salvation Army today.

THE SALVATION ARMY

Crossley gave over £100,000 to the Salvation Army. This would have paid for the building of roughly forty Hale Road Baptist chapels. It is no wonder that Crossley was known as the paymaster of the Army.

He was attracted to the 'Army' in part by its views on holiness and in part by its sense of radical and holistic mission. He even considered joining at one point, but Emily was less enthusiastic. The Booths, founders of the Army, were frequent visitors to Fairlie[1].

The Salvation Army's first local base (or 'citadel' as they called them) was in Altrincham and they then set up in Bowdon in 1880. The Army used the Bowdon skating rink, which had been a short-term electric-lit wonder, but was short of seating space. The local newspaper noted dryly, 'The Salvation Army has at last sent a detachment to Bowdon, which will shortly open fire. The place according to latest advice awaits the shock with tranquillity'. In 1883 it noted in the same dry vein that the Altrincham audiences 'though not large, have been somewhat select'.

The newspaper soon regretted these words as the Salvation Army grew substantially in numbers. The Army was very much a movement designed to appeal to the working classes. Its natural constituency was in the poor Newtown area of Altrincham.

The Army brought controversy with it, perhaps sometimes deliberately. In 1881 one John Kelly was arrested for being drunk and disorderly and assaulting someone at a meeting. Matters came to a head with Altrincham residents in March 1887. The Army used to assemble a crowd of 200-300 on George Street for public preaching. They were outside the shop of a certain Mr Cowsill. He or someone on his behalf threw half a gallon of peas over them from an upper window. Cowsill then complained to the police that they were obstructing the highway. The Army refused to move until they had finished their preaching and the two leaders were arrested. The fine of one was paid, but the other refused to pay and went to Knutsford Prison for fourteen days. She was accompanied by a large crowd of sympathisers.

It is likely that this is the same incident where Crossley, himself a JP, is reported as having come off the bench to sit with the defendant. In any event, Crossley wrote a strongly worded letter to the local newspaper in which he criticised the 'blunder' of the magistrates, saying the Army's only offence was street preaching, and that to deny them this right amounted to religious discrimination.

Soon the correspondence in the local newspapers was expressing displeasure at the disturbance of tranquil Sunday afternoons by the sound of the Army bands. In May 1889 the local newspaper reported: 'The Salvation Army was on a war path on Sunday. At half-past six in the morning they marched through the streets headed by a brass band blowing more vigorously than usual'.[2]

---

[1] Crossley, op. cit.
[2] Altrincham Division Chronicle.

73

Over time however, some of the local churches came to respect the evangelistic and practical work the Army was doing amongst the poor. In May 1887 General Booth headed a holiness convention in Altrincham with the Methodists. In 1901 the Army demolished some cottages in Beggar's Square to the left of the Bricklayer's Arms on George Street and a new barracks was built, which was accessed off George Street. Their old building on Shaw's Lane became a theatre. In 1902 General Booth spoke on 'Lessons of my Life' at the Literary Institute, and the meeting was chaired by the influential John Thompson, brother-in-law of Frank Crossley. In 1904 Mrs Bramwell-Booth spoke at Bowdon Downs Congregational and later that year their bazaar saw the respected Jesse Haworth presiding, supported by the then Baptist minister. The Army had gained Nonconformist support.

The Salvation Army outside the market hall in Altrincham. Their evangelism was a little more direct than that of most local churches. One banner reads 'Heaven or Hell. Wither bound? Answer!' Another says, 'Seek the Lord while He may be found' and another 'What a friend we have in Jesus'.

Advertisement for Cowsill's in 1904. It was from a window at Cowsill's shop that the peas were poured.

Salvation Army Harvest Festival, probably at Shaw's Lane.

The Salvation Army was, however, not the only mission organisation in uniform in Altrincham.

MANCHESTER CITY MISSION

It was not only the Salvation Army that Frank Crossley encouraged and funded.

In late Victorian times, you would have seen men and women, often in uniform, knocking on doors throughout the poorer areas of Manchester and Salford. These people were missionaries working for what was known as the Manchester and Salford City Mission.

You may not be surprised by now to learn that Crossley joined the main board of the Mission in 1884/5. He was stated to be 'a worthy and generous member'.[1] Crossley was also linked with the Mission by marriage as we have seen. John Thompson, who was also on the board of the Mission, married Leila Kerr, Emily Crossley's older sister.

The Mission was not a church; rather it was an organisation to support churches in local mission or to set up missions in areas where there were no effective churches. Its aim was to bring people to churches. In this, it was not always successful. It would often set up mission halls and then find that new converts did not want to leave them. These then became quasi-churches. The still-flourishing Ivy Cottage Church in Didsbury is an example.[2]

The Mission worked mostly in poorer areas. The gospel they presented often went hand in hand with social assistance.

The newspaper report of the 1870 Annual Meeting in Manchester quotes the Chairman as saying that the Mission consisted of 'churchmen and dissenters who, sinking their differences on church government, had worked together with perfect harmony'. The work of the Mission was to go into districts and 'not to proselytize'. It was a genuinely ecumenical project.

The Mission was enormous in scope, even extending its efforts to Blackpool and having evangelists and numerous mission stations throughout Manchester.

The Mission's centenary book does not even mention Altrincham, and yet research has shown that the Mission was actively working in Altrincham for many years. It is even possible that the Mission provided one of the two lay preachers for Bowdon Baptist Church after Betts left.

The Mission started in Altrincham in fact in 1853, and began feeding new converts into existing churches. It was usually called the 'Town Mission'. Bowdon Downs supported the Town Mission for many years. In 1855 for example it donated £27-12s-6d. It may also be significant that it gave a much higher donation of £43-11s-6d to Manchester City Mission on 23 October 1871 at the same time as Bowdon Baptist was being formed.[3] Was this to give a boost to the new Baptist church, or just to mission generally in Altrincham?

We do not have full records for all the 1870s of what the Mission was doing in Altrincham. There is a report in 1877 of a Mr Corfield carrying on the Newtown Free Mission at a house in Islington Street and giving a substantial tea for forty. It

---

[1] Lee, R.: *Mission Miniatures*. Crossley substantially funded the Mission.
[2] Ivy Cottage Church was started in a cottage of that name and, when it built its own building (paid for by one man), it kept its old name. The pastor of Ivy Cottage until 2007 was formerly a member of Altrincham Baptist Church.
[3] Manchester City Mission minutes.

is not clear if he was associated with the Mission, but in 1877 we know that a James Collier was a missionary at a house in Police Street. We also know that by 1880 Manchester City Mission had two full-time missionaries in Altrincham. One of them was a Mr Heard who appeared on a joint platform with the then Baptist minister and Wainwright.

So what did the Mission do in Altrincham? The following examples give a brief flavour for the years 1880 and 1881.

Mostly they visited the poor, knocking on doors and bringing help and the gospel to the occupants.

They held Bible classes in Altrincham on Sunday evenings. The aim was for people from the churches (both clerical and lay) to 'come into contact with people they would not otherwise meet or bring to church'.

In 1881 six young women were taken to the girls' home in Hale and fourteen people signed the pledge (i.e. they agreed to abstain from alcohol), of whom five were stated to be 'great drunkards'.

One eighteen year-old orphan girl came to an open-air service at Goose Green off Railway Street. She later became a Christian at a house meeting.

On Sundays the missionaries would visit the cab stands and talk to the cab men and carry out street evangelism.

During the Altrincham Wakes, the missionaries held open air public meetings. At the end of one such meeting, a man came up to an evangelist. He had previously received a tract. He then came to a missionary's house and was 'led to the Lord'.

The Mission as a whole was obsessed with statistics of its activities. This was no doubt to demonstrate its worth to its funders. The Altrincham Town Mission was no exception. Here are some statistics from the 1870 Altrincham report.

Twenty-two people are recorded as beginning to attend church for the first time. There were 3,409 house visits and 252 meetings, of which fifty-seven were in the open air. Some of these were to large audiences. The aggregate attendance at all meetings was estimated at 10,000. The Bible was read 2,600 times in houses and 2,500 scriptures and illustrated tracts were distributed.[4]

In the summer of 1881 they held meetings at the gypsy encampment on Hale Moss where the gypsies 'appeared to listen most carefully to the message of the Gospel'.

As well as Crossley, there are three other people who we should note were connected with both Manchester City Mission and the Altrincham Baptists. The first is McLaren. It was as early as 1860 that he addressed their rally at the Free Trade Hall. McLaren continued to support Manchester City Mission throughout his life. Its ecumenical endeavours were close to his heart.

The second person is Henry Mowbray, successor as minister to Llewellyn. John Thompson in 1893, in a speech at the Hale Road chapel, spoke of his high esteem for Mowbray and how he was 'most trustworthy' in Thompson's work at the

---

[4] By comparison, the whole of the City Mission in 1870 made 377,981 visits and held 12,236 meetings.

Mission. Sadly we do not know what Mowbray did, but it must have been significant.

The third person perhaps demonstrates a closer connection between the Mission and the Altrincham Baptists than previously known. The Mission records show that a Mr Langley was a Manchester City missionary in 1871. One of the later trustees of the Altrincham Baptists was also called Langley. Whether the missionary and the trustee are one and the same person we do not know, but the Langley on the church trust deeds was the Deputy Treasurer of the Manchester City Mission. In 1883 we find Langley on the same platform at a rally as the then Bowdon Baptist pastor.[5]

The early Altrincham Baptists, like other Protestant churches, may have benefited from and worked closely with Manchester City Mission in Altrincham to help grow their churches.

A Manchester City Mission missionary visiting in
a poor area. Missionaries almost always wore a uniform.

We now look at some of the background to growth.

[5] There is also a Joseph Langley who was later a Baptist minister at Padiham near Warrington. He might have been the same Langley.

THE WIDER CONTEXT

If the initial growth of the Baptists at The Downs chapel in Altrincham was spectacular, this has to be seen in the context of the growth of churches in Lancashire and Cheshire as a whole.[1] There is a myth that Baptist growth was primarily in London and this has somehow turned to criticism of the ecumenical McLaren and praise of Spurgeon. Let us attempt to redress the balance.

The Lancashire and Cheshire Association of Baptist Churches at the time was recognised as one of the most progressive in the country. In 1865, the Baptist Union told the Association at its Liverpool Assembly that one fourth of all its churches had come into existence in the previous twenty years: 'There is no part of the country in which the contrast is more striking between what the Baptist denomination is now, and what it was twenty or thirty years ago'.

By 1888, the Association was the largest outside London. Around 62 per cent of all Baptist churches had memberships of 100 or less, but in the Association's area the average membership was nearly 150.

The *Nonconformist Magazine* on 26 March 1885 attempted a comparison of growth in 'sittings' in denominations by comparing the sittings in 1851 with those in 1885 in Lancashire and Cheshire. The fastest growing denomination was the Roman Catholic church and the second fastest the Baptist. However, both had started from a comparatively low base. The rise in numbers also reflected population growth and the continued migration to the industrial towns and cities of the north.

In 1838 there were thirty churches in the Association with 2,790 members. By 1887 there were 110 churches with 17,512 members. At the time, Nonconformists estimated that two-thirds of all congregations were not members (many, of course, were children).

The fastest period of growth in the north west was probably between 1860 and 1880. Growth was generally steady and not punctuated by bursts of revival. The exception was 1876, which saw the highest number of baptisms in a year, when 1,264 were baptised as believers. This high number is explained by the fact that the Baptists were heavily involved in the Moody and Sankey missions to Manchester in 1874 and to Liverpool in 1875.

J. Lee believes that the Baptists in Lancashire and Cheshire 'increased in number because they evangelised'. They also planted chapels in areas of new population growth such as Altrincham. Lee concludes that 'migration into the region did not contribute to the church's growth', rather most migration was from some parts of the north-west counties to others. In Altrincham's case, it was the migration of poorer and lower-middle-class people into the area that partly contributed to the Baptists growth. This can be contrasted with the influx of richer merchants and industrialists who contributed to the growth of Bowdon Downs Congregational Church.

---

[1] A number of the statistics in this chapter are based on research in *Transactions of the Historical Society of Lancashire and Cheshire*, vol. 124, 1973 by J.Lee: 'The growth of the Baptist Denomination in Mid-Victorian Lancashire and Cheshire'.

Bowdon Baptist Church therefore fitted into a wider pattern: the church was boosted by the Moody and Sankey mission and by immigration into the area, but much of its growth was down to its own efforts.

The *Nonconformist Magazine*'s assessment of growth between 1851 and 1885 was as follows:			
	1851	**1885**	**% growth**
Anglican	389,456	589,803	51.4
Roman Catholic	58,747	141,680	141.1
Baptist	35,694	77,518	117.1
Congregationalist	83,352	149,519	79.5
Various Methodists	188,025	382,060	100.3
Presbyterian	16,715	28,750	72.0

The junction of The Downs and Railway Street in 1897. The Downs Chapel is to the left of the photographer and just out of view.

Postcard of the big lamp at the bottom of The Downs as it was after the coming of the trams in 1907, and in 2007.

The bottom of The Downs as it was, and in 2007 before the later roadworks.

We now return to the true story of the fledgling church.

LOCATION, LOCATION, LOCATION

Let us return to the story of the fledgling church for the next chapters as it enters the most controversial period of its history, one perhaps more controversial than any other church in Altrincham.

Llewellyn proved to be a dynamic leader. Under him, the church grew from thirty to one hundred members. It is worth recalling at this stage that a typical congregation was (and still is) much larger than its members, and attendance at Bowdon Baptist services would have been nearer to 300 (including the Sunday school) according to contemporary estimates. By 1876, the Treasurer reported an income of £305-0s-2d. They had nearly balanced the books.

By 1877, the chapel at the foot of The Downs was becoming not only crowded; its age and poor condition could be hidden no more. Llewellyn had recruited a student pastor to help him cope with the increased numbers, one F. Parker who was attending Brighton Grove Baptist College in Fallowfield. Llewellyn began to wonder if now was the right time to find or even build another building.

The proposal to the church came at the annual tea party in March 1877, which 100 or so attended according to the local press. Llewellyn announced that they had been through a successful year, although perhaps not as successful as the Moody and Sankey years. People had still come to faith. The church should pray for more to do so in the next year. However, no church should ever be satisfied with what it had in terms of those new to the faith. They should be thankful for what they had, but they should seek more.

Spence brought his report as Treasurer. They were only £4-18s-5d short of balancing the books. Llewellyn immediately stopped the meeting and asked the members there and then to make up the shortfall, which they duly did. Simmons as church secretary thanked the ladies for the tea party and then almost nonchalantly proposed that the church should consider constructing a new building: 'I believe that this can be done if half the zeal is shown that has been manifested in clearing off the debt, and it will also soon be filled'. He was glad to say that their Sunday school was getting on exceedingly well; the number of children had considerably increased. They also had a very good library for the young people. A suggestion was made from the floor that 'the idea of having a new chapel should assume a more practical shape' and this became a formal resolution. The search for new premises was on.

We know from other sources that it was becoming difficult to find land to build new chapels in Bowdon. The Downs Chapel was well situated geographically. It was between Altrincham and Bowdon, opposite Bowdon station and not too far from the centre of Altrincham. Could they find anywhere as convenient? Given the name of the church, it is likely the Baptists scoured Bowdon for a suitable site and found none. They probably tried to buy land from the Earl of Stamford but to no avail.[1]

---

[1] According to Cynthia Walker, William Brewer thought the Hale Road land was actually bought from the Earl of Stamford. This was not the case, but the fact that he believed it to be so suggests there may have been detailed negotiations with the Stamford family. The Presbyterians built on land donated by the Earl of Stamford, and in 1872 the Unitarians negotiated to buy land at the junction of St John's Road and Delamer Road, but found the project too expensive. Ashton-on-Mersey (later Sale) Baptist Church was built on land donated by the Earl. The Primitive Methodists on Oxford Road took a lease from him in 1875. It would not therefore be surprising if the Baptists had looked to the Earl as well.

In walking down Oxford Road away from The Downs Chapel, the Baptists would have seen green fields at the end across the T-junction. If they looked to their left at the junction towards the then narrower railway bridge, they would have seen nothing but fields. Turning the other way and looking to the junction of Ashley Road and Hale Road, on the right hand side they would have seen houses and, on the left, fields again. There was no Willowtree Road and no Culcheth Road.

At first sight, this would not have seemed to be a good place to build a new chapel.

On closer investigation, they would have found two landowners. The first was Annie Moss, one of the Leicester family. Peter Leicester owned a lot of land in the area and had once resided at Spring Bank on Ashley Road. He was an attorney and gentleman farmer. The estate of John Tickle owned the other land. The boundary between the two landowners was along the side of the present Hale Road chapel and then continued along the back of the houses on Byrom Street. Would either of them sell any land?

Why would the Baptists want to build in a field right on the edge of town anyway?

We may never know for certain, but this was probably a combination of lack of land elsewhere and remarkable foresight.

What was planned for this area was a massive building programme. The idea was to lay out the streets now called Byrom Street, Bold Street, Brown Street and Bath Street (the 'B streets' as they are commonly called) and build cheap housing. There was also a plan to build Willowtree Road and a road running from the junction of Culcheth Road and Willowtree Road to the junction of Hale Road and Ashley Road which was to be called Leicester Road[2] and a plan to build on the far side of the railway bridge. However, Annie Moss was under a restriction that had a few years left to run that prevented her from selling her land.

Hale itself barely existed and was in fact called Peel Causeway,[3] but with a railway station already there, a town was clearly likely to grow up.

R. N. Dore wrote of the new church: 'Although just over the Altrincham boundary it has always been the "Chapel for Hale Baptists".' With respect to Dore, this is simply not true. The first aspirations of the church were to Bowdon, its catchment area was Altrincham and the predominant part of the membership was most certainly *not* from Hale. An analysis of the church members from the first available records shows that they mostly came from all areas of Altrincham.

The Baptists began negotiations with the estate of John Tickle. The land was within reach of the centre of Altrincham, five minutes' walk from The Downs Chapel and the railway station, halfway to the future town of Hale and in an area of projected new building. What is more, it was still within walking distance of Bowdon, so that they could still call themselves Bowdon Baptist Church.

There may have been one final consideration that influenced their choice. If today you stand at the Altrincham end of Oxford Road a hundred yards or so down, you cannot see much of the chapel. However, with its original tower, it would have

---

[2] This road was never built and this explains the odd configuration of some of the houses and titles on Hale Road. Culcheth Road was built instead, but even that was initially to be called Leicester Road after the Leicester family. For further information, see Appendix 2.
[3] Confusingly, the station was then called Bowdon Peel Causeway.

been clearly visible from the Altrincham end when Oxford Road was opened all the way up into Altrincham.

The Baptists had to move fast to secure the land. The building would take up the site of three houses on Byrom Street and probably two (with oddly-shaped sites) fronting Hale Road. The land was already earmarked for housing by the Tickle estate.

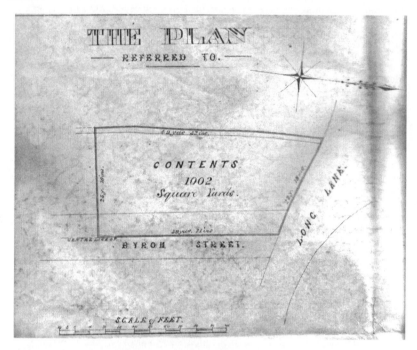

The plan from the 1878 lease to the Baptists. Note Hale Road is still called Long Lane and half of Byrom Street is included in the title. It was common to include half a street as the frontagers were responsible for the cost of sewers and construction of the road.

The Baptists had a problem though: they had no building fund. How could they buy the land? To answer this question, we need to look at how the Victorians in the north-west funded land purchases. The legacy of this is reflected in the strange system of ground rents and rentcharges found on many land titles today.

WHAT ARE THESE GROUND RENTS AND RENTCHARGES?

The Baptists had no cash. They needed to secure the land quickly. How could they do this?

They could not even hope to raise the capital sum to buy the land in the time available. They were unlikely to obtain a mortgage, and even if they did, they would need a further one to cover building costs. Most mortgages were private, and it was not always easy to find a lender at sensible rates. Their only real option was to use a tried and tested system that was then common in the north-west, but one that came with a sting in its tail.

Nowadays, a house-buyer will usually pay the full price for their house and finance the purchase by means of a twenty-five year mortgage. If interest rates are low, this is a good way of raising money relatively cheaply.

The mortgage market in 1878 was only just beginning to develop, and long-term loans of this sort were not readily available. What used to happen instead is that wealthy Victorian landowners would sell their land for a small sum, or even for nothing. In return, the buyer would pay the landowner a perpetual rentcharge and agree to build a building to a minimum letting value within a set period. A similar method was to grant a long lease, usually for 999 years, with a ground rent payable to the landowner.

If all went well, the landowner and his family would manage to convert their land into a perpetual income with a building as security and with the ability to re-possess if there was late payment of the rentcharge or ground rent. They would live off the income generated from the rentcharge or ground rent. Although they seem modest now, these ground rents and rentcharges represented substantial regular payments at the time.

The buyer too was happy, because he had to pay very little (or sometimes even nothing) for the land and was free to raise shorter-term finance for construction costs. The buyer might be an individual who would commission a builder to build a house for him or a builder who might build a series of houses and then sell these and reserve further rentcharges or ground rents. This system today can leave some property owners with a bewildering situation, where they have to pay what is now a small rent and then collect even smaller apportioned amounts from other owners on the street.

This system of freehold ownership coupled with a rentcharge is in fact peculiar to the north-west of England and to the Bristol area. Ground rents with long leases are also a particularly northern system.[1]

The 'B streets' near the new chapel were all developed in this way.[2] If you walk down Byrom Street today past the Baptist chapel, it is easy to see the very different styles of groups of buildings. This was because of the way the houses were developed in lots. There was little like the continental system of uniform town planning; the main development controls were private ones.

---

[1] It is best not to enquire too much how one can own a freehold and pay a rentcharge. The days of rentcharges are numbered, but they represent a strange anomaly in English property law. Contrary to popular belief, 'rentcharge' is the correct spelling. A rentcharge is not a 'chief rent', which was abolished long ago. When the author worked in London, he recalls how southern lawyers could never comprehend the northern system of rentcharges.

[2] The Victorians would be astonished to know they are now regarded as fashionable streets.

Despite the lack of planning restrictions however, houses usually had a common style in order to facilitate economies of cost and design. The 1878 _British Architect_ magazine ran a competition for the design of standard 'cottages'[3] for streets just like the 'B streets'. The winning design was remarkably similar to the design of some of the houses on the 'B streets'.

Many buyers bought to let, just as they do today. By letting the house out, they could easily generate enough income to pay the ground rent or rentcharge and then make a tidy profit. Most occupiers in the area rented their homes.

The system of ground rents and rentcharges generally worked well, and could easily be applied to the building of a chapel. For the Baptists however there was a triple sting in the tail. First, they were faced with paying a ground rent in perpetuity. For years, they struggled to pay it or to raise the finance to pay it off. It came second only to salary in terms of church expenditure.

The second was the level of the ground rent. In order to secure the land quickly before it was sold for housing, they may have been forced to bid high. An analysis of Brown Street, which was built slightly later than Byrom Street, shows that the church indeed paid over the odds for the ground rent. In 1894, the site of twelve houses on Brown Street was leased to a builder in return for a ground rent of £10-0s-10d a year. The Baptist chapel ground rent for land which could have between three and five houses was £25-1s-0d a year. At a conservative estimate, they paid six times the going rate to secure the land.

Analysis of other long lease ground rents in the area shows a similar, albeit variable, story. To further illustrate the point, the yearly rent the Baptists paid for The Downs Chapel on a short-term tenancy was not significantly more than the ground rent for the new chapel.

> The Victorians who sold off their land in return for ground rents and rentcharges could anticipate a life of leisure paid for by ground rents for generations to come. What they did not anticipate, however, was inflation.
>
> It can fairly be said that the hyperinflation of the 1960s was one of the greatest (and probably unintended) social engineering projects of the last century. Without any legislation, the upper-middle and upper classes involuntarily re-distributed their wealth to the house owners as they saw the value of their ground rents and rentcharges plummet. Coupled with inheritance taxes, the economic power of the landed class was fatally weakened.[4]

The final sting in the tail for the Baptists was the covenant to build itself. If they did not build a chapel, or at least three houses, on the site within one year, they lost the land, any partly-built building and all the money they had invested. One year was a very short time indeed.

---

[3] What we would call terraced houses the Victorians romantically called cottages.
[4] Altrincham Baptist Church, like everyone else, benefited from this. It finally bought the ground rent in 2001 for £375.75. The vendors at the time apparently expressed surprise it had taken the church so long to get round to buying it.

THE LOCAL ARCHITECT

One can almost sense the panic of the Baptists as they raced to raise the money and complete the building.

They rushed to appoint an architect. They could not afford an established name. They approached instead the young local architect and surveyor William Owen.

Owen was born on 19 February 1852. He was the son of Joseph Owen, one of the early developers of Ashley Road (then called Peel Causeway), the main road through Hale.

Owen was educated in Bowdon and then studied at the Manchester School of Art. He became an apprentice to the famous Edward Salomons. Salomons is best known for the design of the Reform Club on King Street in Manchester which was built in 1870-71 in Venetian Gothic style. He is also known for the Spanish and Portuguese Synagogue (now the Jewish Museum) in Cheetham Hill, which was built in Moorish style.

At the age of twenty-three, Owen was awarded the gold medal for excellence of architectural design by the Science and Art Department of South Kensington.[1]

When the Baptists approached Owen to design their new chapel, he was just twenty-six but described as a rising star. The age of twenty-six would be considered young today for an architect to undertake a major project.

Whether meetings were held at his house at Ferny Lea, 222 Ashley Road, Hale, we do not know. It is more likely that initial meetings were held at his office at 134 Deansgate, Manchester, where he worked in partnership from 1877 to 1881 with one Owen Edwards, trading under the name of Owen, Edwards and Owen. The firm had a branch in Rhyl.

As we shall see, the very location of Owen's Manchester office may have given some further inspiration both to him and to his Baptist clients as they tried to agree on the design of the new chapel.

Pictures show Owen to be a dapper gentleman. Two years after the Hale Road Baptist Chapel was finished, he married Alice. He was twenty-nine and she was twenty-two. Alice was the eldest daughter of a Vice-Chairman of the London and South Western Railway Company. They had three children, Cyril, Harold and Wilfred.

By the age of fifty, Owen was successful enough to be able to employ two servants. He designed a number of prominent buildings in his career, as well as being involved financially in the Bowdon Steam Laundry.[2] His biography states, 'In all these efforts Mr Owen has displayed much originality, ingenuity, and a perfect knowledge of the styles of the leading schools of architecture, both ancient and

---

[1] Amusingly the local newspaper credited him with the wrong award and published a correction in the next issue, no doubt after a letter from Owen. In the same issue, the newspaper also reported on proposals to build a Channel tunnel.
[2] For the record, examples of his designs include the Presbyterian church at Denbigh, a block of buildings for R. Oldfield in Rhyl and the Rhyl Winter Gardens, a new steam laundry for the Great Central Railway, the Hale Road Cemetery, the post office at Knutsford, alterations to Tabley Hall near Knutsford for the Honourable Cody Leighton, the residence of Sir William Pollitt at Altrincham and a banqueting hall and extensions at the Victoria Hotel, Sheffield, for the Great Central Railway Company.

modern'. He is well deserving 'of the position of prominence he now holds among the men of "light and leading" in Lancashire'.

Owen also worked locally. In 1904 *The Guardian Year Book* said he could claim to some extent "to being a pioneer of Hale as a residential district'.

Owen was to go on to become Chairman of Hale Urban District Council and a magistrate, a position which was to lead him into direct conflict with the very people who now paid for his services.

William Owen in 1905

Architectural design was the subject of much debate at the time. In 1877, *The Manchester Guardian* correspondence columns covered the topic of 'The Unloveliness of Manchester'. One letter was from Edward Salomons. Owen would no doubt have read the letter by his former mentor as he began his designs for the Hale Road chapel.

Salomons wrote: 'Whatever improvements have been made in the last thirty years have been done by our city council according to the best of their lights, the extent of the latter being the forming of a few new streets and widening some old ones. The greatest effort they ever made was the formation of Albert Square, the only open space of importance in the city itself, and the effort was so great that they had to do it at two different times, thereby having to pay compensation to owners for the improved value they (the Corporation) themselves had made. There ought to be someone who had made architecture and art his life study, who has seen and knows well the first cities in Europe, to advise with the Improvement Committee, as also to advise about the numerous matters that almost daily arise wherein art is in some way connected...Look at "the erection" in Albert Square, as also the lamp-posts there, these being a disgrace to our city. See the latter at Antwerp, what a difference! What a disgrace also to our city were some of the so-called triumphal arches erected on the occasion of the visit of the Prince of Wales; see also the new museum at Queen's Park and a number of other instances too numerous to mention.'

Owen designed the chapel at Hale Road Cemetery. This is the memorial stone with his name on it at the bottom right. Owen was also architect to William Marriott. He built two houses for him on Ashley Road near the old Bleeding Wolf public house, and Owen and Alice moved into one of them. Warwick Road, Warwick Drive and Appleton Road were laid out under his influence.

We now turn to a link with Italy.

THE ITALIAN CONNECTION

The church needed to decide on a style for the new building. The Victorians usually based their designs on the architecture of the past, sometimes 'blending' different historical styles in one building.

The Freeman Times of 6 June 1879 carried a humorous article satirising the way Baptists sometimes designed their new chapels. The deacons of the church, the author of the article wrote, would sit down and discuss the design without having any real idea of what they wanted or meant. One would produce a pretty sketch by his young daughter. Others would suggest different styles. They would meet with the architect and indicate their different choices and he would then design their building with Saxon porches, Early English side windows, a perpendicular window to blind the preacher, a Tudor vestry, a gallery supported by Doric columns and an Italian touch. The builder knew this building would not stand up, so he and the architect re-designed it anyway.

The Altrincham Baptists do at least seem to have opted for a uniform style. They wanted a striking design that would be modern yet affordable, visible yet functional. The building had to stand out at the end of Oxford Road.

They were immediately faced with the constraints of the site they had chosen. As the Tickle estate only owned a limited frontage of land on Hale Road, the rest being owned by the Leicester family who were unable to sell, it was clear that the right flank wall would have to be built more or less up to the boundary. The Baptists wanted a large schoolroom, so the only option was to build a long and fairly narrow building with the chapel part raised above ground level and the schoolroom partly sunk beneath ground level.[1] This in turn meant having a large number of steps at the front. As building well below street level could lead to damp problems, there needed to be a physical barrier between the left flank and the road.

To make the chapel more visible along Oxford Road, they decided to build a tower. The front left elevation gave the best sight-line.

Editions of *The Baptist Union Handbook* from 1872 to 1880 show just how many new Baptist churches were being built at the time. There were many retrospective styles, but the distinctive ones can be classified as neo-Classical (often emulating a Greek temple), Gothic, those which were trying to look like a nonconformist Anglican church and (in a minority) those in the Italian style. Of the Italian-style buildings, some are what we call Italianate and some are Romanesque.

The Baptists needed an appropriate style. A Greek temple front would be too wide. What led them to their choice? To find out, we need to do some detective work. Some of the detective work leads to a hypothesis. Whether it is correct is up to you to decide.

The chapel is built in the Romanesque style, and that is partly because the Romanesque style suited a narrow site. It was therefore to Italy that Owen and the Altrincham Baptists turned for inspiration, but we may be able to be even more precise than that.

---

[1] The rooms are so much below ground level that they were used as an air-raid shelter in the Second World War.

Italy was a country with which the Victorians appear almost obsessed, and the reason for this was very much down to one man. The great Victorian Romantic, John Ruskin, took his new wife, Effie, to Venice on their honeymoon. Effie soon discovered that Ruskin was more enraptured by Venice than by her. Ruskin never consummated the marriage and eventually Effie left him for the artist Millais.[2] The result of their honeymoon however was Ruskin's influential book, *The Stones of Venice*, published in 1850. Ruskin produced separate photographic plates to accompany his book. He also published a guide to Florence called *Mornings in Florence* and *Val d'Arno*, a series of lectures on Tuscan art. Venice was, however, his abiding passion.

Ruskin wrote 'Since the first dominion of men was asserted over the ocean, three thrones, of mark beyond all others, have been set upon its sands: the thrones of Tyre, Venice, and England'. His wish was that England would equal Venice in its heyday. He saw a parallel between the maritime merchants of Venice and those of Britain. To Ruskin, the later Palladian and baroque churches represented a fall from the true Venetian standards. To Ruskin, the Doge's Palace and St Mark's represented the authentic Venice.

The influence of *The Stones of Venice* can be seen in the many Victorian buildings designed in the Italian style. Just walking around Manchester with a little imagination, one can see the most unlikely Victorian buildings, ranging from factories to churches and schools, modelled on Venice and other Italian cities.

The Italian influence can be seen too in Osborne House on the Isle of Wight, designed for Queen Victoria and Prince Albert by Thomas Cubitt, and based on a design by Prince Albert. A pair of towers dominates the buildings and parklands. The tower on the Hale Road Church building bears more than a passing resemblance to one of these two towers.

The Italian style can also be seen in some of the mansions in the Bowdon and Dunham area. An example is Fairlie, the home of the Crossleys. McLaren used to visit the Crossleys most Saturday evenings at Fairlie. Crossley was also a friend of Joseph Geldart, an artist much influenced by Italian art. No doubt McLaren's interest in Italy was helped by meeting Geldart through Crossley.

The influence of Ruskin can also be seen in the colours of the Baptist chapel. Ruskin argued for bold and contrasting colours. The ornamental brickwork at the front of the chapel is in this style.

It is likely that McLaren himself had some further influence on the choice of design through his developing interest in Italy. In 1863, after his wife suffered a lengthy illness, McLaren was given a four-month sabbatical from Union Chapel. Like the Ruskins, the McLarens went to Italy. On his return, McLaren lectured on Italian art and architecture. McLaren regularly visited Italy after that for holidays. It is not inconceivable that someone from Altrincham heard one of his Italian art lectures.

One church McLaren particularly liked was San Pietro in Vincoli, Rome. Apart from Michelangelo's famous statue of Moses, the church is well known for its roof. The Hale Road chapel's inside barrel roof (minus the painted ceiling of course)

---

[2] Ruskin is reputed to have been horrified when he saw Effie without any clothes on for the first time after they married and discovered what a woman's body was like.

bears a passing resemblance to the ceiling of San Pietro, although of course there are many other examples that could have been copied.

However, one other chapel may have played a greater role in helping the Altrincham Baptists choose an Italian design. If you live in Manchester, you will have passed this chapel many times, probably without paying it much attention. At the south end of Deansgate is the former Knott Mill Congregational Chapel. The Knott Mill chapel was designed by the renowned Edward Walters and built in 1853. At the end of 1853 he won the competition to design the new Free Trade Hall, pipping Salomons, the mentor of Owen, into second place.

Why is this chapel particularly relevant to the Hale Road chapel? First, it was a Congregational mission church. By 1884 it was mostly funded and supported by Bowdon Downs Congregational Church: indeed, its missioner was at one stage a member of Bowdon Downs. In 1878, it is likely that Bowdon Downs may at least have had links with it, and Bowdon Baptist had a connection with Bowdon Downs. However, the connection with Knott Mill goes further than that.

Knott Mill station (now Deansgate station following the demolition of Knott Mill) would be the station where Owen and his Baptist clients would probably have alighted in Manchester before proceeding to Owen's office. As their train pulled into the then wooden station,[3] Simmons, Llewellyn and the other Baptist leaders would have seen the Knott Mill chapel below them. As they walked onto Deansgate, they could see it even more clearly. The Hale Road chapel front elevation and side elevations (minus the portico) are remarkably similar to the Knott Mill chapel, built in Romanesque style.

The Knott Mill chapel has a decided Venetian influence. This can most clearly be seen from the canal-side elevation and from the campanile tower, which appears to be based on that in St Mark's Square, Venice.[4]

The Hale Road chapel has a completely different tower however to that of the Knott Mill chapel. Perhaps it was best not to make it too obvious where the design was copied from.

Did Owen or his business partner make a trip to Venice? If Owen did visit Venice, would he have admired the brick architecture of some of the churches in Venice? Perhaps the Chiesa of San Giovanni Nuovo with its elongated domed ceiling, appealed to him.

He would have been likely to have climbed to the top of the dome of the Palladian church on San Giorgio Island. Looking out across the main arterial canal of Venice towards Piazza San Marco opposite, he would have admired the architecture of the great cathedral. His eye would have been drawn to the left to the famous tower on which the Knott Mill chapel was undoubtedly based. Just behind it, and poking out to the right, he would have seen a smaller tower. Apart from the change from two to three arches, the campanile tower of the Hale Road chapel bears more than a passing resemblance to this tower, which is that of San Silvestro.

---

[3] It was only in 1896 that the modern station was completed. The original wooden one was considered an eyesore.
[4] It was based on the original tower. Unknown to many tourists, the modern tower in St Mark's Square in Venice is a replica as the original tower collapsed in 1902, with the caretaker's cat the only casualty.

Even this is not entirely satisfactory though, and there are two more candidates. First, there is the tower of Santi Maria E. Donato on the island of Murano in Venice. A more complete and rather startling match might, however, be the basilica of San Francesco in Assisi.

It is up to you to decide, but the author's conclusion is that the Hale Road Baptist Chapel is influenced by the Knott Mill chapel (which in turn was based on a Venetian design) and with the Assisi basilica as the model for the tower.

Perhaps only Owen knew the truth.

John Ruskin at his home at Brantwood, Coniston, in the Lake District. He was influential in bringing the designs of Venice to Britain.

Effie Ruskin left Ruskin for the Pre-Raphaelite artist John Millais. Millais and Effie are shown here with their children, Effie and Mary. The photograph is taken by their friend Charles Dodgson, also known as Lewis Carroll.

Venetian colonnade. The original design of the portico on the Hale Road chapel frontage might have been based on this concept.

The Knott Mill Congregational Chapel at the southern end of Deansgate on which part of the design of the Hale Road chapel might have been based. The offices of William Owen, the Hale Road chapel architect, were on Deansgate.

The Knott Mill chapel was built on the site of the former Grocers' Hall. It later became a mission hall and an auction room. Its owners were intending in 2005 to convert it into a nightclub to be called (ironically) 'Mass'. However, plans were substituted to make the chapel into offices. The chapel's most recent claim to fame is that it was for many years the recording studio of Pete Waterman of Stock, Aitken and Waterman fame. 'Never Gonna Give You Up' by Rick Astley was recorded there.

St Mark's Square, Venice, and tower. The Knott Mill chapel tower was probably based on the St Mark's tower.

St Mark's Square close up. Note the smaller tower to the right...

...and here to the left, which is possibly reminiscent of the Hale Road chapel tower.

This photograph shows why the architect Edward Walters must have been thinking of Venice when he designed the Knott Mill Congregational chapel.

The Church of San Silvestro in Venice.

The Church at Vincoli favoured by McLaren. Note the ceiling. MacKennal visited Venice on his honeymoon. It was a familiar sight to see Victorian tourists from England admiring the architecture of Venice and then bringing back the inspiration for the design of their buildings, especially to Manchester.

The Italian-style ceiling inside the Hale Road chapel.

Was the Baptist chapel also based on the Basilica of San Francesco in Assisi?

The architect William Owen's original model for the new chapel in 1878, showing the front elevation. As one of the author's Roman Catholic friends has pointed out, it is ironic that the Victorian Baptists chose a Roman Catholic Church as the design model for their chapel. They would not have seen it that way of course.

LAUNCH TIME

Even though the church had to make no capital outlay in taking the long lease, they still needed to raise finance for the construction costs in a very short space of time.

They decided to have a high-profile launch and asked eminent people to endorse the project. The best opportunity was to use the laying of the two foundation stones to attract interest. Who should they ask to lay these?

The first person they asked was Peter Spence. This was a natural choice. His son Frank was treasurer and had already agreed to donate £100, which was then a substantial sum. It was felt the Spence family deserved the honour, and it was hoped they might give more. A Mr Houghton was suggested as the second person. He was a rich Liverpool businessman and had personally funded Baptist chapels in Liverpool. Perhaps the hope was that, by asking him to lay a foundation stone, he might do the same in Altrincham. Even if he did not, his presence would give them a powerful endorsement.

Next, they needed an eminent speaker. That choice was easy. McLaren had preached at the inaugural service at The Downs chapel and was invited back.

The Baptists also needed media support to generate local interest. They spoke to the local press and placed an advertisement on the front page of the local newspaper. The newspaper also gave them a free write-up. 'The present chapel is found to be the opposite of a comfortable and cheerful place of worship, and the members are now bent on providing a sanctuary more fitting to their wants...The choice of the site is one which commends itself in many respects'.

So on a Thursday morning in December 1878, a group of people gathered together. The foundation stones were probably laid in the ground. Later they were moved inside the portico at the top of the steps, then to a location at the top of the steps outside the portico, where they still are at the time of writing of this book.

There was a problem, however: at the last minute neither Peter nor Frank Spence could attend, and so it was by an accident of history that the name of the renowned Alexander McLaren came to be on one of the chapel foundation stones.

The winter of 1878 was one of the coldest on record. They had intended to make some speeches at the site, but it was so cold that, after brief prayers of consecration, they hurried down Oxford Road to seek warmth in the Primitive Methodist chapel.

There were eight ministers in the group. As well as McLaren, MacKennal of Bowdon Downs Congregational Church was there. It is possible that this was the first time the two had met. Given what was to happen later, this gives added significance to the event.

Once they were settled in the warmth of the Primitive Methodist chapel, Llewellyn gave a brief account of the history of the church thus far and in particular of the building project. 'I express my thankfulness to the giver of all good for the realisation of a long-cherished hope'. To applause, he thanked the foundation stone layers and the numerous friends who had encouraged and cheered them.

McLaren was next on his feet. McLaren's sermons were always carefully Scripture-based. It was less usual for him to give a public speech. As this was not a sermon, he used the freedom to give his forthright views on some controversial issues, and we will return to these later in more detail.

McLaren was, in fact, a witty and entertaining speaker. He was, he said, only standing in at the last minute for Peter Spence in laying the stone. He was not going to pay his £100 contribution for him! He had warm sympathy for the church and expressed his 'earnest desire for the prosperity of my friend Mr Llewellyn'. The priority for McLaren, however, was not the building of chapels: 'The building of a Baptist Chapel is a matter of small importance except for the hope that you have that the one Christ shall be preached'.

Aware that MacKennal was sitting in front of him and of the added significance that gave, McLaren next referred to the closeness of Baptists and Congregationalists. Pointing directly to MacKennal, he noted they were in practice 'one in heart and sympathy'. Everyone knew he was referring to a possible merger of the two denominations.

He did not think though that there could be much prosperity attending Bowdon Baptist unless there were real ministers and preachers there.

McLaren finished by seeking to make light of his speech: 'I rose without knowing what I was going to say, and I sit down not knowing what I have said; and therefore between the two you have got something very genuine...I hope that God's blessing, which is the root and source of all prosperity, might attend you'.

The records show this controversial but humorous speech was greeted with applause.

All eyes now turned to MacKennal as he rose to speak. He had only been at Bowdon Downs Congregational Church for one year and nine months and had not been able to meet with the Bowdon Baptists, although Llewellyn had attended MacKennal's induction service. To applause, he said he hoped that when they had got their larger and better chapel they would invite him back more frequently.

Clearly he had to respond to McLaren's carefully-put comments on the prospect of the Baptists and Congregationalists merging to form one denomination. He gave a cautious welcome, but was by no means as enthusiastic as McLaren. He said that he newly believed in the Baptists. 'Many of my earlier associations were with the Baptists. In my college days I felt there was very little reason why there should not be the frankest and fullest interchange of services and of sentiment amongst us. During the 20 years I have been in the Ministry, it has not either altered my feeling or judgment on that point'. To laughter, he said that there were some persons who believed him rather more than he believed in the Baptists, but that did not hinder him having a very cordial sympathy with them. Although the distinction between the Baptists and Congregationalists was a real distinction and one of considerable importance, there was much in common.

He concluded by saying, 'I hope that your entrance into your new building will witness a considerable increase in your numbers...I hope you will soon get into your building and, having got into it soon, get free from debt'.

Next to speak was Houghton. He used the occasion to discuss the controversy of differing beliefs on baptism. He then urged each person to take full part in the spread of the gospel. Bowdon needed this very much: it was a 'dark benighted place'. This comment from a Liverpudlian caused some amusement.

The service closed with a blessing by the Revd Jenkins of Salford. The congregation left the Primitive Methodist chapel and crossed over to the bottom of The Downs to have a lunch prepared in The Downs Chapel by Mr Barlow.

McLaren and MacKennal left after lunch. If as is likely this was their first meeting, it was the beginning of a major future collaboration together.

NEW BAPTIST CHAPEL, HALE ROAD, BOWDON. THE MEMORIAL STONES[1] of the above will be laid on Thursday December 12th, 1878, at 1.30pm by Peter Spence, esq, JP and John Houghton, esq. Address will be delivered by Revd. Dr. McLaren and other ministers. A PUBLIC LUNCHEON will take place in the Baptist Chapel immediately after the ceremony. Tickets 2s each.

In the evening at 6 o'clock, a TEA AND PUBLIC MEETING will be held in the British School. Charles Williams, Accrington, and the neighbouring ministers, will address the meeting. Tickets for tea 1s each.

Collection at each service on behalf of Building Fund.

Advertisement placed in local newspaper, December 1879. Note the reference to the chapel being in Bowdon, even though it wasn't.

---

[1] Sometimes 'memorial stones' was used, and sometimes 'foundation stones'. The more modern terminology is used in this book.

The stone laid by the renowned Alexander McLaren at the Hale Road Baptist chapel.

The wealthy industrialist Peter Spence who was to have laid one of the foundation stones. McLaren stood in for him.

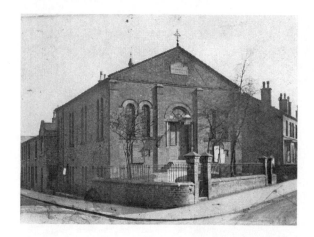

1905 photograph of the Primitive Methodist chapel where McLaren and MacKennal both spoke to the Baptists.

The chapel is now the Club Theatre.

MacKennal as an older man in 1904. When he spoke to the Baptists in 1878 he was thirty-seven and McLaren fifty-two. McLaren outlived MacKennal.

The launch day was not over for the church however. The real business of raising money had only just begun. They had a chapel to build and virtually nothing to build it with. They couldn't admit it, but they were in serious risk of losing the site.

THE VIEW FROM MANCHESTER IN 1878

In the crucial months of October to December 1878, when the temperatures plummeted and the new building was planned, what was the Altrincham reader of *The Manchester Guardian* to make of events? Let us use the newspaper to take a wider view.

The Manchester Guardian was both a local Manchester newspaper and a national one. The fact that a national newspaper was published in Manchester is a reminder of the importance of 'Cottonopolis', as Manchester was nicknamed. Although London was predominant as the capital of the country, much economic power lay in the north of England.

The Manchester Guardian in the months of October to December 1878 carried many articles. However, one can pick out certain themes.

The death in December at the age of thirty-five of Princess Alice, daughter of Victoria and Albert, clearly distressed Mancunians, and brought much sympathy for the royal couple.

Internationally, there were regular reports from Turkey and growing concern over the British intervention in Afghanistan. A Congregational minister wrote condemning the Afghanistan conflict 'as an act of aggression entered upon by the Government of the Country without provocation or excuse'.

Locally, the concern was whether the replacement of the gas lamps in the Free Trade Hall with electric lights would make the Hall too cold.[1] Dr Hans von Bulow, whose wife, Cosima, eventually married Wagner, was scheduled to play with the Hallé Orchestra.

Political rallies were tumultuous. The Conservatives, for example, packed the front rows of a Liberal meeting in Ardwick and sang patriotic songs in order to disrupt it.

Mark Addy received the Albert Medal 1st Class for repeated acts of heroism in saving people from the River Irwell. Later, he was to have a public house on the banks of the river named after him.

However, the main story was the economic depression. This hit Manchester particularly hard. Miners met in Manchester to protest. There was a strike in Oldham as wages were cut. Thousands were unemployed. There were bank failures in Glasgow, Bristol and Rochdale. There was no social security. Poor relief committees were set up in many areas of the

Even the rich Bowdon Downs Congregational Church was acutely aware of the effects of the severe depression. In 1878 they drew up a list of poorer members so that richer members could employ them and raised £22-9s-4d in one month to assist the poor in the area. In his 1879 Church Report, MacKennal highlighted the economic problems in Altrincham. In 1879 soup kitchens were set up and local temperance coffee shops sold tickets for cheap food and drink. Many were sent to the workhouse in Knutsford. Those who were able-bodied had to break stones as their labour. One local minister noted the plight of those who did not want to split their families up through the workhouse.

---

[1] These new electric lamps were probably early filament lamps and arc lamps, as the first carbon-filament incandescent light bulb was only demonstrated on 18 December 1878.

city and regular accounts were published in *The Manchester Guardian* as to their funding. This was the worst depression for many years, only to worsen in 1879 with one of the wettest summers on record, which badly affected agricultural production.

The Altrincham Baptists did not really know it at the time, but 1878 was probably the worst time since the cotton famine of the 1860s to launch a church building fund.

FINDING THE MONEY

What the new church lacked was a single rich benefactor. Most Baptist churches were poor, but there were a number of them which had strong financial support from wealthy donors. Houghton for example, one of the two foundation stone layers, paid most of the costs of three Liverpool chapels. He never paid anything significant to Altrincham.

What gave them encouragement though was that their treasurer was Frank Spence, whose father, Peter, could have easily paid for the construction of the chapel. It was also quite a clever move to appoint Frank Spence as treasurer, and thus give him particular responsibility for the building fund.

On the evening of the stone-laying ceremony, a meeting chaired by George Wood was held in the British School and about 300 people attended. Hymns were sung and the choir also sang. Johnston of the Presbyterian church led the prayers and said, 'I know you are right down good workers.'

Revd T. H. Hoylake gave some encouragement. He said that Llewellyn was to be congratulated on his work in Bowdon. Llewellyn might say that the work was difficult and that they were few in number, but he considered that Llewellyn could feel that these difficulties might turn out to be blessings.

Revd Hugh Davies of Lymm spoke next. Lymm is a few miles from Altrincham and is the older Baptist church, having a history going back to at least 1756. He said that there were three things essential to a Christian church: supreme love of God, sincere love to the brethren and considerable self-denial. Self-denial would be vital to raise any money.

Next onto the platform was Revd J. Stuart of Stretford. What is a man worth if he cannot face difficulties, he asked? 'God put metal into you and made you men and not boys. The church will be very much what you make it. It is erected as a place of worship and a place of prayer. Without the presence of God you will have nothing but bare walls and an empty room.'

Llewellyn now read a telegram from Frank Spence regretting that he was not able to be present with them but stating that his £100 was ready.

Houghton had stayed on after lunch, and he delivered the main gospel address. He was, in fact, standing in for Charles Williams, a man whose name will feature later. At the end of Houghton's address, Revd D. R. Jenkins spoke. He hoped that their good church secretary's appeal 'would be met with a hearty response'. The Downs Chapel was dilapidated, and there was an urgent need for a new building.

What one can sense underlying all the speeches was nervousness about the whole project. Could a church with little money really pull it off? Would you place a construction contract in the middle of a depression and in circumstances where you did not have the money? That is just what the Baptists were forced to do in order to keep the site by complying with the one-year build period in their lease.

It was with some trepidation therefore that Edward Leech as secretary in the absence of treasurer Frank Spence set out in his speech the financial situation. He estimated that the building would cost no more than £2,200. Time would show he was optimistic. He had £376 pledged, of which £103 had actually been paid into the bank. The deficit was £1,824. It looked, he said, as if they had got a very small amount towards the new building, but he assured the congregation that they had done their best. 'All members have been taxed to the utmost, and I hope that our friends belonging to other denominations will come forward and assist us through the means of collecting books, with which I will be very happy to supply them.'

We have to pause here and look at the reality of these figures. The Altrincham Baptists had committed to pay for a large perpetual ground rent, a minister and a new building with *only 19 per cent of the funds needed for the building.*

No wonder Leech looked to help from other denominations. The whole launch day was in the hope that they would attract wealthy benefactors in addition to Spence. Spence was the only person with any serious money in the church. Few benefactors materialised.

> The first fund-raising concert held by the church was not exactly an unmitigated success. The choir performed a cantata called *Nativity*, followed by part of Costa's *Eli*, accompanied in each case by members of the Altrincham Amateur Orchestra. The reviewer in the local newspaper wryly commented: 'We would suggest that if this or any other work be performed by them again that they should secure the services of a conductor.' The review of their 1883 concert was equally acerbic: 'The musical arrangement of the piece cannot be said to be of the very highest order.'

If Leech had known what was to follow, he would probably have abandoned the project and given everyone back their money.

A MATTER OF WEALTH

We should perhaps note at this stage how poor the Baptists were compared to their richer Congregational cousins. The Congregationalists had little difficulty in raising money. The Baptists under Llewellyn, as we have seen, were pleased when they raised just under £5 at one annual meeting to balance the books. By contrast Bowdon Downs in 1887 found it had a cost overrun on building works of £400, and in just one meeting raised £200.

For much of its existence from now on, Bowdon Baptist Church could often not afford to pay all of the salary of their minster. Even the grants they obtained were not enough. In 1876 the local newspaper reported the President of the Baptist Union as apologising for the low pay of Baptist ministers. The very highest income for a Baptist minister at Altrincham until 1905 was £120 a year. The minister was probably better paid than nearly everyone else in the congregation. Let us compare his income with that of others.

In 1874 Sale Presbyterian Church paid its minister £400 a year. In 1875, when Revd Griffiths left Bowdon Downs Congregational, he was given the enormous sum of £2,128-8s-0d as a leaving gift, which the deacons used to buy two annuities of £100 each. This money was raised very quickly. It could have paid for most of the Hale Road chapel.

In 1878, MacKennal was paid £400 a year. When Bowdon Downs had an assistant pastor, he was paid about £200 a year. By the end of his career at Bowdon Downs, MacKennal's pay had increased to a staggering £750 a year, over six times as much as that of the Baptist minister. MacKennal educated his children at public school and lived in one of the Dunham Massey mansions. The Baptist ministers lived in rented accommodation.

Another income comparison is with the two Lang sisters who owned Culcheth Hall School: in 1908 they earned £834 for the year between them.[1]

It would be unfair to say that Bowdon Downs was a church consisting entirely of the rich and influential. Looking through the addresses of church members, one can tell that it became more affluent as time went on, moving from a middle-class church with wealthy backers to an upper-middle-class and

> Like the Altrincham Baptists, Bowdon Downs probably encouraged the practice of 'tithing' income to the church, i.e. paying one tenth of one's income. This produced an enormous income for the Congregationalists, but little for the Baptists by comparison.

wealthy merchant church. Even at its height though, it had a number of servants and lower-middle-class people. Its servants usually did not become full members, but attended communion. Servants of the wealthy at Bowdon Downs were more likely to attend, and feel comfortable in, the mission at the British School on Oxford Road, the Baptist church or the Welsh church.

---

[1] 1908 tax returns show a surgeon on The Downs earned £400 and two dentists earned £345 and £250 respectively. Matthews, Stephen: *Cheshire History No. 39 1999-2000 – A glimpse of Three Edwardian Schools.* The Prime Minister in the 1850s earned £5,000 a year, which is much more (taking inflation into account) than he does today.

It is possible that the Baptist church felt it had a particular responsibility for servants in the area. At one of their annual tea meetings at The Downs Chapel, the visiting speaker, William Birch, had pointed out that there were a lot of governesses and servants in the area who had no church to go to. Once some servants started attending the Baptist chapel, no doubt this attracted more. At the time, Llewellyn quite rightly pointed out that the servants could sit straight down when attending services as there were no reserved pews in the Baptist chapel, whereas in other churches they had to wait until the beginning of the service before being allocated a spare seat.

Analysis, however, reveals that the belief that Altrincham Baptist Church was principally a servants' church is a truth but not the whole truth. The majority of the congregation from 1887 onwards, which is the first period for which we have records, were in fact a mixture of working-class and lower-middle-class or tradespeople. A large minority were servants.[2]

The trust deeds of Bowdon Baptist Church also give a clue as to relative incomes. Although most of the trustees gave Manchester addresses, some were local. Their occupations show they mostly belonged to the middle or lower middle classes. They were likely to have been the wealthiest people associated with the church. Thomas Forster lived on Oxford Road in Altrincham and was a shopkeeper. William Ormond of Altrincham was a joiner and his son a stonemason. William Richard Simmons of Bowdon was a manager and probably the most well-off trustee. Alexander Robertson, William Butler and Charles Southwell were all Altrincham joiners. John Pemberton was a boot and shoe-maker who lived on Peel Causeway with his wife, Eliza, and daughter, Solly who

The national non-parochial registers of 1836 listed Baptists and Congregationalists together. There were seven categories of wealth. Almost 70 per cent of Baptists and Congregationalists came from categories 4-6 out of these seven categories, compared to 41 per cent nationally. Category 7 was 'Other occupations'. These categories 4-6 were the lowest classes and comprised artisans, labourers and colliers/miners. It is likely therefore that the Baptist proportion of categories 4-6 was over twice as high as the national average.[3] A study of a Bradford chapel between 1837 and 1852 shows a predominantly working-class membership with a smaller number of lower middle classes.[4]

in turn was a bootmaker's assistant. William Johnson was a tailor and draper living in Bowdon. None that can be found in the census records had servants, which was at a time when most middle-class people could afford at least one servant. The conclusion is that the local trustees were not well off, so the average church member was probably considerably poorer.

The trustees who gave Manchester addresses were Leonard Thomas Edminson, who was a merchant, Charles Bryer, who was a salesman and Thomas Matthew Nunn and S. Boughey, who were both bookkeepers. Hugh Hunter Stevenson was a 'fancy box maker' and James Abbott and William Spencer were both Manchester merchants. Some of these were also trustees of Sale Baptist Church (then Ashton-on-Mersey), so they were probably people used by the Association to give central support to the local trustees. The large number of trustees was probably to spread

---

[2] A large number of the tradespeople were involved in the construction industry, which is a reminder of how much building was taking place at the time in Altrincham.

[3] Briggs, John: *The English Baptists of the Nineteenth Century*, Baptist Historical Society, 1994.

[4] Radcliffe, C.J.: 'A Textile Workers' Chapel: A Study of a General Baptist Church 1837-1852', in *The Journal of regional and Local Studies*, 9, 1989, quoted in Briggs, op. cit.

the load of the personal financial liability that each carried for the debts of the church. They were brave men, but certainly not rich.

Address books show that most of the church members lived in the poorer streets of the area, unless of course they were servants. They changed address often, as most lived in rented accommodation.

Their disposable income available to give to the church was therefore not great. The servants in particular had negligible disposable income. Their board and lodging was paid for, but a housemaid in London (with higher wages than in Bowdon) earned ten shillings a year in 1871 and fifteen shillings in 1907.[5]

How were these poor people to raise the money? In January 1879 we find them holding a fund-raising concert with a follow-up one in March. These only made a small impact on the funds needed, but their purpose was perhaps also to continue to publicise the project and to give members a focus for their own efforts. These concerts became a regular annual event for the Baptists.

They needed to pay the architect and builders, and so on 17 October 1879 they were forced to mortgage the site to Thomas Thompson, a wealthy cotton spinner and member of Bowdon Downs Congregational. He lent them £1,000 at an interest rate of 5 per cent per annum. This was higher than a commercial rate, but in giving the mortgage he was taking quite a financial risk himself. The Baptists also managed to obtain an unsecured, interest-free loan from the Baptist Building Fund.[6]

Thus the church was financially poor, heavily mortgaged, with a minister to pay and a high ground rent. The financial prospects for the future were not good. Despite economies made, there was a cost overrun of £300, bringing the total cost to £2,500. Then terrible news arrived. Frank Spence, the richest man in the church by far, announced he was moving to Rusholme.[7]

> It is interesting to compare the church with Ashton-on-Mersey Congregational Church. The latter launched an appeal for a new church building seating 350 in 1893 at a cost of £2,500, including buying the land. They received a grant of £250 from the Congregational Union, a loan of £250 and gifts (including two from the Haworth family of Bowdon Downs Congregational of £100 each), which meant that by the time they launched their appeal they had £1,131-11s-0d already pledged or donated, including the £250 loan. MacKennal gave his personal support and donated £5. At the same stage in their own project, the Baptists had just £376.

---

[5] Quoted in James, op. cit.
[6] The author has been unable to trace the loan (and subsequent loans) in any papers of the Fund. It is a good thing the loan was interest-free if it was never repaid.
[7] We do not know the precise date, but certainly by 1881 the family were living at 16 Ansom Road, Rusholme.

Many Nonconformists had ambivalent views about wealth, and encouraged philanthropy. By contrast, in 1876 the Anglican Revd W. Cunningham gave a lecture in Altrincham on political economy including such capitalist topics as 'Wealth: what it is and how to get it', 'Ways of applying and approving labour' and 'Capital in relation to the acquisition of wealth, its profits and the wages of labour'.

The Baptist Sunday school opened a new register in 1897 and listed the employment of those in the school together with teachers who were also working at the time. Two were teachers, four student teachers, three gardeners, three sailors, three electricians, three bakers and three milliners, two were painters, two cabinet makers, two dressmakers and there was one each of draughtsman, carver, clerk, musician, mechanic, confectioner, draper, boot manufacturer, upholsterer and grocer. This gives a further flavour of the composition of the church.

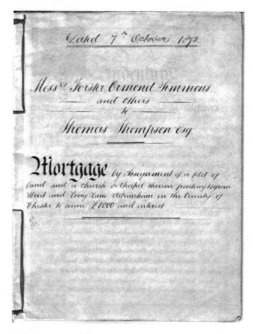

The initial mortgage taken out by the Baptist trustees with Thomas Thompson of Bowdon Downs Congregational Church.

110

The trust deeds of Bowdon Baptist Church. Forster, Ormond and Simmons took the major risk by taking on the lease. They then transferred the risk to the other trustees such as Edminson. Llewellyn later recalled how he thought the people of Altrincham to some extent laughed at the Baptists when they launched a building project with only a few pounds in hand.   He was probably right.

By August 1881 the Baptists had barely managed to pay the interest on the loan and not a penny of capital. They therefore turned to the trustees of the Star Life Assurance Society, which specialised in loans to churches.[8] Star Life paid out Thompson and gave the Baptists a further £200 capital and a lower interest rate of 4.2 per cent per annum. The reason for the re-finance may also have been because the Baptists knew Thompson was dying and did not want to entrust their arrears of mortgage instalments to possibly unsympathetic children.[9]

This is the resolution sanctioning the new loan, proposed by William Brewer and seconded by Richard Trelfa..

---

[8] Many editions of the Baptist *Freeman* magazine contained Star Life advertisements.
[9] In fact the son, T.H. Thompson, later presided at a sale of work at the chapel, so they need not have worried. The Primitive Methodists did have a problem when their mortgagee died and the estate called in the loan, so the Baptists were being sensible in re-financing.

MacKennal's house for part of his time at Bowdon was Haigh Lawn on St Margaret's Road, now converted into apartments. No Baptist pastor of the time could have hoped to live in a house anywhere near this size.

It is quite possible the Baptists would not have embarked on the building project without Spence as treasurer and supporter. Now that their richest donor and financial manager was leaving, he was unlikely to commit further funds. The future looked very bleak indeed.

THE GRAND DESIGN

The *British Architect and Northern Engineer Magazine* of 1878 is surprisingly interesting to read. Nowadays, architecture magazines are usually devoted to the practical needs of the profession. The *British Architect* was devoted to modern design but also to stories that bordered on the libellous. The editor berated ignorant clients and Local Boards, and gleefully reported the evidence from a legal case where a house in Warrington had collapsed.

The magazine even commented in detail on the case of Ruskin v Whistler, which was nothing to do with architecture but was a libel claim brought by the artist Whistler against Ruskin over Whistler's painting, *Nocturne in Black and Gold: The Falling Rocket.* Ruskin had said he 'never expected to hear a coxcomb ask 200 guineas for flinging a pot of paint in the public's face'.[1]

However, buried in the issue of 20 December 1878 is a more sober report on the 'Baptist Chapel and Schools – Mr William Owen architect'.

It is worth quoting from the article about Bowdon Baptist Church:

'The memorial stones of this new chapel were laid last week. The building will be Italian in style, and built of red brick. The lower storey will be used for school purposes, and will comprise a school room 67 feet long and 39 feet wide, with two class-rooms and library and will be provided with a separate entrance from Byrom Street, and also will have communication with the chapel by means of a staircase in the tower'.

The upper floor chapel was 73 feet by 39 feet and 28 feet high 'with a gallery over the main entrance'. It was to accommodate 500 people. The tower was to be 64 feet high. The estimated cost was £2,100.

The Baptists had appointed a construction team under the supervision of Owen.

The main contractor was Mr T. Pennington, a local builder. Penningtons were still in business until comparatively recently.[2] Specialist construction and fitting-out work was either sub-contacted or separately contracted. Mr T. Blease was appointed to do the brickwork. He in turn obtained the ornamental and facing bricks from a Mr Jabez Thompson of Northwich. Mr J. Johnson was the plasterer and Messrs Morton and Sheldon carried out the masonry work. John Peake was appointed to install both the heating system and the railings. You will note that all the tradesmen were local Altrincham men. This was very much a local project.

The Baptist Union Handbook also carried an article about the church design when the building was opened, saying that the centre portion of the ceiling took 'the form of a semi-ellipse, divided into panels by moulded and enriched ribs, and forming an excellent groundwork for future decoration'. The length of the chapel, however, appeared to have mysteriously shrunk to 65 feet.

---

[1] For the record, Whistler won the case, but only gained nominal damages and eventually became bankrupt.
[2] Charles Pennington built the Garrick Theatre in Altrincham in 1931-32.

The new building was finally completed in 1879.[3] It was a striking building, with its ornamental front and campanile tower, but they were forced to economise.

They did this in several ways. The main saving came when they abandoned plans for a large extension at the back and put up a small one instead. The chapel walls and ceiling were to plaster only. Ventilation was rudimentary. The front brickwork was of good quality, but the rest was inferior.

What you may find surprising is that there was no electricity or gas. The building was heated by a small boiler. Services held after dusk were illuminated by flickering oil or paraffin lamps.

There may also have been no toilets. Victorians were expected to think ahead before coming to services or meetings.

On the morning of Sunday 12 October 1879, the Baptists held their last service at The Downs Chapel. The first service at Hale Road was at 7.30pm on the same day. Llewellyn insisted this should be a purely devotional service for church members, focussing on prayer, consecration and the future. Although they needed the money, it was important to start in their new chapel on a spiritual basis.

On the following Tuesday at 7pm they held their first public opening. You will not be surprised to learn that it was McLaren who was the preacher.[4] Funds raised totalled £21, but this was still a drop in the ocean compared to what was needed.

Trade relations were not always harmonious in the Victorian construction industry. In 1875 the Altrincham plasterers went on strike over wages.

John Peake installed the heating systems at the Winter Gardens in Rhyl and in Blackpool. As Owen designed the Winter Gardens in Rhyl, he may have recommended Peake.

NEW BAPTIST CHAPEL, Hale rd, Bowdon, Pastor W.S. Llewellyn-OPENING SERVICES - Monday October 13th 1879, Devotional Service at 7.30pm. Tuesday October 14th at 7pm, Rev. ALEXANDER MCLAREN, D.D. of Manchester.

Advertisement placed in local newspaper. Note again the reference to Bowdon and not Altrincham.

---

[3] There is a myth in the church even today that the building was built in 1878, and this is reflected in the Church Rules at the start of 2009 (now replaced). The building was in fact mostly constructed in 1879 and opened in October 1879; it was the laying of the foundation stones that was in (late) 1878. You can find a full description of what the chapel looked like in Appendix 3.
[4] Sadly, there is no record of what he said on this occasion.

An advert placed by Penningtons the builders in 1904. Note that they had been in existence since 1847 and had a good track record. By 1904, Penningtons had also an established business as undertakers. It was not unusual for people to combine trades like this. It has always been risky appointing a building contractor, as if they become insolvent, there is a huge extra cost in appointing a new contractor. The local newspapers had regular reports of contractor bankruptcy. Fortunately for the Baptists, Pennington did not let them down.

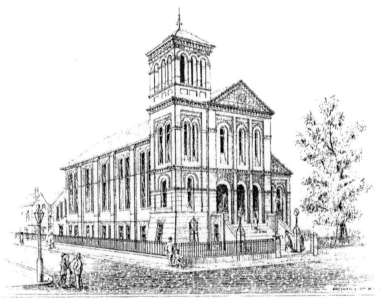

NEW BAPTIST CHAPEL, HALE ROAD BOWDEN.

Architect's drawing of the new building in 1878-79. Note the portico at the front and the ornamental lamps and how the tower is a real feature of the Italian-style building.

115

Harvest festival at Hale Road before 1908. Note there is no pipe organ. The two doors appear to be closer together than now. The choir stalls at the front face inwards. This is the oldest known photograph of the chapel interior.

Another artist's impression of the original chapel.

Original architect's model showing the front left elevation.

At this point in their story, the Baptists had a building they simply could not afford.

LLEWELLYN UNDER PRESSURE

Llewellyn and Simmons personally visited many houses in the area, asking for donations, but the contributions only scratched the surface of the debt.

Llewellyn knew that he had to engage the congregation in further urgent fund-raising, so on Thursday 16 October 1880 the church held its first bazaar, which lasted three days. It was an extraordinary two full years in the planning. The church made it clear that no money was to be raised by lottery, raffle or gambling. These were against its principles. This was to be a straight sale of items made or donated by church members and others.

Llewellyn wrote to many in the Bowdon area asking if they would become patrons of the bazaar. The schoolrooms were decorated with flags, plants and flowers. Adamson of the British School Mission opened the bazaar in prayer and then Llewellyn made the introductions.

He explained that their choice had either been to close down or to move to a new building, such was the dilapidated state of the old Downs chapel. Many had thought them presumptuous, but 'we believe that He who has in His hand the silver and the gold, who has the disposing of all events and all hearts, that He whose glory we seek, will help us out of every difficulty'.

Spence came back to open the bazaar, saying, 'As the ladies are all burning to begin the sale of goods at reasonable prices and give full value for money received, I declare the bazaar open, and may God give you a most encouraging receipt'.

> Part of the 1880 bazaar held at the Hale Road chapel was a demonstration of new-fangled electrical equipment, including a long-distance telephone and a burglar alarm.

The bazaar was, however, to be Llewellyn's last major event at Altrincham. He was suffering from stress. He had built the church up to ninety-eight members, nine teachers and one hundred and twenty Sunday school pupils, but the strain of the building project and chapel debt was too much for him and his health was poor. He and Annie may not have been helped by the fact that their one-year-old daughter, Amy, had mental health problems. Their son, Ivor, was also born in 1880, and the Llewellyns decided it was time for a fresh start before Llewellyn had a breakdown.

There were negotiations with the deacons and then in December 1880, he announced that he was moving to Ogden Baptist Church near Rochdale, where apparently the air was better for his health. His farewell service was on 30 January 1881.

Altrincham's loss was Ogden's gain. Llewellyn stayed there for thirty-seven years, becoming one of its most famous ministers. Under him, the Ogden Church grew substantially. It bought a new burial ground for £1,000, built the New Hey Educational Institute in 1887 and commissioned a British Day School in 1893. It did not have the significant debt problems of Altrincham.

Intriguingly, we find Llewellyn in the thirteenth coach in Spurgeon's funeral procession, with McLaren well behind in the twenty-third.

Llewellyn did not abandon Altrincham, however. He returned from time to time to preach to the Altrincham Baptists: in 1900, for example we find him preaching at the church anniversary service.

The Llewellyns retired to Urmston and celebrated their golden wedding anniversary in 1927. Annie died in 1934 and Llewellyn himself on 10 February 1936. As well as Ivor (who went on to overcome his disabilities and become an analytical chemist) and Amy, who were born in Altrincham, they had two other sons.

> 'Bowdon Baptist Chapel –Many of our readers will regret to hear that the Revd W.S. Llewellyn, pastor of the above place of worship, has accepted a call to the pastorate of the Baptist Church at Ogden, near Rochdale. This regret will be keenly shared by the members of his congregation, to whom he has endeared himself by his many good qualities. He has very largely shared their anxieties and responsibilities in the building of the handsome chapel in Hale-road.[1] Those who have had the pleasure of his acquaintance in social matters will all feel that a good man is going from our midst. We wish him every success in his new sphere of labour.'
>
> Article in local newspaper.

Llewellyn's successor at Altrincham was to be one of Altrincham's most controversial minsters in Victorian times.

---

[1] Actual spelling in the newspaper.

THE CONTROVERSIAL MOWBRAY

The Altrincham Baptists now had their new building, but no minister at a time when they needed clear leadership.

The official story until now has been that after a long search of nearly twelve months, they found their man. The actual story is somewhat different, and we shall now look at the controversial Henry Mowbray and how he came to Altrincham. As you follow his story, you will need to decide whether he was a good man doing his best or the renegade of later portrayals.

Mowbray's parents were Henry and Eleanor (née Brougham) and they came from Scotland. They married on 31 August 1845 in Edinburgh and then moved to Hampstead in London. There they anglicised their surname from Moubray to Mowbray.

Mowbray himself was born in Hampstead on 25 March 1847. Soon afterwards, the family moved again, this time to Cheshire. The family home was near Neston in the Wirral. Henry was the first of four children. His father was a farmer and was prosperous enough to employ two servants.

His parents were both devout Presbyterians. Mowbray took part in services held in his father's kitchen for farm servants and villagers. He became a Christian in boyhood through none other than Wainwright of St John's Church. Wainwright's proximity at St John's might have been what initially attracted Mowbray to Altrincham.

Mowbray was educated at the Collegiate School in Liverpool. He left there at seventeen and went to work in the offices of a Liverpool merchant. In Liverpool, he attended Toxteth Tabernacle, a well-known Baptist

Henry Mowbray. The photograph of Mowbray shows him to be a striking and dapper businessman.

church, and was much influenced there by the preaching of W. P. Lockhart, who became his mentor and who came and spoke from time to time to the Altrincham Baptists. Toxteth Tabernacle had a membership of about 1,500.

In 1874 Mowbray married Jessie from Saighton in Cheshire. He was twenty-seven and she was just twenty-one. The couple decided to move to Bootle, where both were baptised as believers. They had one child, Robert.

Mowbray continued to work in the merchant's office, but he was also appointed to take charge of a mission station of Toxteth Tabernacle. The concept of 'mission station' perhaps influenced his views at Altrincham, as we shall see.

At the church anniversary on Thursday 27 January 1881, before Llewellyn's last service on the following Sunday but with Llewellyn already having moved out of the area, Mowbray was on the platform at the Baptist chapel in Altrincham. He did not speak much, but why had he travelled to this meeting all the way from Liverpool and in bad weather? It seems he was to preach for the next two Sundays on the recommendation of Lockhart, although perhaps the deacons already had an idea they might try him out for another purpose.

The anniversary meeting itself was a little unusual. Mr Woodcock was the president of the meeting as deacon Simmons was ill, although the church was told he might make it later.

The financial situation had deteriorated since Llewellyn had announced his departure, no doubt due to the uncertainty this caused. Southwell read the accounts, and then the supposedly unwell Simmons made a dramatic entry, bemoaning the lack of men at the meeting, although adding (in a rather un-Victorian manner but to laughter) that he always preferred the ladies.

He referred to a dispute with the building contractors over 'extras'. He then said they had asked for permission to ask all the churches in the Lancashire and Cheshire Association for financial assistance, but had been turned down, as there were two other churches which had been given priority. However, the good news was that the marriage licence had finally been transferred from the old chapel and the new one was now available for weddings.[1]

Simmons asked Mowbray to say a few words, and he spoke (ironically with the hindsight of what happened subsequently) about the need for church unity. Mowbray then pronounced the benediction.

Mowbray preached for his two allotted Sundays, and the church liked him so much that they asked him to become temporary minister for three months. As he was still working in the merchant's office, he probably stayed in Liverpool and commuted for Sundays. It is intriguing to wonder whether he stayed with Wainwright.

In this temporary post too he was popular, and so the deacons offered him the post of full-time minister with a pay of £120 per annum. On the first Sunday in July 1881, Mowbray began his new ministry.

After the summer holidays, a public tea meeting was held to more formally welcome him. None other than Robert Lewis, Chairman of the Baptist Union, was there. The church, Lewis said, should treat Mowbray as 'God's messenger'. Lockhart had come from Toxteth and brought what seemed to be a large Mowbray fan club with him. He referred to Mowbray's great energy, but said that was not sufficient to build the church: they needed the energy of Christ.

> BOWDON BAPTIST CHURCH; Hale-road-tomorrow,[2] HENRY MOWBRAY, late of Liverpool, will enter upon his Ministry and preach morning and evening. Services at 10.30 and 6.30. Offertory. All seats free.
>
> Notice in local newspaper.

According to his biographer in *The Baptist Union Handbook*, 'The church was in very low water, the membership small and heavily burdened by debt'.[3]

---

[1] This was a very long delay indeed.
[2] Actual spelling in the newspaper.
[3] This depends on whether you call about eighty-eight members 'small'. The item was written with considerable hindsight.

The Mowbrays left Liverpool and moved into lodgings on Hale Road in a house owned by Elizabeth Mitchell. Mowbray was then aged thirty-four and son Robert was just four years old. The house was quite cramped, as Elizabeth and her sister rented rooms not only to the Mowbrays but also to George Parsons who was a clerk, Fred Townsend who was a schoolteacher and Mary Gale who was a young dressmaker.

Mowbray was not theologically trained. This was not unusual, although the tide was moving towards formal training for all ministers. In 1870, fewer than half of the ministers in charge of English Baptist churches had been trained. By 1901 the proportion had risen to 64 per cent. [4]

When Mowbray arrived, Bowdon Baptist Church was still a respectable size, despite its financial problems. True, membership had dropped by ten to eighty-eight during the interregnum, but Mowbray began the task of rebuilding numbers and these picked up to ninety-four in 1883, ninety-seven in 1884 and reached 101 in 1885. By 1887 he had built the church to 107 members.

Mowbray must have known about the church building debt when he accepted the post at Altrincham. He certainly could not ignore the church's predicament and knew that Llewellyn's health had cracked under the strain.

At first, things began to look better. At the annual meeting in 1883, over 200 people crowded into the schoolroom. Numbers had gone up: some by transfer but more by conversion to the faith. Leech, now the Treasurer, announced £400 of the debt had been paid off in the year. He named Frank

> Bowdon Baptist appeared in the newspapers in 1883 when a Sunday school pupil, Martin Slattery, stole seven shillings[5] from the missionary boxes by sneaking into the chapel on a Thursday while the door was open to allow others into a meeting. William Brewer reported the theft. Slattery 'fingered' three others to Sergeant Cooper who in an early example of police forensic skill, matched the chisel belonging to the father of one of them to the marks on the cupboard door.

Crossley, J. Richards, Thomas Forster and Peter Spence as substantial donors. The church at this stage clearly thought it had pestered Bowdon residents enough for money, and resolved to leave them alone for a year.

Chairing the meeting, William Milne from Bowdon Downs Congregational hit the nail on the head when he said, 'If the pastor, office-bearers, and other workers in the church are burdened with a building debt which is only incidental to the all-important work of the church, they cannot concentrate their efforts on it in the manner they hoped.'

The year 1886 was a watershed for the church in two ways. First, it grew in size and in reputation. Mowbray was a keen evangelist and held a series of evangelistic services with visiting speakers. He was also becoming more influential in the Lancashire and Cheshire Association. The Southern District of the Association held a conference at Bowdon Baptist which Mowbray chaired. On the evening of the day of the conference, Mowbray held a 'Home Mission' conference and persuaded Crossley to chair the meeting and MacKennal to speak. MacKennal paid tribute to Mowbray's support for Manchester and Salford City Mission and his work as a 'home missionary' in Altrincham.

---

[4] Briggs, op. cit.
[5] Now 35p.

This particular year was also a watershed because it was now very apparent that the visible success of the church in terms of growth was fundamentally undermined by its debt.

At the annual meeting in January 1887 Mowbray, Overbury and Simmons tried to put a combined brave face on it. Behind the scenes, however, the strain was reaching breaking-point. They had struggled to pay Mowbray, and he was being reduced to near poverty in order for the debt to be paid. They were in serious difficulties. Much of the income of the church was going into just servicing the debt. The Association grant was £30 per annum and the Association had indicated it wanted to reduce even this to £15. Baptist churches are on their own: they have no significant central funding and they either sink or swim.

> Altrincham Baptists and others were bemused in early 1887 when door locks in Altrincham glowed at night. What had happened was that there had been a demonstration of phosphorescence at the Altrincham Literary Institute and residents dipped their keys into it to light their door-locks, leaving the phosphor on the locks and an eerie glow throughout the area.

The debt cast a cloud over everything Mowbray did. His pay was reduced and sometimes withheld. The congregation, lacking in personal wealth, simply could not afford to pay both the debt and its minister. 1887 was to be a terrible year for a church which appeared to be on the verge of insolvency.

The annual concert on 10 March to raise funds for the building project must have been a surreal occasion. The leaders of the church attended the concert in a display of unity but behind the scenes, battle-lines were being drawn. Mowbray wanted to take a proposal to the Church Meeting to resolve matters once and for all. Overbury and Simmons were united in their opposition to him.

Wainwright of St John's with some of his parishioners. Wainwright was Mowbray's initial mentor and responsible for his conversion to the Christian faith.

Henry, Jessie and Robert Mowbray moved from temporary lodgings into 76 Hale Road and were joined by Margaret Brougham, Jessie Mowbray's sister. She was stated to be living on her own means. If Mowbray had any inherited wealth, it was probably on his wife's side. Also living with them was Caroline Fielding, aged 32, described as a 'mother's help'.

Frank Crossley was an initial substantial donor to the church.

The Spence family were also substantial early donors. Pictured here are their factories at Pendleton (left) and Goole (right). Note how both are similar in design, next to a canal and by a railway. The departure of Frank Spence from the church was a bitter blow.

As the crucial meeting approached, would the other four deacons back Mowbray or Overbury and Simmons?

THE FATE OF THE INDEPENDENTS

The battle-lines were drawn for the Baptists, but before we find out the result of the dramatic events of March 1887, we must return to the story of the independent Congregational church in Altrincham, out of which, you may recall, it is likely the first Baptists came in 1872.

The story of that independent Congregational church has not been fully told before, and is ultimately a tragic one.

This church was the poor relation of Bowdon Downs, sometimes even receiving assistance from its poor relief fund. It cannot however have been that small, as it had outgrown the chapel at the foot of The Downs and relocated to the former Methodist chapel on Regent Road.

Although the Baptists started with a small number when they moved into the chapel at the foot of The Downs, we know that from 1872 onwards there was a steady trickle of resignations from Bowdon Downs Congregational and a transfer of allegiance to the Baptists. Those leaving appear to have been some of the poorer people.

If that is true of departures from Bowdon Downs, it is likely there would have been a larger number who migrated from Altrincham Congregational Church to form the new Baptist congregation. This would have been like going home for them, as they were returning from Regent Road to The Downs Chapel where the Congregational church had previously met.

Although much of the Baptist growth under Betts and Llewellyn was by conversion to the faith, nevertheless they were aided by some transfers from these two Congregational churches.

The departure of the Baptists, although amicable, must have hit the independent Congregationalists. They kept going however. During the 1870s there are reports in the newspaper of regular evangelistic events and musical evenings. In 1874 there is a report of a tea party and the pastor was on the committee of a mutual building society which, rather oddly, took cash deposits only on Saturday evenings between 7pm and 8pm in their schoolroom, perhaps to encourage working class people to save their money before they spent it in the public house. In 1874 we know that the key Micklem family (one was the organist) left the Congregationalists to emigrate to the United States.

What they wanted was a new chapel. They had moved out of The Downs Chapel and bought the Methodist chapel on Regent Road, but this was also in poor condition. Their new building fund clearly struggled to get established.

In November 1876, their fund-raising event received just £7. Their December one received £30, however, but most of it was a gift from the deacons of Bowdon Downs Congregational. When Revd Aylard of the independent church attended the ceremony for the laying of the foundation stones for the new Baptist chapel in 1878, he must have wondered if his own church could ever find the money for its own new building.

In February 1880 these Congregationalists held a fund-raising concert to help pay off their debts, but to little avail. In March 1880 Aylard finally resigned. He had had enough.

A farewell meeting was organised, and MacKennal attended. The meeting became a post mortem as to what had gone wrong, and underneath the Victorian pleasantries, one can detect some real tensions and even animosity. Superficially, the church had been successful. Aylard had started with thirty-five members. Under him, there had been 100 professions of faith and seventy-five transfers, but they still only had seventy-six members. No doubt the Baptist departures did not help. A Mr Turner said they were 'poor people', and indeed that area of town around Regent Road was then one of the poorest : 'We had to be built up on a foundation of poverty.' They had raised £800 to modernise their chapel but had also looked for new premises for five fruitless years. 'Our minister has grown weary with the poor congregation worshipping here, and the poor response he has had to his appeals either for growth or progress. We are here to sympathise with him and to reluctantly part with a good friend... We have been, and we still are, the poor relations of Bowdon Downs Congregational Church.'

MacKennal replied to the attack on Bowdon Downs Congregational. Cryptically, he said he had listened 'with much more of interest than many of you might understand'. As it turned out, he was a good friend of their previous pastor MacWilliam. One can sense real anger in the normally mild MacKennal. Both he and MacWilliam thought the church 'had made a grievous mistake into going into this old building'. This was a 'blunder... I wonder if it had struck you that if the Wesleyan Methodists thought it worth while to sell you the chapel, it was not worth your while to buy it...It is impossible for you to draw to yourselves the sympathy of the religious community in Altrincham and Bowdon if you quitted this place without making any provision for the continuance and carrying on, and even extinction of the work that is being carried on here.'

Given the fact this was a testimonial meeting for Aylard, this is an extraordinary criticism of the departing minister and his church.

One wonders if MacKennal and others felt a similar sense of frustration with the Baptists. Perhaps the message to both was similar: we the rich will support you, but we will not pay for your mistakes. It appears Llewellyn later thought this was the case.

By 1881 the Altrincham Congregational Church was in serious trouble. They approached Bowdon Downs Congregational and pleaded that they should be taken over, the Regent Road chapel sold and the proceeds used to build a new Congregational chapel in Altrincham. The sub-text was clear: in return for the cash from a sale of the Regent Road chapel, they wanted Bowdon Downs' manpower and money. Using Bowdon Downs' resources, they wanted to create a 'vigorous and self-supporting church in Altrincham', independent in due course of Bowdon Downs.

The Altrincham Congregationalists, ever the optimists, stated they hoped to find new premises, probably in the Barrington Road area. Meanwhile they rented rooms on Market Street. These rooms were later to be significant for the Altrincham Baptists.

The congregation on Market Street declined. There is no record of a new minister being appointed to succeed Aylard. There was no help from Bowdon Downs Congregational. They were on their own. By 1885 they had dwindled to twenty members.

On 9 September, a letter was read out to the Church Meeting of Bowdon Downs Congregational which alluded to a decision by the Altrincham Congregational Church acting by its Secretary, a Mr Greenleaves.[1] The decision was, 'That after prayerful consideration the remaining members of the Altrincham Congregational Church, acting on the advice given by the Sub-Committee of the Cheshire Congregational Union, accept the cordial welcome of the Pastors and Deacons of the Downs Congregational Church, and seek admission to the fellowship of their church at the British School with the ultimate object that our long cherished desire of promoting a strong and effective Independent church in Altrincham be attained'. They would like to sell their chapel and 'would probably desire the erection of a new Chapel in the neighbourhood of the British School'.

You will note that they wanted to join with the Bowdon Downs Mission Church at the British School, and then later to move out of the British School and build a new chapel, potentially only yards away from the new Baptist chapel. It may be that they wanted to take the British School Mission with them in doing this.

The Congregational Year Book quotes this letter as if this was a mutually satisfactory solution, and yet that is a cover up. This is the first time the story has been properly told in more recent times. The Minute Books of Bowdon Downs reveal something quite different.

MacKennal was having none of this. His deacons told the Altrincham Congregationalists that MacKennal had no intention of allowing them to build a new church. Presumably the British School was more than adequate anyway, but one wonders, given his growing agreement with McLaren that there should be closer union between the Baptists and the Congregationalists, how MacKennal must have viewed a small church of his own denomination, perhaps still smarting from the departure of the Baptists, trying to merge with his mission church and then to set up a new chapel to rival the Baptists only yards from the Baptist chapel.

It is at this stage that we can understand why the Altrincham Baptists were of strategic importance to both MacKennal and McLaren: if they were to unite the two denominations, it would be inconvenient to say the least if there was a financial problem with a Baptist church near to Bowdon Downs Congregational Church and a rival Congregationalist church setting up nearby which might just push the struggling Baptists over the edge.

MacKennal told the Altrincham Congregationalists he could not countenance the remaining twenty or so members being 'a separate community which had its own plans' within his own mission church; effectively a church within a church.

So the official deal was very different from the truth: they would not join as a whole church. Instead they would simply apply individually to join the British School Mission as members, sell their chapel and do what they liked with the proceeds. Bowdon Downs did not need the carrot of the money and it did not want a challenge

---

[1] We find him later in 1887 on the platform at an Altrincham and Bowdon total abstinence meeting.

to its own mission church or even to the Baptists. The independent Congregationalists had to come on the terms of Bowdon Downs.

That is just what they did. The Altrincham Congregational Church crumbled. Two members joined Bowdon Downs Congregational Church at the next meeting, followed by another twenty-one at the subsequent Church Meeting. They were absorbed into the British Schools Mission and disappeared.

The Regent Road chapel was put on the market and St Margaret's Church bought it for £800 with a substantial gift from one John Grafton. St Margaret's then refurbished the chapel as an Anglican place of worship.

As the Altrincham Congregational Church met its end, were the Baptists to have a similar fate?

THE DOWNGRADE CONTROVERSY

There was a dramatic day for the Baptists in March 1887 which we are about to encounter. At first sight, Spurgeon had no involvement in what happened, but that may not quite be the case. We therefore pause now to look at two magazine articles that were to have worldwide repercussions, and not just for the Baptists.

In March and April 1887, these two articles appeared in Spurgeon's magazine, the *Sword and the Trowel*. They were to herald the bitterest dispute for many years, both within and outside the Baptist denomination, and ended with the mighty Spurgeon resigning from the Baptist Union and McLaren siding with the majority in a vote of censure against Spurgeon. The issues raised by that dispute are still with us.

The articles appeared around and just after the time of the dramatic meeting of the Altrincham Baptists in March 1887 and crystallised what many Baptists had been thinking for some time. They may also have helped to strengthen Mowbray's resolve. Perhaps he saw in Spurgeon's struggle with the Baptist Union something of his own struggle with his own church and the Association.

The dispute between Spurgeon and the Baptist Union was called the 'Downgrade Controversy'.

Bowdon Baptist Church, like all other Baptist churches, cannot have been immune to what was going on. It is difficult to believe that a pastor like Mowbray would not have held strong views over the Downgrade Controversy. Whose side would he have taken?

McLaren did not leave the Baptist Union, but Spurgeon did, and to this day his church, the Metropolitan Tabernacle in London, is a Baptist church but stays resolutely outside the Baptist Union.

Although the articles were not by Spurgeon, it is widely accepted that he was behind them. Why were they so controversial? The author of the articles believed that dissenting theology was on what he called the downgrade, just like a train going downhill. In modern terms, Spurgeon postulated that evangelicals were on the slippery slope to a liberal theology.

Spurgeon felt that a number of ministers had moved away from his interpretation of 'evangelical' and prepared a list of their names. He refused to publish the list, but as we shall see later, one possible name on that list is important in the history of Altrincham.

What is certain, however, is that McLaren was never on the list. Despite not agreeing, McLaren and Spurgeon still continued to respect each other, and McLaren was eloquent in his tributes to Spurgeon when Spurgeon died. At the inaugural service of Bowdon Baptist Church, McLaren quoted Spurgeon approvingly. Spurgeon never criticised McLaren. It is difficult, however, to know precisely what McLaren thought about all the theological issues raised by Spurgeon. He tended to keep his own counsel, and his sermons were carefully crafted on a biblical basis. What we do know is that McLaren was one of the few people who could approach Spurgeon as an equal.

When the dispute erupted and Spurgeon left the Baptist Union, possibly hoping to force a more evangelical breakaway Union, McLaren was on the negotiating committee which tried to bring Spurgeon back into the fold. Spurgeon never succeeded in having more than a small number follow him and the Baptist Union generally held firm. It is possible his heart was not really in a full breakaway Baptist Union.

The specific issues in the controversy are more difficult to pinpoint, but a number can be identified.[1] Spurgeon was asking what it meant to be an evangelical. If one extended the boundaries of evangelicalism, did it cease to be such?[2] How broad church could evangelicalism be? Should there be a statement of faith for Baptists? Could they unite on one which went beyond the shared doctrine of believer baptism?

There was the subject of punishment for the sinner who died without having repented. Spurgeon believed in everlasting punishment. McLaren probably disagreed with Spurgeon, although he did not publicise this, for obvious reasons.[3]

A related area of dispute was the doctrine called 'universalism'. This comes in various guises, but all followers of universalism would disagree with Spurgeon's view that, once someone dies who is not 'in Christ', he is absolutely 'lost' for all eternity. A full universalist would say that eventually God's love is so strong that all will be reconciled to God.

Spurgeon believed in biblical infallibility, while some of his opponents accepted biblical authority, but not necessarily infallibility[4].

There were differences too on the theology of the atonement. One person who publicly disagreed with Spurgeon on this issue was none other than MacKennal, who was chair of the Congregational Union at the relevant time.[5]

In late 1887 the crucial articles were reprinted and re-circulated to all Baptist ministers. What would Henry Mowbray have thought when he read the original and then the reprinted articles? How would he have reacted? Was there in fact more to the events we are about to witness in Altrincham than has been previously suspected? Was the timing of the issue coincidental or not?

We will probably never know for certain if there was a genuine early liberal/evangelical dispute in Altrincham amongst the Baptists. At the very least, the Downgrade Controversy, which was the biggest theological dispute the late Victorian Baptists encountered, must have been on the minds of the Altrincham Baptists, and in particular on Mowbray's mind.

---

[1] This is not a theological work, and so the issues are of necessity dealt with briefly.
[2] As recently as 2003, the Baptist Model Trust Deeds expected members to adhere to beliefs which are 'commonly called evangelical'. The 2008 standard Baptist Constitution has dropped this reference to 'evangelical' in favour of a statement of faith.
[3] This is implicit McLaren's sermon 'The Stone of Stumbling' in *Sermons preached in Manchester First Series*, 1883.
[4] This issue has dogged the Evangelical Alliance for years. Its 1846 inaugural statement of faith did not refer to the inerrancy of the Bible but instead to its inspiration, authority and sufficiency. The 1928 and 1951 statements of faith referred to infallibility, which was dropped again in 1970. See Warner, Robert: *Reinventing English Evangelicalism, 1966-2001*, Paternoster, 2008, for a detailed analysis.
[5] One of the reasons the Baptists and Congregationalists never combined was because of a gradual divergence of theology, the Baptists tending to stay more evangelical than their Congregational cousins.

Spurgeon in his study at Westwood.

As we shall see, there are one or two tantalising clues, beyond just the coincidence of dates, that the Downgrade Controversy did more than just form a backdrop to what happened in Altrincham.

THE DRAMATIC EVENTS OF 1887

As Mowbray woke on the morning of Wednesday 23 March 1887, the Church Meeting that evening was uppermost in his mind. He had discussed the matter with his deacons. They were split, but his mind was made up. He had to push the church to a decision. The church could be wrecked if he got it wrong.

Although a minister, Mowbray was also a businessman. He had tried his best to pay off the church debts, but the income of this poor church was not sufficient. The church simply could not continue like this. He had tried to bring in reforms, but had been frustrated by a minority of members. His own pay as minister had often been in serious doubt. It is likely he had been frustrated by the fact that, for Ordinary Church Meetings, proxy votes were allowed. This meant that, even if the members present at a meeting voted for something, someone could obtain the signatures of absentee members and the vote could go the other way. Better-off absentee members might vote to protect vested interests, particularly concerning the thorny issue of the financial situation of the church.

Mowbray knew he had to force the issue and his solution was simple. A church consists of its members and is not the building. If the building was the problem, the business solution was simple: they should sell it and buy or rent somewhere they could afford. It was his predecessor Llewellyn who had organised the new building, and Mowbray had little sentimental attachment to it. Those opposing him by contrast had probably injected much cash into the new building and did not want to see that disappear in a forced sale.

Mowbray had read the church trust deeds. Although an Ordinary Church Meeting allowed proxy votes, he knew that that the Trust Deeds said that there could be no proxy votes at a Special Church Meeting. He also knew he needed a two-thirds' majority to secure the resolution. He knew he had the support of the majority, but could he secure the two-thirds needed to authorise the sale of the building and buy somewhere within the two-mile radius set by the trust deeds?[1]

If he secured his two-thirds' majority, he could talk with the trustees and put the building on the market and look for somewhere else. If he achieved a majority of less than two-thirds, what was he to do? It might be easier to lose completely, but if he achieved a majority but not the two-thirds vote he needed, there would be stalemate. He might have to leave the area whether he lost *or* whether he achieved a stalemate.

The meeting was packed. Mowbray explained that every effort had been made to pay the debt, but the church simply did not have the resources to do so. He proposed the motion that the trustees should be asked to sell the building and they should move to somewhere they could afford.

A ballot was probably called for. Mowbray must have held his breath as the votes were counted. He had staked his everything on this vote.

His worst nightmare was realised. He achieved his majority but not the two-thirds he needed to sell the building. Mowbray decided he had little option now. As the

---

[1] A Special Church Meeting was required to sanction the sale of the building. This required a two-thirds majority but, unlike an Ordinary Church Meeting, did not allow proxy votes. The trust deeds allowed the sale proceeds to be used towards a new building anywhere within two miles of the Hale Road chapel.

meeting finished, he announced he would cease to be their minister at the end of May.

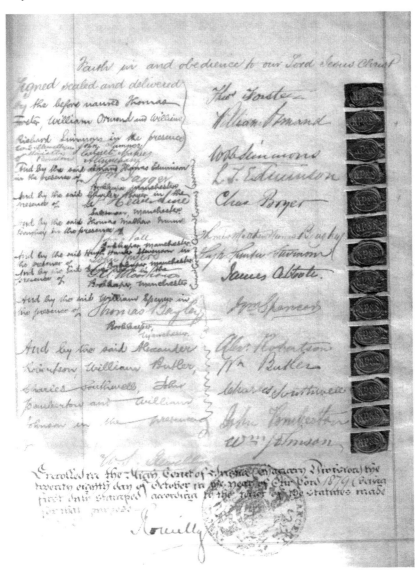

The signatures on the 1879 Bowdon Baptist Church Trust Deeds. Someone, possibly Mowbray, read the deeds carefully before the fateful meeting. One can still see what look like his pencil annotations.

As he left the building for what was likely to be the last time, Mowbray must have wondered where his future lay. His next action though had the result of catching everyone by surprise.

MOWBRAY'S SURPRISE MOVE

Mowbray set up a new and rival church in Altrincham. It is possible that the very first Sunday after the Church Meeting, Mowbray started his own services away from the Hale Road chapel. This was extraordinary, as he was still claiming to be the minister of Bowdon Baptist. Given the date of the Church Meeting, it would have been difficult to place an advertisement in time in the local newspaper. What we do know for certain is that by two Sundays after the Church Meeting, he had hired the Building Society Rooms on Market Street in his own name. He placed an advertisement right at the head of the local newspaper for his 10.30am and 6pm services. Interestingly, the advertisement says, 'All seats free. No collection'. He wanted the people, not their money. The advertisement for the following Sunday stated, 'All are earnestly entitled to attend these services'.

In effect what Mowbray was doing was seeing how many people would follow him in the period between the March meeting and the end of May.

He had an encouraging start. On Tuesday 19 April 1887, just four weeks after his surprise departure, thirty-five members of Bowdon Baptist Church gathered together in the British School on Oxford Road, only a hundred yards or so from the Hale Road chapel. This was a Church Meeting, but a very different one. The minutes of the meeting convey a sense of excitement.

Mowbray was in the chair and recounted recent events. He announced that a total of sixty-two members of Bowdon Baptist Church, including Mrs Mowbray, had decided to resign from Bowdon Baptist. Twenty-seven were not at the meeting but had sent their apologies. This probably left about forty members at Bowdon Baptist. A clear majority had decided to follow Mowbray and leave.

Four initial resolutions were put to the meeting and passed unanimously.

We will look at the fourth in a later chapter, but the first three were as follows:

First: On the Motion of Mr William Franks seconded by Mr James Brewer
            'That is desirable to form a church with as little delay as possible'
Second: On the Motion of Mr Hind seconded by Mr C Southwell
            'That no vote shall be allowed unless given in person (no proxy)'
Third: On the Motion of Mr Southwell seconded by Mr William Brewer
            'That the church have 6 Deacons one third of their number to retire each
            year but the same to be eligible for re-election'.

The thirty-five present then joined hands and sang 'O Happy Day'.

Thus was a new church formed, a church without the proxy voting that had caused them such problems and a church free of debt.

Mowbray read out the name of each person on the list of the sixty-two (including himself in that number as ministers were also members). All had agreed to be the founder members of the new church.

The first six deacons and the church secretary were then elected. In the tradition of the time, they were all men, but it is worth pausing at this moment to look at those forming the new church. Only seventeen were men and forty-five were women.

Newly-elected deacon Southwell then took the chair and proposed that Mowbray be appointed minister. Mowbray was appointed by a unanimous vote. Anything else would have been unthinkable at this stage.

After the fourth resolution and before the meeting closed in prayer, a final resolution was then passed as follows:

'That the great thanks of this Meeting be tended to Mr and Mrs Mowbray for the unwearied and self-sacrificing efforts they have put forth for the good of the cause during the 6 years they have been amongst us.

Especially do we thank them for being the means of uniting us together as a church on honest ground and we pray that God will bless them abundantly in their labours wherever they may be called to labour.'

What was the 'honest ground'? Was it theological or related to the honest approach to the debt crisis? There is certainly some significance in the use of the phrase 'wherever they may be called to labour'. Mowbray made it clear that he would stand by this new church, but once it was a flourishing church, his intention was to move on.

> Mowbray's prominent advertisement for his first services:
>
> > BUILDING SOCIETY ROOMS MARKET STREET ALTRINCHAM
> >
> > The Reverend Henry Mowbray will preach in the above place on Sunday next April Third. Morning 10.30; Evening 6.30. All seats free. No collection.

> For the record, the local newspaper reported next week that the sermon subjects were 'The Church at Antioch' and 'Changes', both on the subject of Christianity and Judaism.
>
> The following week's advert also gave the titles of his sermons which were, 'A better resurrection' and 'Jesus as preacher'.

The first services of Altrincham Baptist Church under Mowbray were held here on Market Street in the Building Society Rooms. The modern buildings shown here form part of the hospital and replaced the Oddfellows Hall which in turn replaced the building society.

The opening page of the Church Minute Book recording the founding of the new church.

Charles Southwell was a young man when the breakaway church was founded. He is shown here later in life at his son's house at Sandiway.

In May 1887, Mowbray wrote a letter to the editor of the local newspaper explaining some of his official reasons for leaving the Hale Road chapel. This is his letter.

Sir,

For seven consecutive Sundays I have been conducting religious services in the Building Society's rooms, Altrincham, to which attention has been called through the medium of your advertising columns. The present seems a fitting time for publicly explaining the cause of these services.

On Wednesday evening, March 23rd, at a largely-attended meeting of the Bowdon Baptist Church, I announced my intention to resign the pastorate at the end of May. As one who, for the last five years, had been most intimately connected with the finances of the chapel, and during the last three and a half years had been practically acting as treasurer of the building fund, I felt it my duty then to make a statement, the substance of which I now repeat: - The church, since entering the new chapel, has never been in a position rightly to support a minister, even with an annual grant of £30 from the County Association.

The trust deed plainly states that all moneys contributed for sittings, &c., by the church and congregation are to be devoted, in the first place, to the payment of interest on mortgage, debt, yearly chief rent, with other necessary incidental expenses, and the remainder to the maintenance of Divine worship. These first claims formerly amounted to about £160 annually. Three years ago they were reduced to £145, and during the last six months to about £135, leaving a very moderate balance, (almost bordering on starvation pay) towards a ministerial stipend. This has necessitated an appeal to outside friends, chiefly resident in Bowdon. Mainly through their generosity the place has been enabled to keep open, and the minister's salary has reached the guaranteed minimum of £120 per annum up to the end of last year.

My financial statement produced a very deep impression upon the large majority of those present at the meeting, who felt that on such a pecuniary basis it was impossible any longer honestly to carry on the services in the building. Accordingly, they determined to make themselves responsible for all debts up to March 31st, 1887, and from that date to worship elsewhere. When I came to Bowdon six years ago, the chapel debt amounted to between £1,700 and £1,800. The church and congregation, by making every possible effort, have succeeded in reducing this to £1,115, and we feel that having strained every nerve to produce this result, there is no prospect of our being able to raise the remainder. Unless from some other source this £1,115 can be procured, we think the most honest course for all concerned would be to get the consent of the trustees to sell the building, and with the proceeds of such sale, first pay off the debt and then devote what is left towards erecting a small inexpensive place, suitable for a congregation of our size and position to worship in. I think there is a general feeling in the neighbourhood that to build a chapel of such a size, and at such a cost, was, to say the least, a great mistake, when the funds in hand were very small, the congregation limited in number and composed chiefly of people of scanty means. Certainly this overwhelming debt has been a constant source of anxiety and unpleasantness ever since the place was opened, and above all a great hindrance to the effective carrying on of a spiritual work.

These being the views of the majority of the friends, they have withdrawn from the old building. Sixty of the church members have formed themselves into a new church, and chosen me as pastor so long as I live in Bowdon. For a number of years I have sought to the best of my ability to serve my friends faithfully, and I am determined, God helping me, before entering on a larger sphere of work elsewhere to see the new Baptist Church worshipping after an honest manner, and under the pastoral care of some suitable minister. Our services are well attended, and for the present are being continued in the Building Society's room. We cordially invite all lovers of simple and earnest worship to join us. - Yours truly,

HENRY MOWBRAY

Bowdon, May 18th, 1887.

A new church was born, but what was it to be called? Was there room for two competing churches in Altrincham, and could both survive?

SHUTTLE DIPLOMACY

Mowbray's resignation took McLaren and the Association by surprise. McLaren must have known there were financial problems, and indeed Bowdon Baptist had made pleas for help, but the swiftness of the split caught them off guard.

Bowdon Baptist Church had been admitted to membership of the Lancashire and Cheshire Association of Baptist Churches on 8 May 1873. McLaren himself had signed the resolution. The Association had given financial support since then. Initially this was £20 per annum but had been reduced in 1875 to £15. On 10 June 1879 the Association resolved to reduce its support to £10 once the new chapel was occupied. Given the debt, this was extraordinarily short-sighted. In 1880, the funding was increased back to £15 per annum and eventually to £30.

Baptist churches are all technically independent and voluntarily associate together in an Association. McLaren could not therefore close Mowbray's new church down; he had no authority to do so. All he could do was seek to persuade him to return to the Hale Road chapel and offer some form of reconciliation. He might use the offer of an increased grant to help persuade Mowbray.

Mowbray knew the breakaway church might not be able to pay him for quite a while, so he quickly found a job working in Manchester to support his family, whilst remaining as minister of the breakaway church.

On 15 April 1887, a meeting of the Association's Council of Reference was held at the offices of Messrs Spencer. McLaren was present. The first item on the agenda was Bowdon. These are the minutes:

'The Secretary reported that the Pastor and four of the Deacons with a number of the members of the church at Bowdon had left the Chapel in Hale Road and had opened other premises of worship. Read the correspondence referring to the matter and detailed the efforts that had been made by Doctor McLaren, Mr Turner and himself to induce that the Seceders return. Those attempts have not yet been successful. After protracted consideration the following resolutions were unanimously adopted:

(i)   That the Council had heard with deep regret of the retirement of Mr Mowbray and other friends from the congregation worshipping in the Baptist Chapel at Bowden (sic) and requested the Secretary to convey to the seceding members its opinion that it is desirable for them to resume their place as worshippers in the Chapel, on which a conference can be had as to the best means of meeting monetary liabilities; and to express to the friends who remain in the Chapel its earnest hope that the worship and work of the Lord will be carried on so as to conciliate the goodwill of neighbours, the confidence of sister churches, and bring down the blessing of God.

(ii) That half of the grant made on December 1886 for the next 6 months be paid to Mr Mowbray vis £7.10.

(iii) That Reverend Doctor McLaren, Thos Turner and Mr Stephenson be sub-committee to work for the Council in reference to Hale Road Church, and the unexpired moiety of the grant made on December 9 (7-10) be placed at their disposal.'

It is worth looking at what lay behind the minutes. First, the meeting took place four days *before* the meeting which launched the new church. This suggests that there had been a previous preliminary meeting of those interested in forming the new church. It also suggests that there had been early discussions with the Association and that the Association was not at the moment taking sides. The Association was prepared to pay half the grant to Mowbray, with the balance to be given either way as the committee decided. The Association may have felt some sympathy for Mowbray. Certainly it was aware that it was financial problems that were the most serious issue.

Further meetings took place, but then the Association appeared to wrong-foot Mowbray. It may be that they thought that negotiations were going well. Mowbray appears not to have discussed these negotiations much with the church, although he would have kept his deacons informed. In any event, an article appeared in the local newspaper of Tuesday 31 May 1887 in which the Revd Lewis of Liverpool, the Secretary of the Association, was reported to have said in Rochdale that there were good hopes of a reunion between the two churches. This was the same Lewis who had once told Bowdon Baptist Church that Mowbray was 'God's messenger'.

The church secretary of the new church was asked by the Church Meeting to write a letter to Lewis asking him for the basis of his statement. Lewis duly replied and his answer was read out to the Church Meeting on 13 July, although we do not know what he said. Clearly the Association still wanted to recombine the two churches.

Simmons, who was one of the deacons who opposed Mowbray at the March Church Meeting, conducted negotiations on the Bowdon Baptist side. Franks and Mowbray represented the breakaway church.

Mowbray now had a body blow. Southwell and Ebenezer Brewer defected back to Hale Road, together with a Hannah Roberts. Southwell was not only a deacon, but also a trustee of the Hale Road chapel, and Ebenezer Brewer was the son of a deacon and one of the founders of the new church. His brother, William James seconded the motion to remove Ebenezer from the membership roll of the new church. Later James Brewer, father of William, left and we find him joining Bowdon Downs Congregational Church, having lost his wife and making the sad journey every Sunday past the Hale Road chapel from his home at 17, and then later 11, Bold Street.

Mowbray was hit hard by these resignations, which in turn completely split the Brewer family. He must have been tempted to abandon the whole project and leave the area. On Wednesday 31 August he brought a 'put up or shut up' proposal to the Church Meeting. He proposed four courses of action for them to consider:

1. Return to the old chapel and humbly confess they had done wrong.
2. Go back, providing arbitration could be arranged.
3. Formally disband and join other churches.
4. Go on as they were, providing satisfactory arrangements could be made.

Mowbray also stated that deacon Simmons had suggested that if he and his family stood in the way of the breakaway group returning to the old chapel, 'he should be willing to leave Bowdon at once'.

Franks then handed in two suggestions to the meeting from Simmons which were the result of a meeting the two had held that day. The first suggestion was for five members of the new church to meet five of the members from Hale Road. The second suggestion was that the members of the new church should go back to Hale Road if Simmons was able to clear off the debt in three or four months.

After a lengthy discussion, it was agreed to proceed with the fourth option.

The church secretary was then asked to write to Simmons and inform him that there could be no meeting until the new church members' names were treated in a similar manner to Mr and Mrs Mowbray. There was a clear suspicion that Simmons was trying to create a divide between Mowbray and the members of the new church. All of them had resigned from Hale Road, but Simmons had only recorded the Mowbrays as resigning. The offer of a meeting was between church members and by-passed Mowbray.

With regard to his suggestion to clear off the debt on the chapel in three or four months, they would 'feel bound to reconsider the question if and when that event took place.' There was some understandable scepticism as to whether Simmons could ever achieve this.

On 5 October therefore, a resolution was passed requesting the church secretary to write to the Association informing them of the true position

> The local newspaper called the split the 'Bowdon Baptist Controversy'.

of the new church and asking the Association to use its influence in getting all the breakaway church members' names removed from the Hale Road church register.

On 12 October 1887, the Association's Council of Reference met. McLaren reported 'that he and the Revd R. Lewis and T. Turner had failed so far in effecting a reconciliation between Mr Mowbray and the 40 friends who had left the Chapel with the few (some 20) friends who remained: and further that it was unlikely that Mr Mowbray will be able to enlist the sympathy of the churches in Manchester with his movements'.

Attitudes were now hardening against Mowbray. At around this time Mowbray appeared with MacKennal and Wainwright on a Bible Society platform. Wainwright had, of course, been responsible for Mowbray becoming a Christian, but MacKennal visibly supported Hale Road, so the conversations on the platform must have been interesting. Reading the local newspaper, it does seem as if Mowbray and his church were ostracised, and all publicity was given to Hale Road.

The church split was all unfortunate timing for McLaren. He was in poor health. On 29 October 1887, Spurgeon finally resigned from the Baptist Union over the Downgrade Controversy. The subsequent attempts by the Baptist Union to bring Spurgeon back into the fold were clearly more important than dealing with a Baptist church split in Altrincham. McLaren, however, found himself in simultaneous shuttle diplomacy between Spurgeon and the Baptist Union and between Mowbray and the Hale Road Baptist Church.

McLaren was on the delegation of four from the Baptist Union appointed to have talks with Spurgeon. It was McLaren who suggested a softer tack in meeting Spurgeon's conditions in January 1898. There was a three-way split amongst the delegation. McLaren wanted to accept Spurgeon's conditions for talks, Booth as President of the Baptist Union and friend of Spurgeon wanted to postpone, but Culross and Clifford were determined to raise issues such as Spurgeon's resignation itself at the meeting.

Spurgeon had also said he had a list of people he could name as being on the 'downgrade' at the Baptist Union, and Culross and Clifford wanted him to withdraw the allegations or bring them out in the open. Spurgeon did not want to discuss this.

McLaren was ill and thus his view did not prevail. If McLaren had been well, the outcome might have been different and perhaps Spurgeon might have come back into the Baptist Union fold. In the end, McLaren was too ill even to attend the fateful meeting with Spurgeon on 13 January 1888.[1] Further attempts were made to bring Spurgeon back into the Baptist Union, but he never returned.

Back in Altrincham, olive branches were still being held out to the breakaway church. Carey Bonner of Sale Baptist Church, having recently preached at Hale Road, agreed in December 1887 to come to a social meeting of the new breakaway church.[2] He was a prominent member of the Association.

The reality though was that the Association could not be seen by its member churches to be supporting a breakaway church, so on 8 December the grant to Hale Road Baptist was increased to £30 per annum and Mowbray received nothing further. Given the fact that the new church had not affiliated to the Association, the Association could hardly support it anyway. The size of grant to the Hale Road Church was almost without precedent. Mowbray was an outcast and on his own.

The next reference to negotiations is in April 1891 when there appear to have been further reunion discussions behind the scenes. The Altrincham rumour mill began working overtime. At a Church Meeting, Mowbray 'flatly contradicted the absurd rumour that was being spread abroad that himself was leaving the neighbourhood, and that the Tabernacle was going to be closed and the congregation going to the Baptist Chapel Hale Road; and explained that the same had no doubt arisen out of the circumstance that the Deacons and himself had been asked by the Deacons of the Hale Road Baptist Church to confer with them concerning the possibility of union between the two churches. This they had done, but beyond a very friendly interchange of thoughts on the subject nothing definite had been agreed upon'.

By 29 April 1891, however, negotiations had clearly reached a more encouraging stage and the breakaway Church Meeting resolved 'that it is desirable if possible that there be reunion between the Baptist Churches of Altrincham and Bowdon'.

It is possible that MacKennal may also have been involved in these negotiations, because in June he invited the breakaway church to a united communion service at Bowdon Downs involving all various nonconformist churches. He must have known this would bring the two Baptist Churches into one united service. Mowbray's church politely declined the invitation.[3]

---

[1] Hopkins, Mark: Nonconformity's Romantic Generation – Evangelical and Liberal Theologies in Victorian England, Wipf & Stock, 2007.
[2] Carey Bonner was later Secretary of the Lancashire and Cheshire Baptist Association. After Sale, he went to Portland Chapel, Southampton (McLaren's old church) and then to the Secretariat of the National Sunday School Union. He wrote many hymns and songs. He was President of the Baptist Union 1931-32. He died on 16 June 1938. In the year after his visit to Altrincham, he temporarily gave up his duties because of nervous depression due to the strain of running Sale Baptist Church. Sale too had financial problems.
[3] The Bowdon Downs Congregational minutes only refer to the Presbyterians and Wesleyans being invited. The Baptists were initially left out, no doubt due to the problem in knowing which church to invite. The service was partly to raise money for the pacifist Peace Society.

Now McLaren became involved again in negotiations. On 1 July Mowbray read out to the Church Meeting an exchange of letters between himself, McLaren and Bowdon Baptist trustee James Abbott. The suggestion by McLaren was that there should be a combined ministry to cover both churches.

Hale Road Baptist Church (as Bowdon Baptist was by then becoming known) now stole a march on the breakaway church and voted to accept this proposal. However, something clearly went wrong at this stage and Mowbray reported to the September Church Meeting that, due to the conduct of certain members at Hale Road, there could be no question of this happening and he had written to Abbott to that effect. That was the final attempt to find a solution.

An interesting thought may have occurred to you by now. There are two Baptist churches at this stage in our history in Altrincham, but today there is only one. Is the current Altrincham Baptist Church the successor of the breakaway church led by the renegade Mowbray, or is it the church that continued at Hale Road and was supported by many powerful figures? Which was to survive? Would they in fact be reconciled after all?

> There were some losses of members after the start of the breakaway church. That is hardly surprising, given the unusual and confusing situation. This must have been agonising for Mowbray. If we look at communicant members of the new church,[4] member number one, Sarah Anne Mitchell, never attended. Hers indeed is a tragic story, as she ended up in an asylum.
>
> Of the sixty-three registered as communicant members in 1887, eight never turned up for communion at all. Ebenezer Brewer and Charles Southwell, a first deacon, were two early departures, both returning to Hale Road. However, after the initial departures, Mowbray appears to have kept his congregation and then grown it. Of the sixty-three communicant members in 1887, nineteen were missing by the end of 1890, but of these eleven had moved out of the area, demonstrating the fluidity of the population, and one had died.

> In November 1887 the following article appeared in the local newspaper:
>
> 'During the past few months the Chapel has been beaten up by a storm of a serious difference between the members. The pastor, who was followed by a number of his friends, took it into his head to leave the church and commence services on his own account. Fortunately for Mr Mowbray, he can afford to preach without salary and his Congregation have no anxiety on the score of payment. His departure has done the cause at Bowdon no good'. The article however, did hint at reconciliation.
>
> Mowbray must have been to see the editor, because in the next issue there was a hasty clarification, saying it should be understood the article was not opening up for discussion any new point; rather, it was suggesting that the Hale Road congregation wanted reconciliation.

---

[4] What a communicant member is will be explained more fully in a later chapter, but briefly there were full members who had been baptised as believers and also those who did not wish to be so baptised but who were still part of the church and who therefore were allowed to take communion but not to attend Church Meetings. In effect the number of communicants gives a better picture of the size of the church.

142

'On Wednesday Mr Spurgeon announced his withdrawal from the Baptist Union, owing to the unsatisfactory situation which he believes has been taken on his charge against the ministry being "on the down grade"[5], both spiritually and theologically. He declines to form a new denomination, saying that there are denominations enough, and assenting that the "thieves and robbers would climb into it, and nothing would be gained'. Baptist churches being self-governing, they would find their own affinities, and keep their coasts clear of invaders. He advocates a growing spiritual life'.

How *The Altrincham Division Chronicle* and *Cheshire County News* reported the departure of Spurgeon from the Baptist Union in 1887.

James Brewer, a local gardener, was a founder of, and then an early departure from, Mowbray's Church.

McLaren, now the grand old man of the Baptist Union and one of the most famous preachers in the world at the time. It must have been daunting for the renegade Mowbray to meet with McLaren.

Which Baptist church was to survive in Altrincham? The answer may come as a surprise.

---

[5] Usually 'downgrade' was used, but not here.

LEONARD

The split became a scandal in Altrincham and amongst Baptists generally.

We now follow the story of the Hale Road Church.

They were in serious financial trouble with the departure of about 60 per cent of their people, but those that remained were determined to continue to try and save the new chapel.

In June 1887 we find them advertising sermons by Revd R. E. Towler of Manchester Baptist College in a bid to attract attention. What they desperately needed though was public backing from the Lancashire and Cheshire Association of Baptist Churches. If the Association sat on the fence, they had no chance of survival. If they had McLaren behind them, they had a fighting chance.

The Association gave public support in October 1887. Hale Road held a sale of work on 28 October and a concert in the evening, followed by sermons by Carey Bonner of Sale Baptist on the next Sunday. Thomas Spencer, vice-president of the Association, opened the sale. The goods, according to the local newspaper, 'offered strong temptation to the feminine fancy'. Overbury read out apologies from Revd Rawes, who worked with McLaren, and from Llewellyn as former minister. Llewellyn's letter said he would have come had he had more notice, which suggests the project was put together in some haste. The former minister was though backing the Hale Road Church.

Overbury, as Treasurer, said the chapel had eventually cost £2,850-1s-10d.[1] The debt was £1,105 and they had raised £3,292. It did not need a mathematician to see there was something wrong with these figures, and the next issue of the local newspaper carried an anonymous letter from 'Perplexed', suggesting that the figure of £3,292 was masking the truth: most of the money in that figure was loans from individuals who had to be repaid. The real sum raised was substantially less. No doubt 'Perplexed' was someone on Mowbray's side.

You will note that the final cost overrun, despite all the savings made, was just over £650, or about 30 per cent. Something had gone seriously wrong with the project.

A subscription list was opened, and McLaren was at the head with a donation of £5. The church also hoped for a donation from a charity called Lady Hewley's Fund, although this may never have materialised.[2]

Spencer in his speech was keen for reconciliation. 'You must pray for those who went away and those who remain. Of course it would have been great pleasure if the efforts of your friends in Liverpool and Manchester had succeeded in bringing back within these walls some of those friends you love.' However, the Council of the Association 'first must help Bowdon in every way it can...You have the full sympathy of the heads of your denomination.'

Kirkland of the Oxford Road Primitive Methodists added his support. They had also been in serious financial circumstances due to their building debt. 'We are

---

[1] £2,850.09.
[2] Lady Sarah Hewley set up the charity in the nineteenth century to supplement the incomes of Nonconformist ministers and transferred seven landed estates into the charity to fund it. The fund still exists.

brothers in tribulation.' However, the Methodists had recently received a legacy of £400 and they only had £200 to pay off. The Baptist obviously needed to pray for something similar.[3]

The sale of work was followed by a concert in the evening.

Hale Road desperately needed leadership and began looking for a minister. In the interim, McLaren took firm and decisive action. The problems at Altrincham were among the most significant the Association now faced. He therefore affiliated Bowdon Baptist Church to his own Union chapel and provided all the preachers. He could not afford to let the church at Hale Road fail.

By 1888 they had found their new minister. His name was the Revd Henry C. Leonard. Initially it might have been McLaren's intention to have a joint ministry with

> The fund-raising concert in October 1887 continued the Bowdon Baptist tradition of poor reviews. The reviewer in the local newspaper wrote of the concert: 'It further embraced several selections by an orchestral band, the performances of which were scarcely what the taste of the audience could have desired. The band essayed several difficult pieces, but lacking time, precision and harmony, complete failure was the result.'

Mowbray, but as we have seen, this was not to be. The Association almost forced Hale Road to appoint Leonard, as it made the increased grant of £30 per annum conditional on his appointment.

Who was the man called in to rescue the Hale Road Church? Henry Leonard was born in 1836 at Brislington near Bristol. He was the youngest son of Robert Leonard JP, a merchant, and was educated at Fishponds in Bristol and then University College London, where he gained an MA. The contrast with the much less well-educated Mowbray cannot have been starker. Leonard was the youngest of six children. Two older brothers were solicitors. The family was rich enough to employ four servants.

In 1855 Leonard attended Regent's Park College and then became pastor of Boxmoor Baptist Church at Hemel Hempstead, where he saw through a new church building project. He was later joint minister with the Revd G. P. Gould at Bournemouth, and they built new churches at Boscombe and Lansdowne. All this experience in steering building projects must have recommended him to the Association, and it is possible that his experience as a joint minister was also considered useful in case McLaren ever managed to persuade Leonard and Mowbray to become co-ministers of a reunited church.

In 1881 he became minister of Clarence Street Baptist Church in Penzance. It was from there that he relocated to Altrincham. He seems to have been involved in the church at Altrincham from the beginning of the year, with his service of recognition as minister being in April 1888.

Leonard was married to Sarah, who was one year older than him, and they had three daughters, Martha, Sarah and Alexandra. The youngest, Alexandra, was twenty-four by the time the Leonards arrived in Altrincham. The other two were two years older (and may have been twins). Their son, Robert, was their youngest child and was seventeen when they moved to Altrincham.

---

[3] One can only assume he was not suggesting they should pray for a timely death.

The Association rallied round to support Leonard with some big names. At his recognition service McLaren, MacKennal and Williams all spoke. Leonard was also invited to be the co-guest speaker at the British School Mission Sunday School anniversary.

At the annual Church Meeting in January 1889, MacKennal, Adamson of the British School Mission and the Secretary of the Association were all on the platform to give public support. Leonard gave a positive speech, encouraging them to look to the future and to put the difficulties of the past behind them. In the previous nineteen months since Mowbray had left, they had added ten members (although he glossed over the fact that most of these were defections back from Mowbray).

Simmons, as Treasurer stated that they had managed to pay their minister and just under £100 off the debt. Overbury, as Secretary, read the Sunday school report. Bowser as Secretary of the Association, said he was there to express his sympathy with them.

In 1889 more support was given at a fund-raising bazaar. Leonard opened by saying that they were seeking a loan of £400 from the Baptist Building Fund to keep them afloat, but to 'do much more than meet the recurring debt is quite beyond the power of the church'. MacKennal himself opened the bazaar. After his now customary stressing of the similarities of their congregational backgrounds, he likened their efforts to that of a swimmer. 'It is very hard work sometimes for a swimmer whose strength has almost gone, and whose conflict with the waves has long continued, to keep up his spirit and continue his strokes, and my most tender sympathies are with those who continue to struggle when the conditions are so hard and adverse, and when there is little to cheer and sustain.'

Simmons said he himself had put £100 towards paying off the debt.

The bazaar closed with 'an amusing farce called "The Dentist's Den"'.

In 1889 they moved out temporarily while the chapel was redecorated. McLaren preached at the re-opening and MacKennal ended the service.[4]

It seemed as if the Hale Road Church might just be able to turn things round.

---

[4] This is the only time we know the subject of an actual sermon by McLaren to the Altrincham Baptists, so for the record the great man preached on John 1:29: 'Behold the Lamb of God which taketh away the sin of the world', coupled with Revelation 5:6: 'The Lamb of God that was slain'.

BACK TO THE BREAKAWAY

The breakaway church was the poorer and less well-equipped church. It had no building it could call its own. Hale Road had the trained full-time minister; the breakaway did not. Hale Road had the backing of the Association. The breakaway church soon lost the Association's support.

Mowbray had been a full-time paid minister, but he gave this up and drew no salary from the new church. He had always in fact been what was called a 'lay pastor', having no formal theological training but still being accepted as a minister. As we have seen, this was not uncommon amongst Victorian Baptists. Many ministers simply could not afford to be trained. In the first half of the century, craftsmen represented the most likely social origin of Baptist ministers. From 1860 onwards, the numbers of white-collar worker ministers began to increase, but only outnumbering artisans after 1880. In 1871 only 58 per cent of ministers had training at academy or college, but by 1911 that figure had risen to 84.5 per cent. Spurgeon's own college played a significant role in this change.[1]

The new church now needed a name. Clearly they could not call themselves anything which might confuse them with Bowdon Baptist or (as it was now more often known) the Hale Road Baptist Church. On 1 June 1887, at their second meeting, Franks proposed and William Brewer seconded a motion to name the new church. The name was Altrincham Baptist Church.

The Independent Congregational Church had used the Building Society Rooms on Market Street until about two years earlier, when they had disbanded and thrown in their lot with the British School Mission. Now Mowbray rented these rooms on Sundays. They had a seating capacity of 150.[2]

As the rooms were only available on Sundays, mid-week meetings had to be held elsewhere. The first Church Meetings of Altrincham Baptist Church were held in the British School, but they soon transferred to a house on Bold Street. This would either have been that of the Brewer family or the Warburtons. William Brewer was a deacon and Warburton was church secretary. Records show the Brewers lived at 17 Bold Street and the Warburtons at 19 Bold Street in 1881.[3] Given the size of the Brewer family, the more logical venue would have been that of the church secretary.

---

[1] Briggs, op. cit.
[2] A newspaper article of the time about a painting exhibition gives this figure.
[3] As they frequently moved from rented house to rented house on Bold Street, we cannot say for certain these were the correct house numbers, although it is likely. However, we do know they were on Bold Street.

17 and 19 Bold Street. The Brewer family lived at number 17 and the Warburtons at number 19. Number 19 was the probable location of the early church Meetings of Altrincham Baptist Church. Members must have had to crowd into the house.

William James Brewer in 1890, aged 24. He was just 21 when he seconded the motion to give Altrincham Baptist Church its name.

Just when they thought they were settled as a new church however, Mowbray dropped a bombshell into the Church Meeting held on Wednesday 4 January 1888.

ANOTHER NEW BUILDING?

Mowbray announced that their use of the Building Society Rooms was 'precarious'. He did not say why this might be the case, but the reason was probably because the Altrincham Permanent Benefit Building Society, founded in 1866, had proved to be nothing like its name and was in liquidation. There was a major dispute brewing between the shareholders and the liquidators, and it was possible that the building might have to be sold.

Before the church could even think about the problem, Mowbray, ever the businessman, proposed the solution.

The church minutes record: 'As there does not seem any possibility for obtaining a suitable place in the town he laid a scheme to purchase a plot of land in Railway Street on the site of the old Bowdon Station and erect there an iron building suitable to seat from 200 to 250 persons. If the friends were in favour of this he would himself undertake the financial arrangements.'

Let us pause for a moment here. Mowbray was working in Manchester to support his family. Altrincham Baptist Church paid him only his expenses. Now he had found a new site for them. Not only that, but he was going to make the financial arrangements himself.

There is a hidden story behind this, because Mowbray may not have been able to give the church the full picture about those 'financial arrangements'. We will return to that intriguing mystery later.

The Church Meeting minutes are rather bland at this point, but the members must have been astonished. Not surprisingly, they resolved it was advisable 'to remove from the Building Society Rooms and that we authorise Mr Mowbray to write to the railway company [MSGVAR[1]] and arrange for a plot of land. In the event of it being successful we authorise him to make such financial arrangements as he may think desirable and that we pledge ourselves to assist him to the best of our ability'.

Mowbray personally negotiated with the railway company. A Special Church Meeting was then convened on Wednesday 22 February 1888 to discuss the results of the negotiations. Mowbray announced 'he had received a reply from the Secretary of the Railway Company informing him that the Directors were willing to let a plot of land to erect a building at the corner of Goose Green (opposite Mr Harrison's shop on Railway Street) for the sum of £10 per annum subject to the conditions in the Agreement'.

The minutes then go on to say that the 'Pastor also stated that he had ascertained what would be the total cost of an iron building to accommodate from 200 to 250 persons and that the estimate to complete the same as per plans and arrangements would be about £300 and the Pastor stated that himself and Mrs Mowbray had decided if the church were willing to erect the place at their own cost then the

---

[1] This is the reference in the minutes, but it should perhaps have been 'MSJARC', the Manchester South Junction and Altrincham Railway Company.

church should rent the building from them subject to the payment of 15 shillings[2] per week which would cover the ground rent and taxes – and hire of harmonium'.[3]

Again, let us pause to consider this. For no cost to the church and for a payment of £39 a year (roughly the Hale Road ground rent), Mowbray was willing to sort out the lease, build a new building seating about half that of the Hale Road capacity (but still a good number and more than ample to seat the combined congregations of the two churches) and to throw in the cost of the hire of a harmonium.

Perhaps he had a point to make, but he made it well. The Hale Road people were wrong to refuse to sell the building. If they had sold, the debt would have gone and they could have built something much cheaper in town. The Church Meeting Minutes record that 'A general conversation ensued'.

Deacon Brewer then proposed 'that we as a church tender our hearty thanks to our Pastor for the trouble he has taken in regard to this matter and that we gratefully accept the offer of himself and Mrs Mowbray and request him to make all necessary arrangements on our behalf for the erection of an iron building'. Not surprisingly, the motion was carried unanimously.

Mowbray responded by saying that, now a decision had been made, he would get the building erected as soon as possible and hoped it would be ready for the first anniversary of the church or Easter Sunday 1 April 1888.

> In January 1888, as Mowbray's church decided on its new building, Spurgeon's own Metropolitan Tabernacle Baptist Church passed a resolution that the church 'in the testimony for the truth he has recently borne by his articles upon "The Down Grade", endorses his action in withdrawing from the Baptist Union, and pledges itself to support him...'.[4]

The timetable for the new building was very fast. The reason lay in the building's design and construction.

---

[2] 75p.

[3] The Church Meeting minutes are difficult to decipher and ambiguous at this point, but the context is clear in that it was the Mowbrays who were taking on the liability for the costs of the building. Certainly the church accounts never make any mention of any payment for it, but later there is reference to a repayment of a loan to the Mowbrays. What may have happened is that they took the lease in their own name and loaned the church the money to build the building, probably interest-free. We shall look later at where the money might have come from.

[4] Quoted in the Altrincham Division Chronicle.

THE IRON TABERNACLE

The new chapel was bought in flat-pack kit form and delivered to Altrincham. The chapel opened in April 1888 and the local newspaper reported that the £40 Mowbray asked to be raised at the opening service was indeed raised. All the furniture was installed by Bagnall & Milne who had premises on George Street.

As Mowbray had done everything to organise the new chapel, he also wanted to name it. He proposed it should be called 'The Tabernacle', and so the 'trading name' of Altrincham Baptist Church became 'The Tabernacle, Altrincham'. Given the materials used in its construction, locals quickly nicknamed it the 'Iron Tabernacle'.

The word 'tabernacle' had theological significance and was quite a common usage in Baptist chapel names. The tabernacle was the tent which signified God's presence amongst his people, the Israelites, in the wilderness. Mowbray's message was that the church was not about buildings, but about God's people.[1]

Mowbray may also have wanted to use the name 'tabernacle' for a further purpose. Perhaps it reminded him of Toxteth Tabernacle where he had first started his ministry, but there may have been more to it. Negotiations had broken down with McLaren and with the Hale Road Church. Spurgeon had left the Baptist Union. Spurgeon's church was the Metropolitan Tabernacle and it too had now left the Baptist Union. We will probably never know, but was this Mowbray's sign of support for the Spurgeon side of the Downgrade Controversy as he too stood with Altrincham Baptist Church outside the Baptist Union?

Building the new chapel was not enough however. The church had to grow in numbers to fill the building. The first recorded baptism conducted by the new Altrincham Baptist Church was of John Walker of Dunham in December 1887.

In 1888 they therefore decided to return to their roots and hold open-air services in Altrincham in the summer. In 1890 they bought a small portable organ to assist with these open-air meetings and ordered between 500 and 1,000 tracts.

Mowbray saw an opportunity for a mission in 1888. Charles Bradlaugh spoke in Altrincham that year. Bradlaugh was an atheist and opposed to Christianity. He had been disbarred from Parliament for refusing to take the oath as an MP, preferring instead to affirm. He was eventually allowed to take his seat in 1886.

The Altrincham meeting was naturally controversial. What is surprising is that Leonard appears to have been there and even publicly supported the motion proposed by Bradlaugh.

Mowbray was an astute operator and promptly arranged for Bradlaugh's Christian brother to lead a mission in Altrincham shortly afterwards. The gap between the two churches was made painfully obvious.

In 1889 Mowbray arranged a second mission led by Henry Lakin, formerly of Manchester City Mission. Mowbray was of course connected with Manchester City

---

[1] The tabernacle in the Old Testament story of the Exodus was a portable structure comprising a wooden framework covered with curtains and carried through the wilderness. It was used as a place of sacrifice and worship. It was in this tent that Moses often encountered God and it was where the Ark of the Covenant was kept. When the Israelites in the wilderness saw the cloud of the Lord over the tabernacle, they stayed in camp, but when it lifted, they set off on their travels, taking the tabernacle with them.

Mission and probably still doing some work for them. At around this time they also began to donate again to Manchester City Mission.

In 1889 they also began testimony meetings which were held every two to three months. Members would explain how they had become Christians or how their lives had been affected by Christ. These were a way of encouraging newcomers into the faith and helping believers to express their own faith.

During this period, a certain Lewis Cole was commended to Spurgeon's College from the Tabernacle. He may have been the first person to be sent by the Altrincham Baptists to be theologically trained.[2]

In the summer of 1891, as part of Mowbray's strategy for growth, the church appointed its first full-time evangelist. He was the Revd James Nankivell, a man of Cornish stock. Nankivell was not, however, a Baptist; he had been the Anglican diocesan missionary for Chester diocese and before that he had been based at St Peter's Church in Preston. It was difficult for Mowbray to recruit Baptist ministers or evangelists because of the isolation of the church from the Association. Mowbray was therefore fortunate to find Nankivell, an Anglican who had now decided to adhere to Baptist principles.

Mowbray intended him to be assistant minister as well, but the decision was deferred because it coincided with further pressure from McLaren to have a joint ministry with Hale Road. When that fell through, Nankivell became the first recorded assistant minister of the Altrincham Baptists, and subsequently Mowbray appointed him as joint minister.

Then in January 1892 Mowbray confirmed to Altrincham Baptist Church certain rumours that had been circulating about the Hale Road Church.

Charles Bradlaugh, the radical atheist MP supported in politics by Leonard.

---

[2] It has not been possible to find out what became of him. It is possible that he emigrated or became a missionary. There may have been students from Altrincham before him, but he is the first person of whom we have an actual record.

Mowbray did not have to look far for an iron chapel. As early as 1878, the local newspaper carried an advertisement for a prefabricated iron chapel having 'good substantial buildings, will accommodate 200 and 300 with chapel, vestry, porch, and fittings complete, also an iron schoolroom'. All he had to do was to apply to C Hemming and Co of 47 Moorgate Street London. Payment could be by instalments. The company was founded in 1851.

The iron used in these chapels was what we would now call corrugated iron, galvanised with zinc. They were often called tin tabernacles, but in fact tin was not used in their construction. The Altrincham nickname of the 'Iron Tabernacle' was therefore correct. The chapels were usually sent out in flat-pack form and assembled on site on a brick base.

There is a puzzle about the Iron Tabernacle. We know more or less exactly where it was, but what did it look like?

This photograph is the oldest one available and shows a building on the right which could be a chapel. The location fits the description. There are no shops and the photograph is probably taken after the railway station had closed.

If the building above was the Iron Tabernacle, then it later became or was replaced by a photographer's studio. One can just make out the word 'Studio' in the window on the first floor of the building on the right. This building existed until quite recent times and it has been erroneously called an old signal box.

The building on Railway Street in more detail. This is almost certainly the Iron Tabernacle, the first building owned by the breakaway Altrincham Baptist Church. Note the possible stained glass window on the side. Although there are horse carriage taxis in the photograph, Bowdon Terminus station had closed as the building stands partly on the site of what was an access road to the station. The building fits descriptions as to its location, and it looks like a mission hall. The chapel was probably demolished later to make way for the photographer's studio.

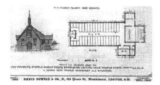

David Rowell and Co also sold prefabricated iron chapels. This is an advertisement for one which shows a typical internal layout. The Altrincham Tabernacle may have looked something like this.

Draycott in the Clay Iron Tabernacle. Note how similar it is to the picture of the Altrincham Tabernacle above.

Avoncroft chapel, another 'iron tabernacle'.

Margaret Heald Hall, constructed for Manchester City Mission in 1886 at a cost of £650. This was a large iron gospel hall.

In 1892 Longsight Baptist Church followed suit and built a similar building.

The photograph on the left, shows Railway Street from outside the location of the Tabernacle. It is possible this was taken while Bowdon Terminus Station was still operational. However, if the photograph was taken after the station was closed but while a taxi rank still remained there, then the Altrincham Tabernacle would be to the photographer's immediate left. Note the small hut to the left in the distance. This was either a ticket office or the cabbies' shelter presented by local church people led by Canon Wainwright.[3]

The photograph shows the same scene today. The modern shops are built on the top of the slope which led down to the station.

The same scene circa 1910. Note the postmen on their bicycles, the tram tracks and the car with its chauffeur and top-hatted passengers. The sight of the car is causing pedestrians to turn and look.

---

[3] Douglas Rendell believes it is a ticket office, but the question then is where is the cabbies' shelter which is mentioned in local newspapers? See his book, *Photographers in the Altrincham Area*, 2006. The author's view is that it was more likely to be the cabbies' shelter as it fits the location and description.

A postcard of Railway Street from near the site of the old Tabernacle after Stamford New Road had been built.

Railway Street from near the location of the Tabernacle. The photographer's studio which replaced the Tabernacle is on the right.

The photographer's studio on Railway Street in the 1980s. The window was north facing as photographers often preferred light from this direction.

The same site in the 1990s.

The junction of Ashley Road and The Downs taken from Railway Street.

The site of the former Iron Tabernacle on Railway Street and near to Goose Green in 2007. If you could stand about 20 feet behind the shop, you might be standing roughly below where Henry Mowbray used to preach.[4]

Matters in Altrincham in 1892 were about to take another dramatic turn.

---

[4] At the time of writing, this whole site is marked for redevelopment so may well look very different in the future.

A NEW MINISTER FOR HALE ROAD

We now turn our story back to the Hale Road Church.

There could be no disguising the fact that times were difficult. This can best be summed up by an article in the local newspaper[1] which quoted in turn an article in *The Church* magazine about Leonard.

'The Church has, as a frontpiece, a very excellent portrait of this gentleman, and a short motion of his ministerial career. It concludes by saying - "As a minister, Mr Leonard has always been marked by his willingness to take difficult rather than easy places. The church at Bowdon, before he became pastor, was described as the 'forlorn hope of the Lancashire and Cheshire Association'. But he has always been enabled to do good work there; nor can we doubt that, with Divine help he will be as successful and as much valued in his future ministry as he has always and deservedly been in the past".'

We can now see a definite contrast in this period between Hale Road Baptist Church and the Altrincham Tabernacle under Mowbray. The Hale Road members paid for Leonard to have his portrait painted in 1889. Mowbray never had time for that; he was working in Manchester and the rest of his time was spent in building up the new church.

Leonard's new idea to grow Hale Road was to form the Bowdon Baptist Mutual Improvement Society. Every week its proceedings were reported in the local newspaper. Its topics included improving reason and memory, free public education, Keats, Ruskin, Walter Scott, an account of Leonard's trip to Ireland and reading. Reading, said the intellectual Leonard, can be a turning-point, 'Yes, the beginning of a new life'. The contrast between the styles of the two men cannot have been starker. Leonard, supported by the establishment figures, tried to educate his congregation. He did not hold a single mission. Mowbray's work was devoted to mission.

Between them, the two achieved a fair amount of press coverage. Sometimes the editor of the *Altrincham Division Chronicle* took mischievous delight in placing articles about the two competing churches very close to each other, but after 1888 Mowbray almost disappears from sight in the local newspapers: his ostracism by the establishment was complete.

There are two puzzles about Leonard. His biography states that he was joint minister with Mowbray in Altrincham. That was never the case, and yet was this the official gloss put on events by the Association? Did they actually work more closely together than the members of their two churches realised? Why was this reference in his biography? Sadly, we may never know the true answer.

The second puzzle relates to the Downgrade Controversy. Given what we know about Mowbray, we have seen he probably favoured Spurgeon's point of view in the Downgrade Controversy and may have seen himself as being like Spurgeon: leading a church out of the Union at the same time to preserve the integrity of the gospel as he saw it.

---

[1] Altrincham Division Chronicle.

Spurgeon stated that he had a list of names of persons at the Baptist Union who he could name as being on the 'downgrade', in other words, as sliding towards an errant liberal theology. James Spurgeon revealed that he and his brother Charles had come close to releasing the names, but they never did. However, Mark Hopkins may have found the list.[2] He states that there exists a scrap of paper in the handwriting of Joseph Harrald, Spurgeon's private secretary, which may date from the time of the Downgrade Controversy and which may be the list. It contains the names of five well-known 'liberal' ministers and two friends of Spurgeon who had turned against him during the controversy.

If there was a liberal-evangelical split partly behind the breakaway in Altrincham over church finances, one might expect the Hale Road Church to call a more liberal minister.

The third name on Spurgeon's list was none other than Leonard.

We know that Leonard quoted Darwin with approval (as an observer of nature only, of course; to be more overt about this would have been a step too far at the time). We know he was regarded as an intellectual. He did state to the church at one point that he was an evangelical, but for Spurgeon he may have been one of those betraying what it meant to be an evangelical Baptist.

Leonard eventually went back to Bristol in 1891 after two and a half years at Hale Road and then to Heston in Middlesex, where at the age of fifty-five the census stated that he was a retired Baptist minister. He had had enough.

In 1890 Hale Road had forty-three members, nine teachers and eighty-six pupils. He had paid £195 off the debt and the Association minuted that there were encouraging signs from Bowdon. However, numbers began declining again.

Leonard was succeeded by William H. Perkins. By the time he took over, Hale Road was down to thirty-five members.[3] In 1890 Perkins was listed as a member of McLaren's Union Chapel, and it is likely McLaren was instrumental in sending him to Hale Road. Perkins was also on one of the district committees of the Lancashire and Cheshire Association at the same time as Houghton, the man who laid one of the foundation stones.

Perkins was born in Leatherhead, Surrey on 5 May 1843, the fourth of five children. His father, Fred Perkins, was a Baptist minister. Perkins graduated from Aberdeen University at a young age and was gifted in ancient languages. In 1868 he went to Hinckley, which was a church with 250 members and with 400 attending the Sunday school. After that he went to Bootle and then to Goodshaw College near Haslingden, where he was a tutor for eighteen years.

He married Ellen and their children were Frederick, Eleanor, Charles and Margaret.

He did, in fact, have a previous connection with the Altrincham Baptists. At the Annual Meeting before the split in 1887, he was on the platform with Mowbray, speaking on behalf of the Sunday Closing Association, a lobby group to regulate

---

[2] Hopkins, op. cit.
[3] There is only one recorded departure to Bowdon Downs Congregational Church, which was Miss Mary Smith in 1888. If people left, it is likely they either went nowhere or drifted to the British School Mission or Mowbray and the other Baptists.

Sunday trading. In March that year, he was also on a combined Altrincham temperance platform with Wainwright, MacKennal and the Methodist Lewis.

Perkins is however a tragic figure. In 1899 he went to Rosebery Park at Bournemouth and was there for nineteen years. Whilst there, Ellen became disabled and the church struggled. His biography states that his later life was dogged by 'illness, sorrow and bereavement', but he carried on ministering regardless and finally died on 14 June 1938.

Perkins was only at Hale Road for three months, and his time at Altrincham does not even feature in his biography. Although he might have been appointed as minister, it is more likely that in practice McLaren simply seconded him to preach and paid for him. Hale Road was, after all, almost part of Union Baptist.

So in 1891, the Hale Road church, in debt but backed by the Association and Union Baptist, was once again without a minister. Could it survive?

THE FATE OF THE HALE ROAD CHURCH

The news was not yet public knowledge, but Mowbray informed Altrincham Baptist Church in January 1892 that the Hale Road Church had closed in the face of a dwindling congregation and its debts. Perkins had left. Bowdon Baptist Church was no more. Altrincham Baptist Church was the sole survivor.

There had been a slow drift of members from Hale Road to the Tabernacle in the period leading up to the closure. It is also clear that there had been an informal agreement that the two churches would not try to poach from each other's Congregations. Now that was no longer necessary, and in February 1892 Mowbray announced that members could invite persons 'lately connected with the membership of the dispersed church of the Hale Road Baptist Chapel to worship with us'.

What was to become of the Hale Road chapel? The trustees would have to sell. They would either have to sell it so it could be knocked down and used for housing or find someone to buy it as a chapel. Who would want it?

The trustees were in a serious dilemma. Nowadays, most Nonconformist churches vest their property in trust corporations. The first reason for this is that it solves the problem of what happens if a trustee dies. The church may find, perhaps a hundred years after it was founded, that it wants to sell its property, and then discovers that the property is owned on its behalf by people who may have no connection with it and do not even know they are trustees. It can be very difficult to track them down.[1]

The second reason is that individuals have to take on serious personal liability. True, they are subject to certain indemnities, but in Victorian times trustees were personally liable for mortgages and rents. To be a trustee was an honour, but it could also be a terrible burden.

With a still functioning church, the trustees knew that the ground rent and mortgage interest would be paid before any other expenses (including that of the minister). That is what the Bowdon Baptist trust deeds required. Once the Hale Road church had been dissolved, the trustees found themselves with an empty building, a high ground rent and a mortgage to Star Life with interest continuing to accrue.

As we have seen, the trustees were probably not affluent enough to be able to carry this heavy financial burden for long. Although Victorian chapel debt was a serious problem, most churches 'traded' their way through any crisis. Altrincham was unusual and of course its crisis was exacerbated when Mowbray left with the majority of the congregation.

The obvious solution was for Mowbray's church to buy the building. Simmons and Southwell had to swallow their pride and negotiate with Mowbray, but would Mowbray want the building he had left and which he had seen as a millstone around the neck of the church?

---

[1] This is still a problem for many independent churches. The law concerning many Baptist and similar churches was clarified in 1916 in the House of Lords. These churches are still mostly what are called 'Unincorporated Associations'. The church cannot sue or be sued in its own name, nor in theory can it enter into contracts. It can only own property through trustees. It is the deacons (and possibly ministers) who in legal theory enter into contracts which do not deal with property and thus they take on the liability on behalf of the church, subject of course to the entitlement to be indemnified from church funds. The solution these days is to form an independent church into a company limited by guarantee or possibly a Charitable Incorporated Organisation.

The trustees offered Mowbray a right of first refusal. Mowbray brought the offer to the Church Meeting. £775 was the asking price, although this appears to have gone up to £800 by the time the deal was done. The church minutes record: 'And after he had given his reasons why the church should accept this offer and a free expression of opinion had been given upon the subject by the Assembly it was unanimously agreed to accept the offer providing that the Pastor could get satisfactory assurances of help in order to work the place, and also providing that the Congregation (the matter having been laid before them) would be willing to support the church in this undertaking.'

Let us pause here and consider the financial implications. The total building cost ended up at just over £2,850. The Hale Road Church had in fact paid off more of the mortgage than might be thought. There was only about £400 of debt still owing with the high ground rent to pay, but it was the loss of members that had really hit them.

The trustees said they would pay off the debt and then sell the chapel for only £800. The reality was that all the other denominations in Altrincham had built their own buildings and no one needed the Baptist church building. For a builder to tear it down and build between three and five new houses would not be good value. Let us also not forget that the trustees probably still preferred to sell to a church, even a renegade one, than to see the building torn down.

Mowbray knew a bargain when he saw one. A chapel built at a cost of £2,850 on offer at £800 was difficult to refuse.

It would still be a struggle though. For the year ended 31 March 1892, Altrincham Baptist Church had *grown* its income to just £180-14s-1½d.[2] It had a minister and an assistant minister. Mowbray should have been paid about £120 per annum, but took no salary. We do not know the precise pay of Nankivell, but ministerial expenses for the whole year in 1891 were £72-10s-0d.[3] The chapel keeper was paid £8-14s-8d[4] a year. The church gave about £22 to missionary work.

The total expenditure for the year was £164-11s-7½d.[5] This meant they still had no hope of paying Mowbray, and would struggle to pay even Nankivell. They had at the end of the year a bank balance of £13-16s-6d[6] and cash of £2-6s-0d.[7]

It took about six months to negotiate the final transaction and raise the finance. New trustees were found to buy the Hale Road chapel on behalf of Altrincham Baptist Church. They perhaps took on the responsibility with some trepidation given what had happened. This time they were all local men.

Intriguingly, three of the new trustees, Joshua Boydell of Fern Lea, Queen's Road in Hale, a merchant tailor, Sydney Brookfield of Thorn Lea on Hale Road, a hosier and later clerk and Edward Hoy of 5 Douglas Villas on Hale Road, a cashier, were members of Bowdon Downs Congregational, perhaps showing the support Bowdon Downs was now prepared to give to Altrincham Baptist Church through individuals.

---

[2] £180.70
[3] £72.50.
[4] £8.77.
[5] £164.56.
[6] £13.82.
[7] £2.30.

Hoy and Boydell were in fact involved in the British School Mission on Oxford Road.

The modern Altrincham Baptist Church is the successor to Mowbray's breakaway church. The centenary of the church was celebrated in 1972, but this was not the centenary of Altrincham Baptist Church but rather the centenary of the original Bowdon Baptist Church. 1987 was the true centenary of Altrincham Baptist Church. However, as we will see, the Victorian Baptist Church wanted to blur these issues and to some extent bury its past split, and so in 1987 the modern church was mostly unaware of its origins.

Chapel debt also troubled the nearby Primitive Methodists on Oxford Road. Frederick Kean was originally from Middleton and one of a family of silk weavers. He spoke with a broad Lancashire accent. The Primitive Methodist chapel was built for the comparatively cheap cost of £1,250 (but still with a cost overrun of £250). By the time of opening, they were £900 short. The mortgagee gave an interest-free loan but when he died, the estate called the loan in and the Primitive Methodists found they were about to be repossessed. Kean roused the trustees into action by pointing out that they had to pay the difference between the sale price and the loan plus interest. He went to see the solicitors representing the estate of the deceased mortgagee and told them it was better to wait to get paid than to get a paltry sum for the immediate sale of the chapel. He then disappeared with the keys and refused to hand them over to the solicitors. Thus the Primitive Methodist chapel too was saved.

Although Bowdon Baptist Church was closed, its name lives on. Bowdon Baptist Church of Georgia, USA, has sent its greetings for this book. In 2008 it renovated its buildings to add a drive-through entrance. The chapel itself still has its traditional pews. Bowdon, Georgia, has a population of about 2,000 and is between Atlanta and Birmingham. Sadly Bowdon in North Dakota (current population 139) does not have a Baptist church. As the North Dakota Bowdon was founded by Richard Sykes from Bowdon in England, residents of Bowdon in England may not be surprised to know that Bowdon in North Dakota has streets called Green Walk Street, Dunham Street and Enville Street.

The Altrincham Baptist Church Trust Deeds.

165

The article in the local newspaper on Wednesday 10 February 1892 announcing the demise of the Hale Road chapel.

'Hale Road Baptist chapel

'It has been determined to close this chapel, and to disperse the remaining members of the congregation. This decision has been arrived at in consequence of the entire inability of the members to direct the financial affairs of the church in anything approaching a satisfactory way. Exactly 5 years ago this difficulty was foreseen by the Revd Henry Mowbray, the then pastor. The position was then fully discussed by Mr Mowbray, and supported by the majority of the congregation. Mr Mowbray took a stand, that in view of the heavy mortgage of the chapel, and the comparatively meagre sources of income, a building more suitable to the limited size of the congregation should be taken, and that the unnecessarily large structure in Hale Road should be disposed of. This opinion was not unanimously shared, but it was evident that Mr Mowbray held the support of the greater part of the congregation. The difference led to Mowbray's retirement from the pastorate of the Hale Road chapel. The establishment of the Tabernacle in Railway Street followed, and under Mowbray's direction, it has become a centre of much religious and social activity. Meanwhile the Hale Road chapel was affiliated to the Union Church, Manchester, and it was hoped that under the fostering care of the Revd Dr McLaren, its fortunes might be restored. The pulpit was supplied from Manchester for some time, but the chapel remained nearly empty. The Revd H. C. Leonard, a scholarly man, and an attractive preacher, spent 2 years in a vain endeavour to increase the congregation, and to strengthen its various departments of church work. His effort was not successful and ultimately he was compelled to relinquish the charge. The scantiness of the congregation has precluded every effort to remove the heavy burden of debt on the chapel. With the present crisis it will be necessary either to sell or let the building'.

Note how press comment had now shifted back in favour of Mowbray.

There was another trustee for the church. This was Mowbray himself. He thus took on personal financial responsibility for the new mortgage. He was without doubt a man fully committed to the church.

THE NEW START

It was a strange coincidence, but at almost exactly the same day as the Hale Road chapel closed, Spurgeon died. At the Tabernacle, a memorial service was held and Nankivell preached, stating that in his opinion Spurgeon was one of the greatest preachers the latter half of the nineteenth century had produced. Bowdon Downs Congregational and other local churches held similar services, for Spurgeon's reputation went far beyond that of his own denomination.

Now, almost symbolically after the death of Spurgeon, it was time for a new start in Altrincham. New paint and varnish were applied to the Hale Road chapel, and on the Sunday evening of 21 May 1892, even before the deeds had been signed, the members of Altrincham Baptist Church marched through the streets to take the chapel back into their possession. Mowbray and Nankivell then led what was billed as a 'solemn congregational service'.

The advertisement in the newspaper listed the luminaries who would attend the public meeting that followed. One might think that this would be organised by McLaren, but in fact it was he who was invited, and then not by Mowbray. It was Nankivell who wrote to him on behalf of Mowbray. This was Mowbray's hour and McLaren had no say in it. McLaren had the good grace to send his apologies and to wish the church 'a prosperous future'. He also said he would be 'glad to render them any service in my power'. Letters of support were received from the Presbyterians at Delamer Road, Williams of Accrington Baptist, the Methodists and Primitive Methodists and many more. The Primitive Methodist Superintendent hoped that 'the glory of the latter be even greater than the glory of the former'.

There had clearly been a 'deal' not to mention the past; indeed, the whole meeting was conspicuously designed *not* to mention the fact that Mowbray had now returned in triumph. Mowbray did say he felt that there

Spurgeon's solemn memorial service at the Metropolitan Tabernacle. Similar services were held throughout the country, including Altrincham.

was the guiding hand of providence in all that had happened. The Tabernacle on Railway Street had been overcrowded, particularly on Sunday evenings. He had felt they needed to move, and then the trustees of the Hale Road chapel, whom he thanked, had given him first refusal.

He also mentioned that Williams had asked to meet with him some months before, no doubt because he knew the Hale Road chapel might have to close, and had urged him to make a new start in every way. He and Nankivell had taken this on board and had set up new trust deeds. As Williams had written a book including sample trust deeds, Mowbray probably found this useful, but he was not prepared to sacrifice one principle: membership would only be for those baptised as believers, although communion would be open to all.

The meeting with Williams was also well timed, because Mowbray in his speech alluded to the fact that he had seriously considered buying back the Hale Road chapel and setting it up as an independent church. Although practising Baptist principles, it would have been outside the Baptist Union, just like Spurgeon's Metropolitan Tabernacle and the breakaway Altrincham Baptist Church at the Tabernacle. It might not have been called a Baptist church at all. It was perhaps this that persuaded the Baptist authorities they had to back Mowbray, despite all that had gone on. They could not afford to have a flagship church become bankrupt, its chapel sold to its former minister who had left the Baptist Union and then have the new church refuse to join the Union.

Mowbray renamed the chapel. Even though this was a meeting to bring the two churches back together, the new church was to be 'The Altrincham Tabernacle' after 'our little Tabernacle in Railway Street'. Apart from in the mane, Mowbray was, however, magnanimous and gracious in victory.

'It is with very much confidence of heart and hopefulness of spirit that we enter upon this work. I might not hit the sense of the meeting, but I have felt it better not to say anything about our past work at the Tabernacle, and nothing about the work that has been carried on there before it was closed. I desire to bear in mind the words of the Apostle, "Forgetting those things which are behind and reaching forth unto those things which are before". I am speaking for my friends when I say that, with one heart and mind, we desire to enter this place humbly and thankfully and confidently, desiring that it might be a spiritual home for all who come, and a hive of spiritual industry for all who are connected with it.'

MacKennal now spoke. He had also brought with him the Bowdon Downs choir. 'The reason why so many are here this evening is to congratulate you that you are one Baptist church again, and not two, and that you have done so wise and so Christian a thing as to seek reconciliation and to bind yourselves together once more in the service of God.' He then went on to give perhaps what was intended as a form of apology, referring to the 'partial judgment' and 'partial knowledge' they had previously possessed about Mowbray. He then alluded to the possibility that Mowbray might have taken the church out of the Baptist Union. 'I congratulate you upon calling your new place a Baptist Chapel and putting it under a Baptist trust... Much is expected of you, and the fact that you have invited other congregations to take part in this meeting is evidence of your intention to engage in wide Christian effort. I charge you to see to it that your church is a house of peacefulness and purity, as well as of fervour and evangelistic actualities.'

Professor Marshall from the Lancashire and Cheshire Association said, 'It is a great relief to many of us to know that the blot and reproach of a closed chapel has been removed. I know that I am treading on delicate ground, but I must say that if the presence of the Holy Spirit is to be here, there must not only be a forgetting of the past, but an entire forgiveness of those from whom you have differed.' This was greeted with applause. Roberts from Union Chapel brought his greetings and so did others, and the meeting closed.

The fact that there had been a church split was in fact not entirely unusual. Paradoxically, J. Lee concludes that the various splits in the north-west led to an increase in overall Baptist numbers.[1] What was unusual was a church split in a prominent town in the north-west where the church was very much a key one for McLaren and the Association, and where the issue was mostly financial. This time, as we shall see, McLaren was determined to see that the church did not fail, but the hour belonged to Mowbray.

 Henry Mowbray's signature

> Extract from newspaper article of Saturday 21 May 1892.
>
> > 'Opening of the new Baptist Tabernacle
> >
> > 'The event is one of singular interest, as it marks the progress made during the past 5 years by the congregation at the Tabernacle in Railway Street, under the direction of Revd Mowbray. The congregation has quite outgrown the limits of its home, and seeks a wider field for its activity and usefulness...The old chapel will, on Sunday next, be reopened as the Baptist Tabernacle, and the congregation from the Railway Street Tabernacle will enter into possession of a building which offers distinctly superior advantages to those enjoyed hitherto. The little Tabernacle, built by Revd Mowbray, has been successful in the highest degree, and the membership fully justifies the new departure. The services on Sunday evening are usually crowded, and the church life is particularly vigorous.'

We now turn back to a puzzle we have already alluded to. Just where did Mowbray get the money from to build the Iron Tabernacle? In the next chapter you will find a solution that may surprise you.

---

[1] Lee, J.: 'The growth of the Baptist Denomination in Mid-Victorian Lancashire and Cheshire', op. cit.

THE MYSTERY OF THE MONEY

In this chapter, we are going to look at some evidence in an attempt to solve two puzzles. Both relate to Mowbray and Frank Crossley.

Crossley could easily have funded the building of the Hale Road chapel. We know that he was a donor when the church was running into serious financial difficulty before Mowbray left. Although the donation was, for the church, a substantial one of about £100, for Crossley this was mere pocket money. Why did he not pay more?

Here we need to go back to Mowbray's own account of events in his letter to the local newspaper quoted earlier. 'I think there is a general feeling in the neighbourhood that to build a chapel of such a size, and at such a cost, was, to say the least, a great mistake, when the funds in hand were very small, the congregation limited in number and composed chiefly of people of scanty means. Certainly this overwhelming debt has been a constant source of anxiety and unpleasantness ever since the place was opened, and above all a great hindrance to the effective carrying on of a spiritual work.'

Mowbray's background was one of mission chapels. It is clear that MacKennal was concerned that the Independent Congregationalists had gone beyond their means, and it is likely that people thought the same of the poor Baptists. We have already noted that Llewellyn thought this was the case. Perhaps Crossley did too. Did Mowbray actually put Crossley off donating more to Bowdon Baptist before the split? We know that at one Church Meeting he said he did not want to further trouble the people of Bowdon. Crossley lived in Bowdon. Did Mowbray ask Crossley not to give too much because he thought the church had to stand on its own two feet? Did he think that moving out of the Hale Road chapel was best for the spiritual heart of the church, so that funding by Crossley would simply make matters worse?

There may also be a reason why Crossley did not substantially fund the church under Llewellyn and that was because it was a Calvinist Baptist Church, when at the time his own theology was moving away from Calvinism.[1]

We also know that Mowbray referred to 'friends from Bowdon' supplementing his salary when Bowdon Baptist could not afford to pay him the full amount. Could this have been Crossley, who funded Mowbray to protect him from financial hardship but would not fund the church directly? Was Crossley a friend and secret supporter of Mowbray? Did Mowbray consult with Crossley before the fatal Church Meeting which led to the split and ensure he had Crossley's secret support in advance?

Here is an even more intriguing thought: did Crossley in fact fund Mowbray in the building of the Tabernacle? If he did, the funding had to be secret because Crossley was a friend of McLaren and McLaren affiliated Hale Road to his own Union Chapel. Crossley could hardly be seen to be publicly undermining McLaren.

At this stage you might well say there is nothing at all to prove any of this. There is no direct evidence, but there is circumstantial evidence. It is for you now to decide.

---

[1] We will examine the issue of Calvinism later.

If Crossley did fund Mowbray in secret at the Tabernacle, we might expect to find four things.

First, we would find a gift or funding from Crossley that did not pass through the church accounts.

Second, Crossley would no doubt want to visit the new Tabernacle soon after it opened to see what he had paid for and what the new church was like. The visit would have to be innocuous and for a purpose that would not attract the attention of McLaren or MacKennal.

Third, we would have to find a motive for the donation.

Finally, we would have to show that Crossley supported Mowbray's actions in walking out of Hale Road and setting up the new church.

Let us look at the money first. Crossley could not donate directly to the Railway Street Tabernacle, as this would have shown in the church accounts and word would soon have reached McLaren. Any funding would need to be more discreet and outside the church books. Let us therefore go back to the Church Meeting where Mowbray said he would fund the building of the Tabernacle. Mowbray told the church that he and his wife would make the financial arrangements. The cost of the building was £300. Mowbray was not a man of substantial means. If he had been, he would not have needed to work in Manchester to support his family during the Tabernacle years. How could he raise the money when he lived in rented accommodation and had no security to offer a lender? The church had no money to pay for the Tabernacle. If Mowbray did not have the money to build the Tabernacle, from whom did it come?

No capital payment or loan appears in the books of the church, and yet when Mowbray finally left Altrincham, one thing McLaren had to resolve was the repayment of an unspecified loan involving Mowbray. The source of the loan is never mentioned. Was this an interest-free loan for the Tabernacle made by Crossley via Mowbray and kept outside the church books?

The second matter to look out for is a visit by Crossley to the Tabernacle. Immediately after the Tabernacle opened, a small article appeared in the local newspaper about a talk given by a Baptist missionary, Miss Cassie Silvey, who was going to the Congo. The meeting was presided over by none other than Frank Crossley.[2]

The third to look for is a motive for Crossley to donate or lend the money. Why would Crossley want to do this? The answer first lies in the fact that the style of Mowbray's gospel mission in the centre of Altrincham would have appealed more to Crossley than a chapel on Hale Road. Crossley's own Star Hall in Ancoats was essentially a gospel and social mission centre. We have to remember that Crossley was also a covert Baptist. Although never baptised as a believer, he deliberately did not have his children baptised as infants; instead, two of his children made their own decisions at age ten and eleven respectively and were baptised in the drawing room of Fairlie by MacKennal.

---

[2] The Altrincham Division Chronicle.

There is, however, more of a motive than that, and one that has not been written about before: Crossley and Mowbray were close friends.

How do we know this? The reconciliation meeting described in the last chapter was chaired by Crossley. Let us look at Crossley's own words in his speech. 'I have had the greatest pleasure in taking part in this meeting. I do not know many of the details that have preceded the change that has led to this gathering, but I have long enjoyed the friendship and warm companionship of your pastor, Mr Mowbray.'

The fourth thing we might expect to find is clear approval by Crossley of Mowbray's actions in founding the Tabernacle. We find this in Crossley's speech. In it he continued, 'I personally rejoice that under present circumstances he [Mowbray] has returned to this place, and that there are so many to give him a cordial welcome, which everyone feels that he deserves (more applause). My heart went out very warmly to Mr Mowbray, and I cordially wish the church with which he is associated the highest possible success. Mr Mowbray has shown by his career in Altrincham that he was prepared to endure hardness as a good soldier of Jesus. He has gone through a great deal, and it was a good thing for him, and those who were acting for him, that it was so. In all the changes of recent years there has been conspicuously displayed in Mr Mowbray, and those immediately round him, that reality which was one of the true qualities for a Christian church. What a thing it is to be real! Even politicians can call out and rejoice when a little bit of reality is displayed. The highest reality is to be found in a Christian church, and if it is not there, it is not a Christian church.'

You will have to decide whether Crossley was a secret supporter of the breakaway church and funded the building of the Tabernacle, but there is certainly substantial circumstantial evidence.

For the reunited church there was however, a problem. Some key players had not returned. Could Mowbray, the man who had walked out, ever really bring about reconciliation?

McLaren had been sidelined by Mowbray. It was time for him to come back into the frame.

MCLAREN'S PLAN

After the reconciliation service chaired by Crossley, an emotional thanksgiving service was held at the Tabernacle and then it closed.

Mowbray now set the tone of how he wanted the combined church to continue. A major mission was held in November 1892, led by a Mr Cairns, an evangelist from Chicago. He sang as well as preached, and proved a great draw. The local newspaper noted that he often enforced his remarks 'with dramatic energy' and gave 'no opportunity for dullness'.

Immediately after the mission, Nankivell left the reunited church.[1] Mowbray must have suspected Nankivell might want to move on, because at the reconciliation service he made a plea for Nankivell to stay, but said that if he decided to leave, they should at least make sure they parted on good terms.

Nankivell made an emotional farewell speech regretting his departure, but he felt called to move on. His last sermon was on the ascension of Jesus and his return. In a side-swipe at other churches in the area, and possibly the now defunct Bowdon Baptist Church, he asked what good it was to have concerts; they needed gospel missions.

Mowbray now needed someone else to work with him, and so it was on 28 December 1892 that he announced to the Church Meeting that one F. Cowell Lloyd was being invited to speak with a view to ministry at the church. The church agreed to hear him. How did this come about? Was he Mowbray's choice?

The church appears to have been in ignorance as to what was actually going on behind the scenes. McLaren and the Association knew that Mowbray's days in Altrincham had to be numbered. He had led a church split and appeared to have been the victor. Some former members would not return until he left. For there to be a true reconciliation, there had to be a new man with no history behind him. Equally, they could not just remove Mowbray. The church members who had supported him at the Tabernacle would not tolerate that. Mowbray had to leave after a decent interval on an ostensibly voluntary basis, and they had to have someone in line to replace him who would be well received by everyone. That person had to be of high calibre, because McLaren was not going to tolerate the embarrassment of another church collapse in Altrincham.

In fact, this all probably fitted in with Mowbray's own plans. You may recall that his letter to the local newspaper immediately after he founded Altrincham Baptist Church suggested he only wanted to stay as minister until a replacement could be found.

It was probably McLaren himself who identified Lloyd as a suitable candidate. It is likely that he consulted with Joseph Angus, the head of McLaren's old college, Regent's Park, to see who his star pupils were. This was not to be a man from Spurgeon's College.

At first, Lloyd was sent to Accrington to work until the way was clear at Altrincham. At Accrington, Williams could keep an eye on him.

---

[1] Attempts to find out what happened to him have failed. All we know is that he left to become an evangelist elsewhere, but probably not with the Baptists.

McLaren knew matters had to be handled carefully, and no doubt he met with Mowbray and explained his thinking. His main bargaining counter was financial. McLaren told Mowbray that the grant from the Association would be withdrawn if Lloyd was not appointed as joint minister with Mowbray. The church was never told this, although the deacons probably knew. It is also possible Lloyd himself never fully knew of the arrangements.

It was thus on 8 December 1892 that the church agreed to hear Lloyd preach and to put him up for a week so that he could meet as many people as possible. Lloyd spoke well and created a good impression. Mowbray and Lloyd appeared to get on well.

The church meanwhile was growing rapidly again. At the annual tea party in January 1893,[2] Mowbray told the press that they had twenty one new members.

Events moved quickly, and on 1 February 1893 the church agreed to 'give a unanimous and cordial invitation to Mr. F. Cowell Lloyd late of Regent's Park College London to be co-Pastor at a salary of £100 per annum' with this arrangement to be subject to 'the sanction of the Committee of the Lancashire and Cheshire Association of Baptist Churches'.

McLaren kept his part of the bargain, and soon after a grant payment arrived from the Association for £15. He also arranged for £10 to be sent from his own church as a gesture of goodwill.

Who was this young Cowell Lloyd on whom so much rested? To understand him better, we now take our story completely outside the British Isles.

---

[2] Note this is linked to the foundation of Bowdon Baptist Church and not Altrincham Baptist. There appears to have been an understandable policy to blur the distinctions and pretend that there had been a genuine re-merger of the two Baptist churches and to bury the split.

SLAVERY IN JAMAICA

It is the Anglican William Wilberforce who is rightly remembered and celebrated for the abolition of the slave trade. However, he did not abolish *slavery* in the British colonies, only the slave trade. Slavery continued unchanged. The heroes of the fight to abolish slavery itself and to resist the powerful and vested interests that supported it were the Baptist missionaries. It is time to tell their story and celebrate them too. In doing so we will find surprising links with Altrincham.

It is commonly thought that Wilberforce was the sole campaigner for the abolition of the slave trade. In fact, he led a coalition as part of a wider Christian campaign involving people such as Henry Brougham. Others of an enlightened nature joined the campaign. Both Josiah Wedgwood and his grandson, Charles Darwin, opposed the slave trade.

The campaign to abolish the slave trade succeeded in 1807, but this left the system of slavery itself completely intact.

The British now took on the role of global policeman against the slave trade. The Royal Navy earned head money by freeing slaves from ships. The slavers themselves were insured if they lost slaves at sea, but not on board. Thus began the practice of the slave ship seeing the navy vessel approaching and throwing all the slaves overboard. Turner's 1840 picture, *Slavers throwing Overboard The Dead and Dying – Typhoon Coming In,* shows such a scene, with the helpless slaves writhing in the water.

British fortunes were built on slavery, but this fact was not really advertised in Britain, where the slave-owning families usually preferred to keep a low profile. The Lascelles family, future Earls of Harewood, built Penrhyn Castle on their profits from slavery, and yet there is little there to indicate the source of their wealth. The merchants of Bristol and Liverpool too built much of their prosperity on slavery, and yet it was easy to turn a blind eye to where all this money came from. Only a few, such as the Liverpool merchant Richard Watt, who built Speke Hall and who incorporated slave heads into his coat of arms, gave tacit acknowledgment as to the source of their wealth. The average Briton simply did not see the slaves and their abuse, and could quietly ignore the issue while drinking slave coffee with slave sugar.

This ambivalence is well typified by the twenty-three-year-old Tory MP for Newark, who voted against the Bill to abolish the slave trade in 1807. The wealth of his family was built on his father's estates in Demerera. Sixty years later, he confessed his regret. His name was William Ewart Gladstone.

Without the wealth from slavery behind him, this reforming Liberal would probably never have become Prime Minister. He knew this, and it haunted him throughout his life.

Demerera is in Jamaica, and it is to Jamaica that we now turn.

Jamaica has a bloody early history. The Spanish took the island and killed off the local Arawak Indians. In 1655 Cromwell's navy took it for Britain. It was the largest island in the British West Indies.

Slave labour was brought in from West Africa to harvest its sugar, coffee, cocoa, pimento and ginger. Sugar from Demerera was immensely popular in Britain.

William Knibb was born at Market Kettering in 1803. He worked as a printer for the son of Andrew Fuller, a well-known Baptist and friend of William Carey, the great Baptist missionary. The business relocated to Bristol and Knibb joined Broadmead church and was baptised there. Knibb's elder brother died in Jamaica, so in 1824 Knibb went to follow in his footsteps, taking his new wife Mary with him. He first taught in Kingston and then moved to Falmouth.

On his arrival in Jamaica, Knibb did not openly oppose slavery, but instead ministered to the slaves. He worked closely with his colleague Thomas Burchell. Burchell wrote home of their reception from the plantation owners: 'No Englishman, except a missionary, would be treated with so much contempt.'

The Baptist and other Nonconformist missionaries were opposed by the Revd George Bridges, a Church of England minister who supported slavery and despised both Roman Catholics and Nonconformists. He wrote, 'The want of employment in the fields or manufactures of England sent crowds of ignorant and itinerant preachers to these shores, where they found, or expected to find, a rich harvest, or a glorious martyrdom'. The Church of England itself owned slave plantations in the West Indies.

The plantation owners would not allow any form of religious instruction for their slaves and banned them from attending Sunday evening meetings. Knibb now began to speak out.

When word reached Jamaica that there was a possibility the British Parliament might free the slaves, the plantation owners threatened to kill them first. The slaves revolted when they incorrectly thought Parliament had already freed them, and the uprising was brutally crushed. Knibb was arrested for incitement and his chapel was burnt down. Burchell was forced to flee the island when he was threatened with lynching. The mobs were often led by local magistrates.

Knibb now left Jamaica for Britain and began a campaign to abolish slavery. First, he had to convince the Baptist Missionary Society, which had always remained neutral on political issues. He received enthusiastic support. He then went on to speak at 154 meetings, often debating with supporters of slavery. He asked how 20,000 Baptist slaves could be denied a place of worship. He pledged that his African brothers and sisters would one day 'both be allowed to bow their knees to that God who has made one blood of all nations'. He also appeared before two Parliamentary Select Committees. The result of his campaign, however, was not a foregone conclusion.

Parliament finally abolished slavery in 1832 and the legislation became law on 1 August 1834. The plantation owners were paid the colossal sum of £20 million in compensation.

However, slavery was not yet over, for Parliament allowed a further four years during which a transitional apprenticeship system operated. Finally, on 31 July 1838, the slaves in Knibb's church met, and at midnight Knibb announced that 'the monster is dead; the Negro is free'. The whole building is reported to have shaken with joy. Knibb took his twelve-month-old son into the pulpit to see the celebrations.

The sheer scale of slavery in Jamaica is demonstrated by the fact that an astonishing 800,000 slaves were set free. Freedom did not bring economic freedom though. The planters paid only sixpence a day. Knibb sided with the former slaves and negotiated a doubling in pay. He also organised the purchase of land in order to set up economically free communities. Eventually over 200 free communities were established.

Between 1825 and 1840, Knibb and the other Baptist missionaries in Jamaica between them planted thirty-five chapels, sixteen schools and twenty-four mission houses.

Knibb died of yellow fever in 1847, predeceased sadly by his son. His wife Mary stayed on in Jamaica until her death in 1867.

By now, you may be wondering what this all has to do with Altrincham. The answer lies in the influence of Jamaica and the abolition of slavery on Lloyd.

One of the missionaries who worked tirelessly with Knibb to free the slaves in the face of constant persecution was Lloyd's maternal grandfather. His name was W. W. Cantlow. Cantlow worked at Crooked Spring where he was responsible for the building of a new church. He lived in Jamaica between 1830 and 1837. Eventually he had to return to England due to ill health. His grandfather's influence in the fight against slavery and his own father's time as a missionary there were to influence Lloyd throughout his life.

Memorial in Falmouth, Jamaica.
To the Memory of William Knibb Who departed this life on the 15th November, 1845, in the 43rd year of his age. This monument was erected by the emancipated slaves to whose enfranchisement and elevation his indefatigable exertions so largely contributed; by his fellow-labourers, who admired and loved him, and deeply deplore his early removal; and by friends of various creeds and parties, as an expression of their esteem for one whose praise as a man, a philanthropist, and a Christian minister, is in all the churches, and who, being dead, yet speaketh.

The coat of arms of Kettering to this day shows two circles which represent the founding of the Baptist Missionary Society in 1792 in Lever Street, and a slave girl. These are to commemorate the role of William Knibb in freeing the slaves. As well as coming from Kettering, Knibb founded a town in Jamaica called Kettering. In a House of Commons debate on slavery in 2005 in preparation for the 2007 celebrations about the abolition of the slave trade, the MP for Hull made a speech about William Wilberforce and was interrupted by the MP for Kettering who wanted to ensure that William Knibb was not forgotten. This chapter echoes those sentiments.

There is record of early anti-slavery activity in the Altrincham area. Joseph Barker and Joseph Moore of Hale Barns spoke eloquently against the slave trade prior to its abolition. Henry 'Box' Brown and Samuel Alexander 'Boxer' Smith toured England in about 1860, speaking against slavery. Smith had bought his freedom and had smuggled Brown out of slavery in a box, hence his name. They stayed with Joseph Moore, who was the village shopkeeper at Hale Barns. Unfortunately Brown turned to alcohol but Smith stayed in Hale Barns for a while, acting as an assistant in Moore's shop. When he returned to America, he gave his gold watch and chain to Moore.

The United States abolished slavery in 1865 after the Civil War, much later than Britain. In 1860 there were about 4 million slaves in the United States, all in the southern Confederate states of course. Manchester played a part in the abolition of slavery there. The Civil War caused a cotton shortage in Manchester. Suffering cotton operatives met at the Free Trade Hall and pledged support for Lincoln and the end of slavery at great financial cost to themselves. The declaration had a significant impact in America and Lincoln wrote in thanks. The statue of Lincoln in Lincoln Square in Manchester presented by the United States commemorates the involvement.

There is a connection between the Altrincham Baptists and the abolition of the slave trade itself. You may have noticed that Jessie Mowbray's maiden name was Brougham. Her great-uncle was in fact Henry Brougham, who worked in Parliament with Wilberforce in the campaign to abolish the slave trade.

In 1886 Mowbray organised a meeting at Bowdon Baptist Church. The speaker was Revd Thomas L. Johnson, a freed American slave. Mowbray had presided at a meeting in Liverpool three years earlier which had commissioned Johnson on behalf of the Baptist Missionary Society to be a missionary in Africa. However, his health had not been strong enough and he had returned eventually to the United States, where he raised support for missionary work in Africa. Mowbray at the 1886 meeting explained his family connection with the fight to abolish the slave trade.

William Knibb. Although Wilberforce was principally responsible for the abolition of the slave trade, it was Knibb and the Baptist missionaries in Jamaica who were largely responsible for the abolition of slavery in the British colonies.

A slave being whipped. Knibb was first spurred into campaigning against slavery when, at a prayer meeting, Sam Swiney, one of his deacons, was arrested for preaching. In fact he had been praying loudly and not preaching. Swiney was a slave and it was illegal for him to preach. He received 20 lashes and Knibb stood with him, then accompanied Swiney in the chain gang until they were forced apart. Swiney was kept in the gang for two weeks. Knibb published an account in a local newspaper and was threatened with libel. However, the newspaper account was eventually handed to the Secretary of State in England, who dismissed the two magistrates responsible for the sentence.

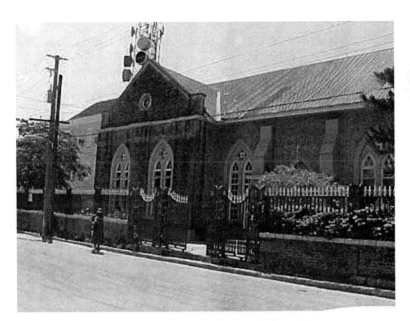

Burchell Baptist Church in Jamaica, named after one of the early Baptist missionaries. Many Jamaicans are still named after those early missionaries. At the time of writing, the Jamaican High Commissioner is Mr Burchell Whiteman.

Mowbray and subsequent ministers were enthusiastic supporters of the Baptist Missionary Society, and encouraged the Altrincham Baptists to raise funds for it at missionary meetings. In 1882, for example, they had a special focus on India.

The first person to go abroad from the Altrincham Baptists as a missionary went to China sometime before 1884. We know this because Edward Leech, in his farewell to the Sunday school before leaving the area, encouraged the young men to emulate their former colleague. Sadly we do not know his name, but it is very likely that Ebenezer Brewer heard Leech speak, as soon afterward he became a missionary to China. China continued to be a missionary focus and in 1903 Revd Byland, a Chinese missionary, gave a talk on Chinese missionary work.[1]

This photograph shows Ebenezer Brewer in Chinese costume.

Altrincham Baptist Church members are shown in this photograph helping to renovate Narambhai Primary School in Jinja, Uganda, in 2007. Narambhai has a link with The Firs Primary School in Sale, one of six schools linked with Jinja schools through the Trafford Jinja Association.

World mission activity has continued to be a feature of the Altrincham Baptists. In the years 1985-2005, 255 people from Altrincham Baptist Church went abroad on short-term mission, twelve on long-term and thirteen were trained as mission workers. Thirty-nine countries have received people from the church to engage in Christian mission work.

Mission is usually in partnership with local Christians. Church members also founded Act4Africa, a health education charity which delivers HIV and AIDS education in Africa using drama and sport. The church has a formal link with Pecel Baptist Church in Hungary where it conducts joint missions, and with the Jinja Christian Centre in Uganda. Every year it sends people to work in Uganda. Church members founded UgandAid, which equips young people with vocational skills which will help them gain employment.

Later in this book we will return to Jamaica, for there is a further surprising connection between Altrincham and Jamaica.

---

[1] Byland was strongly against British policy in China. He wrote a book opposing the British opium trade.

COWELL LLOYD

Lloyd's story is one that has been all but forgotten in Altrincham. As you read about him in this book, you will be amazed at the life of this former Altrincham resident.

Frederick Cowell Lloyd was born in 1866 at Barton Mills in Suffolk. He was the son of Baptist minister Revd William Lloyd and his wife, Sarah Jane. Lloyd had an older brother named William. In 1871 the family had a servant a carpenter living with them. As we have seen, Lloyd's grandfather was a missionary in Jamaica with Knibb, fighting to end slavery and confronting the vested interests of the plantation owners.

Lloyd's father followed in the family missionary tradition and was pastor of Annotto Bay Baptist Church in Jamaica between 1841 and 1848. He then returned to Suffolk. At the age of fourteen, Lloyd himself was baptised at Burlington Baptist Church, Ipswich. Sadly, Lloyd's father died while Lloyd was still comparatively young.

Lloyd's first career was as a teacher and he went to work at a boarding school in Alton, Hampshire. However, he soon decided to enter the ministry and applied to Regent's Park College and received a scholarship paid for by the Ward Trust. The college was originally in Stepney, but by the time Lloyd arrived, it had relocated to Regent's Park and was within walking distance of University College. It was affiliated to London University. The Principal was the famous Revd Joseph Angus. The cost of being a student at the time was between sixty and eighty guineas a year, so training was not cheap.[1]

Lloyd entered the college in 1887 with only two other freshmen that year, who were J. J. Henman and J. W. Kettle. The reason for the drop in numbers was due to a recent raising of standards for entry. Regent's Park intended to provide a longer and more academic course than Spurgeon's own college. The three students became firm friends. Lloyd also became friends with C.E. Wilson, who later became a well-known missionary in India and went on to be Foreign Secretary of the Baptist Missionary Society for over fifty years.

To enter the college, students at the time had to have a reference recommending them 'as having a good moral character and possessed of real piety'. They also had to answer twelve quite searching and personal written questions, all designed to test their faith.

In 1888 Lloyd was awarded first class in the junior class.

In 1889 a Mr Austin came back to the college. He had finished his course at Calabar in Jamaica but returned to Regent's Park due to health problems. He and Cowell Lloyd must have spoken about Calabar and Jamaica. As we shall see, Calabar was to feature later in Lloyd's life.

That year, Lloyd again obtained first class honours and was the highest-achieving student in his year. He was one of four pupils to share the Andrews Prize of £10.

---

[1] Roughly £63-£84.

McLaren was a former student of Regent's Park and a friend of Angus'. McLaren's Union Chapel donated £18-14s-9d[2] each year to college funds. This was the third highest donation to general funds the College received at the time.

In 1890 a student and near contemporary of Lloyd graduated from Regent's Park. He was J. E. Roberts. McLaren took on Roberts to become his assistant at Union Chapel. When McLaren was looking out for a star student to send to Altrincham, it must have either been Angus or Roberts who alerted him to Lloyd, for McLaren wanted a person of high calibre to be minister in Altrincham.

Lloyd got a first again that year, and then in his final year he won the first prize in the first division and £10 for the Hebrew prize. He graduated equal first in his year, obtaining first class honours in philosophy, Greek and Hebrew. Baptists were prohibited by law from becoming a Bachelor of Divinity, so the 'ATS Diploma' Lloyd obtained was the nearest equivalent he could get. Throughout his life Lloyd proudly displayed these letters after his name.[3] The College report says of him: 'His heart is set on the Ministry, and there is every reason to think he will become an efficient preacher of the Gospel'.

One might think that a graduate from Regent's Park would automatically become a Baptist minister, but that was not the case. Many graduates became missionaries, and Lloyd could easily have gone to Jamaica. This was the great period of missionary activity amongst the Baptists. In 1889-90 for example, of the eight who graduated from Regent's Park, one became a missionary with the Baptist Missionary Society in Italy, one went to a mission station in India, one according to the report 'will largely live among the people, and will be content with such an allowance as will supply the necessities of life',[4] two went to the Congo and only three were destined to be ministers of United Kingdom churches. Later in his life, Lloyd was to write heartfelt articles about atrocities in the Congo; perhaps his former colleagues who went to the Congo gave him particular insights.

Lloyd went from Regent's Park to Accrington while he waited for McLaren to arrange matters at Altrincham. He attended Cannon Street Baptist Church. Relying on his previous teaching experience, he was a private tutor to two small boys. He also became friends at Cannon Street with the builder George MacAlpine.

Another person who became a friend at Cannon Street was the minister, the Revd Charles Williams, who was later to become President of the Baptist Union. Williams was also a friend of McLaren's and we have already come across his involvement with Altrincham. You may recall it was Williams who was supposed to speak at the evening service when they laid the foundation stones at Hale Road, but Houghton had to stand in for him. He was present at the reconciliation service.

Whilst at Accrington Lloyd met and fell in love with Alice Green and married her before they moved to Altrincham.

So the new joint minister of the Altrincham Baptists was a highly educated and learned man with a strong interest in world affairs and mission.

---

[2] £18.73.
[3] For Latin scholars, this stands for 'Academicus Theologicus Senatus Diploma'.
[4] It is not clear where he was going, but it was clearly abroad. Today we would call that a 'faith mission'.

Lloyd was twenty-seven when he arrived at Altrincham and Mowbray forty-five. His induction as joint minister with Mowbray was on Saturday 25 March 1893. There was a 'soirée' in the schoolroom to introduce him to everyone, and then the service was held in the chapel upstairs. The great and the good were there. On the platform were McLaren, Roberts (McLaren's assistant), Wilson Cowie of Trinity Presbyterian, James Lewis for the Methodists, Carey Bonner of Sale Baptist, Charles Williams, the Vice President of the Baptist Union, T. M. Morris, who was also from Lloyd's home church in Ipswich, Streuli of the large Moss Side Baptist Church and William Milne of Bowdon Downs, who had long supported the Baptists.

The influential John Thompson was in the chair and he spoke glowingly of Mowbray. Mowbray then in turn read out a testimonial from Lloyd's tutor at Regent's Park. It is worth recording Lloyd's own words in response: 'The basis of my work will be the word of God and the central theme of my ministry will be the loving Christ. The joy and crown of my ministry will be the souls I trust God will give me.'

Williams then spoke of the eighteen months Lloyd had been at Accrington, and how sorry they were to lose him.

McLaren made a number of comments. Lancashire and Cheshire people were reluctant to give any praise to their ministers, but the fruits of a successful ministry could be greater in the area than anywhere else in the country. The curse of Nonconformist ministries, however, was they were often too short to achieve anything. Ministries sometimes failed because of the ministers, but failed more often because of those in the pews. A church would also fail if it was only bound together by the quality of sermons or the fact people lived in the same area. A spiritual quality had to draw them together.

That evening, Lloyd preached his first sermon. His subject was, 'The darkest night and the longest day'.

Within a few weeks of his arrival, Lloyd conducted his first baptisms on 23 July 1893. One of the first to be baptised was Charles Frederick Southwell, the son of Southwell, former deacon of Bowdon Baptist Church and founder of Altrincham Baptist Church.

Lloyd had an immediate effect on the Altrincham Baptists. He is recorded as having a very characteristic smile. He was a man of immense energy and yet liked by all. Whereas Mowbray evoked strong emotions, both for and against, everyone liked Lloyd. There is not one single hint of division or criticism throughout his life.

> Not only did he have a claim to fame as a missionary in Jamaica, but Lloyd's maternal grandfather, Revd W. W. Cantlow, had the privilege of baptising Spurgeon in the River Ken. Spurgeon, then aged sixteen, walked eight miles from Newmarket to be baptised. A few months later, Lloyd's mother was also baptised in the same place, but this time the river was frozen and they had to break the ice.

This photograph of Lloyd is taken when he graduated at the age of 25, two years before he came to Altrincham. The first thing that must have struck the Altrincham Baptists about Lloyd was his enormous beard.

As Lloyd worked his way into the hearts of the church members, what happened to Mowbray? How would McLaren deal with him?

THE SHIFT IN POWER

In the years 1905 and 1906, Charles Nickson wrote a series of articles in the *Altrincham and Bowdon Guardian*. These were later compiled into a book.[1] His comment on Mowbray's time as joint minister with Lloyd is revealing as to how the outside world saw the reunification. 'The Church was re-opened', he wrote, 'with the Reverend Henry Mowbray as honorary pastor, who brought back with him the congregation he had formed at the Iron Church in Railway Street. On 5th March 1893, the pastorate was accepted by the Reverend F. Cowell Lloyd. Mr Mowbray continued to act as honorary co-pastor.' Note the meaning behind the words. Mowbray was not paid by the church. He continued unpaid and earned his keep by working as a book keeper. It was Lloyd who was paid and could work full-time at the church. The minister was Lloyd and Mowbray his co-worker. The balance of power began to shift from the older to the younger man.

To his credit, Mowbray accepted all this; indeed this was probably part of his own plan. The two ministers appear to have worked well together. Almost immediately however, Lloyd began to chair the Church Meetings instead of Mowbray.

McLaren's aim was to remove Mowbray as soon as he could, but in a way that looked as if Mowbray had jumped rather than being pushed. Mowbray had his own slightly different agenda. He wanted to secure the financial future of the church and of Lloyd. He told McLaren he would only leave if there was a guaranteed payment of £80 a year for two years from the Association. McLaren agreed, if the church in return managed to raise a further £20 a year. £80 was a high asking price, being £65 higher than most church grants. Mowbray was in effect requiring the Association to give Lloyd a chance to turn things round by guaranteeing much of his salary for two years.

The deacons received a letter from Carey Bonner of Sale Baptist Church, who had become a sort of honest broker. There was a promise of financial support.

Mowbray replied the very next day. He was willing to go, but ever the businessman, he wanted more than a promise in a letter; he wanted a guarantee.

There were tense negotiations until the Association gave a proper guarantee which in turn was backed up by two individuals who pledged to make full payment if the Association failed to do so.

McLaren knew he needed to show personal support for the church and for Lloyd. He therefore preached at Bowdon Downs (with its larger capacity and richer congregation). Tickets were sold for the sermon and the proceeds were given to the church.

So at the January 1895 Church Meeting, Lloyd was approved as sole minister and a new era began. One immediate consequence of Mowbray leaving was that James Brewer returned from Bowdon Downs Congregational Church.

---

[1] Nickson, op. cit.

Bonner's letter read as follows:

'The Deacons of Altrincham Baptist Church[2]

'Dear Sirs

'As an outcome of our conferences respecting the financial position of your church, I have pleasure in making the following proposition on behalf of the Special Sub-Committee: -for 2 years by this July 1894, we will undertake that Mr. Lloyd shall receive a stipend of £80 a year, apart from anything the church raises, on the following conditions: -

1. That as we are conveying to you our undertaking in the form of a letter, Mr. Mowbray shall in his part, forward a letter to me, undertaking to carry out his promise of retiring at the end of 1894, and leaving Mr. Lloyd as sole Pastor of the church
2. and that the church, for 2 years, undertakes to raise the sum of £20 additional to the amount raised above.

'We trust that this effort to serve the interests of your church will commend itself to you and that your members will respond to the utmost of their ability by doing their part. They have every belief that goodwill be done and a successful future be assured for your church.

'With kind regards

'Cordially yours truly,

'Carey Bonner'

Where would the Mowbray family go now that Lloyd was sole minister?

---

[2] Note that the church is here addressed as Altrincham Baptist Church, its official name.

WHAT HAPPENED TO THE MOWBRAYS?

McLaren knew that Mowbray needed a fresh challenge.

The church had to be satisfied he was going willingly, so McLaren had to give Mowbray an exit route. McLaren respected Mowbray's talents, despite the fact that he had led the church split. He knew Mowbray's heart was in evangelism. Equally, despite the problems between Mowbray and the Association, Mowbray respected McLaren.

McLaren therefore asked Mowbray to work for him and William Crossley as an evangelist in Fallowfield. No doubt Mowbray's friend Frank Crossley (who was of course William's brother), had a hand in this. The post was acceptable to Mowbray, and the Mowbrays bade their farewells to the Altrincham Tabernacle and moved from Hale Road to 22 Amherst Street, Withington.

We can only guess at Mowbray's emotions after thirteen years in Altrincham. However, he knew the future lay with the highly talented Lloyd.

In 1901 we find Mowbray recorded as an undenominational minister. His friend James Taverner, a Baptist minister, was visiting him at the time of the census. The family had a servant, Mary Law.

After Fallowfield, the Mowbrays moved back to Barnet in London. Mowbray's aim was to retire, but he found this impossible and became interested in the Police Mission. In 1910 he became minister of a new church in East Barnet and stayed there for nine years.

The Mowbray's son Robert married Lucy Turner. Robert and Lucy produced a grandchild for Henry and Jessie, Arnold Mowbray. It is believed Mowbray's direct descendants live in Bishop's Stortford.

Mowbray's thirteen years as sole minister at Altrincham made him the longest-serving minister of the Altrincham Baptists up to that time. Given the problems that had occurred in Altrincham, he did not keep in touch. This may have been part of the arrangements made with McLaren. Lloyd needed a clear run. There is a sad footnote to the church members' register, which simply notes that Mowbray's membership ceased 'for non intercourse'. It is likely that most church members knew little of the arrangements behind his departure.

Mowbray died during an operation on 16 February 1927. He was one of the Altrincham Baptists' most colourful, blunt, outspoken, controversial and yet loyal ministers. His obituary says he was 'a forceful preacher, a faithful Pastor and a loyal and generous friend, greatly beloved by all who knew him'.

Without the controversial Mowbray, it is likely that there would be no Altrincham Baptist Church today.

THE DEATH OF FRANK CROSSLEY

McLaren's portrait in Manchester City Art Gallery was unveiled on 15 January 1897. His friend, William Crossley, made the presentation. Frank Crossley was also there, but did not look well. He was, however, 'full of eagerness to right some manifest public wrong and to secure Dr McLaren's help. He made no reference to the proceedings of the day, but at once plunged into the subject uppermost in his mind, and his face brightened when Dr McLaren promised what he asked.'[1] Sadly, we will never know what this request was. Mowbray's friend, Frank Crossley, died in Ancoats on 25 March. It is likely that living in the slums with the poor caused him to die young.

It is estimated that 20,000 people attended his funeral. McLaren delivered the tribute in the Star Hall before the cortege set off. Crossley, he said, 'pricked many a conscience of luxurious and idle and well-to-do professing Christians'. The streets were lined. People of all classes came to pay their respects. Victorian funerals were often dark and morbid affairs. By contrast, Frank's coffin was covered in flowers. MacKennal took the funeral service. At the graveside they sang Charles Wesley's hymn, 'Jesus, lover of my soul, let me to thy bosom fly'.

MacKennal said Crossley was a 'mystic of a severely practical type'. McLaren later wrote, 'Frank Crossley was a nineteenth-century saint, whom Francis of Assisi might have recognised as a brother in faith and spirit'.[2]

The Manchester Guardian was perhaps a more dispassionate observer: 'Few men have been more widely known among us in connection with the movement of recent years for the elevation of public morals, the spread of true religion, the rescue of the fallen, the relief of the distressed, and the awakening of the conscience of the nation to a higher standard of right.'

Crossley wished to be buried where his life had taken him, and so his grave was in Philips Park Cemetery in Ancoats, amongst the poor.

It is almost certain that his good friend Mowbray was a mourner at the funeral.

The memorial to Frank Crossley inside Bowdon Downs Congregational Chapel: 'A friend of God/A friend of men'.

[1] McLaren, E.T.: *Dr McLaren of Manchester*, Hodder and Stoughton, 1911.
[2] Preface to Harris, J. Rendel (ed): *The life of Francis William Crossley*, James Nisbet & Co, 1899.

The name of Frank Crossley lives on in Ancoats. Crossley donated Star Hall to the Salvation Army.[3] This photograph shows Crossley Court, which belongs to the Salvation Army Housing Association and which was built on the site of Star Hall. Behind it one can see a factory reminiscent of the old Ancoats.

Emily Crossley in later life.

---

[3] Some books say it was donated by his daughter Ella after his death, but the local newspaper refers to it being donated during his life.

LLOYD AND THE DEBT MOUNTAIN

It is likely that Lloyd had been given a clear mission by McLaren: build up Altrincham Baptist Church, pay off the remaining debt of £700[1] once and for all and show everyone that even a struggling Baptist church can be turned round and made into the flagship church it was meant to be. He had two years to do this before the subsidy from the Association ran out.

Lloyd quietly and quickly dropped the name 'The Altrincham Tabernacle'. This was Mowbray's name for the reunited church. With Mowbray gone, the usual name of the church became 'Hale Road Baptist Church', although it retained its official name of 'Altrincham Baptist Church'.

Next, he turned his attention to the debt.

Churches such as Union Chapel, Bowdon Downs, Trinity Presbyterian and many Anglican churches would rent out pew space to raise income. A member or parishioner would be able to pay a regular amount to the church. In return, he or she would be guaranteed a particular space in a particular pew, or even a whole pew for the family. Pews were numbered. This worked well in busy churches where there was competition for good seats. Those with guaranteed seats did not need to arrive early, and in return the church had a regular income. The accounts of Bowdon Downs Church reveal this was in fact their chief source of regular income.

The system, however, discriminated against the poor. In 1874 the 'Free and open Churches' Anglican group started a campaign which continued right through the 1880s to abolish pew rents in Altrincham and Bowdon. St John's had half its pews free and half rented, but richer churches had a higher proportion rented.

The other disadvantage of the pew-rent system was that it did not work in a start-up church as there was no competition for places. It also built in class inequality. A richer church like Bowdon Downs tried to make some pews available for newcomers and for poorer people at no rent, but like it or not, this still sent a message to the poor that this was not a church for them.

The Altrincham Baptists had from the start prided themselves on *not* raising finance by renting pews. This was a comparatively egalitarian church. However, the lack of this steady income always hampered them. Lloyd needed to secure a regular income and then raise capital to pay off the debt.

Weekly offering envelopes were therefore used to encourage this regular income, and regular reminders were placed in the church magazine. Raising capital was however the priority. Some of Lloyd's methods of raising funds might come as a surprise to Altrincham Baptist Church members today.

We have already seen that Bowdon Baptist had fund-raising bazaars. Mowbray probably had reservations about raising funds from activities like this, because when he formed Altrincham Baptist Church he discontinued the tradition of the annual bazaar. There is an interesting Church Meeting during the joint ministry when a sale of work was proposed and Mowbray tactfully said he remained strictly neutral. Lloyd had no such hesitations. He had a mission from McLaren to fulfil.

---

[1] The debt had been £400, but the mysterious addition of £300 appears to be to repay the loan Mowbray made to build the Tabernacle and hence probably also to repay Frank Crossley.

He set out three principles in paying the debt which were 'Prayer, Pain and Patience'.

In 1896 he decided to set the ambitious target of paying off the debt in just that one year. The church needed to raise sixty shillings a day[2] when its weekly income was only about thirty shillings. Lloyd led by example. He himself personally collected £320 against a personal target (the highest in the church) of £100 for the year. Over 1,000 people contributed to the fund. One Sunday school member collected 1,200 pennies from those who could only give one penny a week.[3]

There was, however, a famine in India, the Queen's diamond jubilee, a £5,000 extension scheme for the Wesleyan church (who were therefore competing for funds locally) and terrible weather, which threatened to ruin various events including the highlight, the three-day bazaar.

Before we see whether he was successful or not, let us pause and look at what a bazaar was like. We have the records of the preparations for a later one under Lloyd in 1903. It was held on Friday and Saturday 20 and 21 November from 3pm to 10pm each day, with entrance prices of 6d and 3d respectively. Fund raising meetings were held each Wednesday commencing 22 September from 3pm as part of the build up. Teas were provided at a charge of 4d each. Mrs Frank Spence supplied a quantity of flannel. Dr Renshaw and George Faulkner Armitage were considered as speakers. Stalls at the bazaar were provided by the Sunday school, the Christian Endeavour Society and the young men of the church. Each night there were two sets of music lasting fifteen minutes each. Bizarrely to modern sensibilities, there was a shooting gallery run by Southwell, who also loaned his galvanic battery. Mr Whitelow loaned his microscope and ran a photographic studio. There was a fishpond competition. The whole event was publicised by circulars.

Whatever the nature of these bazaars, by the end of the year 1896 not only had the Altrincham Baptists raised sufficient funds to pay off the whole debt, but they also had a credit balance of £35-6s-8d.[4]

With many chapels of all denominations suffering from crippling debts, this achievement was remarkable. The Baptist Home Mission report said:

'The church here rejoices in having freed itself from the incubus of debt, which has so long impeded its work, and looks forward to a period of spiritual prosperity...

'It is Altrincham which records this year the greatest degree of visible success. The huge debt, which might well cause a man of stout heart to despair, has been quite extinguished! Our brother, Mr. Lloyd, and his devoted people, have during the twelve months past raised about £700, and so freed themselves from the burden. With all that, the church reports an increase of 12 in membership, and an earnest activity in all agencies for the spiritual blessing of men and women.'

McLaren decided to make the most out of this. At the 1898 Annual Meeting of the Association, he asked Lloyd to address the assembly. Lloyd's report produced such an impact that he was asked to produce a booklet summarising what he had done.

---

[2] £3.
[3] An old penny was 0.42 of a new one.
[4] £35.33

He called this 'How we paid the debt'. *The Baptist Times* later on recalled how this had 'caused something like a sensation'.[5]

In 1898 Lloyd also felt the church needed a refurbishment. On 7 February 1898 the church accepted an estimate of £50 for renovation of the whole building, both inside and out. In April they also decided to improve the troublesome ventilation in the building. By September, the renovation fund stood at £55-1s-5d.[6] A concert was held in December to raise funds for the decoration.

By 1899 the church was able to honour its promise and increased Lloyd's pay by the agreed £20. Income was £350-9s-0d and expenditure £346-13s-7½d.[7]

On 18 December 1900 a further £45 was raised by a sale of work, £25 more than the original estimate. There was a presentation to Lloyd expressing appreciation of his services. This was accompanied by a purse containing £40 and a surprise fitting out of his vestry with completely new furniture and carpet.

The Association was still paying a record £80 a year. Lloyd knew this had to be reduced. McLaren was no doubt very pleased to receive the following letter from Charles Pierrepont, the Church Treasurer:

'We had a Special Church Meeting on Tuesday evening last, at which there was a large attendance, and the question of the help from the Association, which we have been receiving for so many years, received such earnest and serious consideration that we resolved by increased energy and zeal to endeavour to do with half the amount only, next year, and at the same time expressed a hope that the time would not be far distant when we should be able to say we could manage without financial aid from the Association.

'I am therefore instructed to say that we sincerely appreciate the help of the past years and shall only expect £40 instead of £80 next year.

'It is a real joy to me in being able to send you this message and I feel you will be equally pleased in receiving it.

'If it would be quite convenient to you we would like the £40 to be sent during the first half year instead of a portion then and the remainder in the second half.

'With all good wishes for a very happy Christmas.

'I remain on behalf of the church

'Yours sincerely

'C Pierrepont'

In 1900 Lloyd set up a 'Century Fund' and by 1901 had raised £80-11s-5½d. All this went to a central Baptist fund.

---

[5] It is unfortunate that the church has lost its copy, and there are no copies in any library as far as the author can establish.
[6] £55.07.
[7] £350.45 and £346.68.

From 1902 an anonymous member agreed to pay £50 each year towards Lloyd's salary.[8]

With this help, the church finally became self-supporting in 1903, albeit with a little help from the central augmentation fund.

Lloyd had for a long time wanted to buy out the burdensome ground rent. His hand was forced by two deaths. Ann Fairhurst owned the freehold. When she died in 1895, Peter Weedall Houghton was entitled to the income of the ground rent during his life and then, when he in turn died, Ann Fairhurst's will required that the freehold had to be sold by auction or private treaty. Houghton died on 15 July 1901 and the estate had to sell. It is likely the estate approached the church first. The asking price was £520. Today, one might expect to pay something in the region of £300 to buy out a similar ground rent.

On 12 March 1902 Lloyd persuaded the church to attempt to buy out the ground rent. He set up a special committee. He himself agreed to try and collect £100. The deacons and their wives were required to collect £100, a bazaar was to raise £100, two concerts £20 each and a lecture by a Dr Aked £5. McLaren agreed to join in by preaching, with the congregation paying for the privilege in order to raise £10. There were various other schemes to raise the necessary £520.

The church, however, could not raise the cash quickly enough to buy before the auction. Lloyd bid on behalf of the church but was outbid. He must have discussed with the buyers at the auction how much they would sell for to make a quick 'turn', and the price quoted was £600. Undeterred, he set about raising the balance to reach £600. He and his wife were prepared to take a collecting book and said they would obtain at least £150 and contribute £10 and Lloyd's mother would contribute a further £10. Lloyd always led by example. In the end, he was forced to abandon the project, and the monies were used to upgrade the church building.

Lloyd had no hesitation in approaching members for money when the church needed it. In 1904 for example he announced that he would sit in his vestry on Wednesday 10 February from 3pm-9pm to receive thank offerings. He clearly expected every member to turn up, have a private conversation with him and hand over some cash. This would be almost unthinkable to the church today. His message was reinforced by articles in support in the church magazine by the treasurer and the church secretary and by various scriptures he quoted in the magazine about giving. Eighty-five people visited him and he believed that 'each gift was also the expression of a consecrated purpose to live a life more complete and to the glory of God'. People did not seem to mind his direct methods; he was, after all such a popular man.

Lloyd also organised regular rummage sales, offering to send round a cart to the house of anyone who wanted to contribute. All sections of the church were encouraged to raise funds. In 1899, for example the 'young unmarried ladies' raised £11.

---

[8] This was almost certainly Frank Spence.

Many Nonconformists have followed the practice of giving 10 per cent of their income to the church, seeing this as a scriptural principle. Early Baptists sometimes had a more radical edge than this. Early Baptist John Smyth advocated having 'all things in common, in the necessity of the church, and of the poor bretheren'. In 1660 Thomas Lambe wrote 'an appeal to parliament concerning the poor, that there may not be a beggar inn England'. He was far thinking enough to advocate labour exchanges.

The church magazine was put to good use to raise money. It was sold for a shilling a year[9] to defray costs and carried regular adverts to raise funds. Church members were requested to patronise those advertising. In 1899 we know that 129 magazines were sold a month at a profit of £8, and circulation rose after that.

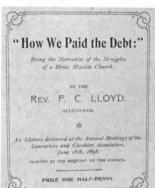

The booklet by Cowell Lloyd, 'How we paid the debt'. McLaren held Lloyd up as a shining example of how Baptist churches might pay off their chapel building debts.

As well as placing the church on a sound financial footing, Lloyd had another task from McLaren, and that was to build up numbers attending. We will now see how he did this.

---

[9] 5p.

HOW DID HE DO IT?

There was a steady growth in numbers. The curtains which had been placed across the side pews at the Hale Road chapel were now removed as the congregation grew. By 1899 there were 141 members, with thirty-one having joined in the previous year.

It is difficult to pin down any one single factor that contributed to this growth; rather, Lloyd appears to have conducted a number of simultaneous strategies. There was also perhaps a feeling that the church had a real sense of purpose and vision again.

One of the secrets of his success was undoubtedly the number of visits he made. Even before he was appointed as joint minister, he had visited most of the church members in their own homes. While at Altrincham, he made over 1,000 visits each year.[1] Newcomers could expect a personal visit and continued personal interest in their welfare. To make sure no one slipped through the net, people were appointed to spot new attenders. He knew not only the name of every church member but also their addresses by heart.

It is also clear that people were drawn by the quality of Lloyd's preaching. He wrote many letters, and if he thought a sermon would be of particular use to a church attender (especially an irregular one), he wrote a personal letter to them suggesting they should come and hear that sermon.

He edited the church magazine and personally dealt with all the advertisers.

Lloyd also appears to have tried to make the church an attractive alternative society. It had its own political agenda, societies, tea parties and meetings. Its members looked out for and cared for one another.

For those who were still uncomfortable about coming to church services, he set up 'Pleasant Thursday evenings', of which more later.

Although he would not have thought about it in this way, Lloyd was also good at public relations. He was constantly writing to the press, passing public church resolutions and engaging in debate, often on political issues. In 1899 for example, he made sure that the press were briefed on the mission for that year. From 1901 he began putting reports of baptism services in the local press and used the services to explain the gospel to the curious. In 1901 his baptismal sermon was 'The confession of Christ and its reward'. There was usually a minimum of two baptisms per month.

Lloyd was keen to make sure that church members played their part in the mission of the church. Duty number seven in his list of requirements for members was, 'Become yourself a winner of souls'. Every member was expected to be involved in mission in some way.

As a focus for much of this effort, there were formal missions most years. On each occasion, Lloyd would appoint a high-calibre outside evangelist. This was possibly because he recognised that his gifting was primarily as a minister and preacher.

---

[1] At his next church, he was nicknamed 'the visiting pastor'.

Lloyd loved getting members to remember things by giving them mottos. The 1899 mission had a motto (according to your faith be it done), a motive (love), a mandate (pray that the Lord will send labourers) and three methods, which were the church 'must be right', 'conversion of our heroes' and 'bring in the outsiders'.

Lloyd required and got enthusiastic support for each mission. In 1899 he got every member at a communion service to stand and agree to 'prepare forthwith by continual prayer and personal preparation'.

Revds C.F. Spurr, W.R. Lane and C.H. Watkins were the evangelists in three separate years. In 1900 the mission was advertised on the front page of the local newspaper and Spurr spoke on the Christian life. In 1902 the mission lasted for eight days.

It is worth looking at the 1904 mission in more detail as an example of how one of these missions worked. This was one of the least successful years by Lloyd's high standards, but we have more information about it than others. The evangelist was a Mr Isaacs. Isaacs was an international preacher from Australia and a well-known speaker at the Geelong Convention, an Australian version of the English Keswick Convention. He was also a past President of the Victoria Baptist Union. 'Wherever he goes he exhibits the special gifts of an Evangelist and is much used by the Holy Spirit in the conversion of sinners and consecration of believers,' wrote Lloyd.

The mission was in mid-September and coincided with missions throughout the country. Lloyd began his build up for the church in early August. A mission choir was formed.

Lloyd decided members should personally visit houses in two specific target areas: 'two thickly populated districts – the district of which Bold Street is the centre, and that quite new district of which Beech Road is the centre'. Each household was to be given a card with details of the events on one side and a 'hearty invitation' on the other. The visitors were given their own motto to encourage them taken from the 1899 mission: 'According to your faith be it unto you.' Eight hundred and fifty invitations were distributed, but in their enthusiasm members sometimes visited houses twice. Lloyd was not concerned; better to visit twice than not at all. If invitees turned up to an event, those who invited them were to be responsible for spotting them and looking after them. Lloyd asked for a good spiritual atmosphere in the church with 'supplication and consecration'.

On 1 September he returned from holiday and published a photograph of Isaacs for members to see what he looked like.

The mission coincided with the weekly separate open-air events held by Christian Endeavour, the Young Men's Mission and the Free Church Council.

There were regular prayer focuses on the mission. During the mission itself there were prayer meetings each day. Lloyd encouraged members to pray for 'many definite cases of conversions before the month closes'. Isaacs duly arrived and stayed with the Pierrepont family.

The Sunday school invited parents. Crucially, the biggest success from the mission came from the Sunday school.

When the mission was over, Isaacs left for Tasmania. Lloyd was honest enough to express some disappointment in the mission and partly in Isaacs himself. The interesting thing about the mission, however, is perhaps not how many new conversions to Christianity it brought, but rather that it forced church members each year to think about their own mission and role in growing the church. Simply by focussing on that, it helped members to think about bringing along their friends and contacts.

> 'He will only infuse his own religion into other minds, whose religion is not a set of hard dogmas, but is fuelled by the heat of personal experience into a river of living fire.' McLaren in 1871[2]

> The church under Lloyd distributed huge numbers of tracts.[3] In 1904 for example, 9,250 tracts were distributed door to door by twenty-three people covering twenty-five districts. Miss Bowland of 27 Bold Street was in charge[4]. The church tended to focus on its own patch and local Nonconformists made efforts to divide up Altrincham by area so as not to duplicate efforts. Streets regularly visited by the Baptists were Brown Street, Bold Street, York Street, Monyash Road, William Street, Hawthorn Road, Tipping Street, Islington Place, Byrom Street, Pownall Street, Armitage Place, Manor Road, Beech Road, Cedar Road, Stamford Park Road, Queen's Villas, Peel Causeway, Rigby Street, Thomas Street, Denmark Street, Finchley Road, Russell Street, Bath Street and Peter Street.

Lloyd knew the name of each Sunday school pupil and each one received a birthday card with a motto on it from him. Here is one from 1906. The Sunday school was one of the big mission success areas. A growing Sunday school meant more families, who in turn attracted further families.

So where did all the new people arriving in the growing church come from?

---

[2] MacLaren, A: *The Pattern of Service*, 1871 (in bound volume of theological tracts). The spelling of McLaren's name changed later.
[3] A tract is a small pamphlet explaining some aspect of the Christian faith.
[4] It is not clear if this was Annie or Ellen Bowland.

WHERE DID THEY COME FROM?

One question that churches often want to have answered is how successful have they been in 'conversion' to the Christian faith, as opposed to attracting people from other churches. We have already looked at the growth of Bowdon Baptist Church and seen that it came from a mixture of transfers and conversions. If the growth of the Altrincham Baptists was simply by attracting people from other churches, that would be illusory growth. Where did all these new people therefore come from?

The church records of Altrincham Baptist Church appear to reveal a mixture of transfers and baptisms. It is not always possible from the records to differentiate between baptisms of people who came from other churches and new converts. However, an early register of members of Hale Road Baptist Tabernacle when the two churches recombined and which takes us up to the end of the joint ministry of Lloyd and Mowbray (we stop midway through 1896 to obtain a convenient figure of 100), gives a good idea.

Of the 100 listed from member number sixty-three onwards,[1] twenty-one were admitted by profession of faith, twenty-eight were transfers and fifty-one were baptised as believers by the church. Of those eleven transfers where further details are given, all are from out of the area, with the nearest being from Sale and the furthest ones from Bridgnorth, and Sharon in the United States. The largest number of transfers is, however, from Manchester, thus showing a pattern of movement into the area. The number of baptisms does suggest a significant new convert rate, which started under Mowbray and continued under the joint ministry.

However, a number of the 100 left or died. They were replaced by a constant influx of new people. The departures are, of course, over a much longer period, but are limited to 1905 for the purposes of this book. Twenty-two left by transfer to other Baptist or Congregational churches (two of these emigrated), thirty-one lapsed or were removed from the books (including Mowbray), seven died and the remaining forty were still in membership in 1905. From 19 April 1887 to the end of 1905, Altrincham Baptist Church had received 440 new full members and lost 288 (including by death), leaving a net gain of 152. This does not include the substantial number of communicant members who were not full members. There were 230 people entitled to take communion in 1905, of whom seventy-eight were communicant (i.e. not full) members. What is striking is that, as time goes on, the retention rate appears to improve, with the highest volatility of congregational numbers being, not surprisingly, during the period of the breakaway church, and the lowest under Lloyd.

So, remarkably, the Baptists do seem to have grown by conversion as well as by transfers. Equally, they gained and lost members regularly due to the increasing mobility of the population, but overall the pattern was of growth, a growth that increased substantially under Lloyd.

---

[1] 1-62 were the original founder members of Altrincham Baptist Church.

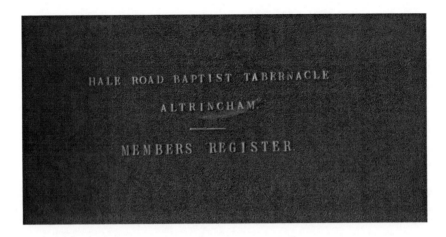

Membership book of Hale Road Baptist Tabernacle when Mowbray came back to take over the Hale Road chapel.

A morning service at the Hale Road Baptist Church in 2004, not long before morning services moved to Trinity United Reformed Church on Delamer Road.

The growth of the church was straightforward enough, but their theology was more complex. We now turn to what the Nonconformists actually believed.

VICTORIAN THEOLOGY AND ROME

This book is not a chronological history book in the usual sense. The intention is to give a sense of what it was like theologically, socially and culturally to live in Altrincham at the time as part of the substantial Nonconformist community, using the Baptists as a focus for this exploration. In the next few chapters, therefore, we pause in our chronological history and take a look at Nonconformist and Baptist theology, and how the Baptists and other churches governed themselves. If you do not enjoy theology, you can skip to the chapter headed 'The Sermon and Popular Culture', but that would be a shame, because there is much here of interest to everyone.

We are not dealing with a dry subject. What the Victorians did and believed affects us today. The Victorian Baptists believed passionately in what they stood for and what they stood against. In looking at what they believed, we will also at the beliefs of others at the time.

We start by referring to a book. It is likely that the Altrincham Baptists would have used a book published in 1879 by Charles Williams of Accrington to aid them in understanding their beliefs. This book was called *The Principles and Practices of the Baptists.*[1] There are good reasons for following Williams. First, he and Lloyd were friends and Lloyd would certainly have read the book and would probably have been influenced by it. Second, Mowbray was counselled by Williams and probably read his book. Third, Williams was a friend of McLaren. Fourth, he was to become President of the Baptist Union and his book would therefore have been widely read by Baptists generally. Finally, Williams has already appeared throughout this book and seems to have taken an interest in Altrincham.

Victorian Nonconformists argued that their beliefs were as old as the Bible, and were founded on the practices, principles and beliefs of the New Testament Church. However, they were not immune to what was going on in the world around them, or to contemporary theological issues. Their theology was partly shaped by, and partly a reaction against, changes in both the Roman Catholic and Anglican churches.

Strictly speaking, what was happening in those churches should have been of no concern to the Nonconformists. They had long ago left the Church of England and refused to conform to its practices. Their religious liberty was finally being obtained in the nineteenth century after years of discrimination, and yet they watched fearfully as they saw changes in the Church of England which appeared to lead it to Rome, and changes at Rome which appeared to harden the approach of the Roman Catholic Church as it tried to wield political power in a changing Italy.

This chapter does not reflect modern Nonconformist views, but is to help us understand the thinking of the Victorians. It is perhaps hard to understand this today, but there was a real and genuine fear that once again the Pope would be the chief spiritual authority in Britain and the perceived Protestant values of much of the country would disappear.

Let us look at two of the chief personalities involved. Henry Newman left the Church of England to become a Roman Catholic in 1845, and later became a cardinal. The Old Harrovian Henry Manning, Anglican Archdeacon of Chichester,

---

[1] Williams, C.: *The Principles and Practices of the Baptists – a Book for Inquirers*, Baptist Tract Society, 1879.

was ordained in 1851 as a Roman Catholic priest and was to become the greatest cardinal of the time in Great Britain.[2] He helped to bring peace to a dock strike as a trusted neutral party and was a social radical, jumping into what would otherwise have been natural Nonconformist territory.

These major defections from the Church of England were concurrent with the growth of the Roman Catholic Church, which was particularly boosted by immigration from Ireland.

Victorian evangelicals in Britain felt the need to come together under a broad umbrella body and to stand firm against what they saw as attacks against the Protestant Church. Thus the Evangelical Alliance was born in Britain in 1846.

When the Pope introduced new Roman Catholic dioceses in England, hysteria ensued, and an Act of Parliament was passed in 1851 to counter them. Queen Victoria took a more sanguine view: 'I cannot bear to hear the violent abuse of the Catholic religion, which is so painful and cruel towards the many good and innocent Roman Catholics.'

Pope Pius IX added to the perceived threat from Rome. Edgar Mortara was baptised as a Roman Catholic by a maid, against the wishes of his Jewish parents. The papal police abducted him at the age of seven. In 1859, his parents pleaded with the Pope for his return at the traditional papal audience with the Jews of Rome, but he refused. Two years later, he paraded Mortara as a Catholic seminarian to the Jewish people in Rome. His actions shocked most British people, including many Roman Catholics. If he could take this sort of action against a Jewish family in Rome, what would he do with British Protestants if he had the chance?

Then came the 1870 Roman Catholic Conclave. The proposal was that the Pope should be infallible when making pronouncements 'ex cathedra'. Officially, all the cardinals rose and gave their assent to the proposal, but in fact a significant number of the nearly 700 left when they saw what was intended. The vote was in fact 451 for, eighty-eight against and sixty-six 'juxta modum' (i.e. don't know).

The Conclave produced a storm of protest from Protestants. Gladstone agonised over how to react to all these events. He was a man of contradictions. He was a devout High Church Anglican and friend of the Ritualist Pusey, and yet also a Liberal whose natural political constituency was the Nonconformists. His sister was a convert to Roman Catholicism, and yet he met a German theologian who was excommunicated in 1871 for opposing the declaration of infallibility. He was in favour of disestablishing the church in Ireland and yet he was a friend of Cardinal Manning.

Gladstone, however, felt an implicit threat to the future of Great Britain from the Pope's actions. The result was his pamphlet, 'The Vatican Decrees in Their Bearing on Civil Allegiance'.

What happened in the Roman Catholic Church occurred at the same time as the move in the Church of England to Ritualism. Many 'broad church' parishes accepted aspects of Ritualism. Nonconformists saw this as a movement of the Church of England from its Protestant heritage and towards Rome.

---

[2] Manning was satirised as Cardinal Grandison in Benjamin Disraeli's 1870 book, Disraeli, B.: *Lothair*, Longmans, Green & Co., 1870.

Part of the theology that moved Anglicans to increased use of rituals was a theology of the sacraments. Nonconformists called this theology 'sacramentalism'. To the Nonconformists, it was the tendency to attribute to the 'sacraments' a power in themselves, regardless of the spiritual condition of the recipient. A Victorian Baptist would, for example, see in believer's baptism an act that came from the faith of the believer. The act of baptism itself achieved nothing. Without the faith of the believer, communion too achieved nothing. To a sacramentalist, the very act of baptism or the taking of communion could achieve something spiritual, independent of the faith of the believer. The believer did not necessarily need to have any faith at all.

As the Roman Catholic Church developed its doctrines and the Church of England embraced Ritualism, many Nonconformists began to see themselves as the guardians of the true faith of the early church.

Many modern Baptists still disagree with sacramentalism, but their attitudes have modified. George Beasley-Murray, father of former minister of Altrincham Baptist Church, Paul Beasley-Murray, wrote in 1966: 'Why do [Baptists] resist sacramental theology so fiercely, and retreat to the defence of a symbolic ordinance...?'[3]

MacKennal had some sympathies with sacramentalism. Perhaps McLaren knew this when he spoke at the Primitive Methodist Church in 1878 at the launch of the Baptist building fund and criticised sacramentalism with MacKennal present in front of him.

Archdeacon Gore, incumbent of St Mary's Church, Bowdon, during much of the period covered by this book. The Church of England in Altrincham saw a move to Ritualism.

---

[3] Beasley-Murray, G.: *Baptism Today and Tomorrow*, Macmillan, 1966.

Altrincham Baptist Church conference held at Blessed Thomas Holford School. Attitudes of both Nonconformists and Roman Catholics are much changed since the period covered by this book.

So we now turn to the book whose truth they sought to guard. In a world of fast developing theology, what about the Bible?

THE BIBLE AND THE EVANGELICALS

The Victorian Nonconformist view of the Bible was one of their core beliefs. To them, Jesus Christ is the true head of the Church and it is principally in the scriptures that his revelation occurs. The Bible was, quite literally, the word of God.

Let us return to Williams as our guide. Williams started his book by stressing the fact that Baptists were (and are) part of the historic Christian Church. They have much in common with all other denominations.[1] Even in late Victorian times, he wanted to stress unity first.

Baptists, he wrote, would, however, regard themselves as 'evangelicals'. We have come across this word in our look at the Downgrade Controversy. The word has been subject to much misunderstanding. It is often confused with 'evangelism'. Evangelism may stem from evangelical beliefs, but that is not the meaning of evangelical. The word itself comes from the word for the Gospels, the 'Evangels'. 'Evangelical' too has often been confused with fundamentalism. A fundamentalist would almost certainly be an evangelical, but an evangelical, although believing the Bible is the inspired word of God, would not necessarily be a fundamentalist.

Evangelicals have in fact always been 'a broad church', including people with diverse beliefs such as Calvinists, Pentecostals and Lutherans. Technically, all Protestants are evangelicals. Many Methodists, Anglicans and others would say they are evangelicals. This has led some in more recent times to define a possible separate group within evangelicalism called 'conservative evangelicals'.

In the late Victorian period in Britain, the understanding of what an evangelical is would have been narrower than it is today, and there would have been a much greater overlap with what we would call fundamentalism. Victorian evangelicals would mostly have been what we now call 'conservative evangelicals'. Even then there was a debate within the Baptists as to how 'evangelical' an evangelical should be[2]. As we have already seen, that debate led to Spurgeon leaving the Baptist Union. In some senses, the legacy of the Spurgeon 'Downgrade' debate still hangs over modern Baptists, even though they often do not realise it.[3]

In common with most Nonconformists, the Baptists as evangelicals took their principal source of authority as the Bible. They did not believe that the church had any power to dictate or alter what the Bible taught. If church doctrine conflicted with the Bible, then it was church doctrine that must give way. Therefore, if the Bible taught believer's baptism and part of the church did not, it was that part of the church that was wrong. With Jesus Christ as the head of the church, the Bible must be the supreme authority for the teachings of the church.

---

[1] Justin Dennison, a senior pastor of Altrincham Baptist Church in the 1980s and 1990s, said he was a Christian first and Baptist second.
[2] The issue is still around today. See for example, Stott J.: *Evangelical Truth, A personal plea for unity, integrity and faithfulness*, Inter-Varsity Press, 2005; Tomlinson D.: *The Post-Evangelical*, SPCK, 1995, and Wright, N.: *The Radical Evangelical: Seeking a Place to Stand, SPCK*, 1996. Nigel Wright is Principal of Spurgeon's College and a former senior pastor of Altrincham Baptist Church. A modern definition describes evangelicalism by characteristics, namely a belief that lives need to be changed, the expression of the gospel in effort, a particular regard for the Bible and a stress on the sacrifice of Christ on the cross. See Bebbington D.: *Evangelicalism in Modern Britain*, Unwin Hayman, 1989. See also page 11 of Beasley-Murray, P.: *Radical Believers: the Baptist Way of Being the Church*, Baptist Union, 1992.
[3] It would be foolish however to read the Victorian debate into much of the modern debate as the issues were very different. McLaren today would be regarded as a conservative evangelical, and yet he stayed in the Baptist Union and Spurgeon left it. Even the more liberal MacKennal would probably today be regarded as a conservative evangelical.

That belief is still today at the heart of a continuing debate between Roman Catholics, Anglicans and Nonconformists. Does the Bible override Church doctrine, or can the Bible only be understood in the light of Church doctrine? Baptists today are still believers in the primary authority of the Bible, and believe their doctrines come from it. In the words of a former minister of Altrincham Baptist Church, Baptist 'emphases are rooted in Scripture and as such they are worth standing for'.[4]

Baptists believe that the Bible teaches the doctrine of believers' baptism. If you deny the authority of Scripture, you can begin to challenge the doctrine of baptism. In the words of H. Wheeler Robinson, 'John Bunyan and his fellow Baptists had a special reason for the appeal to Scripture. It was their one ground for the practice of believers' baptism which could be maintained against the appeal to the traditions of the church.'[5]

Williams and most Victorian Baptists were firmly of the view that the truth of the Bible was paramount. The early church beliefs (as they understood them) were the correct ones. If later on the church re-interpreted those early beliefs, then the Baptists should follow the early church as described in the Bible. They believed that their beliefs and practices, rooted in the scriptures, were as close as they could get to the teachings of the Bible and the practices of the early church.

Many Baptist commentaries of the time traced a direct link between Baptist beliefs and what they saw as the true Church throughout history. Within the wide body called 'the Church', the Victorian Baptists believed there has always been a body of true and often persecuted believers.

In reading the Bible, they used the Authorised Version (King James), although by 1885 the Revised Version was introduced for both Old and New Testaments. All denominations except the Roman Catholics co-operated together in the new translation. However, there is no evidence that the Altrincham Baptists used the Revised Version during the period covered by this book, although they adopted it later.

The Altrincham Baptists took their study of the Bible very seriously. In 1904, Lloyd was able to say that 200 members of the church were signed up to the daily readings of the International Bible Reading Association.

Personal study of the Bible was a core activity of any Nonconformist, coupled with listening to sermons, which were almost always based on Bible passages. God's word was indeed sacred.

---

[4] Beasley-Murray, P., op cit.
[5] Robinson, H. W.: *The Life and Faith of the Baptists*, Kingsgate Press, 1927.

The Victorian debate concerning the authority of the Bible against that of the church has many examples, so let us look at just one which is the question of the marriage of clergy. Most Protestants saw nothing in the Bible to prevent a minister (or priest) from marrying, and indeed some of the apostles and many New Testament church leaders married and had children. Article 32 of the Church of England's Thirty-Nine Articles states: 'Bishops, Priests, and Deacons, are not commanded by God's Law, either to vow the estate of single life, or to abstain from marriage: therefore it is lawful also for them, as for all other Christian men, to marry at their own discretion, as they shall judge the same to serve better to godliness.'

At the Second Lateran Council of 1139, the Roman Catholic Church prohibited priests from being married.[6] Which is right, the Victorian Nonconformists would ask, the later tradition of the Roman Catholic Church or the teachings and practices of the early Church?

The Roman Catholic Church would argue that there is teaching outside the Bible that, together with the Bible, is a 'Deposit of Faith'. Protestants would look only to the Bible and say that one cannot add to the Bible new doctrines to suit a part of the church. Thus for example Victorian Protestants would disagree with the existence of purgatory, the sale of 'indulgences' to reduce time there and praying to or with 'saints'.

Another example of the differing Victorian views on the authority and interpretation of Scripture is the very simple one as to whether Jesus had brothers and sisters. The Roman Catholic Church believes he did not. The Bible does have references to the brothers and sisters of Jesus. In Galatians 1:19, Paul says: 'I saw none of the other apostles – only James, the Lord's brother.' Another example is Mark 6:3: 'Where did this man get these things?' they asked. 'What's this wisdom that has been given him, that he even does miracles! Isn't this the carpenter? Isn't this Mary's son and the brother of James, Joseph, Judas and Simon? Aren't his sisters here with us?'

Victorian Nonconformists would argue that the Roman Catholic doctrine of the immaculate conception interfered with a straight-forward understanding of the Bible, which is that Joseph married Mary, he had no prior wife and Mary was a virgin when she conceived Jesus. The couple then lived a normal family life and had further children. Josephus refers to James as being the brother of Jesus. Non-Protestant churches, by contrast, thought that the references to brothers and sisters were to spiritual brothers and sisters, that Joseph had a prior marriage or that people like James were cousins or stepbrothers of Jesus.

---

[6] It is possible that the earlier Council of Elvira in the fourth century may also have done so.

Dr Jim Perkins preaching in the 1960s at Hale Road Baptist Chapel. The layout of the chapel is not vastly different from the layout under Lloyd. Note the centrality of the cross and the Bible. Nowadays, although there are still disagreements between the Protestant and Roman Catholic Churches on theology, practical co-operation is much closer than it was in Victorian times.

> Many Nonconformists regard the major theological problems in the Church in fact as having arisen when Emperor Constantine nominally converted to Christianity. Until then, the Church had been happily expanding and quietly subverting the assumptions of Empire. When it became the State religion, its whole nature changed – for the worse, they would argue.[7]

Having looked at something that united the Victorian Nonconformists – their belief in the authority of the Bible – we now turn to an issue that divided them. That issue was the doctrine of election.

[7] For a modern Baptist view, see Wright, N.: *Disavowing Constantine: Mission, Church and the Social Order in the Theologies of John Howard Yoder and Jurgen Moltmann*, Paternoster, 2000.

ELECTION

You might think that the word 'election' to a Victorian Baptist would be associated with the growing enfranchisement of the electorate. Election was, in fact, based on a theological tension in the Bible itself and had nothing to do with democracy.

The debate today may seem almost irrelevant to many modern Nonconformists, and indeed it is fair to say that most Baptist churches, if they ever address the issue, would be either 'Arminian' or very moderate 'Calvinist'. We will define these terms below, but the issues these doctrines raised for the Victorian Baptists actually affected which Baptist denomination they belonged to. Even when the two main denominations united, individual churches would be either Arminian or Calvinist.

This debate affected all Protestant denominations. The Church of England has its Thirty-nine Articles of doctrine. These are decidedly Calvinist. You would be hard put today to find an Anglican vicar, however, who subscribes to all of the Thirty-nine Articles. MacKennal was no Calvinist.

This Victorian debate about Calvinism was paralleled (and perhaps influenced) by a scientific and philosophical debate. That debate was about evolution, determinism and free will, and it is worth looking briefly at this as a backdrop to the religious debate as the two are inter-linked.

The theory of evolution was highly controversial. Most Victorian Nonconformists would have derided the theory, but they could not ignore it. Darwin's theory was actually not new. It was the conclusion of the thinking of many others. More popular than Darwin's books at the time was the 1844 book *Vestiges* by Robert Chambers, who argued that all life had a common origin and that life and geology had come about as a result of discernible or deducible evolutionary laws. Darwin quite possibly should not even have been the one to publish the crucial work on evolution. Alfred Wallace sent his text on evolution to Darwin to approve, and this spurred Darwin to write his own book which had been in gestation for many years. The two had their essays read out at the Linnaean Society on 1 July 1858, but it was Darwin, who had taken twenty years to get to where the unassuming Wallace arrived almost in a flash, who took the final credit and whose name has endured, although this was never the intention at the time.

The debate about evolution was paralleled by one about determinism. Marx dealt principally with economic determinism. Hobbes, Hume, Kant, Mill, Wordsworth and Bentham all grappled with determinism in their own ways. What could liberty and free will mean in a deterministic universe?

If one can analyse every single part of the universe and every aspect of it, can one in theory predict what will happen at all times in the future? If so, there can be no free will and humans are bound to follow a particular path. Quantum theory eventually affected the scientific debate: if everything is uncertain, if by the act of measurement itself one affects the outcome, the future cannot be determined. Even then, the debate still resurfaces today: if there is one theory of everything to be discovered which combines Einstein's relativity and quantum theory, could there be an underlying order which allows only a deterministic future with no chance for free will?[1]

For theologians, the question was not whether there was a God, but what the nature of God was. If God had created everything, had he simply left the universe to run like a ticking clock, never interfering with it and letting it run its predetermined course? Where did that leave miraculous intervention? Where did that leave free choice? If God knows everything in advance, where and how can human beings exercise free will?

A Calvinist would not see this as a problem. He would answer that God created everything. As God knows the past, present and the future, free will is an illusion. Jesus died to save people who God knew in advance would respond to the call of salvation, and they have no choice in the matter; God's will is irresistible.

The Bible contains many references to the 'elect'. These are the people God has chosen. However, are the elect chosen by God in advance so that only they will be saved, or does God allow anyone to be saved who repents and believes? To put it another way, are believers predestined to be saved, or does God allow the individual choice as to whether to be saved or not?

If one takes the first possibility to its extreme, it means that Christians do not need to preach the gospel; if God knows in advance who will be saved, then he will bring those people into his kingdom. To most modern Baptists, this seems an extraordinary position to take, but this was the stance of the so-called 'hyper-Calvinists'.

However, during the course of the nineteenth Century most Calvinists moderated their theology. Spurgeon was a Calvinist by conviction,[2] but a comparatively mild one, famously praying: 'Lord hasten to bring in all thine elect, and then elect some more'. It was probably the evangelical revival and the Baptist worldwide mission that contributed most to this process of modification.

William Carey[3] was possibly the most famous Baptist missionary of his time. It was under his influence that Calvinists began to realise the need for mission. Carey was inspired by Captain Cook's journal of his explorations. The people Cook met had never heard the gospel. Carey was spurred into action. If God had already chosen whom to save, there was no point in mission to save people. Carey simply could not accept this. The global mission of the Baptists changed their theology and influenced other denominations.

> 'We are not to look to Genesis for a scientific cosmogony, and are not to be disturbed by physicists' criticisms on it as such. Its purpose is quite another, and far more important; namely, to imprint deep and ineffaceable the conviction that the one God created all things.'
>
> McLaren in *Expositions of Holy Scripture*. McLaren was not a fundamentalist.

> Calvin married a converted Anabaptist, but never changed his views about baptism. He bitterly opposed the Anabaptists.

---

[1] For a modern view of this debate from a neurobiological point of view, see Searle, J.: *Freedom and Neurobiology: Reflections on Free Will, Language, and Political Power*, Columbia University Press, 2007.
[2] Hopkins, op. cit.
[3] 1761–1834.

A good example of the early debates between the hyper-Calvinists and the Baptist missionaries is an encounter between William Carey and John Ryland. Ryland told the young Carey to sit down at a meeting in 1776. 'You're an enthusiast,' he told the budding missionary. 'When God pleases to convert the heathen, he'll do it without consulting you or me.'

Carey, of course, disagreed and went on to become one of the most famous missionaries of all time.

Calvinism is more than just about election. This is a brief summary of the five core beliefs:

Total depravity: there is no aspect of our nature that is left intact by sin.

Unconditional election: God chooses whom he wills.

Limited atonement: Christ died only for the elect.

Irresistible grace: God saves those whom he wills to save.

Perseverance of the saints: once saved, the Christian is always saved.

The convenient acronym for these beliefs is 'Tulip'.

The Bowdon and Altrincham Scientific and Literary Institute on George Street where many debates on science were held. The lecture and concert rooms were designed by Waterhouse. In December 1876 the society held a lecture on 'The Origin of Man', which dealt with the contemporary and rival theories of Chambers and spontaneous generation, and Darwin and evolution. Another lecture was given in 1877 by a Mr Broderick, a proponent of the theory of evolution.

When Bowdon Baptist Church was formed, whether a church was Calvinist or not still affected which Baptist denomination it would belong to.

A PARTICULAR VIEW

The 'Particular Baptists' were the largest Baptist denomination in the nineteenth century, and perhaps the most traditionally evangelical. They were Calvinists, but during the latter part of the eighteenth century, they began a re-assessment of their Calvinism.

The word 'particular' has changed its meaning over time. 'Particular' in the context of the Victorian Baptists referred to 'particular redemption' and 'particular election', two key points identifying them with Calvinism. The word meant something like 'limited'.

The 'General Baptists' by contrast were open to differing theological views. Most were Arminian. This meant that, in common with Wesley, they believed that God saves anyone who repents and believes in Jesus Christ. They therefore rejected the narrower Calvinist doctrine of the elect. Their openness to differing views carried the risk, however, of leading them away from orthodox Christianity. Together with some Presbyterians, some General Baptists even became Unitarians (i.e. they rejected the doctrine of the Trinity[1]) and left the Baptist fold.

Dan Taylor, a West Riding Methodist, came to Baptist convictions in 1763. He could not agree with the Particular Baptists in their Calvinist theology, nor could he agree with some of the liberal tendencies of the General Baptists. Thus in 1770 he helped found the New Connexion of General Baptists: a non-Calvinist evangelical Baptist denomination. Its heartland was in Yorkshire and the West Midlands. Many more orthodox General Baptists then transferred either to the New Connexion or to the Particular Baptists.

This left three main Baptist denominations: the Particular Baptists (the largest group), the General Baptists (the smallest) and the New Connexion.

The Baptist Union was reconstructed in 1832 and its revised constitution paved the way for closer links between the two largest Baptist denominations. The previous doctrinal clauses were dropped in favour of a union of churches and ministers 'who agree in the sentiments commonly called evangelical'. By 1860 the Baptists were coming even closer together, and in 1860 *The Times* was able to say that the 'denominations of "General" and "Particular" as applied to the communities of Baptists do not denote any diversity whatever on the fundamental points of their creed'.

Ministers trained in New Connexion Bible colleges began to serve in Particular Baptist churches and vice versa. In Lancashire during the cotton famine of the 1860s, the Baptist Lancashire Relief Committee collected funds for those most affected and distributed them without distinction as to denomination.

In 1886, our guide Williams was President of the Baptist Union and addressed the Assembly. He asked, in the context of their mission, what held them back from uniting. The resolution after the address was proposed by McLaren. Significantly in terms of the closeness of the Baptists and Congregationalists, it was spoken to by Edward White as Chairman of the Congregational Union. McLaren's resolution was that the Assembly 'deeply impressed both with the importance of the

---

[1] A complex doctrine held by all main Christian denominations and which they regard as being implicit in the Bible. There is only one God, but He is manifest in three persons: God the Father, God the Son (Jesus Christ) and God the Holy Spirit.

evangelisation of our country and with the special needs of our village churches, earnestly commends to the denomination the appeal made this morning from the Presidential Chair on behalf of the Home Mission of the Baptist Union'. That appeal was that they should consider uniting as one denomination. You will note that it was the drive for mission that was the prime motivator.

The 'Downgrade Controversy' overshadowed the subsequent debate, but most Baptists did unite together in 1891 as one denomination under a broad evangelical umbrella. The legacy of those debates is still with us. Spurgeon appeared, for example, to want a Baptist statement of belief, and yet this would have almost been impossible except in fairly broad evangelical terms, especially bearing in mind the Calvinist/Arminian issue.

It is worth looking briefly at the Holiness Movement in all this. The annual Keswick Convention was founded in 1875 and helped to propagate this theology. Crossley and MacKennal were much influenced by the Movement, as was the Salvation Army.

The Holiness Movement took many away from Calvinism. Both Crossley and the Army held campaigns in Altrincham on the subject of holiness. It seems likely that Lloyd too was influenced by Keswick.

The Holiness Movement can probably be traced back to Wesley. Whitfield and the Countess of Huntingdon[2] in the Methodist movement were Calvinists, but Wesley believed not only in justification by faith, but also in sanctification. Salvation he believed begins at conversion but is a process which can lead to a moment when 'the heart is cleansed from all sin, and filled with pure love to God and man'.[3]

The idea was further developed in America. Robert Pearshall Smith arrived in England in 1874 and proclaimed that one could have intimate companionship with Christ all day long, that God's will and one's happiness were one, and that the Holy Spirit and not the believer overcame temptations. However, the believer had to make a deliberate act of full surrender and enter a 'rest of faith'. This was far removed from Calvinism.

Smith's preaching led directly to the foundation of the Keswick Convention in the summer of 1875 under the guidance of the local vicar in Keswick. Although the convention was led primarily by Anglican clergy, Baptists and Brethren were also well represented and as such, the convention began to represent the conservative evangelical mainstream. Keswick had a clear emphasis on spiritual experience, teaching that victory over sin was available if claimed by faith.

George Jeffreys, a Welshman who was to become the founder of the Elim Pentecostal church, said that he had been taught to receive by faith and went to conventions such as Keswick seeking 'an experience that would satisfy'.

Although perhaps in more recent times overshadowed by events such as Spring Harvest, the Keswick Convention continues to this day. The motto of the convention is 'All one in Christ Jesus'.

---

[2] The Countess founded a denomination called the Countess of Huntingdon's Connexion, which still exists as a denomination. The nearest Countess of Huntingdon church to Altrincham is in Middleton. The denomination is particularly strong in Sierra Leone.
[3] Quoted in Dayton, D.W.: *Theological Roots of Pentecostalism*, The Scarecrow Press, 1987.

So where did the Altrincham Baptists stand in a period where the Baptist denominations were coming closer together but when the debate about election was very much a live one?

The first indication we have of a view on Calvinism is in the Abstract of the Lease of the Hale Road site, where the church is referred to as 'the Altrincham Calvinistic Chapel'. Llewellyn was a Spurgeon man and a Calvinist.

In 1889, Mowbray persuaded the church to adopt a statement of faith. It is actually quite moderate in view of the theology of the times. This doctrinal statement promulgated by Mowbray is perhaps more relevant than the 'standard' one set out in the trust deeds: that is because the Church Meeting approved the statement, whereas the trust deeds do not appear even to have been put by Mowbray to any Church Meeting. Lloyd also produced a statement of faith, but sadly we do not appear to have it.

The trust deeds of both Bowdon Baptist and Altrincham Baptist Church show that they associated with the then majority denomination: the Particular Baptists. This placed them in the Calvinist camp, but probably on a reasonably moderate basis. By the time of Lloyd, there is little evidence of an overt Calvinist theology. We have seen that in 1904 he used an evangelist who was linked with the Australian version of the Keswick Convention to conduct a mission. It seems that the church, in common with many others, either moved away from or heavily moderated its founding theology.

The Altrincham Baptists therefore followed the national trend in moving away from, or at least moderating, their Calvinist beliefs.

This photograph from 1909 shows just one of the many tents used at the vast Keswick Convention.

The core belief of the church was, of course, based on believers' baptism. It is to that doctrine that we now turn.

BAPTISM

Believers' baptism was fundamental to the very existence of the Baptists as a denomination. Without it, they would have been Congregationalists.[1]

The vicar of Bowdon wrote in 1856, 'There is a lull just now, in the great Baptismal controversy'.[2] In 1872, the arrival of the first Baptist church in Altrincham locally reignited the debate, but in a very different manner.

Lloyd no doubt read a book on baptismal regeneration by Joseph Angus, his Principal at Regent's Park College.[3] Lloyd himself later in life wrote a book about baptism[4] and this probably reflected his developing views while at Altrincham. Many of the Altrincham Baptists would also have read Williams' book, which contained a long section on believer's baptism.

So what did these Victorian Baptists understand by this 'believers' baptism'? It is important to understand this doctrine, which was central to their very existence as a denomination. In many respects, Baptist beliefs about baptism have changed little since.

Baptists held that only a believer could be baptised. An infant was too young to believe and therefore could not be baptised. However, believers' baptism was to them about the baptism of *believers*, which is not the same as adult baptism. The core concept for Baptists was the faith of the individual and not their age.

Jesus was dedicated as a child but baptised as an adult by full immersion in water (Matthew 3:13-17; Mark 1:9-11; Luke 3:21-22).

The early church practised believers' baptism. There are many references in the book of Acts to baptism. The Ethiopian official was baptised by Philip (Acts 8:26-40). Paul was baptised by Ananias after encountering Jesus on the Damascus road (Acts 9:1-19). Lydia, the businesswoman (Acts 16:11-15), and the Philippian jailer (Acts 16:25-34) were both baptised by Paul.

Many baptisms in the New Testament involve large amounts of water; for example, in Acts 8:38-39, it does seem as if there was a baptism by full immersion in water. The very word for baptism implies full immersion in water. The Greek 'baptizo' means literally 'to soak, plunge, drench or sink in water'.

There is little evidence to suggest that any other practice was followed before the third century. Archaeology appeared to backs that up. There were generally no early baptismal fonts; instead, baptisms were carried out by full immersion. Lloyd was clear that the baptisms of the New Testament were always of believers and by full immersion in water. He understood that there were no traces of infant baptism

---

[1] Many denominations other than Baptists also hold to Baptist views on baptism.
[2] Pollock, W.: *Foundations*, 1856. He was probably referring to the case of Revd George Cornelius Gorham, who the Bishop of Exeter refused to recognise as a Church of England vicar because of his theology on baptismal regeneration. The issue was not over believer's baptism. Instead Gorham did not believe that a person must be baptised (as an infant of course in this case) in order to be saved. Gorham eventually won his case. For a classic modern Anglican view on baptism, see Green, M.: *Baptism: Its Purpose Practice and Power*, Hodder and Stoughton, 1985. For a book which looks at the four main doctrines of baptism, see Armstrong J. (ed): *Understanding Four Views on Baptism*, (Counterpoints: Church Life), Zondervan, 2007.
[3] Angus, J.: *Regeneration: The Sonship That Saves Men*, 1897.
[4] Lloyd, F.C.: *18 Axioms concerning New Testament Baptism*.

at all in the first century and all the evidence pointed to full immersion in the early church.[5]

For Williams, conversion was crucial. Baptists believed it was God's command to be baptised as a believer. Peter was preaching to adults at Pentecost. 'When the people heard Peter's sermon they were cut to the heart and said to Peter and the other apostles, "Brothers, what shall we do?" Peter replied, "Repent and be baptised every one of you, in the name of Jesus Christ for the forgiveness of your sins. And you will receive the gift of the Holy Spirit!"' (Acts 2:37-38) To repent, those listening had to be old enough to understand Peter's message. After repenting, those same people were baptised as believers.

Baptists believe that infant baptism is not found in the New Testament – not even when Luke tells us that a person and their family were baptised (Acts 16:15,33; 1 Corinthians 1:16). If one looks at the whole passage, Baptists would say it is clear that the family cannot have included children too young to understand, because Acts 16:30-34 shows that those who were then baptised not only later listened to Paul and Silas preaching at midnight but also believed in God. These were unlikely to have been infants. Williams argued that trying to produce a doctrine (infant baptism) which runs counter to the whole thrust of the New Testament and which is based on something which might (but probably did not) happen is a dangerous thing.

One consequence for those who believed in infant baptism appeared, at the time at least, to be a belief that an unbaptised child might not go to heaven. This was part of the Anglican regeneration debate. To the Victorian Baptists, all this was mere superstition. Baptists did not accept the doctrine that an unbaptised infant would not be 'saved'. They could not, according to Williams, accept such an unjust God and did not agree with the practice of denying them Christian burial, along with suicides and the excommunicated. On the contrary, Baptists believed that infants who die before they commit actual sin go to be with God.

Lloyd focussed on the state of the believer. For him, there were three essential pre-requisites to be fulfilled before a candidate could be suitable for baptism: the new birth,[6] the clear mind and the right life.

McLaren went further than this. To him, even the baptism of a believer achieved nothing in itself. The baptism was a reflection and recognition of the spiritual act that had already occurred in the believer: the new birth itself. When McLaren addressed the Altrincham Baptists in 1878, he stated that the act of baptism was not a saving ordinance and there was no salvation connected with it. Baptists were baptised *because* they were saved, not baptised *to be* saved. This is the same as his understanding of communion.

Lloyd did not hold baptism to be a 'means of grace' but believed it was one of the appointed channels through which God has designated that his blessings will flow. In that respect, he was probably in advance of the times: baptism was a symbolic act but also more than that.

---

[5] Full immersion of infants continued for a long time even in the churches that baptised infants and was only eventually dropped on the rather obvious health grounds. Orthodox churches still fully immerse infants, doing this three times in the name of the Trinity.
[6] Lloyd was referring to the words of Jesus in John 3:33, 'I tell you the truth, no one can see the kingdom of God unless he is born again'.

Lloyd believed that publicity is also essential to baptism. Being baptised in secret defeats one of the points of the action: baptism is a public confession of faith.

'Though Baptism is intended to be an ordinance to be observed at, or near the commencement of the Christian life, yet it is incumbent upon all believers to submit to this command as soon as they realise it to be a requirement, of however long standing their Christian faith may be,' he wrote.

Lloyd, however, was not in this way trying to take people from other denominations; indeed he stressed quite the opposite. 'Christians associated with other than Baptist churches who come to see that the Baptism of the New Testament was always and only of believers by immersion, and to trust this command is in force today, are not, therefore, necessarily bound to leave their own communion and become members of some Baptist church.'

He believed that baptism should unite believers and not be a source of division.

Gladstone was a keen student of theology and read widely about the baptism debate. He had in his library a copy of the book by Angus and a book by Pusey,[7] who of course had diametrically opposite views to Angus. The book was inscribed, 'W.E. Gladstone –With Author's Kindest Regards'. Gladstone was a high church Anglican and as such would have agreed with Pusey. Gladstone heavily annotated his copy of the book by Angus. One can see from his annotations that he was clearly surprised to see that Angus had quoted Gladstone himself in an exchange of correspondence with a Congregational minister about baptism.

---

[7] Pusey, E.B.: *Scriptural views of Holy Baptism*, 1836.

Williams pointed out that early churches had full immersion baptisteries, as did the catacombs in Rome. Seen here is the baptistry at the Basilica of St John at Ephesus. Note the steps going down into the water. The second photograph shows the earlier Basilica of the Virgin Mary where a baptismal pool has been excavated. Both show pools designed for full immersion.

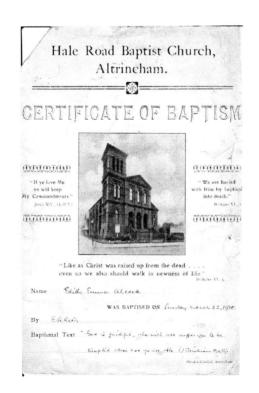

Baptismal certificate of Edith Alcock of 1925. Those baptised as believers received such a certificate.

"One Lord, One Faith, One Baptism."

Eph. iv. 5

"Buried with Him in Baptism, wherein also ye are risen with Him." *Col. ii. 12*

BRIAN DOUGLAS WATERSON

was Baptised on 14th OCTOBER 1956 **at**

Hale Road Baptist Church Altrincham

by Dr. J. R. C. Perkin

Joined the Church 14.10.56

Motto Text: "For I am not ashamed

of the Gospel of Christ"

Romans i 16.

Here is one issued to Brian Waterson in 1956.

An evening baptism service at Altrincham Baptist Church. The candidate, seated on the platform front, is interviewed by one of the three ministers of the church and tells of her Christian faith and explains why she wants to be baptised. Many of her friends are there to support her and pray with her later. The baptismal pool is underneath the platform and uncovered for baptismal services. Steps lead down into it from the platform.

218

Oldfield Brow Congregational Church was assisted by Bowdon Downs Congregational Church and Broadheath Congregational Church. In 1925 the Congregational Church took over the unused St Margaret's Mission Church in Lower Houses. The missioner was Robert Kay. In 1938 the Congregational Chapel on Taylor Road was built. The church was opened on 13 May 1939 by local architect and designer William Armitage.

In the early years of this century, Altrincham Baptist Church assisted Oldfield Brow, and at the time of writing the chapel is home to a combined Baptist-Congregational fellowship renamed 'Church on the Brow'. This is a rare modern example of a 'Union' church, where those wishing to become members can opt for believers' baptism or not.

As the Oldfield Brow chapel is a Congregational building, it has no adult baptistry, which leads to some improvisation, as shown here in a believer's baptismal service.

Revd Glen Marshall, formerly of Altrincham Baptist Church, preaches at Oldfield Brow and is seated front right next to Auriol Bevan. David and Auriol Bevan are co-pastors. Ron Kay, whose family has been involved in the church since its foundation, sits three rows directly behind Glen Marshall. David Hill, a former minister of Altrincham Baptist Church, is on the left front row with his wife Vivien.

Baptists all agreed on the theology of believers' baptism. It was the issue of membership that was to split them.

MEMBERSHIP

When McLaren spoke at the launch service of Bowdon Baptist Church in 1873, the *Freeman* reported him as having dealt with some very controversial topics. This was uncharacteristic of McLaren. Most of his published works are his sermons, and they usually deal with themes derived from specific, and usually very short, passages of Scripture.

Close to the start of his address he said:

'I think that the open fellowship people have solved the question in its relevant importance. I do not care so much about a right, the shadow of a shade, the mode of a mode, but in these days of wild sacramentalism you should bear testimony for the individuality of Christian profession and life. The one thing that binds a man to his Redeemer is his personal acceptance of and adhesion to His great work. Without that nothing is of any account. It is impossible that the leprosy of sacramentalism should creep into a Baptist church, but there is no reason that you should frown at each other over that open baptistry into which Mr Betts is to descend next Sunday. Have you ever refused to stretch out your hands when other denominations stretched out theirs? Dissenters are far more closely knit together than church men, who are only kept from tearing out each others eyes by the fear of damaging their gold spectacles.'[1]

Not exactly pulling his punches, McLaren here deals with sacramentalism, the closeness of Dissenters compared to the Church of England and issues about membership.

When McLaren addressed the launch service for the Hale Road building fund, he returned to this issue of membership. This cannot have been a coincidence. The topic was clearly important to him.

'I do not know what the constitution of this church is; I hope it is broad and liberal, as it ought to be. I believe that all Congregationalists ought to be united more closely together ecclesiastically as well as in sympathy; and while I do not want to ram my shibboleth down anybody else's throat, I do not know anything in the Christian character or in the mutual sympathies of Christian men why they should not have union churches multiplied all over the country.'

He pointed to MacKennal of Bowdon Downs Congregational Church and commented on the fact that they were sitting in the same pew. They were one in heart and sympathy 'in adherence to the one Lord, one in most of the great outlines of our congregation or polity'. He disagreed on one important point, however, a point which it was no use saying was an unimportant one, 'but I do not think it is so important as to constitute a basis of church membership, and it is not so important that you ought to shut out a man from the community of any church. This is my own theory, but I find the people in Lancashire uncommonly hard to convince.' The important point was, of course, believers' baptism, a doctrine not shared by the Congregationalists, but note that he classified Baptists as Congregationalists anyway.

---

[1] The reference to 'church men' is to Anglicans.

The newspaper records laughter at this comment, but it was also a serious point. It is possible that the lunch afterwards at the Downs Church may have been the occasion of the first meeting of these two men who were later to be prime movers in a bid to unite Congregationalists and Baptists and then all Nonconformists into one denomination.

McLaren then went on to take a side swipe at the Manchester and Salford Baptist Union: 'The Manchester and Salford Baptist Union has got a taint of narrowness about it which is not altogether in accordance with my own feeling; still, I have always worked heartily with them, and I hope I always shall.'

So what was this issue of open fellowship which was so close to McLaren's heart; an issue over which the local Manchester and Salford Baptist Union, original sponsors of the church, appeared to take one stance and McLaren another?

The issue was about who precisely could be a member of a Baptist church. Did one have to be baptised as a believer to be a member of the church, or could a Congregationalist join without being required to be baptised as a believer? Churches which allowed the latter were called 'open fellowship' or 'open membership' churches. This issue continues to dog Baptist Churches, sometimes because their trust deeds set out what practice they must follow, even today.[2]

Spurgeon advocated closed membership churches. McLaren's own church by contrast was a 'Union' church. Union churches were combined Baptist and Congregational congregations, with membership open to all believers regardless of whether or not they had been baptised as believers. The only requirement was for the minister to be a Baptist. Union Baptist in fact welcomed Presbyterians as members.

We can now make better sense of McLaren's comments to the Altrincham Baptists, and indeed possibly his side swipe at the Manchester and Salford Baptist Union, which favoured closed membership. McLaren was inviting MacKennal to respond to his public suggestion as to how close Baptists and Congregationalists were and should become.

MacKennal was clearly put on the spot by McLaren and he was cautious in his reply 'The distinction between the Baptists and Congregationalist is a real distinction and one of considerable importance; I suppose there are very few of us big enough and generous enough to hold in our minds similar views of various important points.'

The Altrincham Baptists too were put on the spot by McLaren. Were they open or closed membership? What legacy did that leave in their trust deeds? The answer is an interesting one.

The trust deeds of Bowdon Baptist Church of 8 October 1879 are clear: the Church Meeting could decide to admit anyone to membership who was not of the Baptist denomination, 'but such non-denominational members shall not be entitled to speak or vote at any Church Meeting on any matter in question affecting Baptism or any other principle or practice of the denomination aforesaid upon which they are not in agreement with its members.' Intriguingly, the book by Williams sets out verbatim the trust deeds of his own church in Accrington as well as those of McLaren's Union Baptist. Williams' book was published in the year the Bowdon Baptist trust

[2] Many ignore their trust deeds, particularly if the deeds contain a narrow understanding of membership.

deeds were being drawn up, and it may be that the Altrincham Baptists copied some of the text. If they did, they deliberately altered the Accrington model by adding in the qualification on voting rights. Williams' church was completely open membership without restriction.

Frank Spence in 1880 said that Bowdon Baptist Church was the first Baptist church in the day to have carried out the principle of open membership 'in a just and intelligible manner'. What he was probably referring to was precisely this qualification.

Those were the trust deeds of Bowdon Baptist Church. However, the trust deeds of Altrincham Baptist Church of 22 December 1892 tell a different story. They were drawn up for Mowbray and the deacons of the breakaway church when they bought the Hale Road chapel. These trust deeds omit any reference at all to open or closed membership. It is probable they were drawn up with the first set in front of the draughtsman. It was easiest just to delete the offending clauses. Unlike the position with other Baptist churches, the effect of this was to allow the church from time to time to decide whether it should be open or closed membership. This is perhaps fortunate for the modern church, which has the freedom to decide which practice it wishes to follow.

However, the intention of Mowbray and those who followed him to form Altrincham Baptist Church was soon made clear: notwithstanding the trust deeds, the church was to follow the Spurgeon model and to have closed membership.

We can now look further at the fifth resolution of the first meeting of Altrincham Baptist Church. It was proposed by William Franks and seconded by James Brewer. The first part read as follows:

'That the membership of the church as regards new members be confined to Baptised believers in Our Lord Jesus Christ.'

McLaren would not have been amused.

The issue of church membership has continued to be relevant at Altrincham Baptist Church in more modern times. Dr Nigel Wright, a former senior pastor, favoured more open membership, while George Beasley-Murray, the father of another former senior pastor Paul Beasley-Murray, wrote in 1966, 'If it is believed that open membership should continue, let it be clearly understood that it is solely *for members of other churches transferring into a Baptist Church'.*[3] The issues the Victorian Baptists faced still exist today. The current practice is a preference for new converts to be baptised as believers but people of good standing in other churches can transfer whether or not they are baptised as believers. Ultimately of course it is up to the Church Meeting to decide.

---

[3] Beasley-Murray, G., op. cit. The italics are his.

COMMUNION

In this chapter we look at the theological controversies over communion and find out why so many Baptist and other Nonconformist churches use individual glasses in which to take their communion wine instead of goblets. We start, however, with a Victorian debate about the very nature of communion.

In 1841, the Anglican E. B. Pusey, then Professor of Divinity at Oxford, preached a sermon which shook Victorian England. He argued that the presence of Christ in the eucharist (or communion) was not merely figurative but real, although he fell short of agreeing with the Roman Catholic doctrine of transubstantiation. This is the idea that the bread and wine at the Mass are the literal body and blood of the Saviour. He accepted, though, that the eucharist was a means of delivering spiritual blessing, independent of the faith of the believer. This is just the sacramentalism that McLaren so fiercely opposed.

The *Baptist Magazine* of 1841 commented on what it called 'Puseyism':

'It proclaims the efficacy of sacraments as the channels of grace, imparting regeneration and justification when administered by official hands, whatever be the mental or moral qualifications of the authorized administrator. It is a mode of religion which glories in the observance of forms, and in the pomp of ceremonies; which views holiness as consisting not only in the love of God and man, but as especially exemplified in fasts, and penances, and veneration rendered to holy times and places, to sacred relics, and departed saints.'

Williams stated that Baptists did not believe that the 'Lord's Supper'[1] was a sacrament: rather, it was an ordinance. It was commanded, but did not of itself give blessing. The blessing depended on the faith of the believer. This made most (but not quite all) Baptists what are called 'Memorialists'.[2] Williams wrote that communion 'is neither the cause nor the vehicle of grace'. The bread and the wine 'are signs and memorials of the body broken and the blood shed for them, not the broken body itself and the blood shed…To Baptists, the Lord's Supper is a service designed to bring the love of their dying Saviour, and especially himself, to remembrance, and so to aid the believer in his communion with the Lord.'

> In 1655, Warboys Baptist Church held 'love feasts' before communion, when the church would meet and have fellowship together, sometimes eating together. Baptist practices of communion have varied considerably over time.

Oddly, McLaren took a slightly wider view, preaching that 'the Communion of the Lord's Supper is meant to be a sample of, and not an exception to, our common days: and in the rite there lies a mighty power to make the whole of the rest of life like itself'. All of the items around us, he argued, like the bread and the wine, which are common elements, are to be regarded as symbols and memorials of our Lord. We are to look for Christ everywhere in life. Christians should take their love of Christ 'out into the street and the market-place with us, and work it out day by day, hour by hour, in patient endurance, in loyal love, in simple faith'. To McLaren, all of life was to be sacred and part of the believer's communion with God.

---

[1] I.e. communion.
[2] For a more detailed discussion, see Walker, M.J.: *Baptists at the Table: The Theology of the Lord's Supper amongst English Baptists in the Nineteenth Century*, Baptist Historical Society, 1992.

While most Nonconformists generally agreed on their theology of communion, the Baptists and Congregationalists struggled with a related issue.

In his 1878 address to Bowdon Baptist Church, McLaren said, 'I do not know whether Bowdon Baptist Church is a strict communion church or an open communion church. Whatever it is I wish God's blessing to rest upon it and Christ's spirit to be amongst the members of it.'

As well as choosing whether to be open or closed membership, a Victorian Baptist church had to choose whether it would allow those who were not members to take communion. In the words of the time, were they 'open communion' or 'closed (or strict) communion'.

This issue was most acute in the north west of England, where it split the Baptists more than anywhere else. The Particular Baptists split into the Particular Baptists and the Strict and Particular Baptists. One of the trigger-points for this split was a sermon by Williams himself on the atonement.

'Strict' and 'Particular' may seem quaint expressions to us now, but they were important to the Victorian Baptists. The 'Strict' Baptists were strict about who could attend communion and believed it should only be available to baptised believers. The Particular Baptists allowed those who were not baptised to attend communion, although there were controls to make sure that attenders were genuine believers.

In 1860 these tensions led to the separation of the strict communion North Western Baptist Association from the Lancashire and Cheshire Association.[3] The breakaway Association set up its own theological college at Bury. It only reunited with the Lancashire and Cheshire Association in 1875. One can see that in 1872, when Bowdon Baptist Church was formed, this was a very topical local issue, and is no doubt why McLaren mentioned it. The legacy of the split today is that many churches in the north west of England have trust deeds that prohibit open communion.[4]

Given the recent reconciliation after a split for which he had inadvertently provided the trigger, Williams in his 1879 book trod a careful path between the two opposing views. He did, however, point out the irony that Strict Baptists were similar in theology to Roman Catholics and Anglicans who would only allowed baptised persons (as they would describe them) to take communion, and indeed would require confirmation first.

So where did Bowdon Baptist Church stand? Although a Particular Baptist church, was it in fact also a Strict one? Near neighbour Baguley Baptist Church was a Strict and Particular Baptist church.

Both Betts and Llewellyn were put on the spot by McLaren at the two services. We have to remember that Llewellyn was trained at Spurgeon's College and it is likely that Spurgeon specifically assigned him to Bowdon Baptist Church. Spurgeon

---

[3] It is ironic that the Lancashire and Cheshire Association in more recent times changed its name to the North Western Baptist Association, the very name that the breakaway from the Association took in the nineteenth century.

[4] The Altrincham Baptists in more recent times have helped Milton Baptist Church. Milton was founded as a 'Particular or Calvinistic and Strict Communion Baptist' church. See Nixon, M.: *A History of the Baptist Church Milton Rough, Acton Bridge. From September 1899 to September 1972 and Other Early Notes Preceding*, 1998. As with membership issues, many Baptist churches today ignore the restrictions on communion in their trust deeds.

advocated closed membership but open communion. Llewellyn announced that Bowdon Baptist Church was an open communion church.

Would Mowbray later follow the same line? The fifth resolution of the breakaway church had a second limb to it as follows: 'But that the Communion of the Lord's Supper be open to members of all Christian churches.'

Even Mowbray was unashamedly in favour of open communion. In Lloyd's time, the church magazine regularly mentioned this fact. So the Altrincham Baptists were never in their history closed communion people.

We do not know the frequency of the early Bowdon Baptist communion services, but by the Lloyds' time, communion services were held once a month in the morning and once in the evening, and this practice generally still continues.

Today at Altrincham Baptist Church, communion is open to all believers of whatever denomination. It is a matter of personal decision as to whether to take communion or not. This is a public service.

Even though they were in favour of open communion, the Victorian Altrincham Baptists (and indeed many other Nonconformists) felt they needed to have more control over the process. Although Communion was open, it was not that open. How did one know if a visitor was really a Christian or not?[5] Those entitled to take communion were entered on a special list of communicant members and issued with communion tickets. The communion service took place after the main service and was only for those holding a ticket. The ticket was placed in the offertory so that a record could be kept. Visitors would be asked first where their allegiances lay. Brian Waterson, a former deacon of Altrincham Baptist Church, recalls the practice of issuing tickets and holding a separate and private communion service still continuing into the 1960s.

The ticket system was also a means of checking on attendance. Failure to attend would usually lead to a visit from the minister to see if there was a pastoral or health problem. Repeated failure to attend usually led to an official visit sanctioned by the Church Meeting. If the communicant member was also a full church member, the trust deeds contained restrictions on voting after six months failure to 'communicate', and generally a six month absence could lead to removal from membership.[6]

In effect, in common with other churches, the Altrincham Baptists created a two-tier system of membership. There were full members and a second group who, for whatever reason, did not wish or were not able to become full members by being baptised as believers. They could, however, take communion. In a sense, this went part of the way towards the concept of a Union church. It was also much more open than the Anglican or Roman Catholic churches, where communion was only available for those who had been confirmed into their respective denominations.

So finally in this Chapter we look at why so many Nonconformist churches use individual glasses to take communion rather than the one cup used by other

---

[5] Paul in 1 Corinthians 11:29 writes, 'For anyone who eats and drinks without recognizing the body of the Lord eats and drinks judgment on himself'. The Baptists and other Nonconformists perhaps also wanted to protect unbelievers from judgment.
[6] This has led to some very useful historical records. Nowadays, of course, no one would consider keeping any such records.

churches. Contrary to popular belief, there is no theological reason for this: indeed Paul in Corinthians refers to one cup.

In November 1901 the Altrincham Baptist Church deacons proposed moving away from the custom of only using chalices and suggested that individual cups should be made available as well. This followed a national trend in churches as they became teetotal. They purchased 200 cups and five chalices. The chalices appear soon to have been withdrawn. The new system was so unusual at the time as to merit a report in the local newspaper on the introductory service. Bread was served to everyone and then all partook together. The same happened with the wine. The hymn 'Take my life' was sung during the distribution of the wine.

Today, a choice of individual glasses or a communal cup is usually available. The reason for the change was nothing to do with theology, but was simply because of concerns about the health risks involved in many drinking from the same cup.

> The Marburg Colloquy was held in 1529 to enable the new Protestants to agree on doctrine. What they could not agree on was a doctrine of communion. Martin Luther and Zwingli took differing views, and those differences are still with us. Luther stressed the real presence of the body and blood of Jesus in the bread and wine, but Zwingli believed that communion was a memorial of what had happened and no more. Most (but not all) Victorian Baptists followed Zwingli. MacKennal, however, was no Zwinglian.

> Most Baptists in England in the twenty-first century are not Strict Baptists. Some progressive Strict Baptists in America now call themselves 'Grace Baptists'.

The communion table at Altrincham Baptist Church has an interesting history. Brian and Arlette Young from Altrincham met a German couple, the Hasenkrugs, while on holiday in Corfu. For the Hasenkrugs, it was the first time they had been to Western Europe since the Second World War, as they had lived in East Germany. In conversation, it turned out that Gerhard Hasenkrug had been a prisoner of war at Dunham Massey. Between 1945 and 1947, Gerhard attended Altrincham Baptist Church and repaired and restored an old table, which is now the current communion table. He returned in the 1990s, then aged 73, to see his table again.

The communion table set in the chapel in the 1980s before the refurbishment. Note the chairs behind the table in the photograph. In the 1980s, the deacons would sit behind the table with the minister.

We look next at the ultimate governing body of all Congregational churches.

THE CHURCH MEETING

Baptist churches are independent. This is because Baptists believe that the New Testament model of church is that each church takes responsibility for its own government. This explains why McLaren simply could not just shut Mowbray down when he set up on his own: he had no legal or constitutional right to do so. McLaren's only sanction was ostracism from the Association and the withdrawal of any subsidy. Neither of these sanctions worked.

Baptist churches, however, usually come together on a voluntary basis with other Baptist churches through a local Association, and then through the Baptist Union. The Altrincham Baptists, apart from the period of the Altrincham Tabernacle under Mowbray when the church was independent, associated with the Lancashire and Cheshire Association of Baptist Churches.

Baptist churches themselves are governed by their Church Meeting. Baptists are Congregationalists, which means that they believe that the Church Meeting is where the congregation comes together to decide matters under God. This can break down today if only a small part of the congregation attends the meetings. Victorian Baptists (including Williams) generally believed that the congregational model of church government was the closest to the New Testament pattern.

All ultimate legal and constitutional power in the church was therefore vested in the Church Meeting. It appointed (and could also remove) the minister and the officers of the church, and it alone could admit and dismiss members. It also had certain legal powers set down in the church trust deeds. For example, the sale of the church building usually needs a special resolution of a Church Meeting with a two-thirds majority, as Mowbray found to his cost.

> The ultimate sanction for a Church Meeting was to remove the privileges of membership from a member. Early Baptists sometimes took rather interesting decisions. In 1663, John Christmas of Warboys Baptist Church was expelled by the Church Meeting for 'not loving his wife enough'.

One of the benefits of membership to the Victorian Baptists was that they could attend Church Meetings and vote at them. This gave them a genuine say in the running of the church. The Church Meeting was, however, never intended to be a democracy, but rather a theocracy when the members could come together under God to decide various matters. This was true congregationalism in practice.

The extent of the power and responsibility of the Church Meeting itself was, and continues to be, the subject of much debate. Charles Williams represented one Victorian view, and to some modern ears it was a fairly radical one. He believed that the Church Meeting should only deal with matters of membership, the appointment of the minister and deacons and 'spiritual matters'. Once the minister and deacons were appointed, it was their sole responsibility to lead the church. If they got it wrong, they were accountable to the Church Meeting and could ultimately be dismissed.

This was clearly not the practice of many Baptist churches in Victorian times, and views about the role of the Church Meeting varied then as much as they do today. What happened at Altrincham appears in practice to have depended on the minister at the time and his relationship with the church. In the period covered by this book, there was never any express agreement by the Church Meeting as to how much power it delegated or retained for itself. Each change seems to have been a process of evolution over time. Setting anything down in writing would probably have been too complicated. It was all down to trust.

Mowbray held monthly meetings, but was sometimes prepared to take unilateral action. Key items were discussed at the meetings and sometimes it is fair to say that there was a 'full and frank discussion'. Only full church members were allowed to attend.

Lloyd kept to monthly meetings, but once a quarter he allowed communicant members to attend, and at these meetings he made sure every church organisation gave a full account of its activities. Although weighty matters were sometimes discussed, it is clear that the minister and deacons in Lloyd's time got on with much of the running of the church, probably because the church had more confidence in them than in the time of Mowbray. Lloyd was genuinely popular and trusted. Meetings were much calmer. Lloyd tended to put much more information in the church newsletter to update members, and his monthly Church Meetings usually dealt only with membership matters and major issues.

Both ministers however held an Annual Church Meeting, which reviewed all the affairs of the church and its finances.

What is interesting is that, in the period covered by this book, apart from the trust deeds which only dealt with 'high level' issues, there was never one coherent subsidiary constitution of the church.

The Victorians Baptists in Altrincham never had a set of agreed 'Church Rules'. Lloyd appears to have developed an understanding of what was expected of church members, but any 'rules' were minimal and were adopted almost on an ad hoc basis by successive Church Meetings. This is perhaps because people simply knew how things were supposed to run.

> There were more hymns in *The New Selection of Hymns for the use of Baptist Congregations* on the subject of the Church Meeting than on the birth of Jesus. There were, of course, far more on the crucifixion and the resurrection, but this shows how seriously Victorian Baptists took their Church Meetings or perhaps their ambivalent attitudes towards Christmas.

> John Smyth, one of the early English Baptists, wrote in *Paralleles*: 'We maintain that the power of the Eldership is a leading, directing and overseeing power, ministry or service, both in the kingdom and priesthood of the church, and that the negative voice, the last definitive determining sentence, is the body of the church whereto the Eldership is bound to yield, and that the church may do any lawful act without the Elders, but the Elders can do nothing without the approbation of the body.'

The day-to-day running of the church was mostly left to the minister and the deacons, and it is to them that we now turn.

THE PASTOR AND THE DEACONS

The Baptists believed that every member had a God-given ministry in the church. This stemmed from the teachings of Paul and their understanding of the biblical concept of the 'priesthood of all believers'.[1]

McLaren touched on the subject in his 1878 talk to the Altrincham Baptists. 'If this little church here has in it the real spirit of Evangelistic work, and has not got hold of the pestilent superstition – which the Congregationalists are apt to fall into, and which its Ecclesiastical progenitors in Scotland used to call "the one man system" – if you have not got hold of that pestilent superstition, but believe all Christ's people are priests, and all Christian men and women are Ministers and preachers, you will see a much larger and rapid increase in the future than you have seen in the past.'[2]

To Baptists, the minister held a special place, but equally he was also one of their number. All members had an equal and honourable role to play. This also meant they should not rely on their minister to do everything: all members should fulfil whatever their God-given role was.

It is at this stage in this book that the author needs to apologise to you for a device he has used thus far for convenience. The device is the use of the word 'minister' rather than 'pastor'. This is because the modern reader is more familiar with 'minister'. Victorian Baptists did not, however, particularly use the word in their own churches. They preferred what they saw as the more scriptural word, which was 'pastor'. It implied the role of tending to and leading the flock, all of whom engaged together in ministry. They also felt that a 'minister' had some official connotation. From now on we will use the word 'pastor'.

The day-to-day running of the church was left to the pastor and to the deacons.[3] If there was a period between pastors, the deacons were in sole charge. Baptists based their practice in relation to deacons on what they saw as the practice of the early church, where deacons were to administer the church in order to allow the apostles to get on with their primary calling of preaching and teaching.

At the very first meeting of Altrincham Baptist Church under Mowbray, it was agreed that there should be six deacons, of whom two should retire each year. They could be re-elected.[4] Sometimes, however, the church simply decided not to have an annual election for that year and to leave the existing deacons in post.

The deacons were all male. There was nothing to say this had to be the case, it was simply accepted. However, in 1902, the church appointed 'Sister Edith' as a deaconess. She was not a deacon as such, but a person appointed with specific pastoral duties and retained for a one-year period. The church in this respect was ahead of its time, although Bowdon Downs had earlier instituted separate elections for deaconesses. Today, there is no bar on women being deacons.

---

[1] 1 Peter 2:9: 'But you are a chosen people, a royal priesthood, a holy nation, a people belonging to God, that you may declare the praises of him who called you out of darkness into his wonderful light.' Baptists believed Peter was writing to all believers here and calling them all priests.
[2] The local reporter must have misquoted here. What McLaren almost certainly said (as above) was '…but believe all Christ's people are priests…', but he was reported as saying, 'that believes all Christ's people are priests…'. The latter goes against the whole sense of what McLaren was saying and believed anyway.
[3] Many early Baptists envisaged each church having several elders, but over time the role of elder came to be associated with that of the sole pastor who worked with the deacons.
[4] Curiously, in 1901, the church passed a resolution to have six deacons. Sometimes they simply forgot what they had agreed earlier. There were periods when there were fewer than six deacons.

It was key to the smooth running of the church that the deacons, church secretary, treasurer and pastor got on. It was the deacons who were responsible for paying the pastor. The church could usually rely on the fact that their own representatives were working with the pastor and nothing untoward would happen. The deacons worked as a constitutional safeguard on behalf of the Church Meeting. Sometimes they could take a pastor to task. In his farewell address to the Altrincham Baptists, Nankivell recalled how the deacons had sometimes challenged him, but he added he had never taken offence.

We do not know much about the deacons of Bowdon Baptist Church, but it is likely that Simmons was one of the early deacons. He was very much responsible for raising early funds for the church building. Edward Leech was certainly the church secretary at the time of the launch of the building fund. Overbury and Kenworthy were also deacons at different times, as was Southwell.

The first deacons of Altrincham Baptist Church were Southwell, Brewer, Bailey, Warburton, Franks and Hind. Bailey was the first treasurer. Warburton was the first church secretary.

Quite often, those who took the roles of secretary and treasurer seemed to swap roles. The treasurer and the secretary, however, usually worked closely together.

The choice of a new pastor was the responsibility of the Church Meeting under God's guidance. That is still true today, but in early Baptist churches, when a new pastor was to be appointed, the belief was that such a person could be called by God from the midst of the Church Meeting. Thus it was that, in early Victorian Baptist churches, a church member could suddenly find a hand on his shoulder and learn to his surprise that the Church Meeting had called him to be the pastor!

> During the Civil War, Baptists revived the tradition of the deacons washing the feet of church members, just as Jesus washed the feet of the disciples. It was a reminder that those in leadership were to serve the church.

By mid-Victorian times, this practice had more or less died away and it never happened at Altrincham. The procedure instead was very similar to that used now, in that the deacons led a search for a new pastor from outside the church and proposed that person to the Church Meeting, which had the final say. The Association would make recommendations but could not impose its choice, although we have seen that McLaren did his best to ensure Lloyd was appointed.

Pastors were appointed in accordance with the provisions of the trust deeds, which meant a Special Church Meeting had to be called and a two-thirds vote in favour obtained.[5]

The procedure for appointment of deacons, however, was subject to much debate amongst Baptists, and was not governed by the trust deeds. The Church Meeting therefore agreed on the relevant procedures from time to time. This could lead to some unusual results.

At a Church Meeting, everyone wrote down on a ballot paper who from the church members they thought should be appointed as deacons, secretary and treasurer. Those with the highest votes were appointed. In a similar manner to the early

---

[5] This is still what happens today.

appointment by Baptists of their pastors, a church member might suddenly find himself appointed as a church officer or deacon when he did not want to be one and had no idea he was even a possible candidate. Quite regularly we find that those appointed declined the post, leaving a period of total confusion. This happened at McLaren's church. It was only in 1876 that a system of nominations was introduced at Union Baptist.

Bowdon Downs, as a Congregational church, operated a similar system of appointment of deacons and regularly got itself in a muddle for the same reasons. A list was circulated of all male members and each member put a cross by five names. No one had any idea who would come out top, and regularly one or more chosen deacons refused office. At one election, all four chosen deacons refused to accept the honour.

The temptation for the church members was therefore to play safe and only to nominate those they thought might want to be elected. This was usually the existing deacons. In 1860 the Bowdon Downs deacons begged the church not to follow 'the system almost universally followed on these occasions by congregational churches' of electing the current deacons.

A similar system of voting appears to have been used at Altrincham Baptist Church, but because the church was smaller, it usually caused less difficulty, as it was fairly obvious who should be appointed to leadership positions. However, on 27 November 1895, the system failed at Altrincham too. Mr Whitelow was almost unanimously elected as a deacon and immediately announced he could not take up the post.

Early Baptists often laid hands on both those baptised and those elected to office that they 'may receive the promise of the Holy Spirit'.

Relations between the pastor and deacons were sometimes difficult under Mowbray. By comparison, Bowdon Downs Congregational was reasonably harmonious, but even there problems could arise. All the history books gloss over the departure of Professor Griffiths as pastor and what actually happened. This is the true story. In 1874, after ten years in office, there was a breakdown of trust between Griffiths and the deacons. Griffiths found another post and asked the deacons if he should accept. The deacons said he should. Griffiths effectively appealed over their heads by reading his own resignation letter to the Church Meeting. 'I am sorrowfully forced to the conviction that as there appears little hope of continued cordial co-operation, it is best for me at once to retire from this place.'

When the Bowdon Downs Church Meeting found out what had happened, they voted convincingly (sixty to nineteen) to ask him to stay. The deacons saw this as a vote of no confidence in them, so they resigned. Griffiths said he would stay if the Church Meeting elected deacons he could get on with. The Church Meeting re-elected the same deacons so he left anyway, albeit, as we have seen, with a substantial annuity arranged by the deacons.

This photograph shows the church office of Altrincham Baptist Church at Hale Road in 2007 before it moved to Pownall Road. In Victorian times, the pastor and deacons ran the church without a church office. In 2008, the church office relocated to the former Pownall Road Centre, re-named 'The Hub'.

Lloyd (front row second from left) and his deacons (precise date unknown).
Charles Southwell Snr is front left.

We now turn to look at what the Victorian Nonconformists regarded as the key role of any pastor: that of preacher.

THE SERMON AS POPULAR CULTURE

The pulpit was king. In the days before television and radio and before the cinema gained in popularity, the Victorians loved a good sermon. The essential quality of a pastor was usually his ability to preach. Thousands flocked to hear preachers such as McLaren and Spurgeon. The sermon was the centre-piece of any Nonconformist service. This reflected the central place that the scriptures held in their beliefs.

What were these sermons like? To a generation with a short attention span and used to little detail, Victorian sermons would probably seem dull and too full of scriptural detail. To the Victorians, they were riveting and full of interest.

McLaren was a scholarly man. He would spend many hours in sermon preparation each week. This paid off in the depth of knowledge and understanding he brought to a passage. He has, in fact, been credited with inventing the three-point sermon. This was a radical new way of preaching and was much imitated.[1] Throughout his preaching life, however, he never went into the pulpit without extreme nervous anxiety. He was fundamentally a shy man but once in the pulpit, he managed to master his nerves, and his congregations were usually unaware of his worries.

His sermons were always Bible-based and he rarely ventured into the political arena. Usually, he would preach from just one or two verses, expanding and expounding to obtain every last nuance and meaning. Although the tone of his sermons was mostly sober and delivered in a quiet Scottish way, there were flashes of humour. People spoke of his words thrilling them like electricity. His church was packed. He always left his hearers with a challenge to their spiritual walk.

Someone transcribed each sermon, and they were then compiled and published. Even today, they contain much of interest.

In his 1901 address to the combined Baptist and Congregational Unions, McLaren himself described what he saw as the three essential qualities of a preacher: he must be an evangelist, a teacher and a prophet.

> Robert Hall, a pastor at Cambridge who died in 1831, was such a powerful preacher that people would spontaneously stand during his sermons. By the end of his sermons, a good proportion of the congregation was usually standing.

McLaren and Spurgeon admired each other, but had very different preaching styles. Spurgeon was much more effusive. McLaren said of Spurgeon's sermons: 'There is a passion of love to Jesus, and a grand fullness of trust in Him which have stirred and rebuked me.'[2] Of his own style, Spurgeon wrote in his autobiography: 'For my own part when the Lord helps me to preach, and after I have delivered all my matter, and I have fired off my shot so fast that my gun has grown hot, I have often rammed my very soul into the gun, and fired my heart at the congregation, and this discharge has, under God, won the victory.'

MacKennal by contrast was much more literary and philosophical in style than either McLaren or Spurgeon. As an amateur poet himself, he would often quote from Wordsworth or Tennyson. His series of sermons on the seven churches in the

---

[1] The three-point sermon divided the talk into three distinct sections, and often each section had its own subsidiary three points. This prevented preachers from rambling and provided a clear structure. It is out of favour with most preachers these days. In the ancient world, bolstering an argument with three points was a well-tried device.
[2] McLaren, E.T., op. cit.

book of Revelation is peppered with poetry.[3] However, he could also preach a fairly hard-hitting political sermon.

Sadly, we have no notes of any sermons preached by the early Altrincham pastors, although there is brief mention of Mowbray's second sermon to Altrincham Baptist Church in the local newspaper on the subject of the differences between Judaism and Christianity. We do however have some information about their styles of preaching and their ability as preachers.

They would all, of course, have been much influenced by Spurgeon and McLaren. Some forty volumes of Spurgeon's sermons were printed, and McLaren's sermons appeared in just about every issue of the denominational newspaper, the *Freeman*. The Altrincham pastors had much material to use, and could hear McLaren in Manchester anyway if they wished.

Betts was a friend of Spurgeon's and Llewellyn was a student at his college. Mowbray was almost certainly an avid reader of Spurgeon's writings.

Betts we are told had a fine presence and was nearly six feet tall and 'his powerful and musical voice and his ready command of words were remembered by all'.[4]

Llewellyn 'regarded his spiritual work as preaching'.

Mowbray was 'remembered as a forceful preacher and held in high esteem by all who knew him'. There was, however, a curious resignation which perhaps illustrates that his style of preaching was not to everyone's taste.

A certain John and Emily Griffiths returned from America in June 1888 to settle down again in Altrincham. There was going to be a long delay in transferring their membership from the American church and therefore it was agreed that they should be accepted into membership without transfer. They went to Mowbray's Tabernacle rather than to Hale Road. It is possible that John Griffiths was the same person who was one of the original trustees of Bowdon Downs Congregational. They were certainly well known in the area.

By 1st May 1889 Griffiths had become a deacon at the breakaway church, but in June 1890 he resigned. His resignation was over Mowbray's sermons. The change in tone from the sermons he had heard in America was clearly too much for him. He found Mowbray's style too 'declamatory and autocratic'. The church members, however, did not agree. They enjoyed Mowbray's direct style of preaching and they agreed to accept the Griffiths' resignation. Griffiths and his wife left and went to Bowdon Downs, where they perhaps found MacKennal's intellectual and refined style more to their taste.

We know more about Lloyd's preaching. As we have seen, he was a highly educated man, more so than any of his predecessors. His sermons were always 'marked by a brilliant yet restrained and dignified gift of illustration, by a topical relevance boldly presented, and above all by a timeless appositeness which, in fundamental Christian exegesis, would have made them acceptable to any congregation at any time in the Christian era'.[5]

---

[3] MacKennal, A.: *The Seven Churches in Asia Considered as Types of the Religious Life To-Day* (sic), 1895.
[4] All quotations in this chapter are from Baptist Union handbooks unless otherwise stated.
[5] Comber, L.T.: *Colour Blind: The Life of the Rev F. Cowell-Lloyd, ATS, of Jamaica*, The Carey Kingsgate Press Limited, 1959.

He prepared his sermons thoroughly, writing them out in full in his own handwriting. Then he did an extraordinary thing: he left his notes behind when he went into the pulpit to preach. He knew well what he was going to say, but this technique of preaching without a single note in front of him enabled him to be more spontaneous, to adapt his sermons to the reaction of his congregation and to vary them if he felt there was a special message to deliver at a particular time.

We even know something of Lloyd's preaching topics, at least for 1904 and 1905. He would generally pick a series of passages or a theme. In 1904, the church's motto was 'Be ready in the morning, and come up in the morning'. The first sermon series was on the Christian's spiritual armour. The following series was 'Gideon's Band', 'exploits', 'house-building' and 'the slave owner'. This was followed by a morning series of four sermons on the burnt offering, the peace offering, the sin offering and the guilt offering and on Sunday evenings he spoke on the death of Jesus with 'I thirst', 'It is finished' and 'Into thy hands'.

It is sad that we have no transcripts of any sermon preached in a Baptist church in Altrincham for the period covered by this book. We do, though, have the text of two sermons preached by Lloyd after he left Altrincham. One is described in Appendix 4.

> Although they did not invent the sermon (early Baptists used to devote every Sunday morning to a series of sermons), the Victorians developed the concept. Victorian sermons were longer than the sermons of today. John Betjeman gently satirised the Strict Baptists in *Archie and the Strict Baptists*,[6] a story in which the preacher would preach for an improbable five hours. When the pastor was not there, Archie the teddy bear would preach for eight or nine hours until the chapel had emptied. A Victorian Altrincham Baptist sermon was probably quite long, but considerably shorter than that preached by Archie. Archie was, in fact, Betjeman's real teddy bear and became the model for Sebastian Flyte's bear, Aloysius, in *Brideshead Revisited* by Evelyn Waugh.[7]

[6] Betjeman, J.: *Archie and the Strict Baptists*, John Murray, 1977.
[7] Waugh E.: Brideshead Revisited: The Sacred and Profane Memories of Captain Charles Ryder, Penguin Books Limited, 2000.

Union Baptist Church was demolished to make way for St Mary's Hospital in Manchester, but the successor church at Fallowfield has preserved McLaren's pulpit. The caption on the pulpit reads 'A man of God. A prince of preachers.'.

The congregation listening to a sermon at a morning service of Altrincham Baptist Church in 2007. From 2005 to the date of publication of this book, morning services have been held at the former Trinity Presbyterian chapel in Delamer Road.

By an amazing accident of history, we have the entire text of one early sermon that it is very likely the early Altrincham Baptists would have heard. That sermon was preached in 1872 at the independent Congregational church out of which the first Altrincham Baptists probably came.

The sermon covered disease control and the latest theory on global cooling. Who preached it, and why did he choose such topics?

GLOBAL COOLING AND SUFFERING

Professor Griffiths spoke on what was called Hospital Sunday, a day when many churches supported local hospitals. Griffiths was then the pastor of Bowdon Downs Congregational Church before MacKennal, and Bowdon Downs supported Lloyd's Fever Hospital. We have already looked at his unfortunate departure from Bowdon Downs, but in 1872, (the year of this sermon) that still lay in the future.

His congregation was the independent Congregational church where he was the visiting preacher. His sermon is therefore particularly interesting as the Baptists, although already planning their departure to set up Bowdon Baptist Church, would probably have been present to hear him at the old Wesleyan chapel on Regent Road, now the home of the independent church.

His passage was Lamentations chapter 3: 'For the Lord will not cast off for ever. But though he cause grief, yet will he have compassion according to the multitude of his mercies. For He doth not afflict willingly nor grieve the children of men.'

Victorian sermons often dealt with the realities of suffering and death. Griffiths was no exception in tackling such topics, but despite that, his sermon is surprisingly modern and forward-thinking. Like many Victorian evangelicals, he had a passion for social justice. First he began with an explanation of the use of the twenty-two letters of the Hebrew alphabet in Lamentations 1 and 2 and then the use of a three times twenty-two pattern in chapter 3. This had absolutely nothing to do with his sermon, but perhaps he felt a scholarly beginning was essential for his audience.

He then plunged into his first theme. There was great suffering worldwide and in the towns and cities of Britain. There was 'social outlawry, extreme poverty and want, monstrosity, disease...'

Eleven years before Krakatoa, he told the story of an island in the far east of 12,000 people devastated by lightning, floods and 'fire streams', leaving twenty-six survivors.[1] Even in 1872, there was famine in Persia. Much of man's misery, he believed, was brought about by man himself. In a passage which resonates with issues relevant today, he said: 'If they will trample on the laws of organic life – consumption, decrepitude, fever, paralysis, are to be expected as matters of course! If they will hasten to be rich, they must pierce themselves with many thorns!'

Next, he turned to his main theme. Smallpox, which was creeping through the 'towns and villages, might very soon be stamped out of the world, if we would only agree to do so (as I believe to be the fact)'. He went on to say, 'It is confessedly one of life's deep mysteries, that there should be so little apparent connection between piety and personal prosperity.'[2] The key, he thought, is compassion. Whatever happens on the earth, God is in charge and wants us to exercise compassion. God will never destroy the whole earth until the end of time. Whatever current scientific thought on the end of the world, God is in control.

---

[1] This was probably the eruption of Mount Merapi in Java in 1872. Krakatoa is in the same general area and is between Java and Sumatra. Merapi was a precursor of the massive Krakatoa explosion in 1883, over 13,000 times the power of the Hiroshima nuclear bomb.
[2] Most Victorian Nonconformists would have had little sympathy with the 'health and wealth' doctrine that has come out of America in the late twentieth century.

He then went on to deal with the concepts of suffering: 'Can a just God cause suffering?' 'God does not afflict willingly'. 'God will not forsake those who put their trust in Him'.

Griffiths then came to his conclusions:

1.   Suffering is a corrective force. It is not natural to God's universe and will disappear when Christ returns.

2.   As children of the light, we must do everything in our power to mitigate the violence of suffering.

3.   There is a higher duty 'on which our public have much need to be instructed - that is, the duty of scrupulous personal attention to the laws of public health, as far as those laws can be discovered'. All children must be vaccinated, especially the congregation's own. They should support the hospitals but first 'stop disease spreading'. In answer to the question, 'Am I my brother's keeper?', he would reply 'yes', particularly in this context.

4.   They should also attend to their own spiritual and moral condition. 'What may be the average number of deaths from PREVENTABLE PESTILENCE[3] from licentiousness, overcrowding, neglect of ventilation, and want of proper nourishment, I have no means of estimating. Their sum total must be sometimes terrible to think of! And is this to go on to the end of time? We have not so read the analogies either of Providence or of Scripture!...His will is, that to our utmost, we should always and everywhere, carry on against them a war of extermination!...We do not say, that sickness is ever to disappear entirely from our world; but we may do so without hesitation, that many of its most loathsome, and most fatal epidemical forms ought to have disappeared long ago, and will infallibly disappear as soon as men come to form right notions of the laws of health.'

It was a very Victorian sermon, but also a very modern one, and thought sufficiently important at the time to be printed and distributed locally.

In his sermon, Griffiths referred to two contemporary scientific theories. One was that the earth would spin into the sun and burn up, and the other was global cooling. The latter was the accepted scientific wisdom until the 1980s, although some global warming theories still predict severe cooling for the United Kingdom.

As the sermon touched on disease, we look now at disease and the Victorian way of death.

---

[3] The capital letters appear to be those authorised by Griffiths.

DISEASE AND THE VICTORIAN WAY OF DEATH

The Victorians were familiar with death. It was, so to speak, an everyday part of life. Children died, women died in labour; life expectancy was short; fatal infectious disease was common.

Funerals were a routine sight. The middle classes would have a lavish funeral after the coffin had lain open in the parlour for all to see. The hearse would be a glass coach full of flowers but covered in sable and crepe. Horses nodding with black plumes would pull the hearse and might be preceded by paid mutes who were swathed in black shawls and with drapes over their hats. The mourners would process down the streets behind the hearse.

Lower-class funerals were less lavish, but even then were serious affairs. The burden of paying for funerals was a heavy one for poorer families, so in 1819 the Altrincham Funeral Society was formed. This enabled families to pay subscriptions over time, to spread the cost and then the Society would pay for the funeral.

After a funeral, women were expected to wear mourning clothes for a long time, men for less. A widow was expected to be in mourning for a year and a month for her husband, and to wear bombazine covered with crepe, a widow's cap, lawn cuffs and collars. Given the number of deaths in a family and the differing periods of mourning prescribed for different relatives, a woman could be in mourning for long periods of her life.

Funerals and burials were a source of tension between Nonconformists and the Church of England. Until 1852 Nonconformists had no separate areas in Anglican cemeteries for burials. In 1876 the local newspaper in Altrincham reported continuing problems over this. In 1880 Nonconformists were finally allowed to hold their own funeral services in parish churchyards. The non-denominational cemetery on Hale Road was only opened in 1894, and that was after Home Office intervention, a public inquiry and years of local opposition.

The Baptists were therefore buried in Church of England graveyards (usually St Mary's churchyard), but once it was built, they were mostly buried in the public cemetery on Hale Road.

Infectious disease was a major cause of premature death. Sanitation was poor, causing the spread of disease. In the 1870s the first attempts were made to carry out serious improvements. Oddly, it was the Conservatives under Disraeli who championed public health reform, and it was Disraeli who introduced the great Public Health Act of 1875. The Altrincham Baptists later passed resolutions complaining about the poor state of sanitation and the disposal of ash in the area. These were not trivial issues; people were beginning to appreciate the link between poor sanitation, bad housing and disease.

The Victorians began to grapple with housing provision in the 1870s and to embrace municipal planning. Manchester City Council opened up Deansgate in 1869 and in the same year appointed its first Medical Officer of Health. Housing in the slum areas of Altrincham was still poor. Steps to improve matters had, however, been taken in 1851 with the formation of the Local Board of Health. Dr Arthur Ransome, Professor of Hygiene at Owens College and driving force behind St Anne's Home in Bowdon, lectured at the YMCA in 1876 on 'Foul Air and Lung Disease'.

Tuberculosis was the biggest single cause of death in Victorian England, and Ransome and St Anne's were pioneers in its treatment.

However, the disease that really brought the requirement for decent sanitation to the attention of the authorities was cholera. Cholera was imported into Britain through trade and thrived on poor sanitation. Two-thirds of the deaths in the Crimean War were from illness and hardship, not from battle. Many of these were from cholera. At first, doctors believed cholera was spread by 'miasma' in the air, but a certain John Snow realised this was wrong and in 1849 published *On the Mode of Communication of Cholera*. Edwin Chadwick campaigned for better sanitation, but it was a hard struggle. It was only in 1883 that Robert Koch isolated and identified the cholera microbe. There were three main cholera epidemics in Victorian Britain. The one in 1848-49 killed 61,000; 26,000 died in 1853-54 and 17,000 in 1866.

A hospital was built in Altrincham in the 1840s on Hale Moss. This was a rudimentary structure, so Lloyd's Fever Hospital was opened in 1853, just in time for the cholera epidemic. It stood on Lloyd Street just to the Newtown side of the railway bridge.

With a population for Altrincham alone[1] rising from 4,488 in 1851 to 12,424 in 1891 and with such poor health conditions, there was a clear need for Lloyd's Fever Hospital. It was founded by the widow of Edward Jeremiah Lloyd of Oldfield Hall in his memory. She donated £300 and the other £300 was raised locally. Bowdon Downs Congregational Church contributed to its upkeep, as well as to the main Altrincham hospital.

Fever hospitals at that time did not treat people in isolation: someone with a broken leg could be treated in bed next to someone with typhoid. The chances of cross-infection were dramatically increased, and often it could be worse to go into hospital than to stay at home. Hospital conditions, however, gradually improved during the Victorian period.

Sanitation in Altrincham was still desperately poor at the time the new fever hospital was built. The town lacked a proper water system and even a proper sewage disposal system. Sewage ran through the streets and dysentery and typhoid were common. There were six cases of typhoid in 1872 in Altrincham, two of them fatal. In 1872 the death rate was 19.5 per thousand.[2] Sewage was deposited in Timperley Brook until as late as 1869. In 1877 a resident of Railway Street wrote anonymously to the local newspaper to complain that his cellars had been filled with sewage four times in eight months.

From 1870 to 1905, John Stokoe was responsible for many sanitation improvements in Altrincham, but even in 1899 the Altrincham and Bowdon Provident Society, a pressure group and Christian fund-raiser for the poor in the area, reported through H. E. Gaddum on the poor state of slum housing.

Many diseases were partly a function of poverty. One local newspaper editorial in 1874 stated: 'Still the fact remains that one, if not both the fevers attacking the community, are favoured by unsanitary conditions of dwelling houses; and it is not

---

[1] That is, excluding Hale and Bowdon for example.
[2] Source: Altrincham and Bowdon Guardian.

a little interesting to notice in this regard, the almost entire exemption of the higher ground of Bowdon from these diseases'.

There were still regular outbreaks of the dreaded smallpox. In late Victorian England, it was a fact of life. An estimated 300 million people died of smallpox worldwide in the twentieth century alone. The disease kills roughly one third of those it infects and leaves others hugely disfigured. In 1882, MacKennal noted euphemistically at Bowdon Downs that Sunday school numbers had been 'thinned' by smallpox.

Smallpox, however is entirely preventable. Lady Mary Wortley Montagu is credited with introducing the first inoculation to Britain in 1721. Severely pockmarked herself after surviving the illness, she learnt about the procedures in Constantinople, where her husband was the British Ambassador. She had her children inoculated and persuaded the Princess of Wales to do the same. The procedure was not without risk, and those treated could still be infectious to others.

In 1796 Edward Jenner inserted pus extracted from a cowpox pustule on the hand of a milkmaid into an incision on the arm of an eight-year-old boy called James Phipps. Jenner proved conclusively that contracting cowpox provided immunity against smallpox. In 1801 he wrote, 'It now becomes too manifest to admit of controversy, that the annihilation of the Small Pox, the most dreadful scourge of the human species, must be the final result of this practice.'

It took time, however, for inoculation to be taken up. The 1867 Vaccination Act brought in some penalties for not inoculating children. There were conscientious objectors to inoculation. In 1869 and 1870 Lloyd's Hospital in Altrincham treated twenty-two and twenty-four smallpox patients respectively. Increasingly, however, smallpox was becoming a disease of the poor.

On Saturday 10 February 1872, the *Manchester Examiner and Times* reported that smallpox was once again on the march. The Ebbw Vale Company surgeon wrote that he had 1,235 reported cases of smallpox and 118 deaths. However, he added that 'I have not had a single case of smallpox in a person who has been properly revaccinated'.

Griffiths was right that there could be a recurring smallpox problem in Altrincham. In February 1877 the medical officer reported thirteen cases in Altrincham with a further eight suspected. One man brought his servant, who had smallpox, by train from Brooklands to the Fever Hospital and was fined in court for doing so. Poorer houses were disinfected with chloride of lime. Locals expressed fears that patients were being taken to the hospital in cabs, although this was officially denied.

The last outbreak of smallpox in Britain was in the Rhondda Valley in Wales in 1962. The World Health Organisation only began its campaign to eradicate smallpox worldwide in 1966 but succeeded by 1977. Today, smallpox has been eradicated as a disease and only survives in laboratories, but it is still feared as a potential bio-terror weapon.[3]

Griffiths was also right that smallpox could be eradicated by vaccination, but it took a long time.

---

[3] In a population without immunity, the results would be similar to the devastation caused in the eighteenth century among Native American Indians who had no natural immunity and were sometimes given blankets infected with smallpox.

Lloyd's Fever Hospital and part of the area of
Newtown, now demolished, in 1898.

The site on Lloyd Street of Lloyd's Fever Hospital.   *Altrincham General Hospital in 2009.*

Hale Cemetery, where many Baptists are buried.

THE ASCENDANCY OF THE ORGAN

The organ has a long history. As long ago as the tenth century AD, there was an organ at Winchester Cathedral with forty stops and two manuals. It reputedly took ten men to produce sounds from it. The oldest surviving organ in England is at Wingfield in Suffolk, dating back to about 1530.

In the Church of England, organ use for a long time was mainly associated with cathedrals and cathedral choirs. In contrast, in Lutheran Germany, the organ was used more for congregational worship.

Pre-Civil War organs in England tended to be single manual and quite small. The Dissenters, however, did not approve of what they saw as the Roman Catholic nature of the organ, and destroyed many of them during the rule of Cromwell. After the Restoration, organs were re-introduced into the Church of England. The first swell organ was installed in 1712 at St Magnus the Martyr in London and in 1803 the first separate pedal organ was introduced at St Mary Magdalen in Newark.

What may surprise you is that the use of the organ was generally the exception rather than the rule in most churches until well into the reign of Victoria. The organ replaced unaccompanied singing or the use of musicians.

What happened was that the organ became a status symbol for Victorian churches. Trinity Presbyterian on Delamer Road installed an organ in 1875 and held two special services and a full evening recital to celebrate. The local newspaper even listed each stop, and noted their size and the 'lightness of touch' of the keys. St Mary's, Bowdon, installed a replacement organ in 1875, followed by St Margaret's in 1876.

The early Baptists were suspicious of the organ. To them, it smacked of the established church with all its pomp and ceremony. For them, worship was to be simple and of the heart and to hark back to the worship of the early church. Instead of the organ, they either sang unaccompanied or used musicians, usually in a gallery if there was one, or if not, in a separate area near the front.

Some Strict Baptist churches however even disapproved of musicians on theological grounds. The Gospel Herald, the newspaper of the Strict Baptists, had an extraordinary exchange of correspondence in 1884 about this. The editor wrote an article entitled 'Musical instruments have no place in worship'. A correspondent came back with the query: 'I should be very much obliged for your opinion of the exhortation to praise God with all kinds of instruments, contained in the last Psalm.' Undaunted by the clear biblical precedent for the use of musical instruments of a wide variety in worship, the editor replied by asking why one should therefore leave out the dance as there is the same exhortation for the dance as for music. The editor then simply stated that music has no place whatsoever in the spiritual worship of God. 'By what authority does anyone assume the right to pick out one or more of those typical rites and introduce them into the service of God?' There was no warrant for the 'carnal service of musical instruments in the House of God'.

The introduction of musicians could lead to splits. In 1843, members of Myrtle Street Baptist Church in Liverpool left to found Pleasant Street Chapel 'having conscientious objection to the introduction of musical instruments into the worship of God'.

Particular Baptists, however, as opposed to their Strict cousins, were more likely to welcome musicians. Before the

An example of early Baptist debates about music comes from Broadmead Baptist Church in the seventeenth Century, where the pastor, a Mr Ignello, was disciplined because he 'enjoyed music too much'. The church also disapproved of his 'flaunting apparel; for he, being a thin, spare, slender person, did goe very neate, and in costly trim'.

introduction of the church organ, there was an honourable tradition of musicians playing in a gallery in churches of all denominations. This probably pre-dated any serious use of the organ and gave the service a more 'folk' feel. No doubt the standard of musicianship was varied, and the musicians might sometimes be temperamental, but many churches either could not afford an organ or did not want one. Some claim that modern worship groups represent a more authentic version of worship, with their 'folk' element, rather than the more modern pipe organ. The removal of the organ at Altrincham Baptist Church in the 1990s could therefore be seen in a sense as a reversion to a pre-organ type of music.

When the Revd Oswald Leicester, the first incumbent of St George's Church in Altrincham, arrived at the church he found 'there was a choir, bassoons, violincellos and other instruments with which wondrous sounds were produced'.[1] He used to send his entire orchestra to the Methodist church on Regent Road for combined evening services, but even St George's introduced an organ in 1837.

While the Strict Baptists continued with unaccompanied voices, the Victorian Particular Baptists began to embrace the organ, forgetting that their Dissenting forbears opposed it. Like others, they saw the organ as technological progress in music.

However, there were still Baptist churches being built even in the late Victorian era with space for orchestras. An example is Burslem Baptist Tabernacle. It was built in the Italian style and pre-dated the Hale Road chapel by only two years. It had an orchestra area capable of seating sixty players. The whole church could seat 370 persons and fifty more if needed.[2]

Even the Strict Baptists eventually began to use musicians. W.T. Whitley wrote of the struggle:

'Meeting-houses were presently parcelled out by upright partition, like the stalls in a stable or coffee-house, and the importance of the music began to evidence itself in the space reserved for the performers. Strict and Particular Baptists largely adhere to this type still, as their Chapel at Preston evinces. Here however the ambition of the fiddlers often came into conflict with the feelings of the people generally, and many minutes give glimpses of the struggle, by no means silent.'[3]

---

[1] Leech H.J.: *Tales and sketches of old Altrincham and Bowdon*, 1880. Leech was later organist and choirmaster for the Baptists.
[2] Baptist Union Handbook, 1878.
[3] Whitley, W.T.: *Baptists of North West England 1649-1913*, G. Toulmin, 1913.

We do not know for certain what musical instruments they used in the initial Bowdon Baptist Church on The Downs. We know they used a harmonium played by Miss Simmons, but whether they used a small orchestra or both we do not know, although we do know that concerts sometimes featured a small orchestra. It is unlikely they could have afforded an organ, and there is certainly no record of one being bought from the Congregationalists or Presbyterians or being installed. Even if they had an organ, it would have been hand-pumped as there was no available electricity.[4]

What we do know is that a harmonium was used by the Betts family when entertaining in The Downs chapel and was used for the evening worship at the British School on the occasion of the December 1878 launch for the new Hale Road building. The new Hale Road Baptist Chapel had a harmonium. We do not know whether instruments were used as well, but it seems likely that the harmonium was by then the principal source of music.

The Altrincham Tabernacle under Mowbray also used a harmonium. Mowbray either bought it or hired it and included it in the rent the church paid him. In the 1889 accounts for the church at Hale Road, sixteen shillings was paid for the hire of a harmonium for the year.

A harmonium was a reed organ with a foot pump, and was popular in Victorian houses and for musical soirées. It would not have been as powerful as a full church organ and the congregation had to sing more enthusiastically.[5]

> The introduction of the organ into churches was not a clean sweep at first. Both expense and tradition were factors. *Under the Greenwood Tree* by Thomas Hardy contains a fascinating insight into a pre-organ and pre-Pusey Church of England in this respect.[6]

The only picture of the church harmonium, or was this a piano?

---

[4] The author recalls a hand-pumped organ still being used in Lonan church on the Isle of Man in the 1970s, and the amusement of the younger people when the person pumping sometimes failed to deliver enough air from the bellows during a hymn. Lonan Old Church still uses a pedal harmonium.

[5] Readers at the time of writing can visit the Reed Organ & Harmonium Museum, Victoria Hall, Victoria Rd, Saltaire, Shipley, Yorkshire, where it may be possible to try a harmonium for themselves.

[6] Hardy, T.: *Under the Greenwood Tree*, 1872. Wainwright lectured to the St John's Recreative Society in 1893 on Under the Greenwood Tree using seventy lantern slides. It would be fascinating to have heard his comments on church music.

The organ and electric lighting were installed in 1908.
This shows an early harvest festival.

The chapel before the 1980s refurbishment. The organ
is still there and the pews are still in place, but note the
beginnings of a small music group.

A similar photograph after a morning service from the musicians' area.

Letter from the organ builders Jardine and Co in 1911 about replacement of the organ following rain damage.

The main hall at the time of writing. The organ was removed in the 1990s refurbishment. As well as use for worship, the hall has a variety of uses. Here it is cleared of chairs.

Altrincham Baptist musicians at a service at Trinity United Reformed Church on Delamer Road. The Baptists were renting the chapel from the United Reformed Church.

Below are the youth musicians at a Hale Road Service.

So what did they sing to the sound of the harmonium? We now turn to the new-fangled hymns.

HYMNS AND SONGS

We think of hymns as having been around throughout the history of the church. That is not the case. Certainly the early church wrote its own hymns or songs.[1] However, at some stage the church generally moved into chanting the psalms. Luther wrote hymns, but in England Anglicans and Nonconformists mostly sang psalms. It was the Methodists and Isaac Watts who popularised the use of hymns, but they in turn built on the first collection of hymns by different authors which was published by John Ash and Caleb Evans, two Baptists. The use of hymns was controversial in parts of the Church of England until well into the nineteenth century. It was only in 1861 that *Hymns Ancient & Modern* was published.

By the late Victorian period, hymns were widely accepted in all denominations but the psalms were still sung in many churches alongside hymns.

The Baptists had a real problem though in their use of hymns and songs. The problem was nothing to do with the idea of the use of hymns themselves. The problem was one concerning the words.

The standard Nonconformist hymnbook for many years had been Watts' *Psalms and Hymns*.[2] At first, the Baptists added their own supplements, starting with Rippon's *Selection* in 1787. John Haddon for the Particular Baptists published his *New Selection of Hymns* in 1850 and in 1858 S.G.Green brought Watts and others together in the Baptist *Psalms and Hymns*. In 1866 Spurgeon produced *Our Own Hymn Book*.

The problem for the editors of Baptist hymns was the Calvinist/Ariminian debate. How could Calvinist Baptists include hymns by Wesley which sometimes seemed to amount to anti-Calvinist propaganda, with his optimistic views of salvation and holiness? Even Watts could cause an issue. Some Baptist hymnbooks could not even cope with the vaguely Arminian verse, 'Were the whole realm of nature mine'[3] in his hymn, 'When I survey the Wondrous Cross'.[4]

Looking as an example at the snappily titled *New Selection of Hymns for the Use of Baptist Congregations Enlarged by the Addition of Such of Dr Watts' Psalms and Hymns as are most highly esteemed and generally used in Public Worship*, you would first be struck by the sheer size of the tome. This is partly due to the thickness of the paper used, but also to the 963 hymns in it. All the compilations were heavy volumes, and included detailed scripture indexes.

If you looked a little further, you would find only five Wesley hymns. The rest were deemed not suitable for Calvinists. Nowadays, most Protestants happily sing hymns with contradictory theology with little thought of the nineteenth-century battles that surrounded them.

The cost of buying hymnbooks meant that churches and publishers could not respond rapidly to new hymns and songs, and so there was little development in the repertoire for long periods.

---

[1] There are many references to hymns and songs. See for example 1 Corinthians 14:26.
[2] Bowdon Downs used this book in 1849 and later added Russell's supplement.
[3] Interestingly, another verse is omitted from modern books, perhaps on theological grounds but also because of its graphic portrayal of the blood on the cross.
[4] Watts was a Congregational pastor. His famous poem 'How doth the little busy bee' was equally famously parodied by the supposedly devout Anglican Lewis Carroll in 'How doth the little crocodile'.

All this began to change under the influence of the music of the Salvation Army and composers like Frances Havergal, Fanny Crosby and Ira Sankey. William Booth coined the famous phrase, 'Why should the Devil have all the best tunes?' The Army used strong tunes and sometimes adapted contemporary melodies.[5]

Sankey first published *Sacred Songs and Solos* in 1872 in America. This was revolutionary at the time, bringing contemporary music and tunes into the repertoire. Many were based on music hall styles or folk ballads. They often told a story or used strong imagery. One can get a sense of the priorities of the age in the categories of hymns and songs used.[6]

McLaren chose the hymns at Union Baptist, but his view was that the pastor should sit during the hymns. 'I join in the praise, I do not lead it,' he said. He tended to be conservative in his choice of hymns, according to his first biographer. In 1864 Union Baptist agreed to use Psalms and Hymns. In 1887 it was still chanting psalms during the service and McLaren asked the permission of the Church Meeting to move them to later in the service.[7] More usually, a pastor would choose the hymns and stand to lead them.

By contrast, Francis Collier in Manchester, a Methodist in late Victorian and early Edwardian times, sought out hymns and tunes that would lend effectiveness and power to popular worship. He thought 'the whole spirit of public worship is often chilled and depressed by the use of hymns which congregations find no delight in singing, either because their language is stiff and cold, or because they are set to tunes in which life and fire have been sacrificed to correctness'.[8]

Sale Baptist began a tradition of good modern singing with their pastor Carey Bonner, who wrote many hymns and songs, particularly for children. He introduced some of Sankey's hymns every second Sunday.

Some churches were, however, so fixed in their order of service that the Year Book stated the order for the coming year. Such a formal church was Bowdon Downs Congregational, where in 1882 MacKennal was able to write that the year's order of service was always to be: anthem – short prayer – hymn – prayer – first lesson – chant – second lesson – prayer – hymn – prayer – sermon – hymn – benediction.

Even the Primitive Methodists on Oxford Road, a denomination once famed for their enthusiasm, had a set order of service by 1900: hymn-lesson-hymn-prayer-hymn-lesson-notices-hymn-sermon-collection-hymn-benediction.

So what of the Altrincham Baptists?

It is likely that they would have used *Psalms and Hymns*. However, they were quick to take up the new Sankey songs. John Betts and his musical family gave a

---

[5] The use of secular tunes for religious purposes and vice versa has continued over many years. The author was once tentatively playing an old melody to see what it sounded like. The verse started 'My eyes are dim I cannot see'. When he got to the chorus 'There is power, power, wonder-working power in the precious blood of the Lamb…', he was startled to find his father joining in with the well-known refrain, 'There was beer, beer, lots of bloomin' beer, in the Quartermaster's store'!

[6] Creation, Providence and Redemption; His Life and Love; His Names and Titles; His Humiliation, Resurrection and Glory; His Second Coming; His Office and Work; Songs of Praise; The Lord's Day; Evening and Closing Hymns; Prayer Meetings and Revival; After Meetings; Invitation; Warning and Entreaty; Response and Repentance and so on.

[7] People went to McLaren's church more to hear the preaching than for the worship.

[8] Jackson, G.: *Collier of Manchester — A friend's tribute*, Hodder and Stoughton, 1923.

concert to raise funds, using the occasion to teach the latest Sankey songs. This was followed by the Jubilee Choir which sang gospel 'hits' of the time such as 'Steal away to Jesus', 'Gospel Train' and 'Swing Low, Sweet Chariot'.

Most services probably resembled what today we would call 'hymn sandwiches'. They were not quite as predictable as those at Bowdon Downs; certainly no pastor ever published a standard order of service that we know of. The singing was likely to have been enthusiastic. The Altrincham Baptists clearly enjoyed open-air services. The pastors probably dictated the choice of hymns. They may have sung some psalms. We know that in 1893 the church agreed to use both *Psalms and Hymns* and the Sankey collection for Sunday evening services, but because of their financial hardship they could not afford enough copies of the available hymns supplement. However, in 1897, thanks to increasing numbers, they were able to buy fifty extra copies of *Psalms and Hymns*.

It is probable that the Altrincham Baptists may have later also used Hoyle's *Hymns and Songs For Temperance Societies and Bands of Hope* in their temperance meetings, in Lloyd's day.

The Altrincham Baptists probably had a choir from the earliest days. The choir was used to enhance the worship and to make up for the deficiencies of the harmonium. The choir was also used for evangelistic and open-air events.

In 1878 at the building launch service, we know that the choir sang in the evening. We also know that H. J. Leech, brother of Edward the one-time treasurer, was the choirmaster and organist. In 1893 when the church re-combined, we find him returning and promising to help Lloyd by promoting the choir again. There was a choir at Bowdon Baptist, but almost certainly none at the Tabernacle under Mowbray. His style of service was probably much more in the 'gospel mission' style, with rousing hymns and choruses and a stirring and direct sermon.

By 1904 Lloyd was giving regular reports on the choir and both the choir and Sunday school choir appear to have sung at the main services. Sometimes there were 'Choir Sundays'. By 1899, Miss Simmons had returned after Mowbray left and was leading the choir again. By 1904 Pierrepont was the choirmaster as well as church secretary.

It is not quite so clear where the choir sang in the chapel over time. The early choir stalls were probably at the front of the chapel facing inwards. In 1906 the church tried to raise finance for seating for the choir, and it may be that for a period before that they sometimes stood on the platform to sing. Certainly the oldest picture of the chapel may show they were seated in front of the pulpit in the body of the church and facing crossways.

Lloyd was keen on good singing. On 1 April 1904 he wrote: 'To sing hymns in a slip-shod and half-hearted fashion is a strange contradiction of the avowed purpose we have in view in such exercises.'

In 1904, Lloyd was anxious about the choice of hymns for the mission, but was always willing to experiment. The missioner, he explained, was going to use Sankey's hymns, 'but many of those chosen will be out of the beaten track'. Lloyd organised a band of some sort for the mission and also a choir to sings hymns in the streets before the evangelistic services and to be in the church to sing welcoming hymns. We find Lloyd teaching new hymns at Christian Endeavour meetings. Certainly he was a man keen on good worship and new songs and hymns.

> Probably one of the first hymnbooks in Britain was published by the Baptist Benjamin Keach in the seventeenth century. By common consent Keach's hymns, although some of the first, were generally awful. He wrote the immortal lines: 'Repentance like a bucket is to pump the water out; for leaky is our ship, alas, which makes us look about.' The use of hymns in Keach's church actually led to a church split. Those opposed to the new-fangled hymns left the church to stand out in the yard when the hymns were sung after the sermon. Eventually they left to form their own church. However, the influence of Keach led to Watts writing hymns which were to revolutionise church worship.[9]

So what did they sing at Christmas?

---

[9] For those who think modern hymn- and song-writing is much better today, see Page, N.: *And now let's move into a time of nonsense...why worship songs are failing the Church,* Authentic Media, 2004.

CHRISTMAS AND NEW YEAR

In our tour of the theology and practices of the Victorians, Christmas might not seem an obvious issue at first sight. It was, however, and yet it could not be openly discussed, such was the British respect for the monarchy.

If we go back to the roots of the Christian faith, it is clear that the birth of Jesus is not that important in terms of the thrust of the Bible. The birth of Jesus does not feature much at all. Only two of the four Gospels mention it. True, the coming of Messiah is foreshadowed in the Old Testament, but there is more about the Messiah returning before the end of the age in both Old and New Testaments than there is about his birth. The life, death, resurrection and return of Jesus were far more important to the early church. It is not even known when Jesus was born, but it is almost certain it was not on 25 December and it was probably a few years BC.[1]

What happened was that Christian missionaries added the festival of Christmas to a pagan festival in an attempt to persuade the pagans to abandon their old midwinter festival and turn it into a festival celebrating the birth of Jesus. This was probably done with the best of motives at the time as the missionaries were faced with an intractable pagan population. The equivalent Roman festival was Saturnalia.[2]

The legacy of this early compromise haunts Christians today. Concern about the association of Christmas with a pagan festival goes a long way back in British culture. 'More mischief is that time committed than in all the year besides ... What dicing and carding, what eating and drinking, what banqueting and feasting is then used ... to the great dishonour of God and the impoverishing of the realm,' wrote Philip Stubbes in the sixteenth century. Dissenters were for many years equivocal about Christmas. In 1644 Christmas celebrations were actually banned by Cromwell's Parliament.

The changes to Christmas during the Victorian period were quite dramatic. Christmas, as we know it, is very much a Victorian invention. Before 1843, there were no Christmas cards. Christmas crackers were introduced only in the late 1840s. Father Christmas was partly based on the Norse pagan god, Odin, and came to the fore in the Victorian era.[3] Christmas stockings were a Victorian invention. Mistletoe is of pagan origin. Even many Christmas carols are Victorian compositions. 'Once in Royal David's City', 'O Come all ye Faithful' and 'We Three Kings' were all written in the nineteenth century. They replaced earlier folk carols.

Much of this Victorian Christmas was a German import under the influence of Prince Albert. As loyal citizens, the Victorian Nonconformists could not criticise their Queen's husband, but they continued to try and 'down-play' Christmas as a Christian festival.

We have also to remember that Christmas and New Year were ordinary working days, or possibly half-day holidays, until quite late in the Victorian era. In 1874 the local newspaper noted that drapers were to be given these days off and suggested others should follow their lead.

---

[1] It was certainly not the year '0', as the Romans did not have such a number, so '0' AD never existed.
[2] Or 'Sol Invictus'. December 25 was also associated with the cult of Mithras, a cult which excluded women.
[3] Santa Claus is partly the 1931 embellishment of a Dutch tradition by a well known fizzy drinks company. He is certainly not British.

The Altrincham Baptists did celebrate Christmas, but only by an apposite sermon on the day and the odd hymn.[4] The *New Selection of Hymns for the Use of Baptist Congregations* lumps the small number of hymns on a Christmas theme together in the short section on 'The Saviour – His history'.

'Angels from the realms of glory' and 'Hark! the herald angels sing' were there, but little else in the way of modern carols. There are just four hymns out of 956 on the birth of Jesus. The church even once held its quarterly Church Meeting on one Christmas Day under Lloyd. This was not because they wanted to be spoilsports, but they wanted to respect what they saw as the biblical view of Christmas.

One can sense the struggle the Nonconformists as a whole faced with the new Victorian Christmas in a lecture on carols held at the British School just before Christmas in 1876. The speaker kept a careful balance between 'fun' with Father Christmas and the true meaning of Christmas, between the Puritan tradition of Christmas being a minor festival and the new Victorian secular extravaganza. By 1877 however, the editor of the local newspaper was extolling the culinary fare in the shops. Every table would have its 'juicy joint of savoury goose, with the substantial accompaniment of well boiled pudding on Christmas day'.

Perhaps as a means of down-playing Christmas and trying to return it to its scriptural context in their eyes, the Baptists appeared to take New Year more seriously than Christmas, at least under Lloyd. They followed a Methodist tradition encouraged by Wesley. The watchnight service was a solemn occasion to renew Christian vows for the coming year and to make promises to God. Lloyd took those promises (which were often written down), and a year later reminded the Baptists what they had promised and asked them to search their hearts as to how they had kept them.

If you are Scottish, you may recognise all of this, because to this day New Year is treated as being as more important than Christmas, mostly due to the influence of the Victorian Nonconformist churches, although of course the modern celebration of Hogmanay at Scottish New Year with its alcohol consumption is not exactly what they would have wished.

The Christmas tree was a German custom of pagan origin and nothing really to do with Christmas. It was introduced into England during the Georgian period. Queen Charlotte, the German wife of King George III, is known to have had a decorated tree for her family as early as the 1790s. It was, however, Prince Albert who popularised the tree in England.

---

[4] We can deduce this from the early Edwardian newsletters. There is no mention of anything special in any church minutes.

*Victoria and Albert around the Christmas tree. Many of our
modern Christmas 'traditions' can be traced back to them.*

We turn now to the alcohol problem in Victorian Altrincham.

THE DEMON DRINK

In 1841 there were about twenty public houses in Altrincham. By August 1879 the Brewster Licensing Session reported an explosion in numbers to fifty-two places licensed for consumption of liquor on the premises. By any standard, the ratio of pubs to population was very high. There were a further fifty-seven off-licences and a staggering total of 200 places licensed in some way to sell alcohol in Altrincham. This was at a time when the population was substantially lower than that of today. There was a place to buy alcohol on almost every street in Altrincham.

The problems of alcohol abuse we face today are comparatively minor compared to those faced by the Victorians. Drunkenness was a way of life to many. There are constant reports in the local press of insobriety. In 1878, 206 people were brought to court for alcohol-related offences. Whilst they were at The Downs Chapel, the Baptists were regularly disturbed on Sunday evenings by drunks barging in.

The potential disintegration of society through alcohol abuse was a very real challenge. The nonconformists could not force prohibition, and so in time they had to find an alternative solution.

The Bible has a lot to say about alcohol, although much more about the abuse of power and wealth. It does though roundly condemn drunkenness and over-indulgence in alcohol. Those taking special vows in the Old Testament could forswear alcohol. Moderation is a good scriptural principle. What the Bible does not do, however, is condemn the drinking of alcohol itself. Jesus turned water into wine at a wedding party. With contaminated water supplies, small amounts of alcohol could be beneficial. The apostle Paul told Timothy that he should 'drink no longer water, but use a little wine for thy stomach's sake and thine other infirmities'.[1]

Early Nonconformists drank alcohol, but in moderation. Today, the majority of Altrincham Baptists are not teetotal, although many would support a temperance position. However, during Victoria's reign, as they grappled with the huge social problems society faced and particularly the problems of the poor, the Nonconformists began to embrace temperance and then total abstinence as the solution. Given the fact that the poor could drink away their wages each week, this was an understandable solution.

> Although early Baptists in England sometimes drank alcohol, they did object to drunkenness. In 1670 Philip Seiphard was expelled from Broadmead Baptist Church for 'being overcome in drink'. The same church held a prayer meeting and day of fasting at the house of Jeremy Courtnay to 'cast out ye drunken devil out of him'. The meeting was held at his wife's request.

It is now time to be clear about some important terms. 'Temperance' means moderation in the consumption of alcohol and abstinence from spirits. 'Teetotal' or 'total abstinence' requires a permanent cessation of the consumption of all alcohol. In the Victorian era, just as now, temperance came to be confused with total abstinence, but the ideas were initially quite different.

---

[1] Humankind is in fact genetically divided into two over alcohol. Your ancestors either boiled their water to purify it or added alcohol. If they used alcohol, as most Europeans did, you body is more able to withstand moderate alcohol consumption. This is not good news, however, if your ancestors boiled water. Paul was probably just being realistic.

The first Temperance Society was founded in Bradford in June 1830. It appointed James Jackson, a Baptist minister in Hebden Bridge, to spread the idea. He travelled around the north of England and helped found twenty-three new societies. The Preston Temperance Society was founded in 1832 and it was from here that the idea of the making of a pledge of total abstinence came. Joseph Livesey from Preston was a prime mover and called Preston 'the Jerusalem of the teetotal movement'.

The teetotal movement took hold initially in the north, but the change from temperance to total abstinence was not immediate. For many years, Nonconformists were a mixture of temperance and teetotalism.

In 1870, the Baptist Union supported the Permissive Bill which would allow local councils the right to regulate the sale of alcohol in their areas, but until 1874 the *Freeman* deemed temperance too difficult a topic to discuss, such was the divergence of Baptist views. By the end of the nineteenth century, however, most Baptists were aligned to the temperance movement, with the majority being teetotal.

One can see the struggle as the teetotal movement gained in strength. MacKennal reluctantly supported a motion put to the Cheshire Congregational Union meeting held at Bowdon Downs which favoured the promotion of teetotal views in Congregational churches. That motion was proposed by Francis Milne. MacKennal was not teetotal, but his assistant who joined him later was. In 1887 MacKennal found himself supporting a united Altrincham temperance meeting chaired by Frank Crossley. His compromise position was to call himself an 'habitual abstainer'. MacKennal's dilemma was particularly acute as his brother was a travelling salesman for a brewery.

In 1871 Manchester City Mission received a proposal from the temperance movement to give a lecture to the missioners and to address some workmen's meetings. The Mission Board decided to proceed with caution as it felt the Mission's main object was the diffusion of religion and not the promotion of temperance. They compromised by allowing the lecture to be given to the missioners but not to the workers. However, it was not long after this that missionaries were recording not only those led to churches, but also the number of total abstinence pledges signed.

Frank and Emily Crossley were not initially teetotal, but found themselves drawn to the movement and invited Richard Coad from Cornwall to stay at Fairlie and conduct a temperance mission. It is not clear where the mission was held, but hundreds signed the pledge, including the Crossleys themselves.

Having signed the pledge, Crossley now had a business dilemma related to alcohol. He wrote to McLaren asking if he should sell his machines to breweries. McLaren wrote back that, as Crossley did not know precisely what the use was going to be, he could still sell the engines. Crossley followed McLaren's advice, but gave the profits from these sales to charity.

> When Frank and Emily Crossley agreed to sign the pledge, Emily's remedy was drastic. Frank still had a large cellar of expensive wines and champagnes. He returned home to find that she had simply poured them down the drain.

As more Nonconformists became teetotal, the Baptists faced the difficult issue as to what to do about communion wine. It is clear that Jesus used bread and wine at the Last Supper, but what did one do if one had signed the pledge? The pledge required total abstinence, so teetotal Baptists could not take communion.

Francis Beardsall, a New Connexion Baptist Minister in Manchester, convinced himself that references in the New Testament to wine were to unfermented wine and began a campaign against the use of alcohol in communion services. Again, the process was gradual, but by 1900, 2,077 out of about 2,900 Baptist churches used unfermented wine in communion. Most still do so today, even if the majority of their members drink alcohol. It is difficult to change an historical precedent, even if the use of alcohol may make sharing the communion cup very marginally safer.

In 1856 the Students Temperance Society for all Free church theological colleges was formed. The promotion of temperance in the theological colleges bore fruit, because by 1886 1,000 out of 1,900 Baptist pastors were teetotal and by 1907 211 out of 214 Baptist theological students were.

The movement also realised it had to reach young people. Jabez Tunnicliff, a New Connexion Baptist Minister, was one of the founders of the Band of Hope in 1847 in Leeds. This was a

> In 1825 well before the temperance movement, Walter Aston wrote that the scholars of Oswald Leicester's Sunday school had ale with gin or rum.[2]

children's temperance movement. The Band of Hope Union was founded in 1862. By 1904, it had 2,037 branches in Baptist churches. This reflects the impact of the main temperance movement. Store Street Baptist Sunday School gave its scholars ale to celebrate Queen Victoria's coronation in 1838, but by the time of her death this would have been unthinkable. Union Chapel had a Band of Hope as early as 1874.

Temperance was not exclusively confined to the Nonconformists. Canon Wainwright at St John's Church attended temperance meetings with Aylard of the Independent Congregational Church and Adamson of the British School Mission Church and others. Queen Victoria became patron of the Church of England Temperance Society and a branch was set up in Altrincham in 1876. Wainwright became one of the leaders and in 1878 led the Church of England group in a march with bands around Altrincham. During 1879 alone, the Society recruited 142 new Anglican members in Altrincham.

The Roman Catholics were also active (but not terribly successful) in promoting temperance, with Theobald Matthew being particularly active in Ireland. In 1892 the Bowdon Downs Congregational Temperance Society lamented the death of Cardinal Manning, a staunch supporter of the temperance movement.

---

[2] Quoted in Nickson, op. cit.

John Siddeley owned the brewery in Hale by Hale Station and also the Rising Sun public house in Police Street. He was mayor of Altrincham in 1878. The brewery's large chimney dominated the area. The tragedy of alcohol addiction hit his family when his son Percy died of an epileptic fit brought on by alcoholism.

The first photograph shows the brewery in Hale. The photographer has his back to the level crossing and is looking up Ashley Road to its junction with Langham Road. The second photograph is taken in 1907 and shows the new fountain on Peel Causeway near Hale Railway Station. The land behind formed part of Siddeley's brewery.

By 1900 it is estimated that approximately one tenth of the adult population was teetotal, and substantially more supported the temperance movement. This was an astonishing success for a comparatively new movement, but it also reflected the real concern at the time about the increasing problems caused by alcohol and binge drinking.

THE ALTERNATIVE SOCIETY IN ALTRINCHAM

Those promoting temperance saw that they had to provide an attractive alternative form of society to the camaraderie of the public house.

Entertainment and excursions became a regular feature of the temperance movement. Thomas Cook, a Baptist, organised his first railway excursion in 1841 as part of the movement. The Methodists were particularly good at entertainment. Collier in Manchester organised Saturday evenings at the Central Methodist Hall, using some of the best entertainers of the time. The performances were purely secular and had no overt Christian content, but were of high quality. The only thing that Collier insisted on was that they must not be incompatible with the Christian faith. As a result, many came to Central Hall, and so did not go to the pubs. Ultimately, some of these came to church and to faith. Sobriety and belief increasingly went hand in hand.

The Manchester City Mission record of 1880 for Altrincham contains the story of a tramp who had come to Altrincham twelve months earlier: 'A Christian couple found him work and he settled into the neighbourhood and attended one of the cottage meetings. He became sober and was led to see the truth of the Gospel. Ever since he has been consistent in his attendance at, and membership of, the House of God.'

We do not know which church he attended, but the reader will note the connection made between sobriety and then faith.

In Altrincham, a group of Christians met together to set up The British Workman, a temperance pub in 1875. We know that there was a predecessor to this on Lloyd Street in the 1850s, but it had closed. Wainwright was involved in the new venture with John Thompson. Together, they bought and fitted out a building, triangular in shape, at the corner of Ashley Road and Oxford Road. John Attenborough was the manager and lived at the premises.

> Even the local newspaper began to see the problems of drink in Altrincham by 1874. The editor could not himself give up alcohol, but wrote, 'It is important that every man who abhors intemperance, whether he be a teetotaller or not, should add the weight of his own character and the power of his own sympathy to stopping this evil.'

The pub had a bar, games room, smoking room and meeting room. It sold tea and coffee at two pence a cup plus various other drinks. A decision was made to serve only good coffee. The new aerated water was sold at one halfpenny a cup. The only thing it did not sell was alcohol.

There were many such 'pubs' throughout the country, and the attempt was to create a viable alternative to the atmosphere of the normal pub.

Regular Saturday evening events were held at The British Workman. In March 1876 for example, a series of electrical experiments were held and the upstairs room was packed. In January 1877 they held a 'microscopic soirée'. By all accounts, the British Workman was successful and soon self-funding, so much so that discussions were held to open one in Bowdon.

There was a seasonal teetotal pub in Islington Street in 1878 which became the full-time Islington Arms by 1879, replete with a billiard table donated by William Crossley. Charles and Eleanor Mair were the proprietors. Tragically, Eleanor died at the age of thirty-nine in 1890, and Charles died three years later.

St Margaret's Church opened a tea and coffee house at 19 Chapel Street. Coffee was sold at a penny a cup. Both men and women were welcome and there were newspapers, books and a smoking room. Two years after its foundation, such was its success that adjoining land had to be acquired.

As well as providing an alternative to the conventional pub, members of the temperance movement acted as a local lobby group. A meeting in September 1875 claimed there were fifty-six pubs for 15,000 people and petitioned for the number to be limited. In 1880 the local temperance movement (including the Baptists) lobbied for Sunday closure, or at least restrictions on hours of opening, and reported publicans in breach of the existing laws to the magistrates.

There was a division of opinion, though, amongst the temperance movement. Some wanted to close all pubs, some to limit the number and some such as Wainwright did not see pubs as a problem in themselves. Instead they saw the problem as how they were run.

What increasingly happened was that many churches met together under a temperance banner, as they could unite on that ground, but then some went further and became teetotal. A temperance demonstration was held on a Saturday in July 1894 which united MacKennal, Wainwright and many others with differing views. The intention was to hold a rally at the

> The temperance movement in Altrincham, despite its different groupings, was broadly cross-denominational. Naturally, it had its opponents. When Revd George London of St George's joined a temperance platform, an anonymous writer to the local newspaper criticised his talk (and indeed all his sermons) as 'twaddle'.

Devisdale, but the rain was so great that they had to hastily re-convene in the Literary Institute.

By the turn of the twentieth century, we can see the predominance of temperance in Altrincham amongst the Nonconformists. In 1904 the Altrincham and District Temperance Federation was formed and met at the British School. In the 1905 combined mission (which we will look at later), eighty temperance pledges were taken, perhaps showing the increased Nonconformist confusion between abstinence and salvation. In October 1905 the local Nonconformists organised a temperance rally at the Literary Institute, with Holden, Lloyd and Armitage on the platform. Gone, Lloyd said, are the days when a minister took a glass of wine after a sermon: 'Now we invigorate ourselves by the strength of God.' By 1905 most churches in the area joined in Temperance Sunday each year.

In Altrincham, politics and temperance became increasingly linked. The Liberal William Crossley advocated temperance but the Tory Conningsby Disraeli did not; indeed, he very much supported the brewers. The local newspaper reported with some glee in 1904 that on the same night that Disraeli addressed the Licensed Victuallers' Association in Altrincham, Crossley addressed the Sons of Temperance. There was increased tension between the brewers and many Anglicans on one side, and some Anglicans and most Nonconformists on the other.

What brought matters to a head in Altrincham however was the Licensing Bill, which was intended to transfer some licensing power away from local magistrates into more centralised hands and so potentially allow more public houses. A public demonstration was organised for 20 May 1904 in the Market Place by none other than Lloyd. At the same time he preached an entire sermon against the Bill. The demonstration received ecumenical support and Lloyd persuaded Archdeacon Woosnam of St Margaret's to speak alongside himself and Armitage. William Crossley would have attended but was ill.

So we see the Nonconformists in Altrincham uniting with some Anglicans in public protest against the increasing power of the brewing industry.

There is a story of members of the temperance Band of Hope serenading the cab drivers at the foot of The Downs. They are reputed to have sung, 'My drink is water bright from the crystal stream', at which point the cab drivers signed the pledge, probably in attempt to be left alone, but went back to their old ways a week later.[1]

The Altrincham cab drivers had a reputation for reckless driving, usually by racing each other.[2] The cabmen were not unused to Nonconformist approaches. In 1874 they enjoyed a free dinner at the British School.

William Hoyle of the Lancashire and Cheshire Band of Hope Union compiled *Hymns and Songs for Temperance Societies and Bands of Hope*. The first verse and chorus of 'My drink is water bright' are typical of some of these temperance songs, which often told a story.

'Merry Dick you soon would know,

If you lived in Jackson's Row;

Each day, with a smiling face,

He is ready at his place;

Should you ever with him meet,

In his shop, or in the street,

You will find him blithe and gay,

Singing out the merry lay,-

'My drink is water bright,

Water bright, water bright,

My drink is water bright,

From the crystal spring.'

---

[1] Quoted in Bayliss, H.: *Altrincham: A Pictorial History*, Phillimore, 1996.
[2] 1899 local newspaper report.

The Altrincham and Bowdon Total Abstinence Society on an outing. Note that some of them are clearly working people. The Baptists were heavily involved in the society and it may be that some of them are in this photograph. Annie Bowland's father may be the man standing with a walking-stick in the centre of the group. We will come across him later in this book.

Even before The British Workman pub, there was a temperance influence in the area. This 1876 survey shows the junction of Oxford Road and Peter Street before Oxford Road was continued through to meet Ashley Road, and before the Primitive Methodist Church was built. Note 'Temperance Terrace'.

1898 map. The British Workman teetotal pub was located in the triangular building at the junction of Oxford Road, Ashley Road and John Street. This map shows Oxford Road now completed.

The British Workman pub, shown in the first picture after it had become a coffee shop but looking much as it would have done as a temperance pub and, in the second picture, as it is now. At the time of writing the building houses an optometrist's shop.

The photograph above shows a different view of The British Workman pub.

TOBACCO AND ALCOHOL: HOW ONE CHURCH CHANGED ITS VIEWS

The Baptists illustrate the dramatic change from the middle years of Victoria's reign, when many Nonconformists would drink alcohol, to the end of her reign when most had signed the pledge.

There is little mention at all of temperance under the pastorate of Betts. He was probably not teetotal.

At first Llewellyn was conspicuous by his absence from temperance meetings, but then in 1877 he appeared at the Altrincham and Bowdon Temperance Society and it seems his conversion to the cause happened in Altrincham. 'I am not a very old teetotaller, but I feel my interest in the movement increasing and growing stronger every day...I have become an abstainer because of the many lamentable instances of intemperance which I have witnessed in my own experience.' This may have been a reference to the number of drunks who interrupted services at The Downs Chapel. Llewellyn then asked anyone present who had not done so to sign the pledge.

Llewellyn went on to second an ecumenical temperance motion to restrict Sunday opening hours, but then rather oddly set up his own Altrincham Baptist Total Abstinence Society in 1878. When challenged about the need for a separate society, he gave the rather illogical reply that if the Anglicans and Methodists could have their own societies, why could not the Baptists?

The inaugural Baptist meeting on 19 October was a disappointment. The church was still not a total abstaining church, but Llewellyn was able to say that most were by then total abstainers. The guest speaker was Revd Davies, who referred to the debate between the total abstainers and those who advocated moderation. The total abstainers had won the debate, he argued.

Parker, the student minister, was secretary of the new society and spoke in support. Simmons rounded up the evening. However, there was a clear lack of enthusiasm by church members, and Llewellyn lamented the lack of support at the meeting. Effectively the church members voted by not attending in any great numbers. The separate Baptist society was short-lived, and they soon threw in their lot with the others in Altrincham.

> Rather than just campaign against alcohol on social grounds (which were very strong), the teetotal movement tried hard to find a theological basis for total abstinence. One can see this in the 1886 lecture entitled 'Was the Lord Jesus Christ a total abstainer?' at Bowdon Baptist Church, delivered by Revd John Pyper. He studied the marriage at Cana, where Jesus turned water into wine, the wine used at the Last Supper and the wine and myrrh presented to Jesus on the cross, and still somehow managed to argue that Jesus supported total abstinence.

Mowbray is conspicuous by his absence from Altrincham temperance meetings. He did in 1885 welcome a total abstainer to the church and referred to the fact that most (but not obviously all) the Baptists were total abstainers and implied he might be too, but did not actually say he was. In September 1886, when a temperance lecture was given at the Hale Road chapel, he promptly handed the chair to Simmons. It is not clear therefore whether Mowbray was teetotal or temperance, but the likelihood is that, like Betts, he was not a total abstainer.

Lloyd was a complete contrast. He had signed the pledge before he arrived at Altrincham. It is significant that there was no mention of temperance under the joint pastorate between Mowbray and Lloyd, but as soon as Mowbray left, total abstinence was immediately on the agenda.

The Altrincham Baptists now faced the issue of whether to use wine at communion. It is possible that the first Altrincham Baptists may have used wine. We simply do not know. The accounts of 1889 show fifteen shillings being spent in the year on communion wine, but this could have been fermented or unfermented. We know, however, that by 1901 they were using unfermented wine. The introduction of individual goblets provoked a complaint at a Church Meeting about the poor quality of the unfermented wine.

Lloyd set up a specific group to try and persuade youngsters to sign the pledge and Mr Whitelow organised a Band of Hope. It is interesting that the proposal for the Band of Hope came to the Church Meeting on the very day Mowbray indicated he was near to finalising terms with McLaren for his departure from Altrincham. In 1903 the Altrincham Baptist Band of Hope received eighteen pledges and had received eighty over the previous four years. Before a child could sign the pledge, they had to undergo a three-month probation period to test their resolve.

The Altrincham Baptists were poor at the start of our story, but were also upwardly socially mobile. To what extent this was a function of the temperance movement is difficult to say, but certainly an analysis of some of the early families of Altrincham Baptist Church shows them as predominantly labouring and trades people, with their children taking up more middle class occupations. The savings brought about by total abstinence must have helped.

The proposed change in the licensing laws in 1904 that we have seen in a previous chapter brought Lloyd into conflict with the brewers. In May 1904 he asked the church to pray 'that God will save England from the plighting influence of the Drink Trade and avert the terrible peril lurking behind the Government proposals on behalf of the owners of licensed houses'. He urged them to pray 'day and night for the speedy dissolution of a Government which will, if it is allowed to continue, soon injure the very foundations of our religious liberty, civic justice and national prosperity'.

On 1 May he called a Special Church Meeting after the evening communion service specifically to pass the following resolution, again by a unanimous standing vote: 'That the Government's Licensing Bill, which seeks to deprive local Justices of their power to refuse the renewal of Licences, and directly aims to give local perpetuity to the Liquor traffic, is an unwarrantable surrender to the Brewers and Publicans, and an outrageous affront to the Christian and Temperance sentiments of the country, and ought to be vigorously opposed by every good citizen; and that the members of this congregation pledge themselves to do all in their power to avert the passing of the Measure.'[1]

In the autumn of 1904 we find him writing 'I take it that the evil consequences that are following hard in the wake of the Boer War, the Education Acts and the Chinese Ordinances, all told, pale into insignificance in the presence of the appalling

---

[1] The debate still continues. The January 2009 edition of The Publican suggested that the Government is now in favour of temperance and the old values may be making a comeback.

calamities hidden behind this gigantic conspiracy of the brewers of Britain'. He personally gave 200 copies of a brochure by a licensing barrister to 'thoughtful young men in the neighbourhood' and at an evening service on Sunday 15 May he preached a sermon against the proposed legislation. Lloyd was never one to sit on the fence. The following Sunday evening nine adults signed the pledge.

The pledge by then included a promise not to smoke. However, the Victorian attitude to smoking was less clear than the attitude to alcohol.

While the drinking of alcohol and the smoking of pipes had been around for a long time, cigarettes in Britain were largely a Victorian introduction. Most Victorians did not perceive tobacco as a health hazard.

Robert Gloag brought the idea back from the Crimean War when he saw both Turks and Russians smoking cigarettes. He then manufactured his own 'Moscows' and 'Tom Thumbs'. These sold so well that he founded St Stephen's Church in Peckham in gratitude. In 1871 he introduced the highly successful 'Don Alfonso's Whiffs'.

At first, smoking in public places had to be in designated areas. In respectable households, those wanting to smoke had to go outside or sneak into the kitchen. Gradually however, smoking came to be allowed in most places. In 1860 smoking was first allowed in railway carriages.

Mass production of cigarettes really began in 1883 when the Bristol firm of W.D. and H.O. Wills bought the American Bonsack cigarette-making machine. In 1888 they introduced the Wills Woodbine Penny Smoke and by 1891 made profits in excess of £120 million, a huge amount now and a colossal sum then.

Tobacco was not seen as a social evil like alcohol. The Band of Hope was against tobacco, but one can see the struggle in

| Spurgeon is quoted as saying that he smoked 'to the glory of God'. |

the setting up of The British Workman temperance pub in Altrincham. Thompson abhorred alcohol, but he successfully argued for a smoking room as smoking 'did not do the harm drinking did' and confessed he enjoyed the odd smoke. It is possible that some of the Altrincham Baptists may have smoked. Charles Southwell Jnr enjoyed a Woodbine or two. We do know that McLaren enjoyed the odd quiet smoke and Spurgeon was a convinced pipe-smoker.

The truth is that the Victorians had no real idea of the health problems that smoking could cause.

| Brian Waterson recalls how as a young man in the 1950s he noticed that most church members were still teetotal, but quite a number smoked. |

The Market Place in Altrincham where Lloyd led the protests against the Licensing Bill.

The temperance movement created 'para-church' organisations. The 'Sons of Temperance' was one such organisation, creating its own world for adherents. The picture above left is a certificate given to Eva Brewer to mark 50 years in the organisation. The motto says 'Good life, good health, the reward of temperance'. The picture above right is one from 1907 accepting William Brewer into membership, as long as he continued to pay his subscriptions and keep the principles of the organisation.

One of the advantages of joining the Sons of Temperance was that it was also a funeral society, paying funeral benefits on death.

The main condition of membership was the pledge 'I promise to abstain from the use of intoxicating liquors and tobacco'. If the pledge was broken, re-admission was allowed on payment of a fine of 3d. Children between the ages of 14 and 16 could also join, but their parents had to guarantee their adherence to the pledge.

Brian Waterson, a member of Altrincham Baptist Church for many years. His father refused to let him sign the pledge until he was 21. He never did, but many Baptists did sign the pledge. Joan Hunter (later Joan Southwell) signed the pledge early in life but then changed her mind. Charles Frederick Southwell probably signed the pledge, but later in life enjoyed a drop of whisky, although purely for medicinal purposes, of course. It was not uncommon for people to sign the pledge but to drink spirits as medicine. This was often considered acceptable.

THE CHURCH AT TEA

One is struck by contrast by how central to the life of the church were tea, the tea party and the picnic. The Victorians and Edwardians saw tea as an essential and rewarding part of their daily life.

Part of the reason was, of course, due to the temperance movement. Tea was a good substitute for alcohol. Those who drank alcohol, however, often added rum or other alcohol to their tea. Teetotal or not, most Victorians and Edwardians added copious amounts of sugar.

Tea itself first came from China. However, it was often adulterated in cheap brands with old reused tealeaves, leaves from British trees and dangerous chemical substances. Local newspapers carried reports of tea adulteration. During the 1870s this tea was gradually replaced by less expensive tea from the colonies of Ceylon and India. The initial selling point of Lipton's tea was that it was unadulterated.

Tea merchants sprang up in Altrincham to meet the growing demand. Edwin Cryer, a tea dealer of 27 Stamford Street, advertised in the church magazine and Nathaniel Gould of George Street specialised in Ceylon tea in the late 1890s.

Tea was popularised by the new cafes. Well-known chains were ABC (the Aereated Bread Company), Lyons and the Kardomah.[1]

Tea was often more than just a cup of tea. This was a time when food prices fell in relation to wages. Distribution of food was now easier thanks to the railways. Imported American wheat meant cheaper bread, and first canned and then frozen meat began to arrive from Australia, America and Argentina. Steam trawlers brought back cod in ice, and cod became the mainstay of the new fish and chip shops. Canned fruits were also imported from the New World. Tea, therefore, came increasingly to be accompanied by food.

Tea could be the drink itself or any meal at which tea was served. Gradually, high tea and afternoon tea emerged during the Victorian period. High tea was more common in the north and was probably a continuation of earlier traditions of this being the main meal. Afternoon tea was a lighter meal and more the privilege of the leisured classes.

So what was served at high tea? Clearly tea was the central item. There was much home baking. Cakes, bread and butter, preserves and jellies were a feature. There might be toast and crumpets. A treat might have been the new tinned salmon from British Columbia or Alaska.[2] High tea also featured meat, with ham being particularly prized. There would be sandwiches and sometimes galantines,[3] chaudfroid of chicken and simply dressed fish. Occasionally there might be eggs with the ham, tinned sardines, hot sausages and flaked haddock. Whatever food was served, it was substantial fare.

Tea parties were a feature of nearly all the churches in Altrincham. The contemporary local newspapers were rarely without a report of a church tea party.

---

[1] Perhaps the Baptists enjoyed a joke about this; Altrincham Baptist Church is often today referred to as 'ABC'.
[2] Poorer households usually couldn't afford a tin opener and had to go to the local grocer to have their tin opened.
[3] A dish of boned, stuffed meat or fish that is poached and served cold coated with aspic.

Bowdon Downs Congregational, for example, had a tea party at the British School in 1874 and went to great lengths to make the room look like a large Victorian drawing room. In 1888, the Altrincham Baptists received a donation of £5 to purchase a tea service.

Tea meetings were often used to raise money for church funds. In 1889, the church made a profit of twelve shillings on tea meetings in the year. Those profits increased each year. Jessie Mowbray organised annual tea meetings and sold tickets for them. The high point of church bazaars was always tea.

Lloyd often had a 6.30pm tea before a Church Meeting, although this was usually with an eye to raising funds as well as being a social occasion. Those who prepared (and usually paid for) the teas were always thanked. Lloyd later institutionalised the pre-meeting tea into a quarterly tea for church members and communicant members. Sometimes the Lloyds would also hold an 'at home'.

In 1890 we read that the Church Meeting was preceded by a meeting 'taking the form of social tea for members attended by Pastor, Deacons and about 40 other members. After tea a friendly chat while the Pastor was busily handing round new membership cards.'

Tea was popular on picnics and church outings. In *Shirley* by Charlotte Brontë, a church tea was provided for the parish children and consisted of large currant buns and sweetened tea. Bowdon Downs Congregational Sunday School organised an outing by train to Tatton Park. There the children played games in a field adjoining the park and then consumed an extensive picnic tea, the teachers having their own tea in the adjoining orchard.

If we look just at 1904, we can see the popularity of outings for the Altrincham Baptists. There were two Christian Endeavour picnics. The seniors went to Mr Hope's farm on the banks of the River Birkin. The church mothers went on an outing to Heaton Park. The older Sunday school scholars went to Disley and were joined by the Primitive Methodists. The combined group was able to charter a special train. The junior Sunday school scholars went to Castle Hill Farm in Ashley and got soaked by the rain. However, according to Lloyd (who as Sunday School Superintendent naturally accompanied them), the homeward journey was 'advertised far and wide by the deafening hurrars and laughter of the merry youngsters'. The Sunday school choir had a separate outing to Ashley.

Tea was almost always a central feature not only of these outings but of every event.

One thing the Victorian Baptists did not appear to do was to fast together. They took their food seriously, although the refusal to fast may have been a reaction to what they saw as a Roman Catholic tradition. However, there is an older tradition of Baptists fasting. Seventeenth-century Baptists saw fasting as a religious duty. Broadmead Baptist Church, for example, had days of fasting when ministers or church officers were to be appointed.

Making the tea was almost exclusively the role of women. Lessons in 'economical cookery' were held at the British School and Bowdon Church of England School in 1877 and 1879, where leading local men extolled to a female audience the need for good cooking. 'Man is said to be essentially a dining animal and to make (him) comfortable, he must have his meals attended to properly,' wrote the local newspaper as the class produced wild fowl, treacle pudding, stewed liver, fried plaice and custard (although hopefully not together).

Unknown Altrincham Baptist Church group on a picnic, no doubt with tea.

Advertisement for Skippers from 1904 in the Baptist church magazine. Locals might have bought sixpenny cakes from the Skipper premises on The Downs or at 34 George Street, and later on Stamford New Road.

ENTERTAINMENT AND SELF-IMPROVEMENT

One of the issues that challenges churches today is how to reach those who have never been to church, to whom stepping into a church can be a strange cultural experience. How can one make church more accessible without diluting the Christian message?

In the period covered by this book, most people who did not go to church were still familiar with what a church service would be like and had a basic understanding of the Christian gospel, and yet the churches still grappled with a similar issue.

Censuses were carried out on religious attendance in London by Robertson Nicoll for the *British Weekly* in 1886 and R. Mudie Smith for the *Daily News* in 1902-03. These showed a small decline in Nonconformist attendance and a larger decline in Anglican attendances. Charles Booth of the Salvation Army carried out a census between 1897 and 1900. He concluded that Nonconformity held its own better than Anglicanism. Churches strong on ritual were short of men. Churches that did well were those that catered for secular as well as religious interests. The poorest people, he concluded, (except the Roman Catholic Irish) tended to attend the less formal mission halls.

Nonconformist churches probably reached a peak shortly after 1900. The new practice of the weekend was beginning by 1905 to make inroads into church patterns of attendance. From 1905, attendance declined slowly until the First World War, after which there was a huge change in patterns of attendance and indeed belief.

What the Victorian and Edwardian churches needed was something that would interest people who would not normally go to church and which would then be a gateway into the church.

Bowdon Downs Congregational Church grappled with the problem in its own way. Its congregation was generally well educated. By 1865 it had a library of over 1,000 books. There is reference to a library in the original design of the Hale Road building, but it is more likely that this was an aspiration only, although there was a Sunday school library.[1] There is no reference in the accounts we have of books being purchased. Many of the congregation would not have been very literate in the early days.[2]

Bowdon Congregational also formed the Bowdon Scientific and Literary Club, holding regular lectures on matters of interest for the inquiring Victorian mind. It is fair to say that MacKennal was genuinely interested in science and nature. In 1883, lectures covered topics as diverse as Wordsworth, the rain-band in the spectrum, bacillae in tubercular disease, notes of a visit to Baalbek, the construction of the proposed Manchester Ship Canal, safety lamps and the stones of Carnac.

---

[1] The later library was, sadly, disposed of in the 1980s refurbishment.
[2] Some of the early church minutes are poorly written, and these would have been taken by the church secretary, who would usually be one of the more literate church members. The Brewer family appear to have been an exception, being keenly interested in reading.

Bowdon Baptist as we have seen held self-improvement meetings, but these were too intellectual to appeal to the poorer people of the church. It was Lloyd who made the difference. He wanted to use different means of attracting people, ranging from direct evangelism to more indirect methods. In doing this, he had to take into account the natural Baptist constituency, which was less likely to be interested in what interested those at Bowdon Downs Congregational. Amongst many other things, Lloyd was therefore responsible for starting the Mothers' Meeting, the Women's Pleasant Sunday Afternoon Society, the Christian Endeavour Society, the Tract Society and the Lads' and Girls' Life Brigade. The church calendar became full of events and activities.

Lloyd was, in fact, ahead of his time in starting one particular event. This was the so-called 'Pleasant Evenings'. On 27 March 1895 he brought a proposal for what he called a week-night service and asked for permission to form a provisional committee. This would consist of people from both within and outside the church. It would, he said, be strictly on religious and evangelical lines and yet would be independent of the church itself. This initiative developed into Pleasant Thursday Evening Meetings. Although Lloyd initially called these services, this may have been in order to persuade the congregation that they were not agreeing to a dangerous new development. In fact, they soon became mostly secular events with small touches of Christianity, and were designed so that members could bring their friends without them feeling that the gospel was being rammed down their throats.

All this was Lloyd's gateway to allow outsiders to come to church without attending a service. He still, of course, held special missions and gospel services, which were a more direct way of reaching people.

The Pleasant Evenings were not as intellectual as the meetings held at Bowdon Downs Congregational and had a wider appeal. They started at 8.15pm. Usually there was a speaker, and sometimes a soloist. In 1899 Lloyd reported that the average attendance was about 100 and he gave out prizes for good attendance. He was able to persuade the mayor and mayoress, Mr and Mrs S. Thompson, to attend in 1900.[3] In the same year the group went to Peacock Farm at Styal for the day.

Examples of the 1904 entertainment included a solo of 'I was glad when they said unto me, let us go into the House of the Lord', a concert by the Broadheath Congregational Choir, a lantern lecture on 'A Visit to the Yosemite Valley USA' and the Revd John Holden of Bowdon Downs Congregational reciting 'The Sky Pilot' by Ralph Connor. Thirty new members joined in 1904.

A similar movement swept the country at the turn of the century, but focussed on Sundays. This was the 'Pleasant Sunday Afternoon' movement. Usually meetings were held in a chapel. Apart from a short prayer and a hymn or two, they too were non-religious in character. There might be songs or solos and an address on a secular subject. Sometimes this was political.

In Altrincham, George Faulkner Armitage was the main leader of the movement. It began to bring the Nonconformists into even closer contact.

---

[3] Mrs Thompson was a friend of Mrs Lloyd's, and later laid one of the foundation stones for the rear extension of the Hale Road chapel.

The Pleasant Sunday Afternoon Movement was started by John Blackham. The name came to him during a train journey. In the carriage with him were a number of men who he thought might be ex-convicts. To forestall what they might have been planning for him, he asked them, 'What sort of Bible class would you rather have than go to a horse race or a cock fight?' They answered that they had nothing against the Bible, but asked in turn why church services needed to be so blessed dull?

Blackham decided to start meetings which would show that church need not be dull, and used the word 'pleasant' to describe them.

THE BRITISH SCHOOL

In later chapters, we will see how education helped politicise many Nonconformists. First, however, we shall look at the principal local Nonconformist school. Few people at the time of writing of this book will realise that, when they park in one part of the carpark of a local supermarket, they are parking on the foundations of the British School.

In 1859 Bowdon Downs Congregational Church decided to provide schoolrooms to replace those at the bottom of The Downs. The Building Committee comprised Messrs Rigby, Whitehead, Milne and Joseph Thompson. The building cost £2,600 and opened on 4 January 1861. The British School was situated off Armitage Place, which in turn was off Oxford Road. The Earl of Stamford donated the land in return for payment of a rentcharge.

The school played a key role in Nonconformist life in Altrincham. First, it provided education, and second it provided a convenient venue for meetings, having the largest public meeting room available for use in Altrincham for some time.

For the Baptists, not only was it the location of the evening launch meeting for the Hale Road building fund and the first Church Meetings of Mowbray's breakaway church, but it was also the place where some of the early Baptists would have educated their children.

The school was, in fact, part of a movement which dates back to 1808 in the north-west of England when The Royal Lancastrian Institute for Promoting the Education of the Poor was founded. This had a non-sectarian basis, but caused some anger in the Church of England. The movement spread from the north-west and soon there were British Schools across the country.

The British School in Altrincham was technically independent of Bowdon Downs Congregational, but the trustees and its entire funding came from Bowdon Downs. Government education reforms led to Government grants. In 1875 the school received a grant of £206-5s-0d, but in return it became subject to inspection.

Education at the school was principally Bible focussed. In one room under the scrutiny of just one teacher, up to 100 children would be kept in order and taught by child monitors, sometimes as young as six years old.[2] The average attendance

> H. J. Leech in 1880 tells the story of how youngsters would come to the British School on Sunday morning and then go to Bowdon Downs Congregational after visiting 'Old Peggy's' for some of her homemade toffee to keep them going in the sermons and hymns.[1]

in 1877 was 323 pupils, making the school the biggest in Altrincham, although the sheer number of Church of England schools meant total numbers in Anglican education were higher.[3]

Academically, pupils did well. In 1902 it was reported that the British School pupils had won more Cheshire County scholarships than any other school.[4]

---

[1] Leech, op. cit.
[2] Bayliss D. (ed): *Altrincham — a History*, Willow Publishing, 1992.
[3] The Wesleyans also had their own schools.
[4] For the record, A.J. Pearce and Professor Hall were two of the well-known managers. Samuel Butler was for twenty-eight years school superintendent and John Ferguson and W.A. Boucher were two well-known headmasters.

As well as providing education, the school was used for Bowdon Downs Congregational Church's Sunday School for a while.[5]

The school also housed a mission church of Bowdon Downs. This may have been the successor to an earlier mission at Tipping Street.[6] The mission church remained at the British School until 1901 when it reunited with Bowdon Downs. For a while, Frank Crossley was in charge. By 1883 it had sixty-four members. In 1890 Elizabeth Galbraith transferred to the Baptists from the mission church. It was very much a mission to the nearby poorer areas, and much of its congregation was quite local. In 1886, Bowdon Downs raised specific funds for the area and for Broadheath because of the 'considerable distress'.

From 1870, the Welsh Methodists also met in the school and held an annual rally there. At one of these, the future Prime Minister, David Lloyd George, spoke on Welsh music. In 1890 we find Elizabeth Davies transferring from the Welsh church to the Baptists and being baptised as a believer.

Bowdon Downs Congregational Church also met at the British School at one point while its own building was being extended. In addition to its use for education and church purposes, the school was extensively used for all sorts of meetings. It is probably fair to say that more events in Altrincham were held in the 1870s in the British School than in any other location. The nearest competitor was the Altrincham and Bowdon Literary Institution.

The trustees decided in 1902 to cease providing education. The education reforms which brought in state schools made the British School's primary function no longer necessary. Intriguingly, the Baptists may have bridged part of the premises gap between 1902 and 1906 while the new state school was built as they let their Sunday school rooms to the local Education Committee for two years from 1904.

The school rooms still continued to be used for community uses, for example, hosting the first meeting of the Altrincham and District Temperance Federation in 1903.

By 1904, the British School had been renamed the MacKennal Institute in honour of the great pastor of Bowdon Downs. By 1930 the MacKennal Institute was administered by the Congregational Union and was sold on 21 December 1948 to the YMCA on condition the YMCA did not sell it on at a profit for ten years.

The trustees of the British School were quite ecumenical. St Vincent's Roman Catholic Church held meetings and tea parties at the school, in 1883 entertaining the children with a magic lantern show.

---

[5] This was certainly the case in 1892.
[6] There is a reference in 1879 to a contribution by Bowdon Downs to the pension fund of Revd G.J.Pluck of the Tipping Street Mission, although (but less likely) this could also have been Manchester City Mission.

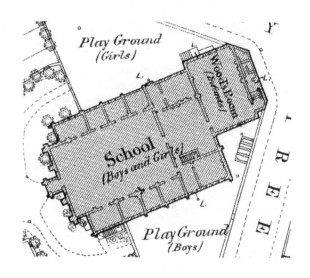

1876 map showing the layout of the British School off Oxford Road.

St John's Church met at the British School while their new building was being constructed. The photograph on the left is of St John's in the late nineteenth century

The photograph on the right is taken from the junction of Ashley Road and St John's Road.

If you stood here at any time during the period covered by this book, you would have seen the British School in front of you.

Oxford Road in 1905. The British School was off a side road just by the tree on the right. Note the ladies shorter skirts 'in the Edwardian period, and the smart but more casual attire of the man on the right.

Nonconformist pupils at the British School circa 1893.

The interior of the British School during a flower festival. This photograph was probably taken in the 1930s. The evening service to launch the Baptist chapel building fund was held here, as was the first Church Meeting of Altrincham Baptist Church.

Stamford Park School was founded in 1906 to replace the British School and the former Wesleyan School. It was intended to be the Altrincham school where Nonconformists would send their children for education. The County Council held a competition for the design of Stamford Park and Navigation Road Schools (the latter replacing the Rigby Memorial School mentioned earlier). The winner was none other than William Owen, the Baptist chapel architect, who won first prize for his design of the new Navigation Road School. Fittingly, Stamford Park School was opened by William Crossley and the opening prayer was by the minister of Bowdon Downs, the Revd J. Holden. When the British School finally closed, a procession marched with a band at its head from the British School to Stamford Park School.

The photograph is an undated early one, but all that is known is that the teacher is a Miss Clitheroe.

The British School had a major impact on the life of Victorian Altrincham. It was the Sunday school however that was the major focus of each church in its youth work.

THE SUNDAY SCHOOL

The National Sunday School Society was founded in 1785 by Ian Fox, a Baptist merchant and deacon. In 1803 he and one William Brodie went on to found the Sunday School Union. By the mid-nineteenth century, the two organisations had merged.

The Sunday school movement was designed to meet the needs of the working class. It has been estimated that the number of pupils in Sunday schools by 1851 was over 2 million and covered a staggering 75.4% of the working class aged between five and sixteen. Together with the Ragged Schools, this was for many years the only real source of education for working class people.

The Sunday School Union became a publishing house and a distributor of Sunday school textbooks and other teaching aids to Church Sunday schools of all denominations. It also provided professional advice to teachers, and in 1870 began teacher examinations to increase standards. The Union also acted as a lobbying group to protect Sunday school education, for example, opposing the Sunday opening of post offices and also the opening of the Crystal Palace.

In 1874 the International Lessons Committee programme was adopted, which led to a scheme of home Bible study. This in turn became the International Bible Reading Association in 1882. The Altrincham Baptists used this scheme. Later in the nineteenth Century, the Boys' Brigade and Life Brigades were introduced and a Boys' Brigade was formed at Altrincham.

The Christian Endeavour movement was imported from the USA in 1888 and placed emphasis on training young people for active service in church life. It ran in parallel to the Sunday school. Worship in Christian Endeavour meetings involved everyone and included the use of sentence prayers, solos and brief addresses. The Altrincham Baptists formed their own Christian Endeavour Society and Lloyd became head of the Society for local churches.

In the 1870s in Altrincham, the local Nonconformist churches worked together to bring young people to Sunday school. We have to remember here that the Sunday school and parallel organisations included teenagers, so the Sunday school was also an early form of youth group. In 1875 there was a combined mission to young people headed up by a Mr Arrowsmith. His religious beliefs were however interesting. The local newspaper reported that Mr Arrowsmith was Church of England, but Nonconformists had 'nothing to fear from that'.

The prayer meeting for the mission was held at Bowdon Baptist Chapel on The Downs and the mission meetings were held at the Independent Congregational Chapel on Regent Road, the British School and the lecture hall at the back of the Presbyterian chapel on Delamer Road.

In 1877 there was a prayer meeting for the Nonconformist Sunday school leaders in Altrincham at which the Baptists were present. By the 1880s there were yearly combined Sunday school meetings for the Nonconformists. In 1886 the annual combined Easter Sunday School Service was held at Bowdon Baptist. In 1887 the Nonconformists also held a combined Sunday school for all children at Bowdon Downs Congregational and Trinity Presbyterian.

The Altrincham Baptists had a Sunday school right from the foundation of Bowdon Baptist Church. As early as 1873, Bowdon Baptist is listed as having fifty pupils. By 1878 this had grown to nine teachers and 120 pupils. This was one of the reasons why the Baptists needed a new building.

At the new Hale Road building, according to the local newspaper, 'the lower storey is to be used for school purposes and will comprise a school room 67 feet long and 39 feet wide with two classrooms, library etc. It will be provided with a separate entrance by Byrom Street and also have communication with the Chapel by means of a staircase and a tower.'

As we have seen, the Sunday school was integral to the design of the Hale Road chapel and explains why the main hall was built so high. This was in order to accommodate the Sunday school without having to place the school too much below ground level, with all the damp problems that would cause.

Numbers dropped after the Baptists moved into the Hale Road new building for some unexplained reason (possibly due to the departure of William Llewellyn to Ogden, as he was a prime mover behind the Sunday school). By 1883, however, numbers had climbed to 120 again.

Was Mowbray less committed to the Sunday school than Llewellyn? By the time of the split, numbers had dropped to ninety-three. After the split, Hale Road initially still recorded eighty-six scholars (unless they were conveniently still including the breakaway church in their returns) and then declined. One year after the churches reunited, the church only had forty-nine, and this reflected a period of growth. This reinforces the hypothesis that the better off families stayed at Hale Road, and many who followed Mowbray were single women and a smaller number of poorer families. It was Mowbray's evening gospel services on Railway Street that were packed out, rather than the morning services. There is mention of the Sunday school in church Meeting minutes under Mowbray, but the numbers were probably quite modest. A gospel hall would be unlikely to have much space for children's provision. Perhaps this was the reason a number of families opposed the sale of Hale Road. Where would the Sunday school go?

With Lloyd there was a new enthusiasm. Just two months after he became co-pastor, the local newspaper recorded that the morning Sunday school anniversary service was taken by his friend Roberts from Union Chapel. In the afternoon, Carey Bonner came from Sale and gave demonstrations about magnetism, and in the evening there was an evangelistic appeal to the older children by Arnold Streuli, pastor of the massive Moss Side Baptist Church. Indeed, so taken was the local newspaper reporter with Streuli's appeal to the children that he quoted the end of it verbatim.

Showing the importance Lloyd attached to the Sunday school, he became its superintendent throughout his time as pastor. A growing Sunday school meant more families and interest from parents who might never otherwise come to church.

Under Lloyd, the Sunday school grew steadily from about seventy-five pupils. By 1899 it had an average of 103. By 1901 there were 200 and by 1908 there were a staggering 326 pupils. This was a remarkable achievement, as from the 1880s, Sunday school attendances began to decline nationally in the face of the increasing availability of state-run or state-controlled education.

Lloyd's purpose in the Sunday school is revealed in an article he wrote in 1904: 'My chief desire is that each teacher should seek to become a definite soul winner and that the conversion of the child should be his supreme aim. Sound scripture knowledge, good and regular habits, generosity and reverence, and love of truth all are important; but the chief end should be with the aid of the scriptures to make the little folks 'wise unto salvation, through faith which is in Christ Jesus'.'

The Sunday school also gave the church access to parents. In 1903 the Sunday school visitor made 517 visits to parents. Lloyd asked the church to 'pray for our Sunday School teachers, that they may be abundantly successful in winning souls'.

There was a Sunday School Union Certificate for the most outstanding teacher each year and certificates for good attendance, birthdays and baptisms. There were also Bible prizes and, as we have seen, the children were encouraged to undertake the temperance pledge. The Sunday school had its own choir.

Sunday school anniversaries were used to promote the work of the school, particularly among the church members, but they were also used to encourage parents who would never normally do so to come to the chapel. On 1 June 1904, for example, there were three special anniversary services. A platform was erected for the young people in the main hall. They had their own service in the afternoon. 'We especially desire the presence of the parents and friends of the children,' wrote Lloyd.

In common with other churches in the area, the Sunday school and its associated organisations were probably the key strategy for growth.

Sunday school trips were a highlight of each year. In 1876 for example, about 100 adults and children from Bowdon Baptist met at Peel Causeway Station (now Hale Station) and headed to Knutsford and then to Booth Hall Park. There they played games. It was a very hot day. They then had tea at a local farm and at 8pm returned to Bowdon.

Altrincham Baptist Sunday School group, date unknown

Sunday school in 1942 with Arthur Overbury back right. The children are all contemporaries of Brian Waterson's.

The former Hale Road schoolroom laid out for a conference in 2007. The original room was much larger and took in the rooms currently behind it.

Stagelights, the performing arts group involving the younger people of Altrincham Baptist Church, perform at a morning service at the Delamer Centre (formerly Trinity URC) on Delamer Road.

AN EVER CLOSER UNION

We will now look at a movement which became one of the most significant ecumenical, political and evangelistic movements in Britain. In its creation, Altrincham, Manchester and some of the people featured in this book played a key role.

The formation of this movement involved two men in particular: MacKennal and McLaren. We can now see the importance of their meeting at the launch of the building fund for the Hale Road Chapel and their speeches to those assembled, which were also aimed at each other. Looking back on his life later, McLaren saw the formation of the movement as his life's greatest achievement.

The Nonconformists always to some extent co-operated, but this gathered a new momentum from the 1870s. In 1872 there was a Nonconformist conference in Manchester and by 1878 there was general agreement on the need for joint evangelism. At the same time, there were moves to unite the Congregationalists and the Baptists. McLaren and MacKennal were both in favour, although initially McLaren was the stronger advocate. In 1886 the Baptist Union and Congregational Union went so far as to hold joint meetings at the City Temple in London. In the same year, the Methodist Collier, started services in Manchester for representatives of the Nonconformist churches.

MacKennal visited McLaren in Fallowfield towards the end of 1889 to discuss a new idea. There were many Nonconformist denominations, but they shared many beliefs. They were, in the main, evangelical in outlook. If they could co-operate together, they could make a serious impact in Britain. It was also no doubt in MacKennal's mind that this might be the beginning of a serious ecumenical movement to unite the Nonconformists into one denomination.

MacKennal wanted to organise a Nonconformist conference. He knew he would get nowhere without McLaren's support. A good sign was that McLaren himself had begun to hold meetings of Nonconformist ministers at Union Chapel. McLaren gave his backing to MacKennal, although we know from his addresses to the Altrincham Baptists that he had reservations about any associated political activity, and here he and MacKennal were to differ.

The Nonconformists had been creating a new label for themselves, and now began to use the name 'Free churches'. The idea was that they were churches free from state or foreign control, subsidy or influence.

Having obtained McLaren's approval, MacKennal now approached Collier to see if he could use Methodist Central Hall on Oldham Street for a pilot conference on 11 January 1892. At the pilot, MacKennal proposed a much larger Free Church Congress for later that year, also in Manchester. The success of this second conference was due to his 'unwearied and competent planning'.[1] McLaren addressed the second conference.

Meanwhile in the summer of 1892, the devout Methodist Dr Lunn paid for a conference in Grindelwald, Switzerland. His idea was wider than the Nonconformist vision of unity. His guests included non-High Church Anglican

---

[1] Jordan, E.K.H.: *Free Church Unity – History of the Free Church Council Movement*, Lutterworth, 1956.

bishops and Gladstone himself.[2] The Bishop of Worcester caused a storm in the English press by celebrating a joint communion at Grindelwald. MacKennal too was at Grindelwald. Although the conference was to consider a wider Protestant unity, it appears that the immediate practical outcome was to give further impetus to the move to bring the Nonconformists together.

MacKennal attended the follow-up Lucerne conference the next year and reported to Bowdon Downs Congregational on the possibility of a move to bring the Nonconformists back into the Church of England, with the High Church moving to join the Roman Catholic Church. This was radical stuff, and MacKennal was wise enough to keep his own thoughts to himself.

The first formal Free Church Council duly met in Manchester and was a direct result of the 1892 conference. Meetings were held at the Central Methodist Hall and the plenary session was held in the Free Trade Hall. The conference attracted 3,000 delegates and ended with a joint communion service led by McLaren.

> 'You will not be doing your duty as Christian men unless you cast yourselves with earnestness and sympathy into the work.' McLaren to the Free Church Congress in 1892.

In 1893 the conference moved to Birmingham and was led by the Quaker, Cadbury (of the chocolate company). The conference then moved to Leeds.

In 1897, Rodney Smith was appointed as the full-time evangelist for the Free Churches. We shall return to his story in a subsequent chapter. The Council then changed its name to the National Council of the Evangelical Free Churches. MacKennal was at first Secretary of the Council and then President in 1898.

> At the 1893 Free Church Conference, Cadbury placed national evangelism high on the agenda. He was alarmed at new research that showed that only 27 per cent of the population attended church.

The Council now decided that national conferences were not enough; unity had to work at a local level. Local District Councils were therefore set up, partly funded by the Cadbury brothers. George Cadbury gave every local Council £5 to buy a large-scale map of their area to plan their mission and divide it up between the Nonconformist churches.

In January 1901 the Free Churches held a mission to London followed by one in February covering the rest of the country. There were 660 meetings in Manchester alone, and John Clifford, McLaren and J. M. Jowett were the main evangelists. This 'simultaneous' mission was probably one of the largest initiatives of its type the country has ever seen. The preparatory meeting for the East Lancashire and Cheshire areas was held at Trinity Presbyterian chapel on Delamer Road in Bowdon.

For its own mission, the local Council used the well-known evangelist, W. R. Lane. His first talk was at the Hale Road chapel and he then visited various venues in Altrincham.[3] He recounted his life in the Coldstream Guards and his subsequent

---

[2] Lunn also promoted tours in the Alps to bring church leaders together. The company he founded became Lunn-Poly, later to become part of the German-owned Thomson holiday and travel agency group.
[3] It is possible his main base throughout may have been the Hale Road chapel.

conversion to Christianity under the title 'From the Gaming Table to the Mercy Seat', using lantern slides to illustrate his talk.

We even have a note of how the Altrincham Free churches divided up Altrincham into segments for door to door work. The Baptists were allocated the 'B streets', Ashley Road to Peel Causeway Station, Hale Road to the railway bridge, Victoria Road, Albert Road and Cecil Road to Lisson Grove.[4] After the 1901 mission, MacKennal reported that every local church had received new members.

There were further national campaigns in 1902 and 1905. Despite the lack of a national mission in 1904, Rodney Smith as national evangelist felt it was a 'bumper year'.

How did all this impact on Altrincham? Given his pivotal role in founding the movement, it is not surprising that MacKennal was the first President of the Altrincham and Bowdon Evangelical Free Church

> 'I think all the members of the various Evangelical communions of this country are under an obligation to the Bowdon church for the generosity and wisdom with which they have spared their minister so frequently.' Alexander McLaren[5]

Council. Given McLaren's key supporting role, it is also not surprising that the Altrincham Baptists were keen members of the council.

Signs of Altrincham churches working together however go back further than all this. In 1874 Bowdon Downs Congregational hosted a combined Easter communion service for all the Nonconformists. Perhaps this sort of local event made MacKennal consider more national co-operation, although even before he arrived in Altrincham, the local newspaper quoted him as wanting more church unity.

The first reference to the Free Church Council itself in Altrincham in the Baptist church minutes is in 1898 when Wilson Crossley,[6] Simmons and Southwell were appointed as delegates to the local Council, which was at first named the 'Altrincham and District Evangelical Free Church Council'. The Council was formed at the Bank Street Wesleyan Chapel on 23 May 1898 and Lloyd was appointed as its secretary.

In 1899 the Baptists hosted the local Council meeting at Hale Road. A tea was prepared for the Council and resolutions were passed in favour of the peace congress at The Hague and against seven-day newspapers. Lloyd reported forty-six churches, chapels and missions had affiliated, an increase on the thirty-two of the previous year. Only the Brethren on Ashfield Road had decided to depart. In the evening MacKennal spoke on Cromwell.

In 1901 Lloyd reported on discussions as to whether Sale should continue to be part of the Altrincham Council or set up its own Council. By then, he noted there were thirty-seven churches and the Council had set up libraries at Sale and the British School.

---

[4] The Free Churches in the campaign were Broadheath Wesleyan Congregational and Primitive Methodist churches, Bank Street Wesleyan, Trinity Mission, the Methodist New Connexion, Borough Road Wesleyan, Oxford Road Primitive Methodists, Hale Road Baptist, Hale Road Wesleyan, the new Ashley Road Congregational Church, Enville Road Wesleyan, Delamer Presbyterian and Bowdon Downs Congregational Church.

[5] Quoted in Guardian Year Book, 1905.

[6] He appears not to be a relative of the Crossley brothers. He was a jeweller's clerk and lived over the shop with wife Fanny and daughter Ethel on Ashley Road.

As well as organising local missions, a practical expression of the Council was pulpit exchanges. Lloyd preached at the Wesleyan, Presbyterian and Congregational churches and their ministers preached at the Baptist Church. MacKennal did not preach to the Baptists in 1904 as he died that year and was unwell from March onwards, but he had preached in 1903 at Hale Road.

In 1903 the Baptists raised money to support a Free Church Council nurse to minister to the poor of Altrincham.

In 1904, MacKennal was still the President and Lloyd the Secretary. At a meeting in 1904, the Methodist Warburton Lewis said the Free Churches had never been closer together. The Congregationalist Holden said they were closer together than the different branches of the Church of England.

There were local lobbying activities, and in connection with lobbying against one of the Licensing Bills in 1904, Lloyd wrote: 'The future of England is in the hands of the Free churchmen. If they fail our national decay is sure.' The Council and Christian Endeavour Union held regular and well-attended open-air services at the corner of Grafton Street in Altrincham and in Broadheath.

MacKennal saw the Free Church movement as the precursor to Christian reunion. In 1887 he wrote: 'If Federalisation [of the Free churches] succeeds, it will certainly head to reunion.' He saw no reason why the Congregationalists and Baptists should not merge. Bowdon Downs developed close links with the Delamer Road Presbyterians, having united services at one stage while Bowdon Downs Chapel was renovated. In 1901 MacKennal went so far as to talk locally of a possible rapprochement with the Church of England: 'While we will not have the rule of Rome, we greatly revere the Catholic idea.'

McLaren on holiday at Mentone in Italy on the Mediterranean in 1904.

Rodney Smith, national Free Church evangelist. Smith needed four burly policemen to help him into the 1901 Birmingham Free Church rally as the building was so full. This photograph was taken the following year.

The Nonconformists in Altrincham and throughout the country were working together on an unprecedented scale. There was much more to come.

THE ROLE OF WOMEN

The way a country builds its houses often reflects its priorities and aspirations. On the continent, Europeans socialised in restaurants, in cafés and on the streets. In England in particular, society turned inwards toward the home and houses were turned inwards on themselves. Georgian wrought-iron balconies turned to Victorian thick curtains, hiding the household from outside prying eyes.

This new type of house was seen as an extension of the woman. It was her duty to make it into a home. 'Wherever a true wife comes, this home is always around her,' wrote Ruskin.[1]

Victoria and Albert were seen as the embodiment of marital purity and domestic bliss, although unbeknown to society at the time, Victoria was almost certainly not her father's child.[2] Victoria and Albert married when Victoria was just twenty. With her high sex drive but their often stormy relationship, they were generally a happy couple.

The Victorians saw domestic love and the creation of the home as the ideal to which women should aspire. The woman's place was in that home. In 1876, Revd Alex Hannay lectured at the British School on 'Home and Homes'. Home, he said, was the place for love and family, and rest for the man.

The Industrial Revolution, however, gave women new economic power. Neil McKendrick of Gonville and Caius College, Cambridge, has written that 'with the Industrial Revolution, their earnings became central to the domestic economy'. Indeed, his research shows that women made a significantly larger contribution than men.[3] It was partly the increased purchasing power of women that boosted the demand for British goods that in turn fuelled the Industrial Revolution.

In Altrincham, the majority of working women would probably have been domestic servants. In 1851 there were 751,540 domestic servants in the nation. By 1891 this figure had risen to 1,386,167. It was only in the 1930s that the number of servants fell below the 1 million mark. The majority of these were women.

This was a significant change which took place from the bottom of society upwards, for it was working-class women who first began to achieve economic power.

However, it took a long time for women to use this power, to mobilise in an effective way and for institutions to change. When Victoria came to the throne, women quite literally had almost no rights. By the end of her reign, women still had relatively little freedom, although there had been some slow progress.

In 1858 the Matrimonial Causes Act allowed women and men to divorce at a cost of £100. Gladstone opposed the Bill. The Act allowed men to divorce on the grounds of adultery, but women had to prove not only adultery but also either bestiality, bigamy, incest, rape or cruelty.

---

[1] Quoted in Flanders J.: *The Victorian House, Domestic Life form Childbirth to Deathbed*, W.W. Norton and Company Ltd., 2003. The extract is from *'Sesame and Lilies: Two Lectures'*.
[2] If she had been, she would have inherited the genetic disease porphyria and not haemophilia.
[3] McKendrick, N.: *Home Demand and Economic Growth: A New View of the Role of Women and Children in the Industrial Revolution* in N.Mckendrick (ed): *Historical Perspectives in English Thought and Society in Honour of J.H. Plumb*, 1974.

In 1839 the Infants' Custody Act allowed a divorced woman to try and persuade a judge to allow her custody of her children until the age of seven. After that, she could only argue for access. She lost both these rights, however, if she had committed adultery before the divorce. The reality was that in most divorces, the man gained custody of the children. A woman might not even have access to them, even after 1839, and full and equal guardianship of children was only given to women in 1925.

Until 1882, married women could not sue (or be sued) or enter into contracts in their own right. Engaging in business on her own was therefore almost impossible for a woman. Even after 1882, a divorced woman only had the right to resume possession of her own property. She had no right to anything belonging to her husband.

There was little specialisation in women's medicine. In 1874, however, the London School of Medicine for Women was founded. Elizabeth Garrett became the first practising woman doctor, but encountered fierce opposition.

In 1866 John Stuart Mill made the first attempt to allow women to vote in parliamentary elections. In 1868 the first ever public meeting in favour of women's suffrage was held at the Free Trade Hall in Manchester. The cause was particularly

> Annie Bowland, who joined the Baptist church when she married Charles Frederick Southwell, had suffragette sympathies.[4]

promoted by the former Baptist (and now agnostic) radical Liberal (and later Socialist), Dr Richard Pankhurst, and his wife Emmeline, initially from a Manchester base.[5] There was a meeting in Altrincham in 1874 which was reported to have had a good attendance but not to have been crowded. There was a suffragette meeting in 1880 in Stretford. William Crossley supported the right of women to vote.

In 1902 women were allowed to attend the Bowdon Scientific and Literary Club for the first time. In 1905 the Free Trade Hall was the scene of the Liberal Party rally where Christabel Pankhurst, daughter of Richard and Emmeline, and Annie Kenney unfurled their banner 'Votes for Women' and were ejected from the meeting and arrested.[6] These were early days, however. It was only after the First World War that women would be allowed to vote, and it took many more years for many institutions and societies to open their doors to women.

For a girl from a more wealthy family, there was always the opportunity for education to improve herself. There were a number of private schools in Bowdon and there was also the possibility of having a governess. Even then, access to higher education was limited. In 1871 the ladies' Newnham College was admitted to Cambridge, but it was only after the Second World War that women were able to receive a full Cambridge degree. However, 1870 saw Forster's Education Act and the move towards universal education. Until then, church schools had often been the only opportunity for education for many girls.

For both sexes, the pursuit of happiness was assumed to involve marriage. The weddings of the Baptists were probably not lavish affairs. Not one Baptist wedding

---

[4] The source of this information is her family.
[5] Mike Partridge, a member of Altrincham Baptist Church at the time of writing, is related to Minnie O'Brien who worked with Sylvia Pankhurst, daughter of Richard and Emmeline. Richard Pankhurst is buried in Sale Township Cemetery.
[6] The original banner read "Will the Liberal Party Give Votes for Women?" However, their seats were changed and they had to unfurl a smaller banner. By such a small change was a decisive slogan born.

is noted in the newspapers of the period in Altrincham. Featured weddings were usually at Anglican churches or the richer Nonconformist chapels. When on a Tuesday evening 1000 people or so attended Bowdon Downs Congregational for the wedding of Jesse Haworth to Miss Armitage (who taught in the Sunday school and who was the daughter of the wealthy George Armitage of Townfield House and sister of the well-known Congregational Minister Revd Elkanah Armitage), there was a lavish reception with petals strewn before the couple and the local newspaper reported how the presents were 'numerous and costly'.

Victorian society was undoubtedly patriarchal and this was reflected in the church. There was no question of women ever being priests, vicars or pastors. In all denominations, the minister was always a man. The secretary and treasurer in Baptist and Congregational churches were always men (although the Baptist constitutions generally did not prohibit women from serving as deacons; it was just understood by the Victorians they did not).

There is, however, another side to the story, particularly in Baptist and Congregational churches, because here women did have considerable influence. This was a necessary consequence of evangelical beliefs. The apostle Paul wrote: 'There is neither Jew nor Greek, slave nor free, male nor female, for you are all one in Christ Jesus.'[7] Although women might be denied the ability to be a pastor or a deacon, the Victorian evangelical devotion to Scripture meant that the Nonconformist churches were forced to allow some equality. The Christian gospel message was, compared to the ethos of the day, liberating for women.

Baptist and Congregational Church Meetings were therefore open to both men and women on an entirely equal basis, except for some which were usually reserved for women only. While women had no vote in local or national elections, they had full and equal voting rights in Baptist and Congregational Church Meetings and elections. This meant they could genuinely influence decisions of the church. They could be either full members or communicant members, in each case with full equality with the men. As full members, they could vote in and dismiss the deacons and the pastor, force the sale of the chapel and change the church constitution. They could (and did) hold a variety of posts in church organisations, being particularly influential in the Sunday school.

Women appear to have been particularly loyal to both Mowbray and Lloyd. Whatever the rights and wrongs of the crucial vote when the Mowbrays left, many of those who followed them were the poorer women in the church.

Bowdon Downs Congregational Church was very much run by the men, but even there women had the vote. As the membership of the Baptist Church was roughly two to one in favour of women throughout the period of this book, they clearly had some influence.

The Baptists and Congregationalists, through their belief in the supremacy of the Bible, found themselves ahead of the political times in allowing women full voting rights.

---

[7] Galatians 3:28.

Although women were all treated equally in the Baptist church, as different social groups became friends, they tended to sit together in groups in the chapel. Servants and working-class women attended the weekly women's meeting which was specifically set up for them. They sat together on the Byrom Street side. Those who attended the Women's Missionary Auxiliary Meeting sat on the Willowtree Road side. When Paul Beasley-Murray arrived as a minister in the 1970s, he was surprised to find this still happening. The practice soon changed.

Women were expected to tend to home life. This photograph is of the lounge of 'The Grove', a house in Ramsay in the Isle of Man as it would have appeared in the Victorian era.[8] Victorian homes seem cluttered to modern taste.

Altrincham Baptist women's meeting outing, date unknown.

Perhaps having the 'religious vote' made women question why they did not have the parliamentary vote, and helped to radicalise some of them in their politics.

---

[8] Picture courtesy of Manx National Heritage.

THE CHURCH AND EMPIRE

Richard Henry Trelfa [1] died tragically on 30 December 1902. The church secretary duly noted the decease of member number 185 in the Altrincham Baptist Church records.

His death illustrates the difficulties Nonconformists experienced in the age of empire.

Trelfa was by trade a joiner and died in Altrincham Hospital as a result of an accident while working at the nurseries of W. Clibran & Son in Hale. His death after an agonising period in hospital when he clung to life, was felt deeply by the church.

What is particularly interesting to us, though, is that Trelfa had been a sergeant in the army, which leads us to ask what the Baptists' attitude to the military might have been? Would he have a military funeral, for example?

It is tempting to see the period after the Franco-Prussian War (which ended in 1871) as a slow build up to an inevitable First World War. With hindsight, this may have been the case, but this was a period when Britain, as far as European conflict was concerned, was more or less at peace. The European royal families were mostly related, and European sabre-rattling could almost be seen as a family quarrel.

Britain however was experiencing that Victorian dilemma, the consequences of which are still with us: was it a European power or did it have a different agenda? Disraeli was astute enough to recognise that Britain then was not really a European power at all, but rather an Asiatic one.

Although Britain in Europe was largely at peace, outside Europe there was a different picture. Wars were being fought around the globe. These were principally the wars of empire and annexation. This was the period of the scramble for Asian and African empires. Countries were annexed or created. Nigeria, Kenya and Uganda joined many other parts of the world in becoming 'imperial pink' on the map. Who could imagine a country today simply annexing Cyprus without an international outcry?

> We don't want to fight, but, by Jingo if we do,
> We've got the ships, we've got the men, we've got the money too.
> We've fought the Bear before, and while the Britons shall be true,
> The Russians shall not have Constantinople'.
>
> George W. Hunt

Some of the annexation was done in the name of God. General Gordon was an evangelical Christian. Hannington in Uganda was a missionary Anglican bishop who was killed by the Masai. He is regarded as a martyr, and yet the fact remains that his martyrdom led eventually to the annexation of Uganda. There was a potent mixture for the British of the desire for power, to civilise, to create a Protestant Christian world, to explore and to investigate.

It would be unfair to say that the British Empire was a bad thing. Much of it was not good, and some was misguided, but it did achieve some positive things.

---

[1] His name appears to have been spelt differently by the church and others at different times.

Of British writers, Rudyard Kipling is perhaps most associated with empire, and yet he is a complex character.[2] He saw empire as 'The White Man's Burden', and certainly the Victorians felt a sense of moral duty to bring their concept of civilisation to the world, but they also had a sense of innate superiority.

It is difficult to underestimate how popular this imperial adventure was in Britain. The possibility of British action in the Russo-Turkish War of 1877-78 was supported by most of the country, even though Britain did not have the military strength to make any substantial intervention.[3] The Afghan intervention of 1879 was also generally popular, as were the Zulu Wars.

There were, though, dissenting voices. In 1901 the lecture at the Altrincham and Bowdon Women's Liberal Club was on 'The cost of a false imperialism'. The speaker challenged the notion that one race has a divine right to rule others.

MacKennal was a pacifist and member of the Peace Society. He opposed for example, British intervention in Afghanistan to secure India. In 1878 he gave a sermon that was later produced as a booklet. In it he challenged Britain's apparent move towards war with Russia. 'Peace is the policy of a Christian nation,' he said. 'It is not an easy thing to keep the peace; the easy thing is to go to war.' He went so far as to advocate disarmament of the entire British Empire. Britain, he argued, should lead the way in global disarmament. In January 1881 he invited a Quaker to speak at Bowdon Downs on 'War and Christianity'. Not surprisingly, the man from the Society of Friends was against war. MacKennal lectured on a pacifist theme while on a tour of the United States.

We know little about Baptist attitudes to empire under Mowbray and his predecessors. Certainly there is no recorded overt support of empire-building. It may be that, for much of the time, they were preoccupied with their own issues.

The Baptists were, of course, among the great missionaries of the time, and it is fair to say that they generally distanced themselves from empire building. The priority of the Baptist missionaries was to spread the gospel and to look after the needy. In Jamaica, as we have seen, they brought about a social revolution and opposed vested interests.

Lloyd's first challenge over empire was the Boer War. The war was generally popular in Britain and led to the British annexation of the Transvaal and control of one of the richest mineral resources in the world. The relief of Mafeking was widely celebrated. In Altrincham there were spontaneous marches, led at one stage by a visiting American brass band. It was also a war where General Kitchener first introduced the notorious concentration camps, and which took a British army of a quarter of a million men over three years to defeat the Boers at a cost of at least £270 million.

It would have been difficult, and indeed highly unpopular, to take a strong stand against the Boer War.

---

[2] Many have wondered why he was called 'Rudyard'. His parents courted at Rudyard Lake, the feeder lake for the Caldon Canal in Staffordshire, and named their child after the lake.
[3] When Disraeli asked the Intelligence Department how many would be needed to hold a front at Gallipoli and around Constantinople against the Russians, he was told 46,000 men and then 75,000, leading him to call the Intelligence Department the 'Department of Ignorance'.

However both MacKennal and Lloyd opposed the war, although Lloyd took a slightly different line from MacKennal.[4] He actively supported those fighting, but objected to the war itself. Thus in 1899 the Baptists raised money for the Altrincham Patriotic Fund,[5] an organisation that raised funds for the wives and children of soldiers.

So when Lloyd took the funeral of the highly popular Trelfa, recently retired from the army, there were bugles and drums and three volleys fired by volunteers under the command of Sergeant Instructor Osmand over Trelfa's grave at the Hale Road Cemetery. There were hundreds of spectators. The choir sang. The press were present. No doubt Lloyd would have taken the opportunity to present a gospel message as part of the talk, but he was there primarily to comfort the mourners and the widow of a loyal church member.

In all this, we can see the seeds of the debate that was later to split Bowdon Downs Congregational in the First World War. Should they fight or not? Bowdon Downs had a pacifist minister in the First World War, but the majority of the congregation did not support his view.

The Baptists were also to face the same dilemma, but in their case there was no split. There were both those who went to the front and those who were conscientious objectors. That story is, however, one for another book.

In a foreshadowing of its role in the First World War, Chapel Street off Regent Road in Altrincham claimed to have sent more men to the Boer War than any other street in England. This photograph shows how it used to look before much of it became a car park. A memorial was kept on the side of the chapel to those who died in the First World War, together with a telegram from the King congratulating the town on its patriotism.

---

[4] The Manchester Guardian took a difficult decision and also opposed it.
[5] Part of the entertainment was Lloyd playing records from his new gramophone selection.

Advertisement for Clibrans in 1904, where Trelfa had his fatal accident

Michael 'Chunk' Southwell of the Baptists
fought in the First World War, but his brother Charles did not.

Unlike their Congregationalist cousins, the Baptists appear to have trod a fine
but careful line in their attitude to war and empire.

ALTRINCHAM POLITICS

To what extent should Christians be involved in politics? If they do become involved, should they ally themselves with any one particular party?

McLaren was primarily a preacher, and yet like all Nonconformists of the time, he had political leanings. McLaren was though acutely aware of the dangers not only of political involvement but also of non-involvement. He referred to this as early as 1873 in his address to the new Bowdon Baptist Church.

He could not be blind, he said, to the fact that there might be a dangerous course in some political direction that might be inimical to the religious life of the Altrincham Baptists, 'but when the clergy of the church cease to be political officers, it will be time enough for them to cease'. In other words, it was the duty of a pastor to be politically active. But, he said there was a danger of their mistaking the means for the end. 'This spiritual work you have to do, the spiritual lives you have to lead, must come to the front. My prayer is that Pastor and people here might long strive together for the faith of the Gospel, and as you work together you will have your reward also.'[6]

In his 1878 talk to the Altrincham Baptists, McLaren returned to the same theme, but this time his speech reflected his growing concern that Nonconformists might lose their way by being *too* involved in politics. 'You can make speeches at political gatherings, you can talk into Town Councils and on the hustings, and at Liberal Associations, and the like. Why, in the name of common sense can you not preach Christ's Gospel as well as do the other?'

It was entirely usual for Victorian Nonconformists to be politically active, and it was the Liberal Party to which they were usually allied. Later, many Nonconformists became involved in the early Labour Party. McLaren's concern was that political involvement might overshadow their primary purpose as churches.

The same issues have parallels in the United States, but there the approach has been very different. In Victorian England, Nonconformists might fight to restrict liberalisation of the licensing laws, but they never seriously expected to achieve prohibition. Instead they tried to prevent alcohol abuse by persuading individuals to abstain and to restrict the power of the beer lobby. In England, the Nonconformists generally allied with what might now be called the moderate 'left' as a result of their views on society, whereas in America their equivalents became involved with what now might be called the 'right'. In England, it was with the Tory Party that the Church of England was associated. Thus we find Conningsby Disraeli as Tory MP generally opening bazaars at Anglican churches while the Liberal candidate attended Nonconformist events.

This is to oversimplify: there were Nonconformists who supported the Tories and there were Liberal Anglicans. A local example is Wainwright of St John's Church, who was an officer of the Altrincham Liberal Association. There is also an honourable tradition in America of more 'left' Christian involvement,[7] but the fact remains that the experience of the two countries at times when Nonconformist

---

[6] The Freeman, 1873.
[7] The Baptists in the United States have been involved in both the Democratic and the Republican parties. Former President Jimmy Carter is a Democrat, for example, and former President Bill Clinton (wherever he might himself stand in religious terms) is the son of a Baptist family and also a Democrat of course.

Christians have been able to have serious influence has been quite different. British Nonconformity has had a more radical and social involvement edge to it.

As the electorate broadened, the Nonconformists in Britain began to see that they could wield power and influence on moral issues. The gradual removal of legal discrimination against them was a sign of their growing strength.

That their power was increasing was also plain to politicians. Nonconformists were heavily involved in widening the electorate, the abolition of slavery and the promotion of free trade. They were against an established or state church, and in 1839 The Religious Freedom Society was founded, followed in 1844 by the British Anti-State Church Association.[8]

The real shock to the Nonconformists was the 1872 Education Act. Nonconformists saw state-funded Anglican-run schools as a threat to their own voluntary Sunday and weekly schools. The state, as they saw it, was paying for children to be indoctrinated into becoming Anglicans.

Nonconformists were not able to muster real support in Parliament for their views in 1872, and so they organised a petition signed by at least two-thirds of all Nonconformist ministers. To their anger, Gladstone virtually ignored it. This led many of them not to vote in the 1874 election or to vote for radicals within the Liberal Party who were critical of the leadership. Disraeli won the election, in part due to the voting or abstention of the Nonconformists. Nonconformists and Liberals both remembered this lesson, as we shall see when we look at the events of 1902 onwards.

MacKennal had fewer reservations than McLaren about the growing Nonconformist influence in politics as the electorate widened. In 1886 he gave a lecture to the Congregational Union on the role of Nonconformist ministers in creating stability within a widened electorate. 'England has become an almost unchecked democracy in its political constitution, and this involves serious responsibilities upon Nonconformist bodies. At present the newly-enfranchised electors are the victims of opportunism, and their recently conceived hopes have been rudely dashed. One of the great objects at which Nonconformists must aim is a rehabilitation of political faith in earnest principle and action. The people must be taught that only a small number of public ills can be cured by legislation.' Individual activity was still important.

The Free Church Council was set up primarily to enable the Nonconformist or 'free churches' to work together in mission. However, under the influence of MacKennal and others, it began to move into politics on moral issues and those concerning religious freedom. This move was supported by the majority, but there were reservations, especially from the leading Nonconformist, R. W. Dale, in Birmingham.

The creation of the National Council saw increased Nonconformist involvement in politics, and a determination to have a Nonconformist 'slate' in Parliament.

---

[8] MacKennal was a supporter of the Anti-State Association, which later became the Liberation Society.

There were still concerns about allying too closely with the Liberal Party, or indeed any one party, but the reality was that, over time, this is precisely what happened. An anonymous minister warned against this in a 1909 book.[9] Like most, he was not worried about individual political involvement. 'It is a great thing doubtless, to rank as one of the political forces of the country, as a political force whereof statesmen must take account.' 'There is no reason at all why a Nonconformist should not stay in the forefront of the political ranks.' However, he felt that Nonconformists had become too closely allied with the Liberals, and in the process had lost their spiritual heart. In particular, Baptist and Congregationalists had forgotten their roots: Church and State should be separate. 'The Free Church Councils...practically make the programme of their meetings relate, from beginning to end, to the programme of the Government of the day or to what they think that programme ought to be.'

> 'I know the Dissenters. They carried the Reform Bill...the abolition of slavery...Free Trade, and they'll carry the abolition of church rates.' So said Lord John Russell on the increasing political power of the Nonconformists.

In 1893 the *Review of the Churches* was launched as the mouthpiece for the Free Church Council. John Clifford and MacKennal were on the editorial board. Gladstone, certainly not a Nonconformist, wrote the foreword, a sign that he recognised the political potential of this movement. The relationship was not always easy, and periodically the Nonconformists fell out with the Liberals.

In 1901 the Free churches' manifesto called for an end to the war in South Africa. It asked for an amnesty, eventual autonomy and for the amity and unity of all South African peoples. 5,425 of the nearly 10,000 Nonconformist ministers signed a petition against the war. The Wesleyan Methodists and the Unitarians, however, supported it. The problem with Nonconformist involvement in politics is demonstrated here: there were very few political issues about which they could all actually agree.

The period after their 1900 election defeat saw the resurgence of the Liberal Party, and it can genuinely be said that their 1906 election success was in large measure a result of Nonconformist activity. Nonconformists began to win at by-elections, and after the 1906 election the MPs included some Nonconformist ministers and between 180 and 200 active Nonconformists – a truly staggering number. Eighty-three were members of the Liberation Society[10].

MacKennal's father was an active Liberal, and MacKennal himself joined the Liberal Party at university and became the Secretary at the university branch. In 1878 he and other prominent members of Bowdon Downs Congregational Church were on the Altrincham delegation to the Manchester Liberal Conference. It is interesting that in March 1904 we know he attended a political dinner for thirty key Nonconformist ministers with Campbell-Bannerman and Herbert Gladstone, the Party Whip. The notes provided to Campbell-Bannerman before the dinner stated 'Revd A. MacKennal, Congregational, C.B., represents Lancashire'.[11]

MacKennal sometimes preached political sermons on what he saw as moral but political issues, believing that 'there is no weightier duty at this hour devolving on

---

[9] *Nonconformity and Politics by a Minister*, 1909.
[10] How the Nonconformists used and then lost their influence after 1906 is, sadly, beyond the scope of this book.
[11] Koss, S.: *Nonconformity in Modern British Politics*, Shoe String Press, 1975.

Christian men in England than to speak out on public affairs'.[12] In 1878, he preached a sermon at Bowdon Downs in which he compared British policy in Afghanistan to Baal worship.[13]

There is little in the records of Church Meetings of Bowdon Downs Congregational of a political nature, but we do know that one church member resigned in 1901 because of what he saw as MacKennal's increasingly political sermons. The church, however, rallied round to support MacKennal. Whilst some might disagree with him, 'we unite in protesting against any attempt to "Tune the Pulpit", to hinder you in any way or degree from speaking to us as your conscience and judgment may dictate'.[14]

As one would expect, many of the members of Bowdon Downs Congregational were also involved in the Liberal Party. Just looking at Hale, we find Liberal party committee members included Joshua Boydell (a member of Bowdon Downs and also trustee of Altrincham Baptist Church[15]), W. H. Goulty (a member of Bowdon Downs), Jesse Haworth (member and personal friend of MacKennal), F. Kean (of the Primitive Methodists on Oxford Road) and J.C. Needham (member of Bowdon Downs and a lawyer who was co-opted onto the Committee).[16] John Thompson was also a well-known Liberal.

In 1878 a Liberal Reform Club was set up in Altrincham at a house on Stamford Street. It was backed by the Lancashire and Yorkshire Bank (a bank controlled by members of Bowdon Downs Congregational) and had Armitage and Haworth on its committee.

In 1903/04 the Liberals in Hale held meetings which included a protest against the Licensing Bill, the Education Act, a discussion on Home Rule and a debate on Religion in Secondary Education. It was more than just coincidence that these were key Nonconformist issues.

Bowdon Downs was not the only church involved with the Liberal Party. When a meeting was held in 1877 to consider forming a Liberal Club for Altrincham and Bowdon, Aylard of the Altrincham Congregational Church and Adamson of the British School Mission were both on the committee.

A Liberal meeting in Hale on 24 January 1905 was chaired by Thomas Wilkinson, minister of the Ashley Road daughter church of Bowdon Downs. The meeting covered the favourite Liberal Nonconformist themes of the Education Act, Chinese labour, the Transvaal War and the Licensing Act as well as the finances of the country.

Although outside the historical period covered by this book, in 1906 the Nonconformists helped secure a great electoral victory for the Liberal Party. William Crossley was returned as the first Liberal MP for Altrincham.

Although an Anglican, William Crossley had strong Nonconformist leanings and always kept a pew at Bowdon Downs Congregational.

---

[12] Altrincham Division Liberal Association: Hale Polling Station Minute Books 1903-1905, Cheshire County Council, Archives and Local Studies.
[13] Baal was a pagan god or generic name for pagan gods in the Old Testament.
[14] Quoted in MacFadyen, D.: *Alexander MacKennal BA., DD., Life and Letters*, J.Clarke, 1905.
[15] It is worth mentioning that he signed the pledge at a public meeting in 1892.
[16] There is also a Mr Hawkesworth (sometimes spelled Hawksworth). A Mr Hawksworth was treasurer of the Altrincham Baptists in 1904, but it is not clear if they were one and the same person.

Manchester always had a radical edge to much of its politics. Part of the agenda of the Anti-Corn Law League was the transfer of power from the landed classes to the newly emerging middle class. John Bright was a textile manufacturer from Rochdale, and William Cobden was MP for Manchester. Cobden said, 'The sooner the power in this country is transferred from the landed oligarchy, which has so misused it, and is placed absolutely mind I say absolutely in the hands of the intelligent middle and industrious classes, the better for the condition and destinies of this country.' The mansions of Bowdon and Dunham were perhaps evidence of that transfer, but maybe not quite in the way he intended.

THE BAPTISTS AND POLITICS

Most Baptists could not vote. We can, however, deduce their politics from their pastors.

Llewellyn was an active Liberal and is described as an 'ardent reformer'.[1] This makes McLaren's comments in 1878, when he must have known of Llewellyn's political involvement, all the more interesting. McLaren, you may recall, advised against placing politics ahead of ministry.

We know little of Mowbray's politics. He was probably too busy working in Manchester and running a church to have much time for political activity.

Leonard was an active Liberal, appearing on platforms with MacKennal and indeed, as we have seen, going so far as to second a motion proposed by the radical atheist Bradlaugh to the Working Men's Liberal Club. That probably places Leonard on the radical side of Liberal politics. It also makes Mowbray's subsequent mission in Altrincham with the Christian brother of Bradlaugh doubly interesting. Perhaps his message was a deliberate one: Altrincham Baptist Church (as opposed to the Hale Road Baptist) had its priority in mission and not in politics.

Lloyd was Secretary to the local Free Church Council while MacKennal was President, and Lloyd later became President himself. The Council, of course, was primarily religious in function, but strayed increasingly into politics on moral issues.

There is one reference to Lloyd's own political allegiance on public record. In 1904 William Crossley addressed a Liberal meeting at the Drill Hall in Hale and a letter of apology for absence was read out from Lloyd. He was not afraid to involve both himself and the Altrincham Baptists in politics when he saw a moral aspect, whether or not this coincided with the agenda of the Liberal Party.

Let us look, therefore, at his political stance on various issues, many of which were common to other Nonconformists.

He was passionately in favour of temperance and freedom of religion, and passionately against racism or slavery. He was on the committee for the Sunday Closing movement to try and prevent the sale of alcohol on Sundays and to prevent alcohol being sold to those under eighteen.[2] According to his biographer, he 'used the local press for the expression of Christian opinion...in contemporary events, such as the Congo atrocities'. The Altrincham Baptists always seemed to be able to get stories into the newspapers, but the number of mentions increased under Lloyd.

We have already seen that Lloyd was opposed to the Boer War. He returned to a South African theme on 6 March 1904 when he persuaded the church evening service congregation to stand and pass the following unanimous resolution:

'That this congregation desires to record its dismay at the action of His Majesty's Government in sanctioning an ordinance that will virtually set up a system of slavery in South Africa under the British Flag and urges upon the Government the immediate removal of the permission given for the importation of Chinese labour

---

[1] Baptist Union Handbook.
[2] We know he was active in writing to his MP about this issue.

into the Transvaal; and at the same time desires to affirm the principal that what is morally wrong can never be politically right or necessary.'

We have to recall here that there was no formal apartheid system under the British in South Africa. The background to Lloyd's protest was the decision of the Rand mine owners to import workers. It was the responsibility of the Conservative Balfour Government to enlist these Chinese labourers. By the end of 1904 20,000 had been sent to South Africa with more to follow. The young Chinese were separated from their families, worked long hours for minimal wages and were kept in compounds.

On 1 March 1904 Lloyd wrote this 'tame' little piece in the church magazine summarising his views on current political events (interestingly foreseeing the possibility of a European war):

'The retrograde Temperance Legislation threatened by the Government, and the thinly disguised "Slave Trade" that has just been sanctioned for South Africa, together with the danger menacing our international commercial relationships, through the designs of Protectionist Statesmen, and that other awful daughter of a European war conflagration, which the Russo-Japanese conflict is bringing within the range of possibilities, are big with coming doom, unless God and His mercy can awaken Britain's conscience ere it be too late.'

Lloyd also protested against the trafficking of opium from China and, as we have seen, organised protest rallies against the licensing legislation in 1904.

We can therefore see that the Altrincham Baptists became increasingly politically active on a number of moral issues. These generally coincided with Liberal political views. There was, however, a much closer tie between the Congregationalists and the Liberal Party in the area. This was probably because the less well-off Baptists were not of sufficient status to serve on committees and many were not eligible to vote. However, they *were* politically involved. It is therefore not surprising that the name on one of the memorial stones of the 1908 extension to the Hale Road Chapel is that of William Crossley, the Liberal MP.

There is one final notable story involving the Baptists and politics. Jacob Bowland was elected to the West Ward of Altrincham in 1897. His brother-in-law was the Baptist Charles Southwell Jnr.

It is possible that some of the Altrincham Baptists may have been early supporters of the Labour Party, but it is not possible to prove this from the records we have. It was, however, the case elsewhere.

The early Independent Labour Party held summer meetings in Altrincham around the same big lamp at the bottom of The Downs where the Baptists had gathered for their open-air services. In July 1893 W. K. Hall, the Labour speaker and prospective candidate for South Salford, found an anarchist holding a simultaneous rally next to his own, which proved entertaining for those assembled. Shortly afterwards, the Manchester City Mission had an outing to Altrincham, tea at the Newtown Night School and then combined with the Altrincham and Bowdon Total Abstinence Society for a rally attracting many hundreds, also at the big lamp at the bottom of The Downs. This was a busy meeting place.

In 1905 a Mr Thompson was elected as Labour candidate to the local council but his election was annulled as he failed the residency qualification. William Games, also of the Labour Party, was elected to the South Ward.

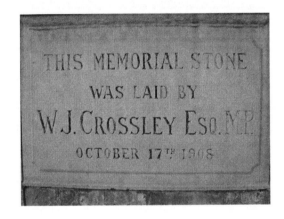

Memorial stone laid by William Crossley at the Hale Road Chapel extension in 1908.

One political issue divided both the Nonconformists and the Liberals, and that was Ireland, so it is to the Irish question that we now turn.

A horse-drawn election cart promoting Jacob Bowland in one of his campaigns for the Liberal Party in West Ward, Altrincham. The three people on the right of the cart (from left to right) are Jacob Bowland, probably Jacob's father and Charles Southwell Jnr. Charles married Annie Bowland, a suffragette supporter and daughter of Jacob.

The cart also mentions other candidates, namely Birtles, Drinkwater, Hughes, MacDonald, Palmer and Smith.

The reference to the ladder is probably a link between his first name of Jacob and Jacob's ladder in the Bible, as well as being a reference to his decorating business.

There is a dog beside the cart and magnification of the photograph shows another one cheekily perched on top.

HOME RULE FOR IRELAND

We have an intriguing glimpse into the heady mixture of politics and religion in Victorian Altrincham over the proposal to give 'home rule' to Ireland. Nowadays, we might simply call this 'devolution'.

The Irish question was never far from the domestic agenda. Between 1845 and 1850, there were about 1.1 million deaths through starvation in Ireland, while the Viceroy continued to draw his salary of £20,000 a year. Little attempt was made by the Government to alleviate this disaster. It was only an alliance of merchant bankers in London led by the Rothschilds and Thomas Baring, together with some aristocrats and Christians, that made any serious attempt to bring relief.

Irish Home Rule was an abiding passion for Gladstone, and he made two attempts to bring it about. It is tempting to ask how much the recent history of England and Ireland might have differed had he been successful. The political reality was that he was not able to force any legislation through the House of Lords. His only option would have been to have a showdown with the Lords to emasculate its power. This never happened.

Both of Gladstone's attempts left the country, the Liberal Party and the Nonconformists deeply divided. Let us look specifically at his first attempt. Gladstone's conversion to Irish Home

> Gladstone's Home Rule plans for Ireland were part of a longer-term devolution plan for the whole of Great Britain.

Rule in 1885 has to be seen against the background of Nationalist attacks.[1] In 1881 a Fenian bomb in the wall of the Salford Barracks injured three people and killed a young boy. There were two attempts to bomb the Mansion House in London and to blow up Liverpool Town Hall. In 1882 an Irish American called Edward McCaffrey and the 'Invincibles' hacked the Duke of Devonshire's brother and an undersecretary to death in Phoenix Park in Dublin with twelve-inch surgical knives. In 1883 there were bombs in Glasgow and London. In 1884 four London railway stations were closed because of Nationalist incidents, there was an attempt to blow up London Bridge and the newly opened underground railway had to be closed due to a bomb incident.

All this sounds comparatively modern, but we need to recall that Irish Nationalists were beginning to learn an important lesson: the British Government may claim not to bow to terrorism, but terrorist acts certainly capture its attention.[2]

Gladstone did not want to reveal his conversion to the cause of Irish Home Rule until he was politically ready, but his hand was forced when his son let the secret slip out. Amid cabinet resignations, Gladstone introduced the Bill before Parliament on 26 March 1886. In a masterly three-and-a-half-hour speech, he outlined plans to set up an Irish Parliament and executive in Dublin. This would have powers of legislation and control over all but certain matters. These exceptions were principally those affecting the Crown, peace and war, defence, foreign and

---

[1] Manchester, with its large Irish community, was the location of Fenian activity. A secret Fenian convention was held there in 1867. In the same year the Fenians launched an attack on Chester Castle which failed. Two of the Fenians were apprehended and then sprung in a daring raid from a police van on Hyde Road in Manchester. A policeman was killed in the incident. Three others were later hanged. This hanging helped move the Roman Catholic Church and moderate nationalist politicians into more overt support for the Fenian cause. See *The Manchester Martyrs* by Mervyn Busteed in *History Ireland*, November/December, 2008.

[2] There is a hypothesis that later Irish attacks were part of a complicated plot involving the British Government and were intended to lead to the assassination of Queen Victoria and thus to discredit Home Rule. See Campbell, C.: *Fenian Fire, The British Government Plot to Assassinate Queen Victoria*, Harper Collins, 2002.

colonial relations, customs and excise, trade and navigation, the Post Office, coinage and legal tender.

There were to be safeguards for the minority. The new legislature was to have a senate and a chamber, but they would meet together. They could, however, meet separately if required, and each could block the other. Irish members would be excluded from the Westminster Parliament, and separate legislation would deal with the buying out of the landlords.

The Bill was defeated by 343 votes to 313. The issue split the Liberal Party, with ninety-three voting against the Government.

Almost immediately there was violence in Belfast, with an official death toll of thirty-one. Hugh Hanna, a Presbyterian minister said, 'The armed servants of that Government are sent to suppress rejoicing loyalty by the sanguinary slaughter of a people resolved to resist a wicked policy.'[3]

Gladstone decided to dissolve Parliament and appeal to the electorate with the supporters of Parnell, but he had misread the mood of the country. He lost the

> In 1930 King George V said, 'What fools we were not to have accepted Gladstone's Home Rule Bill.'

election and the Tory Party under Lord Salisbury returned to office with an overall majority of 118. The debate was not over, for everyone knew that if and when Gladstone returned to power, as he eventually did, he would attempt to re-introduce the legislation.

There had been debates in Altrincham about Home Rule for some time, but until Gladstone espoused it, this was very much an Irish preoccupation. In 1874 for example, a Captain Kirwan gave a talk on Home Rule at the Roman Catholic School on Moss Lane.

After the election, Home Rule continued to be at the top of the political agenda. In March 1887, the Altrincham Workingmen's Liberal Association debated the subject. Thomas Thompson was on the platform. In April, MacKennal and forty Congregational minsters telegraphed Gladstone deploring the Conservative Government's coercive policy in Ireland. The Conservatives then held a meeting at the British School, followed by one organised by the Liberals. Isabel Mills organised a letter from the ladies of Bowdon to sympathise with their sisters in Ireland.[4]

Then in May there was a tumultuous debate in Altrincham between the Conservatives, represented by J. Baron of Salford, and the Liberals, represented by none other than H. J. Leech, the Congregationalist and later organist for the Baptists.

In November, Charles Williams, our earlier guide through Baptist theology and former President of the Baptist Union, spoke at the Hale Road Chapel in support of the building fund on the topic of, 'Ireland and the Irish Question – as viewed by a visitor'.

---

[3] His street preaching in Belfast brought him the nickname 'Roaring Hanna'.
[4] She is called Isabella in the census returns, but she appears to have preferred Isabel.

On 5 July 1888, a meeting took place at the British School. We know that Leonard, the Hale Road Baptist pastor, was present, and it is possible other Baptists might have attended, their interest no doubt raised by the debates in the previous year.

The proponents of Home Rule were clearly Liberals and one of their main speakers was none other than MacKennal. It is interesting to see how MacKennal was prepared to engage in overt political activity on the side of the Liberal Party. What is also interesting is that the trustees of the British School allowed it to be used for both debates.

MacKennal said that it was difficult to get Irishmen listened to in Parliament. Juries would not convict for crimes in Ireland. He compared British Rule to that of Rugby School before Dr Arnold. 'I am against the bullies,' MacKennal said, and then went on to deliver a devastating attack on some of the clergy of Belfast. 'I am sorry to say there are men who call themselves Christian ministers, amongst others Dr Hanna and Dr Caine, two signal examples of most unchristian speech.' He charged the English Government with 'criminal disregard of the people they have governed'.

A meeting in response took place on 24 July 1888, also at the British School, this time held by the Conservatives. The speeches by the anti-Home Rule speakers were amusing, but there was a cutting edge.   There was objection to the alleged misquoting of the Conservative Altrincham MP, Sir William Brooks, by the Liberal press. The main speaker was the barrister Millar Darling. He said that it would be right for Protestants in the north of Ireland to resist if the Act were ever passed. As Conservatives they had an obligation to protect the Loyalists in the north.

> I. S. Leadham was a Liberal barrister and parliamentary candidate. In 1887, he wrote in the *Altrincham Division Chronicles* on the Home Rule debate: 'The Conservative Party cannot be called unconscientious.   It has an exquisitely tender sense of political morality. Its scruples respond to the necessities of the moment as the jelly fish responds to touch.'

> Millar Darling, speaking in the British School, said that there was no man 'so capable as Mr Gladstone of seeing through a brick wall'. He also told a joke about Gladstone's father visiting Gladstone's tutor at Oxford.   'You have told me a great deal about William's ability,' Gladstone's father is alleged to have said. 'What have you got to say about his stability?'

The Altrincham debate about Home Rule illustrates the increasing preparedness of Nonconformists to become involved in political debate. We now look at their involvement with the State.

NONCONFORMISTS AND THE STATE

Let us join the Altrincham Baptists at their first Church Meeting of the new century on 23 January 1901.

The day before, Queen Victoria had died at 6.30pm. The queen's body, dressed in white for the first time since the death of her beloved Prince Albert, left Osborne House, the inspiration of Albert, and crossed the Solent on board the *Alberta* from the Isle of Wight to the mainland. In her lead casket were Albert's dressing gown, a photo of John Brown and a lock of his hair. The fleet was assembled as an eight-mile-long escort, accompanied, perhaps as a sign of things to come, by four bigger German ironclads.

At the Baptist chapel, the Bible stand was draped in black, and white flowers had been placed on the platform. So that future generations could know the feelings of the church, Lloyd recorded the following resolution:

'That this church desires to place on record its deep gratitude to Almighty God for the long and prosperous reign of our beloved Queen Victoria; for her noble example as wife, mother, Christian; her tact and wisdom as ruler, and her unfailing sympathy as a woman; as well as for the happy growth in religious liberty that has characterised her reign. It is the church's hope that all its members will earnestly seek the comforting grace of the Heavenly Father for the Royal household and God's religious blessings for His Majesty the King.'

We should note the crucial reference by Lloyd to the growth in religious liberty during her reign. Let us delve into this issue which shaped not only Baptist, but all Nonconformist thinking. We need especially to understand that Nonconformist theology affected the way Nonconformists thought about the State. These ideas are probably almost unknown to many Nonconformists today, but they were, and may soon be again, of crucial importance. What was essential to most Nonconformists was to be a 'free Church', free from discrimination and living under a benign and even-handed State.

Thomas Helwys, who founded the first Baptist church in England in 1611 on what is the site of Guy's Hospital in London, wrote:

'For mens religion to God is betwixt God and themselves; the King shall not answer for it, neither may the King be judge between God and man. Let them be heretikes, Turks, Jewes, or whatsoever, it apperteynes not to the earthly powers to punish them in the least measure.'[1]

Put in more modern phraseology, what he is saying is that men and women should be free to practise their religion without interference from the State. Baptists and other Nonconformists, therefore, believed that the State and the various denominational Churches had to be separate. In England, of course, the Church of England regarded itself not as a state Church, but rather as an established Church. Nonconformists saw little difference between the two. They believed that all religions should be treated equally and regarded the closeness between the established Church and the State with suspicion. Why should any one denomination be given a special preference over another?

---

[1] Helwys, T.: *A Short Declaration of the Mistery of Iniquity*, 1612.

This belief even influenced American constitutional thinking, where there is a clear separation between Church and State, and full religious liberty is permitted for all.[2]

As former Altrincham Baptist pastor Nigel Wright points out however, 'separation of church and state does not mean separation of church and society. The church is fully involved in society, doing its best to serve and shape it…Individual citizens are certainly at liberty in their capacity as citizens to serve within the legislature, the legislative or the enforcement services. They bring their Christian perspectives to bear upon their task; but they do not formally represent the church as church in these capacities.'[3]

Baptists, he argues, are therefore essentially supporters of liberal democracy, believing it is not perfect but is the best that can now be achieved. Their belief in separation of Church and State, and freedom under law brings them into disagreement with religions that believe that religion and the State should be one, or at least closely allied. Such a State can bring about an abuse of sacred power. This debate is very relevant today.

We have looked at the start of this book very briefly at the discrimination Nonconformists endured. It is now worth going back to see how the discrimination against the Nonconformists helped mould their political thinking.

In 1664 the Conventicle Act made them subject to a fine, prison or even transportation if five or more of them met together and did not use the Church of England *Book of Common Prayer* for their worship. Why should they, when they disagreed with some of its contents? This Act effectively prohibited any legal form of Nonconformist worship. For example, a family of six praying together in their own home without using the *Book of Common Prayer* could be sent to prison.

In 1665 the Five Mile Act became law. Ministers had to swear they would not attempt to try and make any change of government in either the Church or the State. If they refused to take the oath, they were banned from going nearer than five miles to any place where they had previously been a minister. Under the Test Act of 1672, Nonconformist holders of military or civil office were only allowed to take communion under the rites of the Church of England. Many Nonconformists were punished under these Acts of Parliament. John Bunyan, the Baptist author of *The Pilgrim's Progress*, spent twelve years in prison for his beliefs.

This discrimination continued for many years. Only in 1689 with the passing of the Toleration Act were some of the burdens on Baptists and other Nonconformists eased. Until then, they could not even own land on which to build places of worship.

If in reading this you think that things were different for Nonconformists by Victoria's reign, you would only be partly right. Discrimination carried on for a long time. It was as late as 1828 that the Test Act was fully repealed. Only in 1836 were Nonconformists allowed to hold their own weddings. Until then, they had to use Church of England churches for their weddings.

---

[2] Baptists and others who had fled religious persecution were much involved in the framing of the American Constitution. Article 6 states: '…no religious Test shall ever be required as a Qualification to any Office or public Trust under the United States'.. The 1st Amendment states: 'Congress shall make no law respecting an establishment of religion, or prohibiting the free exercise thereof.' American Baptists and others have opposed the government-sponsored display of the Ten Commandments as this would impact on State neutrality in religious matters.

[3] Wright, Nigel G.: *Free Church, Free State – The Positive Baptist Vision*, Paternoster, 2005.

Until 1860 these Nonconformists could not attend grammar schools. In 1868, Gladstone finally abolished the system which forced Nonconformists to contribute to Church of England funds. Until 1871 they could not hold office in a university, although even then, the posts of Professor of Divinity and College Head were barred to them.

We have seen increasing Nonconformist political activity, but in 1902 something happened which set Nonconformists on a collision course with the State and led to their political radicalisation. All over the country there were Nonconformist protests.

Until now, how these protests affected Altrincham has not been fully written about.

THE EDUCATION ISSUE

So now we turn to the source of the national Nonconformist protests. In Altrincham, as elsewhere, they really started in 1902. Today Baptists and other Nonconformists attend local schools of all types, including Church of England and Roman Catholic schools. The Balfour Education Acts, however, meant that Church of England and Roman Catholic schools were paid for through the rates, while Nonconformists' schools were effectively abolished and replaced by state education.

Nonconformists were not against state education, as long as it had religious teaching which was neutral; what they objected to was allowing the Church of England to have its own schools, while those of the Nonconformists were closed.

Many historians have simply dismissed Nonconformist concerns as religious nonsense, and in doing so they have failed to understand what motivated them. To Nonconformists, what was proposed was unfair treatment. The State was not being even-handed. It should not subsidise any one denomination over others and it appeared to be creating a system with little local accountability.

As we have seen, the 1872 Education Act had been opposed by the Nonconformists, but to little avail. This time they were better prepared.

In Altrincham, elementary education was primarily provided by the Church of England. In 1877, although the British School was by far the largest, there were only two other Nonconformist schools (one Congregational at Navigation Road, and one Wesleyan). There were, by contrast, seven Church of England elementary schools and one Roman Catholic.

It was generally accepted that something needed to be done about the education system but the question was what. Balfour, at a meeting in Manchester, explained that 'the existing educational system of this country is chaotic, ineffectual, is utterly behind the age and makes us the laughing stock of every advanced nation in Europe and America'.[1]

The basis of the legislation was the abolition of the School Boards and the assumption of responsibility for education by committees of county and county borough councils. The practical outcome, however, was that many Nonconformists did not have Board schools within travelling distance, and so would have to submit to education in Church of England schools. In Board schools, parental preference could still lead to Church of England teaching. Even worse, Nonconformists would have to pay for Church of England schools through the rates, even if they did not attend them.

The legislation may have had good intentions, but it may also have been a cynical piece of politics by the Conservative Party. It sought to detach the Irish vote from the Liberal Party, the party that had espoused Home Rule for Ireland against the Unionists.[2]

---

[1] MacKay, Ruddock Finlay: *Balfour, Intellectual Statesman*, Oxford University Press, 1985.
[2] My thanks to Mervyn Busteed for this insight.

The well-known Baptist, John Clifford, wrote a pamphlet entitled 'The Fight Against the Foul Bill'.

In 1902 a deputation went to the House of Commons to protest. MacKennal was part of the deputation. The Commons meeting was preceded by a prayer meeting in the House. Despite the support of the Quaker Joseph Chamberlain in the Cabinet, the Nonconformists ultimately lost in 1902, and could only continue to protest.

In May 1903, 140,000 people demonstrated in Hyde Park. Motions were put to the crowd from twelve platforms simultaneously. Churchill, never one to understand Nonconformist feelings with his public school and Anglican background, could not comprehend it at all and called it 'Pantomime Martyrdom'. To the Nonconformists, the new law was a step backwards from all the progress towards religious liberty made during the reign of Victoria.

The March 1904 Free Church Council proposal to solve the education crisis was quite modern in outlook and was as follows:

1. One type of elementary school controlled by a public educational authority.
2. Denominational school buildings should be rented to state schools at fair rents.
3. All schools maintained by public funds should be under the control of elected representatives.
4. There should be no denominational teaching, but instead simple Bible instruction, subject to a conscience clause.

Teachers in state schools will recognise the legacy of the Balfour legislation in their schools even today, but what now happened in Altrincham will come as a surprise to many readers.

THE ALTRINCHAM DILEMMA – HOW TO PROTEST

The Altrincham Nonconformists were united in their opposition to the Education Bill. They were split as to what to do when it became law.

From early on, they recognised that the legislation would be passed in some form. It was likely to be at least three years before the next election. What should they do about an Act of Parliament which many felt was so discriminatory that it had to be opposed as a matter of conscience? These same people opposed the idea of active resistance to Home Rule in Northern Ireland by those in Ulster. Was there another way?

In 1902 Bowdon Downs Congregational passed a resolution condemning the Education Bill. The problem was that they could pass resolutions, but it would get them nowhere with a Conservative majority in Parliament. Should they just give in, or should they continue the campaign by other means? Is there ever a point when Christians should refuse to obey legislation?

What the Nonconformists were faced with was having to pay rates knowing that part of those rates would be used to pay for schools which taught theology with which they strongly disagreed. To turn the matter on its head, how would the local Anglicans have reacted in 1902 if Bowdon Church of England School and St George's School had been closed and their pupils sent to new state schools, while they paid rates which were used to subsidise the Nonconformist British School?

We also have to remember that the Nonconformists claimed they were the largest religious group in the country at the time.

We can get a sense of the agonies faced by the Nonconformists as to what to do in Altrincham from a pamphlet by Mrs John Mills, published when it seemed likely the Act would become law.[1] We have come across Isabel Mills earlier in this book when she organised a letter of support from Bowdon for Irish women. Not only was she a prominent Liberal, but she was also a member of Bowdon Downs Congregational church from 1864. She died in 1919.

She wrote: 'That in view of the possibility of this Education Bill being forced upon the nation it becomes the duty of all women householders to carefully and seriously consider the subject, and act, as to payment or non-payment of a School rate, as their convictions and consciences may direct.'

All Nonconformists agreed that active resistance was not an option, as this would be against the teaching of the Bible, but in refusing to pay rates, the state authorities could still collect the money by direct action against them. Mrs Mills clearly felt she had to tread carefully in view of the split in the Liberals on this very subject. She wrote that it is the duty of the people to warn the Government of passive resistance of this sort if the Bill were passed. 'People say "You defy, you break the law, it will be an unconstitutional act". Well, this is an unconstitutional Bill.' What she felt she could not do was tell other Nonconformists to refuse to pay their rates.

---

[1] Mills, Mrs J.: *The Education Bill: an appeal to women householders by the President of the Altrincham and Bowdon Women's Liberal Association*, 1902.

She had decided to lead by example and not pay the rates. She would not resist seizure of her goods by the courts for failure to pay. 'That is passive resistance, the all-powerful action that killed the church rate.'

Women were denied the vote, she pointed out, but as some of them were ratepayers, they still had a vote of sorts in that they could refuse to pay their rates. 'Rate-paying and representation must go together.' She believed that leading Anglicans themselves opposed the legislation. Even Altrincham District Council passed a resolution against it.

'It is for [the little children], for fair play, better education and sound religious teaching for all, that I would plead, not only as a Nonconformist but an English citizen,' she wrote.

Where would MacKennal and Lloyd stand on this? Was Isabel Mills on her own?

BUILDING THE RESISTANCE

Rumblings of discontent about the Bill can first be seen in March 1902, when Lloyd and others formed the Altrincham Educational League. Isabel Mills was one of the joint founders.[1] Lloyd proposed they should carry out their own poll in the area to see what views might be over the formation of a School Board for Altrincham, but at the second meeting of the League it became apparent that Altrincham did not have a sufficient population for its own Board and would therefore have to be administered by the county council.

George Faulkner Armitage was appointed President of the League and Lloyd Vice-President, and the League from then on formed the nucleus of resistance in Altrincham. There was no talk, however, of a refusal to pay rates; instead they looked to public protest.

Lloyd reported to the League that MacKennal believed the Free Church Council would oppose the Bill.

A letter was written to the local newspaper by an anonymous 'Noncon', who may, of course, have been Lloyd himself. All religions should be treated equally. 'The Nonconformist leaders propose drastic measures if the Bill becomes law,' the letter said.

Next, Lloyd needed to get his own church on board. On 27 April he preached a highly political sermon against the Bill. His text was the epistle of Jude. Nonconformists were being asked to pay for schools where there was no popular control and where it was possible Ritualistic clergy might end up teaching High church doctrine to Nonconformist children. He disagreed with the President of the Free Church Council who said this would not be a death blow for the Free churches; he felt it could be just that. 'Nonconformity stands for truth, justice, freedom, reform, peace and national righteousness.'

At the end of the sermon the whole congregation stood as a sign of their support for his proposal to write a letter of protest to their local Tory MP, Conningsby Disraeli. The letter made no difference at all to Disraeli, who fully supported the proposed legislation, but it helped the church to feel that it was doing something.

In May, the Primitive Methodists on Oxford Road followed suit and held a protest meeting.

On 16 May the League brought the Free churches together in the Literary Institute. MacKennal and Lloyd were on the platform and Armitage chaired the meeting. It is fair to say that just about every Free church in Altrincham was represented. Lloyd addressed the meeting. 'I protest against the Bill as a lover of liberty and a lover of my country.' This, he said, was 'the greatest threat to Free churches for generations'.

In October the Free Church Council met and spent much of its time discussing the Education Bill. Altrincham agreed to join a combined Manchester protest rally at Alexander Park. Lloyd again addressed the meeting. 'How many good things that have come to us through our work as Free churchmen are now being imperilled?

---

[1] She appears to have worked closely with Lloyd throughout. In 1903 she opened the Baptist bazaar.

Many can be mentioned, and it is up to us to stand up for our own rights, to hold intelligently our convictions, to love them, and to realise that they are sacred. We must stand shoulder to shoulder and join hands.'

Lloyd's speech worked, and the Council agreed to start a list of those who would refuse to pay their rates.

Meanwhile, Lloyd's mentor Charles Williams brought a motion to the Baptist Union about the education issue and then an anonymous 'Vox Humana' wrote to the local Altrincham newspaper, claiming from personal knowledge that Bowdon 'is certainly contaminated by Ritualism'.

MacKennal preached in November against the proposed legislation. What was not clear yet was where he stood should the Bill become law, as seemed likely. Would he pay his rates, or would he advocate passive resistance?

The Free Church Council met again in May 1903 and MacKennal finally made his views public. He was unequivocal: 'I cannot understand...persons who take action against a law by disobeying it.' He would pay his rates. He opposed Lloyd's more radical views.

Lloyd himself was now in a tricky position. It would be difficult for Lloyd as Secretary of the Free Church Council to oppose his own President after MacKennal had made such a strong statement. Lloyd had to make his decision quickly and to make it public. The very first item on the next issue of the local newspaper was an advertisement for a sermon he was to preach the next Sunday evening at the Hale Road Chapel. The subject of the sermon was 'Why I cannot pay the Education Rate'. Lloyd and MacKennal were now on a collision course. Would anyone follow Lloyd and Isabel Mills or were they on their own?

This was no easy decision, because a refusal to pay rates, or even the part attributable to the hated school subsidy, could have serious personal consequences.

The first Altrincham person who refused to pay was William Kesselmeyer of Elysee Villa on Manchester Road.[2]

Lloyd desperately needed support, and so he placed an advertisement for a meeting of passive resisters at the Hale Road chapel. Attendance was a disappointment. The local newspaper reported, 'At present their following is not a strong one'. Only three local ministers so far were

> 'PASSIVE RESISTANCE. THOSE PERSONS who have decided to REFUSE PAYMENT of the Sectarian portion of the New Education Acts are invited to attend a MEETING to take counsel together, to be held at the HALE ROAD BAPTIST SCHOOLROOM, ALTRINCHAM, on MONDAY June 29th at 8pm.'
>
> Advertisement in the local newspaper.

prepared to refuse to pay part of their rates. This was a relief to the local magistrates, no doubt, as there had been riots in Bury St Edmunds when goods of passive resisters were sold. It looked as if MacKennal's view would prevail.

---

[2] He was probably the same Kesselmeyer who was a well-known composer of pieces for the piano.

Disappointed but undaunted, Lloyd pushed ahead with the new Altrincham Passive Resistance Movement. Revd A. James of Sale Congregational Church was the movement's Secretary and he wrote to the local newspaper to reassure everyone that the Passive Resisters were serious about their intentions, but would always be peaceful in what they did.

The magistrates now took action against two unnamed Dunham Massey residents. Then Elijah Helm, secretary of the Manchester Chamber of Commerce and a local resident, refused to pay his rates. Four oak chairs were taken from his house.[3]

The Sale Passive Resisters held a protest meeting, and were addressed by Frank Spence. Lloyd was on the platform to support them. Next, Lloyd published a manifesto for the Passive Resisters in the local newspaper.

The Sale magistrates took action against a Mr McCappin of Ingleside in Dunham Massey for non-payment of his rates. This time, several ministers turned up in court to support him. The Resisters cheered McCappin as he tried to speak and the police shouted back at him. 'Dear me, whatever is the matter?', the reporter quoted one policeman as saying. Immediately after the court hearing, Lloyd addressed a protest meeting at Sale Bridge, where a curious crowd gathered. There were further protest meetings in New Market Square in Altrincham and in Sale.

In September 1903 a new group came before the magistrates. This time there were Baptists amongst them. Isabel Mills and Robert Lewis were accompanied by Pierrepont the Baptist Church Secretary and Miss Simmons, the church harmonium player. All had

> The father of the late Professor Fred Langley, a former deacon of Altrincham Baptist Church, went to prison for refusing to pay his rates, although at the time he did not live in Altrincham.

goods taken from their houses and the goods were then sold.

Jesse Haworth, one of the most influential people at Bowdon Downs Congregational, also refused to pay his rates. The complication was that he was a magistrate himself, so found himself being dealt with by people he normally sat on the bench with. His fellow magistrate Pollitt[4] said he did not agree with the law, but had to enforce it.

Lloyd too was in court, but he was there to protest for an additional reason: his goods were not going to be taken and sold. He explained to the magistrates that he had refused to pay his rates, but that someone had gone behind his back and paid them for him. He wanted it to be acknowledged that the payment was without his authority and demanded that his goods should be taken from his house. Not surprisingly, the magistrates refused this rather unusual request. Outside the meeting, Lloyd begged the gathered crowd not to pay his rates in future. There was, of course, every suspicion that it was Baptist church members who were making the payments on his behalf behind his back.

In October Lloyd addressed the Free Church Council about the education issue and this time received enthusiastic applause.

---

[3] He was the author of the centenary book of the Cotton Exchange and "The Joint Standard" on monetary policy. See Helm, E.: *The Joint Standard; a Plain Exposition of Monetary Principles and of the Monetary Controversy*, Macmillan and Co, 1894.
[4] This is the same Pollitt whose house was designed by Owen, the Baptist chapel architect.

Sad news now reached Altrincham. MacKennal had been taken ill while on a trip, and for weeks the local newspaper had carried the story of his health and the possibility of him returning to Bowdon. In January, however, he died.

In February 1904, the Tory MP Conningsby Disraeli said in a speech that passive resistance was dying out. Lloyd was determined to prove him wrong, and it was clear there was a growing momentum. He wrote in the church newsletter that the Passive Resisters were again to the fore: 'On Monday, February 22, a magnificent demonstration was held at the Literary Institute,' he wrote. The following Monday 'saw a number of us in the Police Court once more, and some eighteen champions of religious freedom and the rights of conscience, had, in consequence, orders served upon them for the distraint of their goods. What a strange spectacle for the opening years of the 20th Century to witness! Passive Resistance is to my mind, speaking from a human stand point, our only hope and the only way left to us to win back the heritage that has already been lost in so large a measure.'

In March Frank Spence, now back as an Altrincham Baptist Church member, had his goods distrained for the first time. When asked if he had any legal objection to paying, he replied 'Yes, the law of God'. He was accompanied again by Isabel Mills, Mary Simmons, Pierrepont, Thomas Meldrum of Ashley Road, William Tattersall of Cambridge Road and Robert Lewis.

Following MacKennal's death, everyone wanted to know where his successor at Bowdon Downs Congregational Church, the Revd John Holden, would stand. Would he pay his rates? To Lloyd's delight, he joined Lloyd and refused to pay. At the same court hearing his goods too were taken and sold.

The protest meeting afterwards at the Primitive Methodist chapel on Oxford Road showed the growing strength of the movement and was attended by most of the Free Churches, including an increasing number of Methodists. Lloyd explained, 'I feel that the witness we are making is helping England to get further freedom, justice and truth.'

The opposition fought back. An anonymous writer in the local newspaper commented that no Passive Resister would ever give a vote to a Unionist candidate. Their protests were therefore pointless in Altrincham. 'Neither their speeches nor their rates, therefore, can have the slightest effect upon Mr, Disraeli or his candidature. Passive resisters cannot influence an election in Altrincham.' This was particularly significant, as the Liberal candidate for the 1906 elections was to be William Crossley.

The local magistrates included Owen. The architect of the Baptist chapel found himself ordering distraint on the goods of the members of the very same Baptist church whose chapel he had designed. Another magistrate now came off the bench and refused to pay his rates. This time it was George Faulkner Armitage. He was joined by William Thomas, the minster of the Congregational church at Broadheath, and George Mitchell of the Primitive Methodists.

Finally, and much to his relief no doubt, Lloyd had his goods taken. He attempted to make a speech to the magistrates in court, pleading the

> Lloyd was delighted when his mother joined the protests and was arrested by the police.

Toleration Act of 1650 in his defence, which was supposed to guarantee some freedoms to Nonconformists. He said he doubted if the magistrates knew what the Act was. Mr Harris, the magistrate, retorted that he doubted he could talk as much as a minister.

This time the protest meeting after the court hearing was at the Methodist New Connexion chapel in George Street. Afterwards, one Charles Pidduck wrote to the local newspaper in support of Lloyd's unsuccessful attempt to plead the Toleration Act.

The Passive Resisters needed a local martyr. So far, no one had gone to jail. The first to receive a prison sentence was Robert Lewis, but his sentence was initially suspended for seven days to allow him to pay. He refused. The second was Edwyn Holt of Athol Dene, Arthog Road in Hale, a local Nonconformist solicitor. Both had engineered it so that the bailiffs could not distrain against their goods.

Gaddum on behalf of the magistrates, said he thought Holt should spend seven days in prison, but the clerk to the court suggested a suspended sentence. Holt pleaded to receive the full sentence. Lewis asked if his previous suspended sentence could be converted so that he and Holt could go to prison at the same time. Gaddum, however, ordered that they should go separately. They also requested that they should be treated as common criminals.

Holt decided to arrive in style at prison and paid the court for a first-class rail ticket. He travelled wearing his silk top hat. At Knutsford Station he was met by the police and the prison chaplain. Lewis arrived later. The local Liberal Party noted in its Minutes that Robert Lewis, one of the Hale committee members, 'for conscience sake had suffered imprisonment'.[5]

In March 1905, Pierrepont, Mary Simmons, Isabel Mills, Lloyd, Armitage, Spence and Haworth appeared together before the magistrates and Lewis and Holt spent another seven days in Knutsford Prison, this time together. In September all appeared again, and this time there were two Congregational ministers plus the Primitive Methodist minister and others.

Revd W. D. Thomas objected to the magistrates that he had been summonsed as a 'clerk in holy orders'. He was, after all, but a humble Congregational minister in Broadheath and not a vicar. Lloyd, as a Baptist, raised a similar objection. He was a preacher of the 'gospel of the grace of God'. This, he also reminded the magistrates, prevented him from ever becoming an MP. The magistrates had taken advice, and refused to change anything. More household possessions were taken.

There we leave the Passive Resisters. For them, it all hinged on the elections in 1906. Who would win? If it was the Liberals, and locally if William Crossley defeated Conningsby Disraeli, what would happen to education?

This book finishes in 1905, and so that story must be left for now, with the Passive Resisters risking property and prison for their beliefs. What happened to their protests and education policy will have to be left to another book.

We have, however, uncovered an extraordinary new chapter in the history of Altrincham.

---

[5] Hale Polling District minutes, 1904, ibid.

The term 'passive resistance' was first used by the American naturalist and writer Henry David Thoreau. Thoreau refused to pay war taxes as a protest against slavery. He believed that a citizen has the right to disobey any law he or she thinks is evil or unjust.

The Passive Resisters foreshadowed Gandhi in their techniques. Gandhi went to South Africa and campaigned against the treatment of the Chinese, just as did the Nonconformists in Britain. Only three years after the Passive Resisters started their campaign in Britain, Gandhi took part in passive protests against the Transvaal government's treatment of Indian settlers. Gandhi encouraged the boycott of British goods. He believed that acts of violence against the British only provoked a negative reaction, but passive resistance would lead more people to support his ideals. It would be intriguing to know if he ever looked to the Nonconformist Passive Resisters for part of his inspiration. This is not beyond the bounds of possibility.

Thoreau and Gandhi had a profound effect on the Baptist Martin Luther King Jnr. who 'became convinced that non-cooperation with evil is as much a moral obligation as is cooperation with good'. Studying Gandhi, King was moved by the way he practically applied a key Christian principle: 'Love your enemies and do good to those that hurt you.'

Once the goods of the Passive Resisters had been distrained, they had by law to be disposed of. This led to some entertaining scenes. The first auction was of the effects of McCappin. Before the auction, two people walked the streets of Altrincham with a portrait of the well-known Baptist, Dr John Clifford, encouraging people to attend the auction.

The auctioneer of J. Percival and Co., 7 Market Street, may have been expecting the usual quiet sale of goods in his office. Instead, a large crowd burst in and sang 'O God, our help in ages past'. At the end, the auctioneer vowed never to conduct a sale like this again.

The scene was repeated many times, but the Resisters learned that they could bid for the goods of others. Thus the Resisters would pack the auction room and each would bid for and buy the goods of one of their colleagues. After the auction, they passed the goods back to the former owners.

In 1905 Edward Isaacs was the evangelist for the Altrincham Baptists in their mission that year. Soon after his arrival, Lloyd took a surprised Isaacs to see Passive Resisters' goods being sold by the auctioneer. Isaacs was prompted to write to the local newspaper, comparing the religious liberty established in Australia where there was no established church with the lack of liberty he saw in England. He wrote that he left the auction rooms 'shocked and indignant'.

MacKennal died on 23 June 1904 at the height of the rates protests. This is the memorial to him and his wife, Fanny, in Bowdon Downs Congregational Chapel. MacKennal was minister at Bowdon Downs for twenty-seven years. Although they disagreed over passive resistance, Lloyd wrote in tribute: 'My people will never forget his beautiful sermon preached at Hale Road Baptist Church, on the occasion of the local annual interchange of pulpits, some 12 months ago, when he preached from the words: "We have this treasure in earthen vessels".'

Memorial to MacKennal's son Alexander and daughter-in-law Clara in Bowdon Downs Congregational Chapel. Tragedy struck the family again when the couple drowned in an accident on the River Severn in 1908.

Ashley Road Congregational Church as it used to look. The minister here was a key ally of Lloyd in the rates protests.

The influential George Faulkner Armitage worked closely with Lloyd in the rates protests. He was a magistrate and was later to become mayor of Altrincham. He is seen here processing as mayor to church.

Bowdon Church of England School pupils in 1919. Nonconformists earlier had objected to having to close their schools and then to subsidising Church of England schools as well. Nowadays children from Nonconformist churches happily attend the school.

THE RETURNING TIDE

Bearing in mind the apparent inter-connectedness of Christian circles in Manchester, it is not surprising to find that the two people we are about to look at were good friends of McLaren's. They would have certainly influenced Nonconformists and possibly Anglicans in Altrincham.

We start with Samuel Francis Collier. We have already seen him promoting the Free church movement in Manchester and pioneering new hymns and secular entertainment as the first stage in drawing people to church.[1]

Collier was born in Runcorn on 3 October 1855 and was to be one of the foremost forward-thinking evangelists of his time. Many of his ideas would, even today, be regarded as radical.

Collier started his career as a minister at the Methodist Chapel at Lever Street in Manchester. There was, however, a sign of times to come, as on his very first Sunday evening he went out onto the streets with a small band of Sunday school teachers and visited houses in the crowded areas around the chapel. Soon he began to hold Saturday afternoon open-air services for children, both to reach them and their parents. Often he walked the streets until midnight in order to understand the problems of the area.

The Oldham Street Methodist Church in Manchester had, by 1883, dwindled to a congregation of between fifty and 100. The church might have been closed, but a group of far-sighted men decided that it needed rebuilding. This decision, according to Collier's biographer, 'checked that facile and fatal policy of abandoning the centres of great cities which has become so grave a reproach to Protestant Christianity alike in the Old World and the New'. This, to him, symbolised the much-needed returning Christian tide into the inner cities.

When the new Methodist building came to be opened, these bold men took a risk and selected the young Collier as minister. What we now know as Central Methodist Hall was opened on 27 October 1886. Twelve months after its opening, the crowds at the evening service were so great that the St James's Theatre on Oxford Street had to be hired for a second service. This started a little later so that people who could not get into the first venue could rush round to the second.

Two years later in 1889, the Free Trade Hall became available and every Sunday night for the next twenty-one years was packed out.

Although after the period covered by this book, it is worth noting that by 1910 congregations had become so large that the Albert Hall was built on Peter Street, not far down the road from the Free Trade Hall. A number of nearly-deserted Methodist churches in the centre of Manchester were brought into the circuit [2] and many old churches were rebuilt or re-modelled. 'Indeed, so swift and strong was the returning tide, that in 1904 Collier was able to announce that the attendances at the various Sunday Services of the Mission numbered not less than 16,000, independent of the still large number that were reached every week by house-to-house visitation, open-air and lodging-house services, and other means.'

---

[1] Much of the information in this chapter is from Jackson, G., op. cit.
[2] Methodists have 'circuits', or groups of connected churches.

We just need to pause here for a moment. In the centre of Manchester, every Sunday, week by week, more than 16,000 people were attending the Methodist churches at a time when most historians believe that Nonconformist chapel attendances were beginning to decline.

Collier's evangelism went hand in hand with social mission. He helped to establish a women's home, maternity home, hospital and guilds for the infirm. In 1891 he transformed a disused rag factory in Hood Street, Ancoats, into a men's home and shelter.

Central Hall was deliberately not called a chapel or a church because Collier's stated intention was to be Methodist but also to be ecumenical. According to his biographer, he also helped to put an end to the era of the cheap mission by spending well on buildings as he thought 'only the best would work'.

Like McLaren, Collier was a modest man. He published no books and there are only a few of his early sermons available. He rarely asked anyone for money. People seemed to give spontaneously. William Crossley once joked with a Manchester audience that he used occasionally to ask Collier to drink a cup of tea with him but gave it up as he found that each cup cost him about £500. Collier himself only drew a modest stipend.

He was much admired by successive bishops of Manchester. 'But perhaps the commendation which Collier himself prized most highly and which, in Manchester at least, was of most real service to him, was that expressed again and again by Alexander McLaren,' says his biographer. The 'great Baptist preacher' regularly attended Collier's anniversary meeting at the Free Trade Hall, and once even went so far as to say that if he had his years to live over again, he would try and shape his ministry according to Collier's pattern.

People who came to Collier's meetings were of all classes, but a large proportion were poor. Hungry men who followed the crowd into the popular Sunday afternoon services were given food and drink. Homeless men were supplied with a ticket of admission to one of the city's lodging houses.

Collier insisted that the Central Hall doors must be open twenty-four hours a day, every day of the year. He was proud of the fact that these doors were designed to be like those of a public house, as he said that he wanted them always to be easy to open and familiar to those who entered.

In the evenings, Collier would send two brass bands out into the centre of Manchester. The street scene, particularly at weekends, would be recognisable today. Those with the bands would gather together about 200-300 people, many of whom were drunk, and bring them into a midnight service as they followed the bands. To keep their attention, Collier used the latest technology and showed them pictures projected by lantern. He also used the lantern to show the words of hymns on the screen. Rodney Smith recounted how he saw many burst into tears when they saw the words of the hymn 'When I survey the wondrous cross' projected in this way.

Collier was perhaps the forerunner of modern thinking on how to reach the unchurched.[3] We have already looked at his Saturday night concerts which were intended to be a competitor to a Saturday night on the town. He refused to have ambitious amateurs and instead engaged competent artists and paid them full fees. He charged a small admission charge. He even showed early films. He always made sure, however, that everything was decent.

His purpose was two-fold: first, he wanted to provide an alternative to the rough, binge-drinking culture of his age. Second, he wanted people to be used to the venue so that they would come through its doors without fear on a Sunday.

Politically, and this will by now come as no surprise to you, he was a Liberal and a member of the Manchester Reform Club. Friends recalled he was a man with humour, but also a driven person.

In terms of worship, we have already seen that his approach was very modern. His services used good tunes and modern hymns.

Collier and his wife had five sons. One died in infancy and two were killed in the First World War. He himself died on 2 June 1921 of a recurrence of the devastating 1918 influenza. He was one of the great Christian pioneers in Britain, and Lloyd would have been familiar with his work.

Collier at his desk. His name still lives on. At the time of writing, there is a suite named after him in the hotel that occupies the site of the former Free Trade Hall in Manchester.

We have seen Collier was a good friend of McLaren's, but both Collier and McLaren were friends of a man we have briefly come across already, and who for a number of years worked for Collier in Manchester. That man was a gypsy. His name is Rodney Smith.

---

[3] We must mention here the Baptist, Arthur Mursell, who pre-dates Collier in giving talks with secular content to attract non-believers. About 7,000 attended the Free Trade Hall every Sunday to hear him. William Birch of Homer Street Mission also packed out the Free Trade Hall on Sunday evenings before Collier used the building. The Free Trade Hall was a busy venue for Nonconformists. A modern successor to these pioneers is the 'Reaching the Unchurched Network' or (RUN), with which Altrincham Baptist Church became involved through Revd Roger Sutton.

MCLAREN AND RODNEY SMITH

McLaren, Moody and Sankey, Collier, the Free churches and the Salvation Army were all connected with a man who called himself 'Gypsy Smith'. He was one of the most unusual evangelists of the time, with a worldwide reputation, but at one stage he was based in Manchester.

Rodney Smith was born on 31 March 1860 in a tent near Epping. He was the son of Cornelius Smith and Mary Welch. He was their fourth child and travelled with his parents and five siblings.

Smith's father and two of Smith's uncles decided they would like to know more about Christianity. For some reason, they walked into a beer shop in a village and asked the lady owner if she could help explain this religion to them. Having no Bible and not really knowing what to say, she lent them a copy of *The Pilgrim's Progress* by John Bunyan. That Sunday the brothers went to the Primitive Methodist Chapel on Fitzroy Street in Cambridge and attended all three services. An appeal was made to those who might be interested in following Christ and Smith's father went for prayer. Later he went to a mission hall and there he became a Christian, followed soon afterwards by his two brothers.

Smith as a young man came across Ira Sankey and others while they were on a mission to the area. Although he had never met Smith before, Sankey felt called to place his hands on Smith's head and told him that one day he would be a great preacher.

Later, Smith visited Bunyan's Baptist chapel and felt some sort of a calling from God. He too visited the Primitive Methodist Church in Cambridge and there he dedicated his life to God at the age of sixteen.

Smith was illiterate, but as he now wanted to study the Bible, he taught himself to read. Soon he was singing and preaching. He came to the attention of William Booth of what was then called the Christian Mission and which was later to become the Salvation Army. Smith went to work for Booth as an evangelist in various parts of the country.

Smith married one of his converts whilst working for Booth. Ultimately, he and his new wife moved to Hanley in the Potteries. There he set up a mission, using an old circus as a base. However, he fell out with Booth and was dismissed from the Salvation Army in what, for Smith, was a painful episode. Booth had a tendency to be fairly autocratic. Smith therefore continued working successfully in Hanley on his own account. By now he was known as 'Gypsy Smith'.

His fame as an evangelist spread and he visited America and Australia, holding highly successful missions there. Many thousands in the United Kingdom, America and Australia came to hear him and were brought to the Christian faith.

Collier too heard of Smith and invited him in 1889 to work for him in Manchester. Smith toured many towns around Manchester. Union Chapel records show that McLaren invited Smith to hold a mission there in 1896. Strangely, this was McLaren's first serious mission at Union Baptist, which had been mostly built up on McLaren's reputation as a preacher rather than on direct evangelism.

In preparation for the mission, thousands of home visits were made and in just three days 100 women visited 6,000 people. McLaren and his assistant, Roberts, personally signed thousands of invitations.

Smith himself thought he was not up to the challenge of matching the eloquent preaching of his friend McLaren, but McLaren reassured him and Smith went on to preach in his usual and highly individual style.

Smith's mission was the talk of Manchester. It is likely that the Altrincham Nonconformists would have taken people to Union Baptist to hear Smith. People thronged to the mission. Ten or twelve Anglican churches sent people. The roads were blocked, and when McLaren's cousin, Alick, went out to calm the waiting crowds on the last day, he lost his hat and then couldn't get back into the chapel, so great was the crush.

During the eight-day Manchester mission, there were 600 converts to Christianity. Not to be outdone, the Metropolitan Tabernacle invited Smith to hold a mission in 1900 which in turn produced 1,500 converts to the Christian faith.

In 1897 Smith became the special missionary of MacKennal's national Free Church Council.

Smith was awarded the OBE. His wife died before him. At the age of seventy-eight, he got married again to a lady who was twenty-seven. Today this would have perhaps caused a tabloid sensation, but did not do so at the time. He died on the *Queen Mary* on his way back to England in 1947, aged eighty-seven.

Smith was a modest man, and always remained true to his Romany past, often visiting nearby gypsy encampments wherever he was.

The foreword to Smith's autobiography is by McLaren. McLaren described his friend as a 'character of rare sweetness, goodness, simplicity and godliness'.

He was one of the greatest evangelists the United Kingdom has produced.

A young Smith with his parents. While he was still young, his mother died of smallpox. His father then brought Smith up on his own and earned his living by making wicker goods and playing his fiddle in pubs, where Smith collected the money.

Smith, aged 26, while in Hanley.

Smith's first wife.

LLOYD AND THE HOLY SPIRIT

We now return to our chronological history of the Altrincham Baptists, where something unusual happened in 1904. Its origin lies in Wales.

Off-shoot Keswick Conventions were held in Llandrindod Wells in Wales in 1903 and 1904, and they may have sown the seed for these extraordinary events. What we now call the Welsh Revival, however, started in 1904 with Florrie Evans from New Quay in Cardigan. This young teenager declared in a youth meeting in February that she 'loved the Lord Jesus with all her heart'. Something in what she said, or how she said it, profoundly affected the meeting. Contemporary accounts say that the Holy Spirit appeared to fall upon all those in the meeting. Thus began a revival in the Cardigan area.

Seth Joshua, an evangelist, had been praying for many years that God would raise up a young man from the coal pits to revive the Welsh churches. That September, he addressed a convention that included the people from the Florrie Evans' youth meeting. One of those who heard him was a man called Evan Roberts.

Roberts was twenty-six and an ex-coal miner. He in turn had been praying for revival in Wales for eleven years. Roberts was very moved by what Joshua had to say. As he responded to the prayer 'Bend me O Lord', he received what he later called a fresh 'baptism of the Spirit'.

Roberts now returned to his old Church of Moriah near Llanelli and spoke with the young people there. What he said in turn had an impact, first on the young people, and then the whole church. Meetings continued into the early hours of the morning. People did not want to leave. Soon there were conversions to the Christian faith. People discovered a new joy, with spontaneous prayer and hymn-singing.

Roberts, his brother Dan and his best friend Sidney then travelled around Wales, spreading this revival. Roberts' message was a straightforward one: people should confess all known sin, deal with and get rid of anything doubtful in their lives, be ready to obey the Holy Spirit and confess Christ in public. Florrie Evans herself went as part of a team to north Wales with her friend, Maud.

Singing was a feature of the revival. One song from the Welsh Revival still sung by churches today is 'Here is love, vast as the ocean', but perhaps the most famous at the time was sung by Sam Jenkins, a tin-plate worker from Llanelli: 'I Achub Hen Rebel Fel Fi', 'For saving an old rebel like me'.

In our current age, it is almost impossible to conceive of the enormous and profound impact of the revival on Wales. It is estimated that at least 100,000 new people joined churches. The crime rate dropped. The revival was linked with total abstinence from alcohol and public houses reported substantial losses in trade. Allegedly many pit ponies failed to understand the colliers as they no longer swore.

The revival was characterised by prayer, repentance and joy, and it was very much led by, and a movement of, the working classes, the poor and the young. It was not really a precursor of the charismatic renewal of the later twentieth century. There were no gifts of the Spirit associated with the Welsh Revival, but it transformed Welsh society and is the reason we see so many chapels and former chapels in the country today.

You might wonder what this had to do with Altrincham which, after all, is in Cheshire and not Wales.

Moriah was a Welsh Presbyterian (or Calvinistic Methodist) church, as is the Welsh Chapel on Willowtree Road in Altrincham. Lloyd spoke at the inauguration service for the new chapel in 1903. In 1903 it had seventy members and a congregation of 200. In 1905 it appointed its first minister, and it is likely that it too grew and was influenced by the Welsh Revival.

We do know that Lloyd himself, a man of Welsh ancestry, was much affected by the Welsh Revival. How he came into contact with it we do not know, but we do know that by the time he came back from his summer holiday in 1904 (which may of course have been in Wales), things began to change for the Altrincham Baptists. Lloyd was a changed man.

He announced to the church in October 1904 that he would choose for the morning sermons a series of Bible studies on the Holy Spirit. This, he wrote, would 'result in a glorious outflow of evangelistic enthusiasm and irresistible power. There are few more important topics, and yet there are few less intelligently dealt with nor more vaguely comprehended. Yet "not by my might, nor by my power, but by my spirit, sayeth the Lord".'

For the next few weeks he spoke exclusively on the person of the Holy Spirit, his character, his work (two parts), his coming, the Holy Spirit as teacher and 'His Pentecostal coming'. For what had not that long ago been a Calvinist Baptist church, this was an extraordinary change. The church was asked to pray that they would see a real impact from the sermons. Lloyd asked for the Thursday evening prayer meetings to be 'thronged with worshippers'. He clearly wanted a revival in Altrincham.

In January 1905 he announced that he felt 'there was a revival coming'. Conversions were taking place. In February he addressed the Free Church Council. 'For the wonderful revival of religion in Wales, I give hearty thanks to God, and call upon you the churches of the neighbourhood to wait upon Him for the power of His Spirit to fall upon the land.' Lloyd, already a dynamic pastor, was transformed, and the church found a new vitality.

Evan Roberts.   *Florrie Evans.*   *Seth Joshua.*

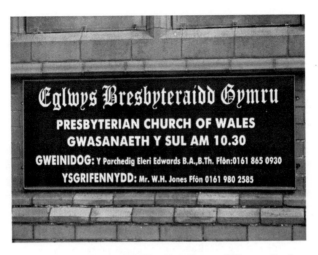

Services in Welsh are still held in Altrincham on Willowtree Road.

Lloyd was much influenced by the Welsh Revival.

Lloyd now stunned everyone by announcing that he was leaving Altrincham.

LLOYD ON THE BRINK

Lloyd's announcement came as a complete shock to the church, but there was a reason behind it. The Association had seen how successful Lloyd was in Altrincham. They regarded him as their man, brought in to reunite and save a church deeply in debt and struggling to find its way after a damaging split. Now they wanted to replicate Lloyd's success in Broughton, Salford.

Lloyd was also approached by a church in Sheffield, but quickly turned this down. Broughton was different though, as McLaren was behind the proposal and spoke to Lloyd personally about it.[1]

Lloyd did not immediately say 'yes' to Broughton, and so the Altrincham Baptist deacons used the opportunity to start a campaign to keep him. First they went to the press. On 11 January a notice appeared in the Bowdon Guardian calling a public meeting that very day. 'All friends desiring he should remain in Altrincham are requested to attend a public meeting at Hale Road Baptist Church Wednesday, 7.45pm.'

Lloyd agreed to come to the meeting to explain his position. He said that the call from Broughton and the position there was a responsible one. However, he did not yet feel it was a call from God. That was the crucial test for him.

Lloyd was not only popular with his own church members, he was also popular with other ministers. Holden of Bowdon Downs Congregational Church wrote to the Church Secretary: 'The Free Churches of Altrincham will greatly rejoice if Mr Lloyd sees it should be possible for him to remain the Pastor of your church.' W. D. Thomas of Broadheath Congregational Church wrote, 'In the removal of Mr Lloyd the Free churches of Altrincham would lose one of their most devoted workers, and we Ministers would lose as brotherly and kindly a fellow worker as one could desire to meet.'

The deacons had hastily arranged a petition by the Sunday school choir which was presented at the meeting. Pierrepont said that the 'Pastor seems to see in that call the mysterious moving of God and feels that a revival is coming'. A resolution to keep Lloyd was proposed, seconded by Hawksworth (the Treasurer) and carried unanimously by the congregation standing together and clapping vigorously.

Lloyd had still not made up his mind, but he responded by saying, 'I feel confident that a revival is coming. This meeting will very much help me to a decision. If I go where my heart leads me I would not go at all. I intend to make very much of the future and trust it will bring a tremendous spiritual knowledge.' His speech was both interrupted and rounded off by applause.

Pierrepont knew further action was still needed and called an emergency Church Meeting on 18 January. He insisted that Lloyd should be there. The church unanimously passed the following resolution:

'We are deeply conscious of his invaluable and self-sacrificing labours in our midst during the past 11 years, and feel it would be a dire calamity to lose him. We therefore, earnestly urge him to remain with us assuring him of our most hearty

---

[1] The Bowdon Guardian story quotes Lloyd as saying McLaren was behind the proposed move.

appreciation of past services and pledging ourselves to loyal co-operation in the future.'

Fresh letters in support were read out. A Revd Carter led the church in prayer and the meeting was closed by Lloyd after he had 'feelingly responded to the resolution and messages of appreciation'. He still did not, however, commit himself to a decision either way. He had McLaren to contend with. These were anxious days for the church.

Decision day was 18 January. After the emergency Church Meeting, it was the church's annual tea party in the lower church hall. The press was there as this was definitely a newsworthy local event. H. V. Thomas, Secretary of the Association, was also present. The church members and guests gathered. The tea must have been a strange event. Lloyd made small-talk but revealed nothing. It seems that he actually made his decision during the tea party. He probably told the Church Secretary and Treasurer, but no member dared ask him.

After tea, they all moved up to the main chapel and Lloyd sat in the centre of the platform, flanked by Thomas and the deacons.

Lloyd stood up to address them. Before announcing the opening hymn, he said that his deacons had asked him to relieve their intense anxiety as to his decision. 'It is not without much prayer and serious consideration that I have been enabled to know the Lord's will in the matter. Now in no uncertain manner I feel a decision has been arrived at, and although feeling sorry for the church at Broughton, from whom I have received the greatest kindness, I feel compelled to continue my work in Altrincham. The love of my people, their many expressions of affection, the number of appreciative letters received, and above all else the conversion of two brethren last Sunday, conduced in no small measure to help me to this decision.'

This announcement, according to the newspaper report, 'was received with the most enthusiastic outburst of applause'. The whole congregation then spontaneously stood and sang, 'Praise God from whom all blessings flow'. For good measure they repeated it. McLaren and the Association had lost. Lloyd was staying.

Thomas made the best of it and asked those who had joined in the singing, 'to consider you have pledged yourselves to a new cooperation with Mr Lloyd and the work of the church, and with the spirit of prayer and consecration'.

The combined church and Sunday school choirs then sang a hymn with a Mr Mossop playing the harmonium. Overbury sang the Magnificat and then they sang the doxology a third time for good measure. It was an emotional meeting.

The church minutes record more precisely why Lloyd stayed: '...the chief inducement being the appeal of the children and the conversions which have recently taken place through which he recognised the guidance of the Holy Spirit.'

'Cowell Lloyd was a man often in my thoughts when I was at ABC. My dream was to build the church up to the size it reached in its heyday under Cowell Lloyd.'

Paul Beasley-Murray, Senior Pastor of Altrincham Baptist Church 1973-86.

Ulundi Villa on Hale Road where Lloyd lived at one time while in Altrincham. The name of the house is on the front wall.

Lloyd also lived at Vona on Willowtree Road, near the Welsh chapel, where he was guest speaker at their opening ceremony.

Willowtree Road as it was and today. The spelling of the road changed regularly. The author uses Willowtree because that is the name on the oldest road sign, which is on the wall of 12 Hale Road.

Memorial stone laid by Lloyd in 1908 for the rear chapel extension.

Lloyd was convinced something special was going to happen in Altrincham and he didn't want to miss it. He was right.

THE GREAT MIDNIGHT EVENT IN ALTRINCHAM

If you had been standing at Hale Station at 10 o'clock at night on Saturday 24 June 1905, you would have seen an extraordinary sight. This sight was replicated in other parts of Altrincham.

The united congregations of Ashley Road Congregational, Bowdon Wesleyan, Bowdon Downs Congregational, Hale Road Baptist, Hale Road Wesleyan, the Welsh Chapel, the Oxford Road Primitive Methodist Church and the Pleasant Sunday Afternoon and Pleasant Saturday Evening Societies all assembled together.

The marshal was none other than Lloyd himself, assisted by a Mr Birchall[1] and others. The pair eventually managed to get the huge procession in line. Then, led by the Altrincham Borough Band, the combined churches marched up Ashley Road and turned right. No doubt, Lloyd, as one of the main organisers, had requested that they march past the Baptist church, and this they duly did by marching along Byrom Street. The procession turned right onto Hale Road, left into Tipping Street, then onto Lloyd Street, then onto Railway Street and made its way up to Market Street. They sang on the way 'Come ye that love the Lord'. To give a theatrical effect to the night-time processions, they all carried Japanese and Chinese lanterns, were surrounded by torch-bearers and were led by people carrying a massive illuminated lantern. They even used acetylene lamps to give added brightness.

Meanwhile, two other similar large processions had assembled, one at Borough Road and the other at Dale Square in Broadheath. They too sang the same hymn. The three groups represented nearly all the Free churches of the Altrincham area together with the Salvation Army.

The people of Altrincham gathered to watch. Tracts were handed out, public houses were visited and the crowds were invited to join the procession, which many did.

The three processions met together in one giant assembly, packing New Market Place. There they sang 'All hail the power of Jesus' name' to the tune 'Diadem'. Then they processed along Market Street, Stamford Street and Station Road. This time they sang the somewhat lighter song 'Count your blessings'.

The processions were followed by outreach events. As there were so many people, the meetings were held simultaneously in the Literary Institute, the New Connexion Methodist Chapel and the Salvation Army building, and even then an overflow meeting was required.

The main meeting was in the Literary Institute. Mrs Graham sang 'the glory song' and there was a solo of 'I gave my life for thee'. This was a very public meeting and there were some hecklers, but they were soon silenced. Finally, at midnight, the Revd G. H. MacNeal of Manchester and Salford City Mission began his address, urging people to follow Christ and not the churches which so often let him down. The appeal produced a good response, with about fifty people positively responding and a further seventy being talked with at the end of the night. The service ended at the extraordinary time of 1 o'clock in the morning. In addition, eighty people signed the pledge.

---

[1] Not a known relative of the author.

Lloyd was delighted. This was a united mission organised by the Free Church Council in which he played a leading role. One year after MacKennal's death, the Free churches were working even more closely together.

The local newspaper dealt with the story with banner headlines reading 'Revival at Altrincham'. Nothing like this had ever been seen in Altrincham before. The Welsh Revival, it said, had arrived in Cheshire.[2]

Hale Station, where one of the enormous processions assembled late at night.

Byrom Street. Lloyd led the Free church procession along here in 1905 past the Baptist chapel.

The local newspaper ran a further story about an event planned for later in July. Lloyd had even bigger ideas.

---

[2] Altrincham Bowdon and Hale Guardian, 1 July 1905.

BAPTISMS IN THE BOLLIN

On a sunny morning in July 1905, you would have seen a strange sight at the Hale Road Baptist Chapel. A lorry arrived, a number of men came out of the chapel and then heaved a heavy harmonium onto the lorry to join a large tent that had already been loaded.

The lorry then proceeded to a field belonging to a Mr Spilsbury near Primrose Cottages off Vicarage Lane in Bowdon Vale. The field led down to the River Bollin and the tent was erected near the river. Above it, the bank led up to a level area. The lorry was parked a little distance away.

At half past two in the afternoon, you would have seen an even stranger sight as the pastor of the Baptist church led the whole congregation and the Sunday school out of the chapel onto Hale Road, along Ashley Road and down onto Vicarage Lane. They too ended up in the same field and found an estimated 4,000 people waiting for them there.

Many of the citizens of Altrincham had heard or read about an extraordinary spectacle that was about to take place. They were so curious that they had arrived early at the field to get good positions. What they had been told was

> A report appeared in February 1905 in the local newspaper of an estimated 8,000 witnessing baptisms in the River Dee. It may be that Lloyd got the idea from this article.

that believers' baptisms were to be held in the River Bollin itself. Most would never have seen a believer's baptism before. This was the climax of an increasing number of baptisms at the Hale Road Chapel which came as part of the revival. There had been five baptismal services in six weeks.

Pierrepont, the Church Secretary, now realised he had a logistical problem. The intention was to hold a service around the lorry with the singing being led from the trusty church harmonium. However, the crowd did not want to give up their places on the river bank. After a brief struggle to persuade the people to move to the lorry, Pierrepont bowed to the inevitable and ordered the lorry to move to the river bank by the crowd.

Pierrepont himself conducted the crowd in the singing as he stood on the back of the lorry. Brookfield played the harmonium. They began appropriately enough with a song called 'Shall we gather at the river?'

There was a slight distraction for the crowd as two dogs ran into the river, but Pierrepont pressed on. Those waiting to be baptised now went into the tent to change. The tent had been erected about halfway down the river bank. Whilst they changed, Lloyd addressed the crowd to explain what was about to happen. He then went into the tent himself and emerged in robes to conduct the baptisms.

The first candidate was a man and the second, according to the local paper, 'quite a youth'.[3] There were some hecklers, but Lloyd calmed them down and the third baptism passed quietly. Lloyd perhaps recalled as he carried out the baptisms how his grandfather had baptised Spurgeon in a river.

---

[3] Altrincham Bowdon and Hale Guardian, 26 July 1905.

Lloyd then gave a closing address, ending with the words 'God be with you till we meet again'. The service closed with another hymn. The crowd, clearly intrigued and impressed, walked back to Altrincham.

Lloyd is in the water about to baptise a young man. One can just make out the hats on the pegs in the changing-tent. Note the large crowd and the newspaper reporter in the foreground with his notebook.

A close up of the changing tent and some of the crowd.

The candidate is immersed in the waters of the River Bollin. The reporter is in the foreground.

The river was swollen by recent rain and was quite fast flowing. Note the two men on the bank. One holds a towel to give to the person baptised as they come out of the water. The other is almost certainly Charles Southwell Snr. The Downes family believe one of their number was baptised in the Bollin, which probably means the person being baptised is Ernest Southwell.

The River Bollin was a favourite area for the people of Altrincham. The photograph above on the left shows a lady in romantic pose and the one on the right shows the use of the river as a recreation area within easy walking distance of Altrincham. The photographs are taken at Ashley Mill.

The baptisms in the Bollin would be spoken about in the town for many years to come and were one of the lead stories in the local newspaper.

WHAT HAPPENED TO LLOYD?

It is at this point that our history of the Altrincham Baptists draws to a close, for we have reached 1905. It will be for other books to continue the story.[1] However, we cannot just leave Lloyd. His is a truly amazing story.

Lloyd was pastor of Altrincham Baptist for an astonishing twenty-four years. In all the period covered by this book, there is never a hint of a word being said against him or any disagreement with him. Lloyd long outlived the older McLaren, who died on 5 May 1910, his final great speech being to the first Baptist World Congress in 1905.

Tragically, Alice Lloyd died young in 1915. Her memorial plaque is still in Altrincham Baptist Church. She was ill for a long time before her death and Lloyd nursed her throughout. The emotional stress of all this coupled with his duties of leading the church meant Lloyd nearly did not make it to her funeral, such was his exhaustion.

At the funeral was a Mrs Louie Bentinck, Alice's best friend and now a widow. She was profoundly deaf. Sometime later Cowell Lloyd and Louie Bentinck started courting. Lloyd was clearly not a man to move slowly, and just a year after Alice's death the two were married. Louie proved just as popular with the church as Alice.

In December 1916, during the dark years of the First World War, the Lloyds finally left Altrincham. The church tried to keep them, but Lloyd had decided it was time to move on. The Church Meeting minutes state that the church members 'gratefully acknowledge our indebtedness to him for his unremitting zeal and earnest work, so faithfully and disinterestedly rendered without relaxation to the very end'.

Under Lloyd, the Altrincham church membership increased from seventy-three to 316 and Sunday school attendances rose from 100 to 350. If one adds communicant members and simple church attenders to this number, this meant that the church, even with its much larger capacity than now,[2] was absolutely packed on Sundays. 'The Church was united, confident and strong, and above all the members were united in Christian love.'[3]

Lloyd took up the post of pastor of Denmark Place Baptist Church at Camberwell in London in January 1917. During his six years there the membership increased from 355 to 652. Denmark Hill was at that time a much better-known church than Altrincham.

One might have thought that Lloyd would have finished his career at Denmark Hill. However in 1923, at the age of fifty-seven, when many people would be looking forward to retirement, the Lloyds took an extraordinary decision. Lloyd's father must have told him much about Jamaica and of the family involvement in the fight against slavery. Jamaica was in his blood.

Before Denmark Hill got wind of what was going on, Lloyd sent a cable to Jamaica accepting the post of pastor of East Queen Street Church in Kingston. The reaction

---

[1] Not forgetting, of course, Cynthia Walker's excellent shorter book on the first 100 years.
[2] Pews seat far more than chairs.
[3] Comber, op. cit. It is worth bearing in mind the relative size of Bowdon Downs Congregational. Taking communicant members, their high point was in 1902 with 367 communicant members, although this discounts the separate church plants of the Congregationalists. The younger Baptist church caught up with, and eventually overtook, Bowdon Downs.

of the Camberwell Church was even more extraordinary than that of the Altrincham Baptists in 1904. Before they could do anything, the Lloyds found that virtually the whole congregation had marched the mile up the hill from the church to the manse to try and persuade them to stay. The congregation then surrounded the house, taking up the entire garden and blocking the road. They would not let the Lloyds leave.

On the left: Cowell Lloyd, aged 50, in the year he left Altrincham Baptist Church. One can see the change from the radical long-bearded student to the mature pastor. However, at fifty, his most famous ministry was still ahead of him.

On the right: Cowell Lloyd's first wife Alice died at Altrincham. There is a plaque in her memory in the chapel. This is a photograph of his second wife Louie.

Fairhaven on Norman's Place in Altrincham, where Lloyd lived in 1904 and 1905 – years when so much happened in Altrincham.

The efforts of the church were all to no avail: the cable had been sent, and so the Lloyds packed their bags and headed across the seas to Kingston to start a new life.

LLOYD IN JAMAICA

Altrincham Baptists may find this difficult to comprehend, but possibly their greatest pastor[4] is far better known for his work in Jamaica than for his twenty-four years in Altrincham.

East Queen Street Baptist Church in Kingston, Jamaica, was founded in 1822 and its ministers had been associated with the campaign to end slavery. At one time the church reputedly had the largest congregation of any Baptist church in the world. It was destroyed in an earthquake in 1907 and the minister at the time lost a leg in the disaster. Numbers had, however, subsequently declined.

True to form, under Lloyd, church membership grew from 300 to over 1,000. The growth was so great that Lloyd built an additional hall seating over 1,000 people. It was named the 'Lloydon Hall'.

It is a testimony to Lloyd that the Jamaican church of which he was minster is still flourishing, as indeed are his previous two churches.[5] However, Lloyd did more than just help to build up East Queen Street. For twenty-nine years he was Baptist chaplain at Kingston Prison where he held a Thursday Bible class which, according to his biography in the *Baptist Handbook*, 'produced remarkable results'.

Lloyd must also have remembered the conversations he had with Austin all those years ago while a student at Regent's Park College. Austin had been teaching at a school at Calabar in Jamaica. Lloyd duly visited the school, and thus began a long association between the pastor and the school. To this day, Calabar is a thriving Christian school. Lloyd established two scholarships there for under privileged children.

Not only was he on the Board of Calabar, but he was also on the Board of Shortwood College. He also supported and regularly attended the East Queen Street Literary Association and was President of the Jamaican Christian Endeavour Society.

Lloyd edited the *Baptist Reporter* for the Jamaican Baptist Union. Given his love of editing the Hale Road Baptist Church newsletter, it is not surprising to find he also edited the *Equester*, the magazine of East Queen Street Baptist.

He still found time to be Vice-President of the Mission of Hope in Camberwell, which specialised in looking after unmarried mothers and illegitimate children.

In 1930 he gave the presidential address to the Jamaican Baptist Union, which he entitled intriguingly 'Malignant Mistakes and Manifold Mercies'. This was his commentary on the social problems of Jamaica. His speech was so popular it was published and ran to two editions.

Lloyd supported the poor in his area and fought for social justice. The Lloyds personally lent money to the poor through a trades union that they supported. The union was part of the early Labour movement in Jamaica. Andrew Bustamente, leader of the union, organised strikes against plantation owners for better wages.

---

[4] I am speaking here of the period up to 1945. For subsequent years, as any wise historian would say, it is too soon to make judgements.
[5] By an interesting historical irony, some Jamaican emigrants arrived in Britain and attended Denmark Hill Baptist Church, not realising Lloyd had been pastor there. They were startled to see a picture of 'their' pastor on display.

In 1937 ship passenger records show the Lloyds arriving on the *Cavina* from Jamaica and staying at Baptist House in London.

Most men would have retired by this stage in life, and Lloyd resolved to retire in 1939. However, East Queen Street persuaded him to stay on as pastor when the Second World War broke out. In 1943 he held his jubilee as a pastor. The mayor of Kingston presided at the celebrations, and friends from Altrincham and Camberwell, despite the war, managed to send him messages of goodwill. The church seated 1,200 and there was twice that number outside.

He finally retired in 1950 at the age of eighty-four. A grateful East Queen Street Church made him Pastor Emeritus. At ninety-three, he was still driving a car, preaching and writing in Jamaica.

> Even as recently as 2003, a book has recorded the impact of Lloyd in Jamaica.[6]

Louie Lloyd died in 1964. Lloyd died in 1966 just before his hundredth birthday. The funeral service was a triumphant one and held at East Queen Street. The church by then had over 1,800 members. Lloyd was buried at sea.

His Baptist Union biography says, 'Few Englishmen have been more widely known or more greatly loved by Jamaicans from all walks of life than Frederick Cowell Lloyd for he was the friend of all, from the Governor-General to the poorest peasant.' His biographer hoped that Lloyd's example and his story would 'inspire and encourage youth and age to be Lloyd-like in the devotion to service for Christ and humanity'. His official biography is called *Colour Blind*, for he was known for remembering everything about everyone he met and treating all equally, regardless of their race or creed.

A Jamaican schoolteacher wrote: 'He is surely one of the greatest authorities on the Holy Scriptures we have had the good fortune of seeing in Jamaica.' A Jamaican periodical called *Labour and Capital* wrote of him in 1943:

'For the past twenty years he has endeared himself to the people of Jamaica by his sacrifices, by his Christian ministry, by his Christ-like simplicity, by his willing hands and purse, by his self-denial, by the hours days and nights he spent in the service of suffering humanity, regardless of race, creed, religion, class or colour, in the by-ways and hedges of Kingston; joining in wedlock hundreds of poor persons; burying the dead who had not tasted the joy of a Christian life and thus had no church that they could call their own; giving letters upon letters to every heart-torn and weary, unemployed person who knocked at his door from morning till night in the quest of employment...emulating the traditional glorious deeds of the early Baptist missionaries...who helped break the links and chains of slavery from the feet of our ancestors.'

Brian Waterson recounts how the Altrincham Baptist Church Treasurer was surprised when, in 1966, the church received a generous legacy from Lloyd. Lloyd never forgot Altrincham Baptist Church.

---

[6] Wright, M.: *Rebecca, My Father's Dream: a Memoir*, iUniverse.com, 2003.

He was a prolific writer and wrote at least nine books.[7] Remarkably, his last book was written when he was eighty-seven. It is called *Titles for the Psalms* and the accompanying photograph shows a still dynamic man. The book contains the following dedication:

'This book is dedicated by the Author first of all to God Who has continued to give him mental vigour long passed the allotted span of life, enabling him to lay at His feet this perhaps last gift of public service; then under God to his comrade-wife whose success in creating a home atmosphere conducive to health and congenial for work has been a continuous inspiration; and to his brother Mr. John P. Lloyd, whose assistance and advice has been of the greatest value; and also to the three churches which he has had the honour of serving during his public ministry – Hale Road, Altrincham (Manchester, England), for 24 years; Denmark Place, Camberwell (London, England) for 6 years and East Queen Street, Kingston (Jamaica) for 27 years of which he is still Pastor Emeritus.'

Portrait of George Liele in East Queen Street Chapel, Jamaica. Liele was a freed American slave who came to Jamaica as a missionary. He was probably the first ordained black minister in the United States and one of Lloyd's predecessors as minister at East Queen Street.

---

[7] His books include A wonderful chain; The Poverty of Jesus; What the Bible has to tell us about Hell; Beautiful Words; The Fellowship of the Cross; Divine Mnemonics; The Messenger, the River, the Gift; The Limits of Forgiveness; God's Way with Man and Keywords for the Books of the Old Testament. Near the end of his life he was still working on a book of keywords of the New Testament. He also wrote in Christian journals and the Christian World Pulpit.

Calabar College in 1922, the year before Lloyd arrived. The school is still thriving.

The photograph shows the Lloyds in Jamaica with Bustamente at the foundation of the Bustamente Industrial Trades Union in 1938. Bustamente went on to the take the centre left Jamaica Labour Party into government and Jamaica into independence.

Cowell Lloyd

Lloyd in Jamaica, aged 92. As recently as 2003 a speech reported in the Jamaican newspaper the Gleaner recorded Lloyd as one of the heroes of faith in Jamaica and a pioneer ecumenist.

Fittingly, the last words of the last book of this great man are taken from the last Psalm: 'Hallelujah – Praise ye the Lord.'

AND FINALLY...

Here we leave Altrincham, Cowell Lloyd and all the people featured in this book. We end our history in 1905, with the Welsh Revival in full flow, baptisms in the River Bollin, the Liberals poised to win their great election victory of 1906 and William Crossley about to become the first Liberal MP for Altrincham.

This is not the end of the book though. In the Appendices you will find biographies and photographs of some of the people mentioned, both famous and ordinary. The story of Ebenezer Brewer and his fiancée in the Boxer Rebellion in China is a particularly interesting one, but you will also find much about families such as the Spences and Southwells. There is also an historical walk round Altrincham which will show you some of the places mentioned, together with a timeline, further photographs and other useful information.

It is, I am convinced, only by understanding where we have come from that we can face the challenges of the future, both by learning from the mistakes of the past and by looking to our predecessors for inspiration.

We owe these people of the past a huge debt. What they did challenges us to achieve great things in our own time. What will a book written in a hundred years' time say about the people of Altrincham?

I hope that you have enjoyed, and will continue to enjoy, this book.

APPENDIX 1

BIOGRAPHIES

This Appendix contains insights into the lives of some of the people featured in this book who have not had chapters devoted to their fascinating stories. They range from ordinary people to people who were famous throughout the country.

We start with a great local Nonconformist with an international reputation.

George Faulkner Armitage

William Armitage lived at Townfield House in Altrincham and died in 1893. He was a cotton manufacturer in Manchester in his firm of Armitage and Rigby, first Chairman of the Lancashire and Yorkshire Bank, a JP, Treasurer of the Lancashire Congregational Union and also of what was then Henshaw's Asylum for the Blind.[1] He was also a founder trustee of the Newtown Free School with Canon Frederick Wainwright.

William's fourth son **George Faulkner Armitage** was not a Baptist, but he worked closely with the Baptists and with Lloyd in particular.

George was born in Longsight in Lancashire in 1849. He qualified as an architect and furniture designer and became internationally known. He was influenced by John Ruskin and William Morris. He represented the country at the Paris Exhibition in 1900 where he won a gold medal. He lived at and ran his business from Stamford House, Church Street (where the Cresta Court and offices are now), later buying the building adjoining Sandiway House. Part of the Armitage workshops are also believed to have been once on the site of the modern Tesco.[2] Armitage married his cousin Annie (nee Rigby). She was the sister of his business partner John Rigby. George Armitage was a devout Christian, and every morning household prayers were said with the staff. In 1891 he had eight servants.

After Nonconformist students were allowed to attend Oxford in 1871, Armitage and Basil Champneys designed Mansfield College, a Congregational foundation, where MacKennal was Chair of the College Council. Armitage remodelled the interior of the Fine Art Society in London and his company was responsible for carvings in the choir stalls at Chester Cathedral. Armitage was the architect for William Crossley's home in Ambleside in 1901.

Armitage employed Charles Southwell Jnr of the Baptist church (see below). He founded the Pleasant Sunday Afternoon Society for Altrincham, whose headquarters were at Sandiway House. Trelfa was a member (see below), and at Trelfa's funeral Armitage met the coffin at the Baptist chapel. Armitage was a member of Bowdon Downs Congregational Church and Mayor of Altrincham between 1913 and 1918.

---

[1] Thomas Henshaw from Oldham founded the Bluecoat School there and left a legacy of £20,000 to found what is now Henshaw's Society for Blind People.
[2] This is according to some information from members of the Southwell family.

He became President of the Manchester Free Church Federation. Like his father before him, he was also a JP, and in 1904 we find him sentencing a man to one month's hard labour for deserting his wife and four children, leaving them with no alternative but the workhouse.

Although a JP, he supported Lloyd in the rates protests of 1903 onwards and his goods were regularly subject to distraint on the orders of his fellow magistrates. He was a manager of the British School with Gaddum at one stage, but lost his post because of his refusal to pay his rates.

He also supported Lloyd in the Nonconformist protests against the proposed legislation in 1904 to liberalise the licensing laws and transfer responsibility away from magistrates. In 1904 he joined a protest demonstration in Market Square with Lloyd. In the same year he also wrote a paper for the Cheshire Congregational churches, writing that Congregationalists had become too prosperous for their own good.

In 1905 he spoke at a Baptist Pleasant Thursday Evening with slides on 'The perils of ice and snow in the high Alps'. Armitage opened at least one sale of goods for the Baptists.

He never liked the new-fangled car, preferring always to use his single horse brougham.

He was a deacon of Bowdon Downs Congregational Church from 1885 to 1891.

Armitage died in 1937, but it is believed that a bequest from his estate went towards the cost of building Oldfield Brow Congregational Church, now a joint Baptist-Congregational church.

Townfield House on Church Street, home of the Armitage family. By the time of this photograph in 1917 it had become John Leigh hospital.

George Faulkner Armitage.

An Armitage chair.

William Armitage was the first Chairman of the Lancashire and Yorkshire Bank. The Altrincham branch is on the right. The photograph is taken in or after 1907.

Joshua and Emily Boydell

Joshua Boydell was a member of Bowdon Downs Congregational Church but also a trustee of Bowdon Baptist Church. He was born in 1855 and lived at Fern Lea on Queen's Road and later on Ashley Road and was active at the British School. He was a member of Hale Urban District Council.

He signed the pledge at a Bowdon Downs temperance meeting in 1892 because of the evils of drink he said he had witnessed recently among the working classes.

He and his wife Emily helped found Ashley Road Congregational Church, but Emily died in 1901. He presented the Ashley Road Church with its organ in her memory. They had four children.

The Brewers

The Brewers were, of course, teetotal. They were one of the key Baptist church families for over 100 years, and also one of the most volatile in the early days.

James Brewer was born in 1832 in Berkshire. He was a gardener. **James** was 54 in 1887 when the breakaway church was formed. He and his wife **Rebecca** had three sons: **William James**, aged 20 in the crucial year of 1887, **Ebenezer**, aged 18 and Frederick aged 16. Their eldest child was their daughter **Ellen** (or Helen) and their youngest child was their other daughter Louisa Jane.

The families of James and Rebecca appear to be long-standing Baptist ones. James was the youngest of at least four children. A letter from his brother Joseph written in 1868 talks of various evangelical churches in the Henley-on-Thames area. Joseph used to preach and hold house meetings. Rebecca was born Rebecca Mayo and her family had Baptist roots going back to at least the beginning of the nineteenth century when they were associated with a Baptist church in Chesham.

James and Rebecca moved from Hillingdon in Uxbridge (Middlesex) to 116 Byrom Street, but moved from time to time within the same area of Altrincham, at one key point in the history of the Baptists living at 17 Bold Street. They always rented their houses.

Rebecca died on 30 March 1887 at the age of 56, around the time of Mowbray's first service at the Building Society Rooms on Market Street. Mowbray gave an eloquent eulogy at the second service he held in the Building Society Rooms after he walked out of the Hale Road chapel.

James proposed the motion for the founding of the breakaway church and was one of its earliest deacons, but left for Bowdon Downs Congregational Church in 1890 when his son William resigned, returning to the re-combined Baptist church in 1895 only after Mowbray left. In 1901 we find him at the age of 69 sharing a house on Albert Road East with Annie Warburton aged 35, as a lodger (they were related by marriage –see below). She was a housekeeper and widow. Thomas North, 32, was living with them and he was a fellow gardener.

James died on 18 April 1910 aged 78.

His daughter **Ellen** married **Alfred Warburton**, the Baptist Church Secretary in 1890. They had no children.

His oldest son **William James** was associated with the church from 1876 and wrote an early account of its history (now lost). In 1881 he was a clerk in a coal office. In 1883 he appeared in the newspapers when one of the Sunday school children stole from the missionary boxes.

William James was also a founding member of the breakaway Altrincham Baptist Church with his father. He proposed the resolution giving the new church its name. In 1890 Alfred Warburton resigned and William wrote a letter of protest to Mowbray. The Church Meeting told him either to withdraw his remarks or leave. He left, returning later to become a member of the re-combined church. Lloyd noted in the minutes on his return that the source of the original dispute had gone and William was welcome back, but added that the original Church Meeting's decision to ask him to recant or withdraw was not being overturned.

A. W. J. Brewer appears at the St John's Church Debating Society from 1893 onwards, so it is likely that William James Brewer attended St John's under Wainwright while absent from the Baptists. This also may explain why his son William (see below) was not baptised as a believer until 1940. William James is mentioned in debates at St John's about the compulsory early closing of shops (most shops opened for twelve hours a day), Home Rule (which is recorded as a rowdy debate where he spoke for the Government), total abstinence against temperance (he supported the former), conscription (he opposed it - see below as to his son William's review on this topic), strikes and their remedies (there was a coal strike at the time), whether women should be eligible for municipal election (his views are not recorded) and whether women ought to be allowed to compete with men in all the pursuits and vocations of life (he voted against on health grounds and because of the adverse effect, as he saw it, on home life).

William James married 38-year-old **Alice Downes** on 3 January 1901 at Bank Street Wesleyan Chapel. They had a daughter **Kathleen Alice**. Alice was the daughter of another gardener and she too was one of the founding members of Altrincham Baptist Church. Kathleen was baptised and became a member in 1919. Brian Waterson knew her.

In 1901 the family lived at Albert Terrace. When his wife Alice died after just two years of marriage, William James married **Winifred Mullins** on 19 January 1905 at the Hale Road chapel. They had been baptised at Hale Road on the same day in 1898. They had three children, **William, Eva** and **Audrey**. Eva and Audrey were baptised and became church members in 1925. William James died in 1944.

Audrey and Eva never married, but the family lived at 5 Midland Terrace at Ashley Road in Hale for over seventy years, at one stage next to the Woodalls who were also a church family.

William (or Bill) was the son of William James. In 1946 Bill and Audrey volunteered to help the Manchester and Salford Baptist Union start a new Baptist church at Newall Green in Wythenshawe. At its height, it had about 400 Sunday school pupils. Bill was the Treasurer. Eventually he moved to Sale Baptist Church and then back to Altrincham Baptist Church.

Bill's only son was **David**, who at the time of writing attends Lymm Baptist Church. He has five children, of whom **Sarah** is the family historian.

We now go back up the family tree to James's second son, **Ebenezer Joseph** Brewer.[3] Ebenezer in 1891 was a clerk in an assurance office. He left the breakaway church only a month or so after it was founded, and returned to Hale Road with Charles Southwell. His departure meant the Brewer family were probably living in one house but attending three churches, two of which were intense rivals. Conversations around the dinner table must have been interesting.

Ebenezer studied at Bible college and then became a missionary to China. He became engaged to **Elizabeth ('Lizzie') Burton**, who was also a missionary to China. In 1899 the Boxer Rebellion in China forced Ebenezer to flee hidden in a haycart and he returned home on furlough in the spring. Lizzie stayed on. Her story is set out in her own biography below.

Following his escape, Ebenezer returned to Altrincham and composed a gallery of 'Real Life in China' for the Baptist church bazaar and spoke at a Good Templar's teetotal meeting. We find him in 1901 staying at a manse in Sawston, Cambridgeshire (where he was probably giving a missionary talk), but he returned to Altrincham where he addressed a temperance meeting. Apart from furloughs in England, he spent a total of seven years as a missionary in China.

He then emigrated in 1902 to Trenton in New Jersey and worked in a children's home where he followed his uncle, the Revd **Walter L. Mayo,** as superintendent. There he met and married **Mary Lillian Howard** and they had one daughter **Florence Rebecca** (her second name being that of course of Ebenezer's mother).

Ebenezer died in 1934 aged 66.

We now again go back up the family tree to the third son of James Brewer, **Frederick Thomas**. He was initially a joiner by trade, but in 1908 is recorded as a builder. It is possible he may have worked for Alfred Warburton. In any event, he married Warburton's daughter **Clara Warburton** in 1900 and they had three children, **Marjorie, Claire** and **Freda**. Mr and Mrs Fred Brewer were baptised at Hale Road in 1903. Clara was listed as a draper in 1908.

The youngest child of James Brewer was **Louisa Jane**, who was a milliner and born in 1874. She never married and in 1921 moved to join Ebenezer in America.

From 1881 a Mr **H. Brewer** Jnr organised a concert at the British School in support of the two teetotal pubs in the area, and he may have been a distant relative of the Baptist Brewers. One 1883 concert was so successful that many had to be turned away.

The author recalls Bill Brewer and his sister Eva in the 1980s, the last of the Brewers to be members of the Baptist churches in Altrincham.

The Brewer family grave is in Bowdon parish church graveyard and later burials were at Hale Road Cemetery.

---

[3] One wonders if he was named after the famous Ebenezer Cobham Brewer who compiled a well-known dictionary of phrases and fables containing such gems as 'Better wed over the mixon than over the moor', which he interpreted as a Cheshire saying that it was better to wed a Cheshire woman than a Londoner who lived over the Staffordshire moors. The Brewers enjoyed literature.

James Brewer and his daughter Louisa in a photograph taken in a studio in the Isle of Man. The Isle of Man became a favourite Victorian holiday destination, and the local newspapers in Altrincham contained accounts of intrepid adventures to the island. One account was of a day trip leaving from Timperley Station.

James Brewer in a posed joke photograph taken in Altrincham but showing him in Blackpool.

Baptismal certificate of William James Brewer, 30 December 1883. The original is missing, but this is the oldest known baptismal certificate of the Altrincham Baptists.

Rebecca Brewer, wife of James. She was a ladies' nurse.

An old William J. Brewer in 1939 behind the family house at 5 Midland Terrace. Standing left to right are Kate, Audrey and Eva; his wife Winifred is seated.

The training home in China where Ebenezer Brewer trained as a missionary.

Ebenezer Brewer later in life in America

Part of the churchyard at St Mary's Bowdon in 1906, where many Nonconformists (including the Brewer family) are buried.

17 Bold Street, one of the houses where the Brewer family lived.

Bill and Edith Brewer. Bill was a conscientious objector in the Second World War. He was asked to become a professional for Altrincham Football Club, but turned this down as he might have been forced to play on Sundays which would have conflicted with his Sunday school duties.

361

Sydney and Susan Brookfield

Sydney (or Sidney) Brookfield was born in Camberwell, South-East London, in 1856 and moved from London to Altrincham in 1881. You will recognise the site of his shop, which is the triangular building at the corner of The Downs and Ashley Road. He was at one time in partnership with a Mr Wilson. He was a silk merchant, draper, hosier, glover and gentlemen's outfitter.

He joined Bowdon Downs Congregational Church, where he was briefly a deacon. He lived at Thorn Lea on Hale Road. He and his wife Susan had three children.

In 1903, he sold the lease of his shop to Union Bank of Manchester, liquidated his business and re-invented himself as an estate and insurance agent.

He was one of the trustees of the Hale Road Chapel from the time it was bought by the breakaway church. In 1899 we find him holding a sale of work in his drawing room to support Dr Barnardo's. In 1904 he was loaned by Bowdon Downs Congregational Church to the Baptists for six months as organist, and played the harmonium at the baptisms in the Bollin. He died in 1938.

Advertisement by Sydney Brookfield, showing the location of his shop at the junction of Ashley Road and The Downs. Brookfield later had a business at Stamford Chambers on Moss Lane.

Elizabeth Burton

Elizabeth Burton (or 'Lizzie' as she preferred to be known) was a member of what is now Sale Baptist Church. She was the third of four children and her father died young, leaving her mother Harriet to bring the family up on Baguley Road in Sale.

Lizzie's interest in missionary work was first kindled at Frank Crossley's Star Hall in Ancoats when a Miss Taylor gave a missionary appeal. At first Lizzie was turned down for missionary work on the grounds of ill-health. She persisted, and after six years was accepted as a missionary.

She became engaged to Ebenezer Brewer (see earlier) and the couple went separately to China as missionaries with the China Inland Mission. On arrival in China in 1898, she was greeted by Hudson Taylor, one of the greatest missionaries of all time, before going to a training college at Yeng-Cheo,[4] a city which Marco Polo once governed. She wrote poignant letters home during her voyage to China.

Her description of her arrival in what is modern-day Yangzhou gives a hint of what was to come:

> 'I wish I could truly describe Yang-Cheo. It is a city, and is supposed to be one of the richest in China, though the numerous beggars and poverty-stricken appearance of the people make one inclined to doubt the truth of this statement. When our boat drew up to the landing-stage a large crowd of natives stood on the jetty, and we heard cries of "The foreign devils," &c. Very inviting, was it not? In a very real sense missionaries have fellowship with Jesus in this city; He was despised, so are we. Foreigners are considered by the majority of the people an unwelcome intrusion. Nevertheless there is a large band of earnest Christians among the people, and a glorious work being carried on by the small band of helpers; so it is well worth being despised.'

The Boxer Rebellion was a violent uprising against foreigners which was eventually put down by a multinational force. The Rebellion was led by a secret martial arts society called the 'Harmonious Fists', hence the name 'Boxers'. A hundred and eighty missionaries and their families were killed in the Rebellion.

When the Rebellion broke out, Lizzie and a group of five other missionaries and one child decided to flee towards the Yellow River on 17 July 1900 where they could perhaps find a boat to the south and to safety. They met a group of men on the banks of the river who said they would take them across, but instead they took them to a lonely place further down the river and ordered the missionaries down to the ground with the words, 'All get down your time has come to die, this is the place'.[5] One of the missionaries, a Mr Young, prayed for them all and then the men hacked the missionaries to death.

---

[4] It was sometimes called Yang-Chao.
[5] From a letter of Miss May Nathan, quoted in Marshall Broomhall, M. (ed): *Last Letters and Further Records of Martyred Missionaries of the China Inland Mission With Portraits and Illustrations*, 1901.

It is partly thanks to the work of pioneer missionaries such as these people that there is a flourishing Chinese church. There is a memorial to Lizzie in Brooklands Cemetery.

Lizzie Burton in China. On arrival at the training school in China, all missionaries with the China Inland Mission had a photograph taken in Chinese clothing, which they wore from then on.

Plaque showing the names of missionaries killed in the Boxer Rebellion. The name of Lizzie Burton, Ebenezer Brewer's fiancée, appears on the right.

Thomas and Jane Forster

Thomas Forster was born in 1833 and was from Grappenhall near Warrington. He moved to Altrincham and started in business as shopkeeper, dairyman, milk purveyor, confectioner and tea dealer. He lived at 26 Stamford Street in 1881 and then moved to 32 Oxford Road. He was a trustee of Bowdon Baptist Church but there is no record of him ever holding office there. In 1883 he was named as a substantial donor to the Baptist building fund along with Frank Crossley and others. However, during the period of the breakaway church we find him attending the Bowdon Baptist Mutual Improvement Society at Hale Road, so he did not support Mowbray. There is a Thomas Forster who later joined Bowdon Downs Congregational and he may also be one and the same as the Thomas Forster who was a member of the Liberal Reform Club in Altrincham and vice-chair of the Liberal Workingmen's Club.

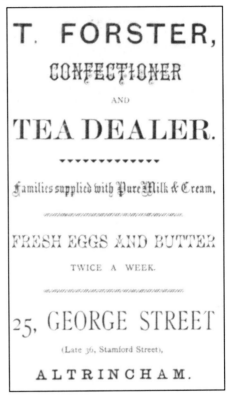

His wife **Jane** was ill for quite some time, and the couple took regular trips to the Isle of Man for her health. Jane died and was buried there in 1901.

Forster effectively then moved to the Isle of Man and in June 1903 he too died there, aged 72. He was a member of Broadway Baptist Church in Douglas when he died, so he must have been a Baptist sympathiser while remaining at Bowdon Downs Congregational Church when he lived in Altrincham. His funeral service was conducted by Revd W. Forster, who was presumably a relative.

His grandson became a professor of music.

Mr and Mrs James Hawksworth

James Hawksworth and his wife joined Altrincham Baptist Church in 1899 and lived on Hawthorn Road. James was later Church Treasurer, and in 1904 was one of those who helped to persuade Lloyd to stay in Altrincham. He was a syrup mixer by profession. The family later moved to Longsight.

Jesse and Marianne Haworth

Jesse Haworth, aged about 76.

Jesse Haworth was one of Lloyd's most influential supporters in the churches' rates protests. He was a JP and deacon of Bowdon Downs Congregational Church for 25 years. He was instrumental in bringing Alexander MacKennal to Bowdon from Leicester, and the MacKennals and Haworths became friends.

Haworth was born in Bolton in 1836 and the family then moved to Pendleton. His father died and his mother **Marianne** was left to bring him up. She was a housekeeper and Jesse became a salesman.

He married another **Marianne**, who was five years his junior. In doing so, he married into the Armitage family as she was the daughter of George Faulkner Armitage. By 1881 he was a cotton agent living at Green Walk in Bowdon and the family had two servants. He was a partner in the firm of James Dilworth and Sons. Clearly he did well in business and the household expanded, acquiring adjoining properties. Haworth was a member of the Royal Exchange and collected paintings and ceramics. The Haworths' children were **Elizabeth, Goodier, Arthur** and **Frank**.

However, it is not for supporting Lloyd in refusing to pay his rates that he is best known, but rather for his love of Egypt, and more particularly Egyptology. Howarth's interest probably began in 1877 when the novelist Amelia Edwards published her book, *A 1000 Miles Up the Nile*. The Haworths followed Edwards' route twice.

They met the archaeologist Flinders Petrie through Edwards, who was by then a mutual friend. The couple agreed to finance Petrie's archaeological digs without condition, although said they wanted to be kept out of sight and did not want any plunder to take place. Petrie is most famous for his pioneering work on the Great Pyramid at Giza.

In 1890 the Haworths presented their Egyptian collection from Kahun and Gurob to the Manchester Museum. In 1912, with the collection rapidly expanding, Haworth made a substantial contribution to the museum building fund. In recognition of his generosity, and of his position as one of the first patrons of scientific excavation in Egypt, the University of Manchester conferred upon him the Honorary Degree of Doctor of Laws. He went on to donate another £10,000, and in his will left a further £30,000. These were very substantial sums at the time. He died on 23 October 1920, aged 83.

The great archaeologist Flinders Petrie on a dig in Egypt.

Edward and Margaret Leech

Mrs Leech Snr transferred from Bowdon Downs Congregational Church to Bowdon Baptist Church only three months after its foundation under Betts. By 1881 she was a widow and lived on Oxford Road with her son **Edward**. It is possible therefore that she and her husband were founder members of Bowdon Baptist Church. Edward was born in Preston and was just 25 when he launched the building fund for Bowdon Baptist Church. He was sometimes the Treasurer and sometimes the Secretary of the Church.

He and his wife **Margaret** lived at modern-day 54 Oxford Road in 1881 with their one-year-old daughter Mabel and had one servant, Ellen Vaughan from Wales. Edward was a cotton salesman.

He was also in charge of the Baptist Sunday school. His departure from the Sunday school merited a moving address from Mowbray and an article in the local newspaper. He moved to Stockport in 1884 where he and Margaret had two further children, **Percy** (who was also to become a cotton agent) and **Elsie**. The family then moved to Eccles. Leech kept in contact, however, and appeared on the platform with Mowbray at the last Annual Church Meeting of Bowdon Baptist Church.

Like his brother H.J. Leech, he gave recitations at the Newtown Institute. In 1889 he gave visible support to Mowbray after the breakaway by chairing a public tea meeting. He returned later to Altrincham.

367

Henry Leech

Henry James Leech was a journalist and Edward's older brother by two years. In 1881 he lived with Edward and Margaret on Oxford Road. Henry married, but his wife died young in 1887. The Liberal Reform Club, of which he was a member, expressed its condolences. He moved in with his mother at 54 Oxford Road where, in 1891, they had a lodger and a servant.[6] By 1901, after his mother had died, he was a lodger at a house on Elm Road and was by then listed as a journalist and author.

He was the author of *Tales and sketches of old Altrincham and Bowdon* and wrote a book in 1897 proposing the incorporation of Altrincham.[7] He was on the committee at one stage of the Bowdon Scientific and Literary Society. In 1879 he gave a lecture at the British School on 'Charles Dickens, his life and works'. In 1880 he gave a lecture on the House of Commons. He was a speaker at the Altrincham Workingmen's Liberal Club and published and edited the *Altrincham Division Chronicle*. He represented the Liberals in the 1888 Home Rule debate with the Conservatives at the British School. He presented a petition to the Local Board on behalf of a meeting at the British School in 1893 about the alleged unfair dismissal of the keeper at Stamford Park. He also helped Manchester City Mission.

Leech was organist of Bowdon Baptist Church in 1878 and sometime choirmaster. He was certainly a Baptist sympathiser but probably never a member. Later he helped Lloyd as organist, and when the churches re-combined, he played the harmonium at the reconciliation service and promised to help Lloyd with the choir. His base was, however, at Bowdon Downs Congregational, where he also led the choir at one stage.

Newtown Free School or Institute just before it was demolished. Henry Leech gave recitations there and was also librarian.

---

[6] Like many people, they rented the house. Their first landlord was John Watson and James Percival the second.
[7] MacKennal commented on this favourably in 1900 in a talk to the Primitive Methodists, although he did say that he expected Bowdon in thirty years to be a suburb of the expanding Broadheath.

Henry and Jane Overbury

Henry (or **Harry**) **Leonard Overbury** was born in 1844 and was originally from Houndsditch in London. He was a life assurance agent but also trained as a Baptist pastor. He married **Jane** and they had six children. In 1881 the family lived in Stockport while Harry was lay (i.e. unpaid) pastor of Ancoats Baptist Church. They then moved to Altrincham and lived at Holly Bank on Hale Road. They joined Bowdon Baptist Church and Overbury became Treasurer under Mowbray. The Overburys did not follow Mowbray in the church split, staying on at Bowdon Baptist Church until its demise.

The couple had a daughter **Ethel** and son **Roland** who were both commended in the Sunday school in 1889. They also had **Gilbert, Oswald** and **Bernard**. Their third son **Arthur** was head of the Baptist Sunday school for many years and a life deacon. He was, according to Brian Waterson, born at 78 Hale Road. Brian became a deacon of Altrincham Baptist Church in 1958 when Arthur Overbury was still a deacon. **Betty Overbury** was Arthur's daughter and died in June 1941.

The Overburys attended Altrincham Baptist Church after Mowbray left and rejoined as members of the combined church in 1902 under Lloyd. When Lloyd agreed to stay on at Altrincham instead of going to Broughton Church in Salford, Overbury sang the Magnificat to the church in celebration.

Wedding, showing Arthur Overbury with the bride. The photograph is on the steps of the Hale Road chapel.

Unknown Baptist church group, date uncertain, but the man on the right is Arthur Overbury.

Sunday school with Arthur Overbury.

Sunday school in 1942 with Arthur Overbury (back centre) and Charles Frederick Southwell Jnr (back right). The children are all contemporaries of Brian Waterson. Some families were members of the church for generations.

Charles Frederick Southwell Jnr later in life with Arthur Overbury.

Charles and Annie Pierrepont

Charles F. L. Pierrepont was born in 1871 in Lincolnshire but his parents then moved to Rusholme. He married **Annie** and their children were **Edith** and **Mary**. He was a railway clerk. He was baptised as a believer in 1898 when he and Annie joined the Baptist church. He later became Church Secretary. They lived at Holm Lea on Ashley Road and then at Fairholme, Claremont Grove in Hale, where church member May Massey was their domestic servant. He helped persuade Lloyd to stay in Altrincham when McLaren wanted him to move to Salford. He was choirmaster for a while and we find him on the lorry at the baptisms in the Bollin, conducting the singing.

He negotiated a lease of the church schoolrooms in conjunction with the church lawyers, Brett Hamilton and Tarbolton of Kennedy Street, Manchester, to the Cheshire County Council Education Committee before the new Stamford Park School moved into its new buildings.

The Pierreponts played and sang for the Altrincham and Bowdon District Total Abstinence Society. Pierrepont was a Passive Resister with Cowell Lloyd, and regularly appeared before the magistrates for refusing to pay his rates. His mother joined the church in 1902.

He resigned as Church Secretary in 1905 on health grounds and due to outside commitments. It may be to him that Lloyd paid tribute (from Jamaica) for bearing a long-term unspecified illness with Christian grace and fortitude while being Church Secretary. However, only a few months after resigning as Secretary, Pierrepont replaced James Hawksworth as Treasurer when the Hawksworths left the area.

George and Julia Shiner

George Shiner was born in Frampton, Dorset, in 1856. He was a gardener and domestic servant. He married **Julia** and the family lived at Rose Cottage on Langham Road.

The Shiners were members of Bowdon Baptist Church during the time of Leonard at Hale Road, and Shiner was also a member of the Bowdon Baptist Mutual Improvement Society. Their children were **Wilfred**, **Walter**, **Annie** and **Ethel**.

The Shiners joined Altrincham Baptist Church under Mowbray after it took back the Hale Road chapel in 1892 and were baptised at the same time. Shiner became a deacon and Sunday school teacher under Lloyd. Wilfred in 1900 was involved in taking 160 Sunday school children to Tatton Park.

The Simmons

William Richard Simmons was at different times church secretary and treasurer of Bowdon Baptist Church. He was the first to propose the building of a new chapel. He worked as a life assurance agent and lived at Post Office Place on Rose Hill in Bowdon with his wife **Jesse**.

He took the lease of the Hale Road site in his own name together with Ormond and Thomas Forster, and then created the trust deeds which allowed Bowdon Baptist Church to occupy the chapel.

William opposed Mowbray's resolution to sell the chapel. He and Mowbray were the principal protagonists during the period of the split. He then conducted negotiations with Mowbray and the Altrincham Baptist Church Secretary to try and bring the two churches back together, volunteering at one stage to leave the area if that would help. He is probably responsible for paying off much of the early debt, and we know that he and Llewellyn personally knocked on many doors to raise funds.

In 1889 Jesse Haworth nominated him to be a guardian of the local workhouse, but he declined.

Simmons returned after the two churches reunited and Mowbray had left, but was never a deacon or officer again. In 1898 he was appointed as a delegate on behalf of the church to the Free Church Council. He was a supporter of the teetotal movement.

Mary E. Simmons was the couple's daughter. She was born in 1849 and died in 1915. When she died, she had been with the church for over thirty-eight years. She played the harmonium for a number of years and organised some of the early fund-raising concerts. In 1899 she organised the tea for 100 Sunday school pupils when they went to Frodsham and in 1900 organised a tea at Tatton Park with the Southwells and Shiners. She was also the librarian of the Free Church Library at the British School.

She was a Passive Resister and refused to pay her rates. In September 1904 at the age of 56 she bravely attempted to address the magistrates, producing laughter in the court when she said of Lloyd and her fellow protestors, 'As I look round at my companions in misfortune, they do not look like very dishonest or dishonourable people.'

The Southwells (with the Downes and the Bowlands)

Charles Southwell was born in Lincolnshire in 1845. The Southwell family believe that he and others in the family moved to Staffordshire and then brought a canal boat from there up to Altrincham. The canal boat connection would fit with the family trade as joiners. Apparently when they had delivered the boat to Altrincham, they decided they liked the area, sought work and then settled. This illustrates the growing mobility of the population as they followed new sources of work.

Southwell was an early member of Bowdon Baptist Church and then became a deacon; indeed, it is possible he was a founding member. He was treasurer under Mowbray in 1885 and 1886. He married **Mary** and they had three children, **Charles Frederick Jnr**, **Michael Ernest** and **Louisa** (or 'Lily').

The Southwells were a young family during the turbulent Mowbray years. Southwell was forced to bring his young family up on his own after Mary died, although he had a housekeeper called Elizabeth Whittaker. The family lived at 46 Lloyd Street, 10 Osborne Road and also at Victoria Villas, 128 Hale Road, before ending up at The Limes on Norman's Place.

Southwell walked out of Bowdon Baptist Church with Mowbray to form the breakaway church, but soon afterwards he changed his mind and returned to Hale Road, probably because as a trustee he had considerable personal financial liabilities if Bowdon Baptist Church became insolvent. He later re-joined the combined church under Mowbray in 1892.

Southwell was active in the Sunday school. In 1900 he organised a Sunday school trip for 160 children with Wilfred Shiner and others to Tatton Park, with games and a tea. He was a deacon under Lloyd. In 1903 he ran a shooting gallery at a church bazaar.

Michael was born in 1877 and nicknamed 'Chunk' as he became a wood-carver. He and Charles Jnr were commended as Sunday school members in 1886. Chunk fought in the First World War, whereas Charles Jnr did not. On his return from the war, Chunk had a tragic motorcycle accident at Ringway and died later, from his injuries.

Lily was born in 1880 and later in life became a teacher in an elementary school. She was baptised as a believer in 1903 and later married Hugh C. Mills. She moved from Victoria Villas and emigrated to Hawkes Bay in New Zealand.

We now turn to the Bowland family, as they became connected with the Southwells through marriage.

Peter and **Mary Bowland** were both local gardeners. Their children were **Jacob**, **Ellen**, **Mary** and **John**.

John became an artist.

Ellen was born in 1850 and looked after her father Peter at 33 Denmark Street, Altrincham, when her mother Mary died. Ellen was a seamstress. She and her younger sister Mary moved to live at 27 Byrom Street. Mary was a nurse. Mary joined the Baptists in 1891 and Ellen then joined them in 1889 from an unnamed church, being baptised as a believer at the same time.

Jacob became a painter and decorator and his shop was at the corner of Regent Road and Norman's Place. He married **Ruth**. They lived at The Limes just round the corner on Norman's Place. We know that in 1901 they had one servant named Alice Mutch. Alice was baptised as a believer and joined the Baptists in 1892.

Jacob and Ruth had four children **Annie, Mary, Elizabeth** and **Wilfred**. Jacob and Ruth did not attend the Baptist church but Annie went to the Baptist Sunday school. She was baptised as a believer and then became a member of the church in 1893.

Charles Southwell Jnr was born in 1875 and baptised by Lloyd in 1897. He attended the Baptist Sunday school at about the same time as Annie and Wilfred. Charles and Annie started courting. Annie had a reputation as quite a fiery lady. They eventually married in 1902.

Charles Southwell Jnr was at first a furniture draughtsman and then a designer for George Faulkner Armitage (see above). He worked for Armitage and successor companies for seventy-eight years (although in latter years was only called upon to give consultancy advice when needed). He was also an amateur painter and painted a picture called 'Oldfield Brow' out of a window at Duncot, 314 Oldfield Road, Oldfield Brow. He became a deacon of the Baptist church after the period covered by this book.

As well as being a decorator, Annie's father Jacob was a local politician and was elected to the West Ward of Altrincham in 1897. Charles Southwell Jnr helped his father-in-law on the campaign trail. Annie too was politically involved, but in her case it was as a suffragette.

By 1927 the couple had moved to Sandgate, 13 Sandiway, Altrincham. They had a son **Dennis** who married **Bessie Tomlinson**, an Anglican. Dennis was in the cotton trade in Manchester and Bessie was in the fashion trade and they met when they commuted into Manchester. They ran the Stamford Drapery store on Stamford Park Road. That branch of the family attended St George's Church but also sometimes the Baptist Sunday school. Their son **Desmond** married **Joan Hunter**. Joan was born on Pownall Street and then moved to Bold Street. She attended the Primitive Methodist church but also the Baptist Sunday school, until she succumbed to the pleasures of a Sunday morning cycling club. Desmond and Joan had three children, **Jonathan, David Michael** and **Joanna**.

Charles Jnr and Annie also had a daughter **Dorothy Mary**, born in 1907, and a son **Charles Geoffrey**. Dorothy married **Frank Downes** in 1930 who ran a chemist's shop. They moved back to The Limes on Norman's Place and then to Duncot, where Charles did his painting.

Frank and Dorothy had three children, **Barbara** (born 1932), **Frances Marjorie** ('Dinky') and **Geoffrey Francis**, all of whom had children.

The Southwells were in fact quite literally involved in saving the Hale Road Baptist chapel. When the organ was installed in about 1908, an organ loft had to be constructed. The wall at the front of the main hall was scaffolded and the brickwork cut out to form an arch. During the night at the weekend there was a terrific storm and high winds. Charles Southwell Jnr got the men out and worked throughout the storm. They added more supports. Without this, it is thought that part of the chapel might have collapsed. There is still a drop of some inches that can be seen when looking at the last arch before the organ arch.[8]

Charles Southwell Snr died in 1916 and the Church Meeting recorded his forty-four years of service 'so ungrudgingly rendered'... 'His faithfulness and loyalty were his distinguishing features'.

At the age of 64 Charles Southwell Jnr contributed his reminiscences to Lloyd's biographer. He died in 1971, aged 96. Brian Waterson remembers Charles Southwell Jnr as his Sunday school superintendent. John Campbell recalls that he used to be called 'Mr Force', after the super-hero from a brand of cereals at the time.

Wedding photograph of Charles Frederick Southwell Jnr and his suffragette wife Annie Bowland. The photograph is possibly taken outside The Limes on Norman's Place, the Bowland family home. On the front row (left to right) are Charles Southwell Snr, possibly his housekeeper Elizabeth Whittaker, unknown, possibly Lily Southwell, Charles and Annie Southwell, unknown, Annie's parents and unknown. On the very back row on the left just in front of the door is probably Lloyd. The wedding itself would probably have been held at the Hale Road chapel.

[8] My thanks to John Campbell, former fabric steward of the Baptist church, for this insight.

Charles Southwell Jnr and his new wife
Annie on their wedding day.

The three children of Charles Southwell
Snr: Lily, Chunk and Charles Jnr.

Charles Southwell Jnr and his daughter Dorothy on her 21st birthday.

Charles Southwell Jnr designed and carved the war memorial by St Margaret's Church, Dunham for his employer George Faulkner Armitage. The memorial was subsequently moved from its original location. Southwell also carried out work at Chester Cathedral for Armitage, and at Ampleforth College.

Armitage's design studio circa 1897.

Charles Southwell Jnr was responsible for many of the designs produced by George Faulkner Armitage. Shown left is an Armitage chair.

On the right is a sitting- room interior dating back to 1891. Armitage designed sitting-room interiors for the Paris Exhibition with the help of Southwell.

Charles Southwell Jnr both painted and designed. Here is a combination of the two in a painting of his own front room which he designed at Sandgate.

*'Chunk' Southwell home on leave
during the First World War.*

Charles Geoffrey Southwell
married Betty during the Second
World War at St George's Church
in Altrincham. They had a daughter
Gillian. Charles was involved in
the parachute drop at Arnhem and
landed in the river. He developed
tuberculosis after this and was ill
for a long time after the war.

*Back row: Dorothy and her father Charles
Jnr; middle row: Bessie Barbara and
Frances; front row: Geoffrey and
Desmond. Barbara recalls being taken,
aged 4, around Dunham Park by her
grandfather Charles Southwell Jnr and
'planting' halfpenny coins. She was
amazed when she came back next week
and found they had grown into pennies.*

Charles Jnr and Annie later in life with son-in-law Frank Downes, the chemist.

Four generations of Southwells: Dennis, Charles Jnr, Desmond and baby Jonathan.

The Spence family

But for his last-minute unavailability, the name of the great industrialist **Peter Spence** would have been on one of the foundation stones of the Hale Road chapel. Instead, McLaren's name was substituted. Peter and his son **Frank** were substantial donors to the building fund. The family is an interesting case study of Victorian self-made men with strong religious convictions.

Peter Spence was born in Brechin in Scotland in 1806. His father's family were hand-loom weavers and his mother's family were farmers. He left home at an early age and was apprenticed to a grocer in Perth. There he set up as a grocer with his uncle and married **Agnes Mudie**, daughter of a linen manufacturer. He started reading science books and developed an interest in chemistry. When her coffee shop and his business both failed, the couple moved to Dundee to live with Agnes' mother and Peter worked at the local gas works. Each night he would experiment with gas products in the twelve foot square wash-house.

In 1834 they moved to London where he registered his first patent. His new business failed, however, and they moved to Burgh in Cumberland where Peter again worked in a local gas works.

Spence's constant experimentation finally paid off when he discovered a process for manufacturing alum by treating coal shale with sulphuric acid. Alum was used in the printing and dyeing industries. Spence spotted the opportunity and quickly patented this new process in 1845.

His discovery was actually a complete accident. One night all his experiments had failed, and he forgot to take the materials out of their basin. The next morning he found they had turned to alum crystals.

Spence set up his new business in Pendleton in Salford with Henry Dixon. He chose the location because the Manchester area had good labour, coal and a big demand for alum. He located the factory right by the canal and near the railway, giving him good transport facilities. The family lived at Arlington House in Stretford.

Spence's new process revolutionised the alum industry. He went on to register a remarkable fifty-six patents, one of which led to a new type of cement. Production at Pendleton by 1850 was 20 tons of alum a week and by 1870 he was producing 250 tons per week. He became the largest manufacturer of alum in the world, setting up other factories in Birmingham and Goole. Many of his processes used waste from gas production.

Manchester entrepreneurs in Victorian England were often blithely unaware (or sometimes perhaps deliberately ignorant) of pollution issues, and Spence had the unfortunate distinction of being one of the first to have a claim brought against him for pollution offences, namely 'conducting an unacceptable nuisance at Pendleton'. The factory had been emitting toxic waste products such as hydrogen sulphide and sulphuric acid.

In the summer of 1857, the Manchester photographer brothers James and Robert Mudd were commissioned to take eleven photographs as evidence for the Pendleton Alum Works indictment. The case was heard in the Summer Assizes of the Northern Circuit in Liverpool and commenced in August that year. The Mudd photographs show trees stripped of their foliage. The jury returned a verdict of guilty on the nuisance charge but not guilty that the nuisance was injurious to health. The Pendleton works were closed down and the business removed to Miles Platting in east Manchester.

To be fair to Spence, he had already realised the problem and employed someone to find ways to reduce the pollution. However, that person turned against him and gave evidence for the prosecution. Ironically, Spence was a campaigner for better sanitary provision for the poor in Manchester. He was also a member of the Manchester Literary and Philosophical Society. It was there after a railway accident that he took up the challenge of Dr Joule to show that freezing iron and steel makes them more vulnerable to cracking.

Disaster then struck, because Spence opened up a new process that failed commercially. Spence was at the time a deacon at McLaren's Union church. McLaren suggested that his fellow deacon, the wealthy iron manufacturer Richard Johnson, should call on Spence. Johnson asked Spence what he needed to turn the business round. Spence told Johnson it would take £5,000. Johnson promptly lent him the money and Spence was able to pay him back within the year.

Spence gave evidence in 1881-82 to a House of Commons Committee on railway rates, stating that the railways were killing industry and the canals. He subscribed £1,000 to the formation of the Manchester Ship Canal and was a JP and also Director of the Mechanics' Institute. He turned down the opportunity to stand as a Liberal for Parliament.

Spence was also a total abstainer and campaigned against what he saw as the evils of alcohol and tobacco. He did not tolerate drinkers in his workforce, but was regarded as a good employer and generally paid above average wages.

Spence died in 1883 shortly after his wife Agnes. It is said he always had a strong sense of humour, even joking on his death bed. McLaren wrote of him: 'His devout Christianity was of an unfortunately rare type; his conscientious liberality of rarer type still. To a green old age he kept much of the interest, the vigour, the buoyancy of youth, and he died in peace, calm of mind, and clear of heart, not eager to go, but satisfied with what God had given him...'.[9]

Spence's children were **James** (born 1836), **Frank** (born 1838), **John** (born 1840), **Mary** (born 1844), **Deveril** (born 1846) and **Margaret** (born 1849).

Frank was born in Greenwich while his father Peter was conducting his first business in London. He married **Frances** (usually called **'Fanny'** to avoid confusion) and their children were **Wilfred, Peter, Malcolm, Harriet, Jessie** and **Howard**. It is Frank's story we will now mostly follow. Frank was a manufacturing chemist.

The family moved to Ardwick and then to 72 The Downs in Altrincham (where they shared with the Gelchrist family).

Frank worked with his father and in 1875 they registered the first patent for the treatment of bauxite, which was a good substance to use in water and effluent treatment. The Spences timed the patent well as it coincided with the passing of the Public Health Act which required better water purification. Bauxite was also used in the manufacture of paper.

Frank joined Bowdon Baptist Church and was at one stage Treasurer. He contributed £100 to the building fund, which was about 5 per cent of the then estimated total building cost.

Frank left the church when in 1881 he and Fanny moved to 16 Ansom Road in Rusholme. Frank came back to open the first fund-raising bazaar. By 1891 the family had moved to 162 Bury New Road, Broughton, in Salford. It is possible that they attended Broughton Baptist Church. It was interesting to note that it was this church that tried to persuade Lloyd to be its pastor at around the time the Spences rejoined Altrincham Baptist Church.

By 1901 they were living in Dalfield on Arthog Road in Hale (now called Miramar) and were rich enough to employ three servants. Dalfield was named after Fanny's home town in Scotland and one of the windows in the house is believed still to have a 'Spence' etching.

The couple rejoined Altrincham Baptist Church in 1905, although they seem to have been regular attenders before then. Spence was a Passive Resister and had his goods taken when he refused to pay his rates.

Just how hard the Baptists were hit by his departure in 1881 can be seen from the impact on the church accounts on his return. In 1905 he contributed over £75 to church funds. Harry Overbury was the next highest contributor at roughly one tenth

---

[9] Quoted in *Chemical Trade Journal: Industrial Celebrities,*

of this level. It is possible that the departure of Spence in 1881 led ultimately to the bankruptcy of Bowdon Baptist Church, and that if Spence had not been a member when the Baptists were looking for their new building, they might never have embarked on their ambitious project. They may have relied too much on the support of Spence and his father. It is likely that the departure of Spence forced the 1881 re-financing exercise undertaken by the church.

Malcolm, Frank and Fanny's third child, had five children: **Geoffrey** and **Gwen** (who were twins), **Reginald**, **Molly** and **Marguerite** ('**Peggy**'). Gwen married **Clive Duerr** and they had two daughters **Pamela** and **Gillian**. Molly married **Norman Duerr**, brother of Clive, so the two sisters married the two brothers. Geoffrey's son is **Paul**, who lives in Kenya and still of course has the Spence surname.

The Duerr family are world famous for the manufacture of preserves. The first jams were produced in the family kitchen in Heywood. F. Duerr & Sons Limited was then founded in 1881. Norman and Molly's children are **Anthony** (OBE and Chairman of the company at the time of writing) and **Shirley**. It was Shirley's great-grandfather who established the company. The company's reputation was for paying and treating its staff well. The company name was firmly established when it provided preserves to troops in the trenches in the First World War.

The Duerr family were active in Ashley Road Congregational Church, so the Congregationalists inter-married with the Baptists.

Frank Spence died in 1907. Peter Spence and Sons was sold to Laporte in 1960.

Molly Spence, born in Bowdon in 1909.

383

John Thompson

John Thompson illustrates how the Nonconformists became increasingly bound together, both by family, politics and religion. By offering support to and dealing with each other, they formed a religious grouping that had tremendous economic power.

Thompson was the son of a prominent Liverpool merchant. He spent three years in Bombay and then moved to Bowdon, where he joined Stewart Thompson and Co. He was a member of the Manchester Chamber of Commerce, Chair of the Bowdon Institute, Director of the Lancashire and Yorkshire Bank, Chairman of Manchester City Mission, on the committee of the Boys' Refuge in Strangeways and supported the YMCA. He was also a Governor of Manchester Royal Infirmary and a Manchester JP.

Thompson was a keen supporter of the temperance movement. He married **Leila Kerr** and **Frank Crossley** married Leila's younger sister **Emily**. He was a friend of Wainwright for over forty years. He was also a member of McLaren's Union Baptist Church. Mowbray helped him at Manchester City Mission and Thompson was effusive in his praise for him. Thompson also spoke at Lloyd's induction at Hale Road as co-pastor with Mowbray.

The photograph above left was taken in 1897 on the occasion of Queen Victoria's diamond jubilee and shows Railway Street and the new Stamford Street. The building on the right is the Lancashire and Yorkshire Bank where Thompson and Mills, with others from Bowdon Downs Congregational Church, made much of their money. The photograph above right shows the scene in 2007.

The Trelfa family

Richard Henry Trelfa and his wife **Ann** were members of Bowdon Baptist Church. Trelfa was a deacon. In 1881 he was on the building committee when the church was running into serious financial difficulties. In 1887 he gave a recital at an Altrincham and Bowdon total abstinence meeting.

The Trelfas did not follow Mowbray when he left Bowdon Baptist Church. Instead they moved to Sale Baptist Church, returning to the re-united church in Altrincham in 1895 after Mowbray left. In 1891 they lived at 94 Byrom Street and later at 8 Charter Road.

Trelfa was a cabinet maker by trade, but he joined the army and became a sergeant, probably fighting in the Boer War, even though Lloyd was opposed to it. Trelfa was at one point choirmaster of the Baptists and on his return from the army became an enthusiastic member of Armitage's Pleasant Saturday Evening group.

In 1902 Trelfa was sawing wood at the top of a shed at the Hale nurseries of W. Clibran and Sons when he fell fifteen feet to the ground, landing on his head. For weeks he lingered on at the hospital with a fractured spine, and then died on 30 December 1902.

The Trelfa's son **Fred** was commended in the Sunday school in 1889 and baptised as a believer in 1900. He was also a cabinet maker. **Lucy** was their daughter and was recorded as a Sunday school member in 1897. They also had sons called **Bernard ('Bertie')** and **Norman**.

Brian Waterson remembers the Trelfas as elderly people in the church.

Frederick Wainwright

It may seem strange to place a biography here of **Canon Frederick Wainwright**, but his story is connected with that of the Nonconformists and the Baptists and, although he never appears to have preached at the Hale Road chapel, he was prepared to work with the Nonconformists and they with him.

Wainwright was born in London on 16 June 1837, just before Victoria came to the throne. He was educated at what became Liverpool College. He gained an exhibition to Trinity College, Cambridge where he went on to win a scholarship and then graduated in classical honours. He was an assistant master at his old college for four years. It was probably while at Liverpool that he became the spiritual mentor of Henry Mowbray.

He then became curate at St Mary's, Bowdon, under William Pollock. From there he was sent to St John's Church, which first met in the British School whilst the church waited for their new building to be completed. Wainwright stayed at St John's for most of his life, although he did think of leaving at one stage when he contested the Proctorship in the Convocation of York and lost. It is a testament to Altrincham that it could attract a man of such high calibre to lead a mission church.

Canon Wainwright of St John's. Note the Bible in his hands.

Wainwright supported the Altrincham Provident and Dispensary Hospital and was on the committee of the Provident Society, a Christian charity for the poor in

Altrincham. He was on the Bucklow Board of Guardians (the workhouse for Altrincham).

He married **Elizabeth** and their sons were **Frederick, Leonard, Ernest** and **Arthur**. In 1874 he lost his eldest daughter **Maud** who died when she jumped into a scalding bath while the maid was not looking. In 1882 Elizabeth died. The mission church of St Elizabeth's in Newtown, built in 1890, was supposedly named after her.

Wainwright went on to marry **Edith** who was thirty years his junior and they had children whom they named **Hilary ('Larry')** and **S John**. In 1901 tragedy struck again when they lost Larry. All three losses are commemorated in stained glass windows in St John's.

Wainwright retired to Altrincham and in 1927 collapsed on Hale Road bridge, dying shortly afterwards.

He was responsible for the conversion of Mowbray to the Christian faith and worked with the local Nonconformists throughout his life.

The Warburtons

Alfred Warburton became the first Church Secretary of Mowbray's breakaway church when he was 35. Warburton was a stonemason and contractor and an Altrincham man. There are many Warburtons in Altrincham, no doubt because of the proximity of Altrincham to the village of Warburton. He may have been related to, or even employed by, Hercules Warburton who built some of the houses on Hale Road and who was later on Hale Urban District Council. His wife **Ellen** was three years younger and one of the Brewer family; the families became closely related through marriage.

In 1881 the Brewers and the Warburtons even lived next door to each other on Bold Street. The Warburtons' daughter **Clara** was the Brewers' housekeeper and later married **Fred Brewer**, one of the Brewer sons and three years her junior. She was born in Sheffield, so the family may have lived there at one stage. In 1888 she lived in Queen's Road; she became a member of Altrincham Baptist Church but left in 1890, to return later under Lloyd.

Warburton was involved in the Altrincham and Bowdon District Total Abstinence Society.

In 1890 the Warburtons resigned from the church after a dispute with Mowbray. William Brewer also resigned in support. The Brewers and Clara returned under Lloyd, but the remainder of the Warburtons never did.

Alfred died in 1898 and Ellen married **Thomas James Edwards** in 1902.

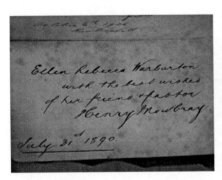

Note from Henry Mowbray to Ellen Warburton dated 31 July 1890 shortly before they fell out: 'With the best wishes of her friend and pastor Henry Mowbray.'

19 Bold Street where the Warburtons lived.

The front of the Hale Road Baptist chapel in the snow. The joiner's yard is visible. The photograph is taken before the triangle at the junction of Hale Road and Oxford Road was created. Oxford Road has had tarmac laid, although the original cobbles can still just be made out. There is an advertisement for the Pleasant Sunday Afternoon Society to the front left of the chapel. The post-box on the right is in a different location from the current one. To the right of the chapel is a large advertisement for tea from Seymour Mead's, a grocer's shop on Chester Road. The lady on Byrom Street is wearing a long dress. The date the photograph was taken is unknown but is after Lloyd became sole pastor in 1895 and is likely to be before the First World War. It might have been part of a small series taken in the locality (others are shown elsewhere in this book).

APPENDIX 2

A WALK AROUND VICTORIAN ALTRINCHAM

This interesting walk takes you around Altrincham to look at some of the places and people featured in this book. The walk is about 3.5 miles long and should take you about an hour (if you are a fast walker and reader), or it might be better to take your time and allow a more leisurely two hours or so. You can easily split the walk up into segments. You can all follow the walk in your imagination.

The first half is easier to walk as one-way streets can lead to complications if you drive, although it is feasible with a good navigator. Although designed as a walk, the second half can just about be done by car. By walking you will see much more. If you are in a group going by car and you are the driver, you can drop your passengers at the junction of Hale Road and Oxford Road and then leave your car somewhere in the area of the junction of The Narrows and Woodville Road. However, parking is difficult around there and you may need to park a little further afield. When you have parked, walk to join your passengers on Hale Road at the start of the walk and you can then drive them round the second half.

If at any stage you wish to take a break, you will find you are never too far from your starting point, or hopefully a café. If your walk is significantly after the date of publication of this book, be aware that some things will inevitably have changed.

The walk begins at the Hale Road chapel site. 1878 is the base year and we will look both forwards and backwards in time from it. It is the year when the Baptists were searching for a site for their new chapel and launched their building fund. You will find the walk makes a lot more sense if you have read the book first. A good historical imagination will also be useful. You need to try and recreate in your mind what things used to look like.

The start: junction of Oxford Road and Hale Road

Start your walk by standing on the central triangle at the junction of Oxford Road and Hale Road in Altrincham, facing the Hale Road Baptist chapel. In 1878, the triangle was not there, and Oxford Road ran on your left straight into Hale Road. There was no branch to your right. In 1878 the chapel did not exist either; where it now stands there was a field.

The street running down the left-hand side of the chapel was a rough track used for construction traffic. Wagons laden with construction materials would be making their way down the muddy road. There were problems with the sewers in the area. Mr Buck, the land agent, wrote to the local newspaper explaining that the sewer was laid in 1874, and the problems were caused on a Mr Pownall's land, not that of the owners of the street. Pownall developed land on the left side of Hale Road as you look down it towards the railway bridge.

This street down the side of the chapel is Byrom Street and was the first to be developed of what are called the 'B Streets', namely Byrom, Bold, Brown and Bath Streets. Confusingly, at one stage Bold Street was to be called Brown Street and vice versa.

The land on which the chapel now stands was originally intended to be developed as five terraced houses. Two would have fronted Hale Road and three would have been numbers 2-6 Byrom Street. The first house on Byrom Street after the chapel is number 8. If you look at the houses to the left of Byrom Street on Hale Road and follow their line across the front of the chapel, you will see where the original building line was intended to be. This also explains why the chapel fronts Hale Road at an angle, as it had to line up with the houses on Byrom Street. Byrom Street does not come onto Hale Road at ninety degrees.

The reason for this was because of the land boundaries at the time of construction. In 1898 on the right of the land on which the chapel stands was a fence marking the boundary between the two land owners. The line of the fence was tight up against the boundary of the current chapel. Byrom Street therefore had to be parallel to this and so had to enter Hale Road at an angle. If you are interested in these matters, Box A at the end of this Appendix will give you details of the old land ownerships of the area and shows why the site came to be in this awkward shape.

To the right of the fence were fields. There was no Willowtree Road. You can see to your right the date on one of the houses as 1896; none of the houses on the left side of Hale Road as you look up it to your right existed in 1878. The houses on the right-hand side, however, did exist in 1898 and date from the 1840s.

Hale Road itself to your right was much narrower than now and was tree-lined. Children played in the street.

Look at the photograph immediately before the start of this Appendix which shows the chapel as it used to be and compare it with how it looks now. Notice incidentally how the Baptists spent a lot of money on the brickwork of the facade compared to the ordinary bricks for the rest of the building.

Now cross over Hale Road from the triangle of land and look at the front of the chapel. The portico at the top of the steps was originally open. In 1879 the two memorial or foundation stones were inside the portico, but have since been moved. One was placed by Alexander McLaren, the famous Baptist preacher who has featured much in this book. The other was placed by the rich philanthropist Mr Houghton of Liverpool.

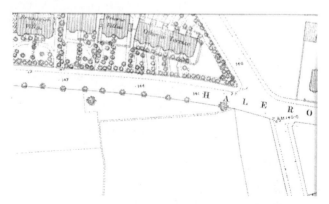

1876 map showing the site of the Hale Road chapel before the Baptists built their chapel. The junction is Hale Road, Byrom Street and Oxford Road. Note there are no houses on one side of Hale Road, only fields.

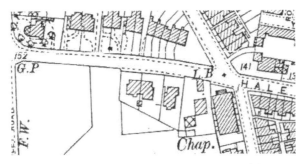

1898 map showing the chapel when built. The mystery of the map is that there is not even a small rear extension shown. Note that some more houses have now been built on Hale Road.

This memorial stone was first laid in the portico but moved when the portico was refurbished.

If you are able to view the inside of the chapel, go to Appendix 3 which will take you round the inside of the chapel and show you what it looked like in 1879 as a brand new building.

If not, begin to walk down Byrom Street on the right-hand side with the chapel on your right.

Byrom Street

The 'B Streets' were part of the primary mission area for the Victorian Baptists.

The Byroms were a well-known local family. In 1851 James Byrom started a drapery business in Altrincham with John Brownell. In 1868 the business relocated to Stamford Street. The business was the first in Altrincham to be lit by electricity. Byrom was on the Local Board. He was mayor of Altrincham in 1880 and also later. One of the domestic servants of J. W. Byrom in 1905 was Florence Cowell, a communicant member of the Baptist church.

As you walk down Byrom Street, look at the chapel. Notice the wide well down the side. This was partly to allow light into the schoolrooms and partly to try and keep damp away from the side of the building. At the end of the chapel were memorial stones for the 1908 extension. Lloyd was the Baptist pastor who features much in this book, Mrs Thompson was a friend of Mrs Lloyd (Thompson had been mayor) and William Crossley was the first Liberal MP for Altrincham.

At the end of the chapel extension is 8 Byrom Street, part of Enville Terrace. If you are interested, Box B at the end of this Appendix will give you more information about how this and adjoining houses were developed. As you walk down Byrom Street, notice the type of housing. These were streets for the working class and tradespeople. Most of the houses were rented.

At number 17 in 1886 lived Emma Longstaff. She was one of the members of the independent Congregational church in Altrincham. When that church disbanded, she joined the British School Mission Church on Oxford Road.

Brian Waterson, a long-serving deacon of the church, grew up at 26 Byrom Street. Further down at one time lived the Peers family, who you will come across later in this walk.

J W Byrom, mayor of Altrincham in 1901.

Advertisement for Byrom's shop in 1904.

Brian Waterson (back row, third from left) at Altrincham Boys' Grammar School.

Mildred Robb, later to marry Brian Waterson, visiting Brian at 26 Byrom Street. Note the bath hanging up in the yard. This would have been taken into the front room at bath-time. The houses on Byrom Street changed little for many years. Electricity only came to the street in the 1950s.

Alice Downes, one of the sixty-two who founded Altrincham Baptist Church when Mowbray walked out of the Hale Road chapel, lived at number 30. It is not known whether this Alice Downes was part of the Downes family mentioned in this book, although it is possible.

The Southwells lived at number 42. You can read about the Southwells and the Downes in the biographies' section in Appendix 1.

Stop at the alley on the left and look further down the street. The Trelfa family lived at number 72 at one time. At the far end on the right is 116 Byrom Street where the Brewer family lived before moving to Bold Street. The house was demolished to make way for the current garage. You can also read about the Brewer and Trelfa families in Appendix 1.

Imagine the scene in 1905 when the combined churches in the area, led by Lloyd, assembled at Hale Railway Station (then Peel Causeway) at 10*pm* and marched up Byrom Street with a band on their way to meet many other churches of the area in the centre of Altrincham for the enormous midnight rally described in this book.

Now go down the alley by number 47 Byrom Street and turn left onto Bold Street.

Bold Street

Now you are on Bold Street, head back towards Hale Road. Just before you do, note that number 58 was inhabited by early Altrincham Baptist Church member Liza Ethel and number 96 by Ellen Billington.

Ellen and Mary Bowland lived at number 27. One of them was in charge of tract distribution for the area on behalf of the Baptist church. Every house was periodically visited by the Baptists. You can read more about the Bowlands in Appendix 1.

Numbers 17 and 19 merit a special mention. In 1881 the Brewers lived at number 17 and the Warburtons at number 19. James Brewer was one of the founder deacons of the breakaway church and proposed the motion to found it.

Alfred Warburton was the first Church Secretary. It was probably in his house at number 17 that the early Church Meetings of Altrincham Baptist Church were held after the initial meeting to set up the church at the British School. James Brewer, then a widower, lived in number 11 by 1896.

Nurse Mary Bowland of number 27, seen here holding Charles Southwell Jnr's son.

Joan Hunter (see Appendix 1 under the Southwell family) lived at 12 Bold Street.

Arthur Snape, the part-time chapel keeper, lived with his wife at number 9 in 1904. They were communicant members of the church. Lloyd wrote in the church newsletter, 'Will friends who have odd jobs, such as limewashing, furniture removing, jobbing, etc., remember our Chapel Keeper, Mr. Snape, of 9 Bold Street, who much needs all such further help to his income that he can get.'

Early church member Euphemia Harewood lived at number 1. Now turn right onto Hale Road.

One of the 'B Streets' is Bath Street, which runs at the bottom of the others. This picture shows bomb damage in 1940. The Hale Road chapel schoolroom was used as an air-raid shelter during the Second World War.

Hale Road

Before you walk down Hale Road on the right hand side towards the bridge, you might care to note 18 Hale Road where in 1904 Mary Simmons lived for part of the time when she refused to pay her rates. You can read more about the Simmons family in the biographies' section in Appendix 1.

On the side of Hale Road along which you are walking there were no houses, but Brown Street was under construction. Between Brown Street on the right however and the railway bridge were nurseries, running parallel to the railway line down towards modern Hale.

In 1908 Fred and Clara Brewer lived at number 42.

In 1878, 27 and 35 Hale Road had not been built. This is the old 27 Hale Road as it used to look.

*35 Hale Road as it used to look before 1914. At the time of the
photograph, the shop was Minifie confectioners. To the right was
Harvey Brewer Bicycles and then Tipping Street.*[1]

Walk onto the bridge on the right-hand side. The bridge was in fact much narrower
than it is now at only 30 feet wide. In 1924 it was widened by another 25 feet to its
present width. It was here in 1927 that the retired Canon Wainwright of St John's
Church collapsed and died shortly afterwards. He was the spiritual mentor of
Mowbray. You can read Wainwright's biography in Appendix 1.

In 1878, you might have seen a train passing underneath the bridge, belching smoke
as it passed. As you stand on the bridge, it is worth considering the puzzle of the
name of Hale Road. Hale Road does not lead to Hale. In 1878, however, it did lead
to Hale, but a different Hale from the modern-day one. What is now called Hale

---

[1] The Brewer who owned the bicycle shop is not believed to be a close relative of the Brewers in this book, but may have been a distant one.

Barns was then called Hale. Modern Hale was called Peel Causeway, and hardly existed in 1878.

To further confuse matters, Hale Road was actually called Long Lane. The bridge was called 'Longlane Bridge'. The church title deeds show the Hale Road chapel as being built on Long Lane. Long Lane at the turn of the nineteenth century was regarded as unsafe in the dark. Edith Hall, a Unitarian, recalled how her mother would stay in Altrincham overnight rather than walk along Long Lane to what is now Hale Barns. By 1878, much of it was still a country lane, but it was being upgraded.

It is also worth recalling at this point what is known as the 'Long Lane Tragedy'. Street life then was perhaps not so different from today as we might think. Two gangs from Altrincham and Hale had an encounter on Hale Road on the evening of Saturday 6 September, 1868. This ended with the youths running into Peel Street. Bricks were thrown and one of the boys received a nasty head wound. After helping him, one gang (including a Thomas Jenkinson) went in search of the other gang. This group had gone further up Hale Road and had torn down fences to protect themselves, and the locals did the same. In the fight that followed, Jenkinson was injured and died from a severe fracture of the skull. His grave is in Bowdon churchyard. Six of the youths were captured at various farmhouses but the seventh escaped. They were charged with wilful murder at Chester Assizes on 5 December and all pleaded not guilty, as extensively reported in the *Chester Chronicle*. The trial hinged on whether the prisoners were acting in self-defence. In the end, they were discharged with a warning from the judge.

In the past from the bridge you would have seen, towards the centre of modern-day Hale, Siddeley's brewery, a constant reminder to the Victorian supporters of the temperance movement of what they saw as the evils of drink in the area. The brewery was near Hale Railway Station, roughly where the clock now stands. In 1878 John Siddeley was mayor, to be succeeded two years later by James Byrom. His beer was known locally as 'Siddeley's Purge'.[2]

View from the Hale Road bridge in 1910 looking towards modern-day Hale Barns.

[2] In 1900 there was a scare over beer contaminated by arsenic in Altrincham, and a number of people were taken ill.

In 1878 you would also have seen nurseries on the right of Hale Road, running from Hale Road down to Broomfield Lane and extending quite a way along Hale Road. It was in one of these nurseries that Richard Trelfa fell off a roof in 1902 and later died of his injuries in hospital.

Some of the terraced houses on the right-hand side of Hale Road existed in 1878, but only a few. On the left in 1878 there was no Ashfield Road and you would have seen nothing but fields until Peel Road by the current Methodist chapel. Peel Road was originally called Peel Street and was built in isolation from other houses. The Methodists started a Sunday school there in 1866. After Peel Street, Hale Road became a meandering country lane.

You are not going to go there on this walk, but much further down Hale Road is the war memorial and then the cemetery where many Nonconformists are buried. The chapel in the centre of the cemetery was designed by William Owen who also designed the Hale Road chapel. The cemetery chapel originally seated 350. Owen's name is on the memorial stone on the outside wall. The location of the cemetery was initially opposed by local residents, led by the vicar of Ringway, although supported by all the Nonconformist minsters and St George's, St John's and St Margaret's churches. Trelfa is buried there.

Hale Road from the war memorial looking back down to the railway bridge.
The Methodist chapel is n the right.

398

Hale Cemetery in 1920. Note the still rural feel of the area. The cemetery was originally placed well outside the built up area.

Now walk down from the bridge, continuing on the right-hand side of Hale Road.

The Mowbrays lived on the right at number 76. In 1891 their son Robert was at school and Margaret Brougham, Jessie's older sister, was living with them. To look after young Robert the Mowbrays employed Caroline Fielding, a mother's help, and visiting the household was James Fish, a life insurance inspector.

In 1905 Mary Simmons lived at number 78. Although you are not going there now, you may care to note that Charles Southwell Snr lived at 128 Hale Road in 1908.

Cross over now and look for 77-79 Hale Road. Lloyd lived at Ulundi Villa in 1898 before moving to Norman's Place.[3] The name of the house is on the wall by the road and not on a gatepost.

Now walk back towards the bridge, staying on this side of the road. Just after number 67 you may be interested to note in the wall the old boundary post between Hale and Altrincham. Sydney Brookfield lived at 67 and Henry Overbury at 59. You can read about them in Appendix 1.

Hercules Warburton built the last houses before you get to Ashfield Road. He lived in the house on the corner called Ashfield and was a member of Hale Urban District Council with William Owen.

Go back onto the bridge on the right-hand side and look towards the Baptist chapel as you go up onto the bridge. In 1879 you could see its tower and, of course, the imposing spires of St John's Church and Trinity Presbyterian Chapel in the distance.

---

[3] It is ironic that Lloyd, an opponent of the Boer War, lived in a house named after a British victory over the Zulus. We know that a Miss Adamson lived there at one stage and she may have run the house as lodgings. She is probably the same as the Miss Adamson who joined Bowdon Downs Congregational Church in 1901 when the British School Mission folded and combined with Bowdon Downs Congregational. She was the daughter of the minister of the British School Mission, who retired in 1892 and died shortly afterwards.

Hale Road bridge.
Note the tower of the Baptist chapel.

The office block on the left now called Westgate used to be a garage.

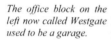

Now walk along Hale Road on its right-hand side. In 1878 on this side between the railway bridge and Oxford Road there were a couple of buildings, but otherwise this was all empty land. Look out for Tipping Street on your right at the bottom of the bridge and turn into it. Tipping Street and Yarwood Street were built in 1878 but the houses on Tipping Street started about 100 yards further away from Hale Road than they do now. William Tipping Pownall was the developer. Tipping Street and Pownall Road were the slightly nicer roads at the end of the whole poorer area called Newtown which stretched to Lloyd Street. Most of Newtown has been demolished to make way for the supermarket, car park and the flats alongside the railway line, so you will have to use your imagination here. Joan Southwell recalls how when she grew up in the Pownall Street/Tipping Street area around the time of the Second World War, her mother would tell her not to go into some of these slum areas which were called 'Calais' and were presumed too dangerous for a young girl to enter on her own.[4]

---

[4] Supposedly the name 'Calais' was a corruption of the name of a well-known Irish family living in the Newtown area. One current Altrincham Baptist Church member recalls that the part of Newtown in which he lived when young was, however, safe enough for all house doors to be left unlocked.

You will see a pub on your right and, just beyond that at the time of writing, the former Pownall Road Day Care Centre, which you may wish to walk up to. This is an important site as it was once St Elizabeth's Church and School. The church was on the first part of the site, which originally comprised 430 square yards and was then extended onto what was originally to have been an extension of Islington Street. Both church and school were missions of St John's Church to the Newtown district. In 2007 Altrincham Baptist Church took a lease of the Centre to run it for the benefit of the community and re-named it 'The Hub', providing facilities such as a Toddler Group, Child Contact Centre, drop-in and refreshments.

The initial land for St Elizabeth's was acquired in the name of the vicar and churchwardens of St John's Church from the Earl of Stamford on 30 June 1876 in return for a rentcharge of five shillings (25p).

The slum area of 'Calais' was almost literally cut off from the rest of Altrincham. You could only enter its inner areas from Lloyd Street or by going down a dark passage besides St Elizabeth's Church and School. Beyond, the traveller would enter into an almost completely separated and often forgotten about area.[5]

On Islington Street in the middle of Newtown was a temperance pub. At the far end of Newtown, just by Lloyd Street, was the Newtown Institute. You can read more about the Institute and see some photographs of one family who lived in Newtown in Box C.

Now turn round and come back the way you came, turning right onto Hale Road. When you reach the junction of Hale Road and Oxford Road, turn right onto Oxford Road.

Oxford Road

Walk down the right-hand side of Oxford Road heading towards the centre of Altrincham. In 1878, numbers 40 to 58 on your left and 47 to 69 on your right were brand new. They are all the larger houses with the decorative elements in white brick. Prior to 1876, when the development started, Oxford Road was called British School Road.

The rider is posing outside 49 Oxford Road. Note the child with her doll and the lady pushing the pram.

---

[5] Jack Peers recalls being warned not to go down the alleyway from Pownall Street into the dangerous area of Calais beyond.

401

Mary Ann Leech and her son Henry J. Leech rented number 54 and appear there in the 1881 and 1891 censuses. You can read their biography and that of Henry's brother in Appendix 1.

Turn right into the first road off Oxford Road. This is Rigby Street and was once simply the entrance road to the British School. At one stage it was named after the Armitage family. It used to be lined with trees. The road forked, with each fork running either side of the school building and stopping about a third of the way down it. The current fork is not quite the same as the original one in fact. If you look at the building on your left, stand so that you are in the road and parallel to the back of the building (watching out for traffic of course). At the time of writing there is a grid in the road. Just in front of you in 1878 was the entrance to the British School. The school building itself went back into the modern supermarket car park.

The British School was the Nonconformist school, and it is likely that many Baptist children were educated here. It was also here that the breakaway church was formed and held its first Church Meeting, only yards from the Hale Road chapel. It was here on Sundays that the Welsh church also met. Later the school became the MacKennal Institute and then the YMCA, before being demolished[6].

This book contains a chapter on the history of the British School which you may now wish to read again.

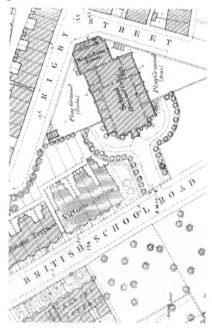

The British School off Oxford Road.

[6] Joan Southwell recalls how as a child she used to sit with friends at the back door of the British School. During the Second World War, Lonnie Donegan of skiffle-band fame was evacuated to Altrincham. Joan recalls hearing some very early concerts by Lonnie at the British School (although by then of course it was the home of the YMCA). She also recalls going to watch films there in the early 1950s. There was usually a religious film followed by a comedy or similar, such as Laurel and Hardy.

Head back towards Oxford Road. Straight ahead of you in 1878 was an orchard, probably with pear trees. Oxford Road was first called Blossom Street because of the sight of pear trees there in spring.

Turn right towards the centre of Altrincham. Thomas Forster was living at number 32 in 1901. You can read his biography in Appendix 1.

On your right you will come to the Club Theatre. The first part of it was vacant land in 1878. In 1921 the extension for the Sunday school of the adjoining Primitive Methodist chapel was built on this land and called the 'Keene Hall'. This was later demolished to make way for the more modern Club Theatre side extension. The Club Theatre has a long history in Altrincham.

The main theatre itself was once the Primitive Methodist chapel. You can just make out above the door the original inscription stone. The design of the chapel was deliberately plain and reflected a desire to get back to the basics of Methodism. It was here that the service to launch the Hale Road building fund took place, and where McLaren and MacKennal both spoke after McLaren and Houghton had laid the Hale Road chapel foundation stones on that cold morning in December 1878.

In 1878 the minister of the Primitive Methodists was Revd J. Collins. The Sunday school originally met in the basement of the chapel. Frederick Keene was one of the main driving forces behind the chapel and saved it from being repossessed by its mortgagees. Lloyd attended Keene's funeral at the Hale Road cemetery. The Primitive Methodists had a history of being involved in radical politics, and many were instrumental (together with the Baptists) in the formation of the Labour Party. In 1904 the Sunday school pupils of the two churches went on a combined outing to Disley and Lloyd spoke here to what he found to be a very receptive congregation. Also in 1904 the Primitive Methodists wrote to the local police to protest against stone-throwing by gangs of youths at their end of Oxford Road.

Just past the Primitive Methodist building you will see what was once a road leading to your right. It also continues up to your left towards Ashley Road and is called Peter Street. This junction was originally a T junction. What is now Oxford Road continuing ahead was blocked by houses. Peter Street to the right led into the poor Newtown area.

Now turn round and face back towards the Hale Road chapel. Imagine it in 1879, newly built, with its Italian campanile tower. That tower would have made the chapel stand out when viewed from this far end of Oxford Road.

Turn left onto Peter Street and up to Ashley Road, just as the Baptists in 1878 would have done after the launch service as they headed to lunch in The Downs Chapel. Turn right onto Ashley Road. Where Oxford Road now runs into Ashley Road, another road called John Street ran parallel to Peter Street into the Newtown area.

As you walk along Ashley Road, you will pass a triangular building (at the time of writing an optometrists) at the junction of Ashley Road and Oxford Road. This was once a teetotal pub (the British Workman) which you will have read about in this book.

Ashley Road looking toward Railway Street. The British Workman on the corner of Ashley Road and Oxford Road in the late 1870s was a teetotal pub set up by local Christians.

Cross over Ashley Road to its north side at the traffic lights. The triangular building on the corner of The Downs and Ashley Road was built in 1877 and was once the store of Wilson and Brookfield. We have already encountered Sydney Brookfield on our walk. Now head up the The Downs.

The Downs and Railway Street

Walk about ten yards up The Downs and stand with your back to the lamp-post, looking across The Downs. Opposite you will see two shops, and above them and slightly set back behind them you can see the outline of a building that was once a chapel. The chapel was first used by the Aitkenites, somewhat eccentric early charismatics, then the Congregationalists before they built their new church, then the Independent Congregationalists with whom some early Baptists may have worshipped, then the Presbyterians before they moved to their new building in Delamer Road and finally by the Baptists.

In 1878, the Baptists were still renting the building from Bowdon Downs Congregational Church. It was here in 1872 that the first Baptist church was formally launched and where McLaren spoke. Betts was the first pastor-evangelist, to be followed by Llewellyn. A baptistry was installed to baptise believers. Its remains are still in the cellar. A frieze has also been discovered above the current false ceiling, showing biblical texts around the perimeter.

Box D at the end of this Appendix tells you more of the very early days of the chapel.

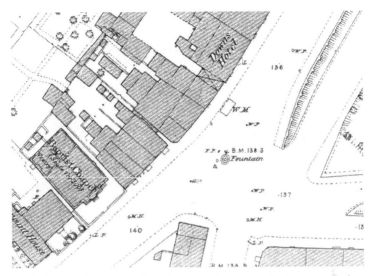

The location of The Downs chapel from an 1878 map. Note the fountain on Railway Street and The Downs hotel.

12 The Downs next to the chapel.

After the Downs chapel ceased to be used for worship, it became a chemist's shop.

The arrival of the first tram on 9 May 1907.
The chemist's shop is on the right.

Now walk the few yards back to the bottom of The Downs to where it meets the main road. Here in 1878 was a large lamp and a hut. This was the front of the queue for hansom cabs, and in 1878 you would have smelt the horse droppings rather than petrol car exhausts. In 1876 a stove was installed for the cab-drivers, plus a small clock to remind them to keep their appointments. It was around this lamp that the Baptists at The Downs Chapel would gather together for open-air mission services on Sunday evenings after their own chapel services. It was probably around here that Manchester City Mission also held some of its open-air services and the early Labour Party and indeed an anarchist held rallies.

You can find a photograph of the 'Big Lamp' in the chapter on Llewellyn.

Look down Lloyd Street, which is the street heading towards the railway bridge in the distance. In 1878 the railway bridge was much narrower. On the far side of the bridge was a large area of land called Hale Moss. Lloyd Street itself became a country lane after the bridge, eventually coming onto Hale Road.

Hale Moss was once a place where horse-racing took place, but in 1878 it was still marshy and often occupied by a gypsy encampment. The head of the gypsies in the 1870s was called 'Emperor Boss'. In 1881 the Boss family on the Moss consisted of Charles, Emperor, Uriah, Eli, Lyari, Walter, Sinai and Agnes, and children Annie, Famie and Rhoda. By 1913 Emperor (this was indeed his real name) had abandoned the open-air life as a horse dealer and was living at 24 Queens Road, Hale, in business as a furniture remover and firewood dealer. His grave is just inside the Hale Road cemetery.

The Downs hotel by The Downs Chapel as it used to look in the 1860s. A hansom cab waits outside the hotel for a passenger. The photograph below was taken in 1910.

On the edge of the Moss on the Altrincham side was St Vincent's Roman Catholic School. In 1880, part of the Moss was drained to form Stamford Park. In 1895 Sanger's Circus paraded through Altrincham to Hale Moss.

Today, only the King George V Pool near St Vincent's School remains as a reminder of the former Moss. There are springs feeding Stamford Park pond out of the remains of the Moss. The outflow on the north side is part of a system dug in 1621 to power the mills on Grosvenor Road and was soon afterwards extended to Dunham Hall. The inflows to the pond are marked by manholes in the park.

Until the 1850s, Hale Moss was home to a primitive wooden hospital for Altrincham, but this was replaced by Lloyd's Fever Hospital. In 1878, you would have seen the Fever Hospital on the right just before the railway bridge. On the right off Lloyd Street was the Newtown Institute.

Now cross over Railway Street and head towards the centre of Altrincham on the right hand side of Railway Street. On your left you would have seen the butcher's shop of John Henson Needham at number 34, with meat strung up outside. On your right you would have seen a road starting a few yards past the junction of Railway Street and Lloyd Street. The road ran parallel with Railway Street but went downhill, then swung into the entrance to Bowdon Railway Station (or more correctly Bowdon Terminus). 24 Railway Street, which was a post office in 1878, is roughly opposite where the road swung into the station forecourt.

In 1878 a cab drovers' shelter was erected somewhere in front of the station, replacing an old railway carriage. The subscriptions for this were an act of kindness by local Christians, led by Canon Wainwright.

If you want to know more about Bowdon Station and the later Altrincham Station and a little about Hale Station, please read Box E at the end of this Appendix.

You now arrive at the junction of Railway Street and Goose Green. Hale Moss was home to geese, amongst other animals, and these geese gave their name to Goose (or Goostrey) Green. At this junction was the other end of the entrance road leading down to the station. When Bowdon Station closed to become a goods and carriage shed, the approach was also closed and area became derelict land.

It was on this derelict land that Henry Mowbray built the breakaway Altrincham Tabernacle. This was the first Altrincham Baptist Church building. The location was probably about thirty yards up Railway Street heading back towards The Downs from the bank building at the junction of Railway Street and Goose Green. Here you would find a gate through the old station railings and, a few feet in, the Iron Tabernacle. The Tabernacle looked like, and had the feel of, a gospel mission hall.

It is intriguing to think that, whenever McLaren came through Altrincham on his way from the new station, he had to pass Mowbray's rebel Baptist chapel.

The Tabernacle site after the Tabernacle was demolished and replaced by shops. This is a map published in 1898.

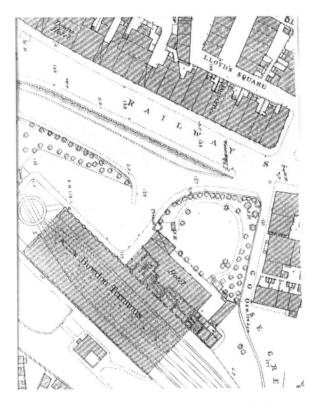

1878 map showing Bowdon Terminus Station before it closed. Note the hotel, the access roads and the turntable. When the station closed, Mowbray's Iron Tabernacle was built across part of the access road.

Later, when the new Altrincham Station was built, it was part of a grand scheme involving the construction of Stamford New Road. In 1872, there was no such road. Instead, Railway Street swung to the left, roughly through what is at the time of writing the Grafton tower block, and up onto George Street. Between the bottom of Regent Road and Goose Green opposite were three public houses in 1878, called the Woolpack, the Orange Tree and the Faulkner's Arms. The last two were thatched. The Faulkner's Arms stood across the modern Stamford New Road.

Railway Street looking back towards The Downs. The photograph is pre- 1907. The photographer's studio is on the left. William Peters was the photographer there from 1897. The studio was probably on part of the site of the old Tabernacle.

The Faulkner's Arms on Railway Street in the 1880s.

Regent Road

Now cross Railway Street and head up Regent Road opposite. Regent Road was originally called Chapel Walks, but its name was changed after a visit by the Prince Regent between 1810 and 1820.

Its original name was due to the fact that it had a well-known Methodist chapel on it. This chapel was on the left, roughly where the public toilets are at the time of writing. The chapel is probably where Wesley preached on his visit to Altrincham in 1761 and found the place so packed he could not get in. 'I believe many were wounded, and some much comforted,' he wrote.[7]

It is also this building that later housed the independent Congregational church which catered for some of the poorest people in Altrincham. One hypothesis of this book is that the Baptists would have belonged to this church, before forming their own church in 1872. It was here in 1872 that Griffiths preached his Hospital Sunday sermon mentioned in this book.

Chapel Street once ran between The Grapes public house (a restaurant at the time of writing) and the chapel. You can still see the sign showing what remains of it, but most of it has been obliterated by the car park. Many from this street fought in the Boer War[8].

Celebrations in Chapel Street, probably to celebrate the end of the First World War.

This photograph shows The Grapes public house and the chapel on the right. The early Baptists may have met in the chapel. The plaque on the wall is the Roll of Honour of those who died in the Great War.

[7] Quoted by Nickson, ibid. Wesley was referring to a wounding and comforting in the spiritual sense.
[8] Between 1914 and 1918 the street sent 161 men to the First World War from its sixty-six houses. Many did not return. King George V is believed to have called it the bravest little street in England. There is a commemorative plaque.

The early Altrincham Association Football Club held its annual meetings in The Grapes. The players would often change on Regent Road and then, kitted out, would run through Goose Green to the Moss Lane football ground.

A further picture of the Grapes pub and the chapel

On your left, look briefly down New Street but do not turn into it. Meetings of local Roman Catholics originally started in George Street and then two cottages at 71/73 New Street on the left were bought and a small Gothic-style building erected in 1858.

Opposite New Street you will see the hospital on your right. In 1878 it was much smaller than it is now. You can still work out which was the original building. This was the main Altrincham hospital, although cases that needed isolation went to Lloyd's Fever Hospital. MacKennal was on the board of governors of the main hospital.

Altrincham General Hospital.

Market Street

Turn right off Regent Road onto Market Street, with the hospital on your right. In 1878 this street was called Bowdon Road. At the time of writing, you can see the extent of the original hospital building as it existed in 1878. Before the hospital was extended, much of the rest of the current site was a volunteers' drill hall and parade ground.

On your left look out for a building which at the time of writing is called Webber House. Stand with your back to it. In 1878 you would have seen the drill yard and to your left in the distance down the hill two chapels: one Unitarian and one Methodist. There was no market.

Opposite you is a building that is now part of the hospital site. On the site of this building at some stage after 1878 the ill-fated Altrincham Permanent Benefit Building Society built its offices. Later these became the Oddfellows Hall and by 1901 this was replaced by a nurses' home. The Building Society Rooms were the location of the first services of Altrincham Baptist Church when it broke away from the Hale Road church and before it moved to the Gospel Hall on Railway Street.

Now head back along Market Street the way you came and cross Regent Road into Norman's Place directly opposite.

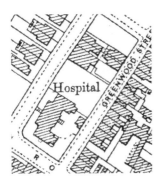

1898 map showing the hospital and a building further along Market Street to the north. This was probably the old Building Society Rooms where Mowbray held his first services as he led the breakaway church.

Norman's Place to Woodville Road

The first house on your right on the corner of Regent Road and Norman's Place did not exist in 1878, but many of the other buildings did. Norman's Place was named after local landowner George Norman. The Methodist New Connexion Church was founded in the kitchen of Walter Watson's home in Norman's Place. The New Connexion Methodists then bought a site in George Street and erected their first chapel in 1821. The minister founded a boarding school for boys in Norman's Place.

On the left corner of Regent Road and Norman's Place were the business premises of Jacob Bowland. See Appendix 1 under the Southwells for further information about him. His decorator's shop was expanded in 1910 to include the balcony and turret you can still see.

On the left was Number 5 Norman's Place, the site of which is a car park at the time of writing. In 1903 George Mitchell lived here. He was minister of the Oxford Road Primitive Methodists. He joined with Lloyd and refused to pay part of his rates in protest over the Education Acts.

Oswald Leicester was vicar of St George's Church until 1832. His father built The Poplars on the right in 1785. This was once a school. Leicester founded the first Sunday school in the area in 1783 on Ashley Road (then Thorley Moor Lane).

The Poplars has been demolished, but you can still see what is probably an original gated entrance. The arch over the original entrance consisted of whale jaw-bones, which must have been rather an unusual sight.

Opposite the Poplars is The Limes. We have already seen the Southwell family living on Byrom Street, but later Charles Frederick Southwell Jnr and his wife lived here in the Bowland family home. Their move here shows the upwards social mobility of the Baptists over time. Their wedding photograph, probably taken at The Limes, is in Appendix 1.

William Johnson, one of the original trustees of Bowdon Baptist Church, lived at 4 Norman's Place in 1891. He was then aged 68 and married to Eliza. He was a tailor and draper, and she was also a draper. Their daughter Sarah, aged 38, lived with them. Their other daughter was Selina Sutcliffe and the Johnsons had grand-daughter Annie staying with them at the time of the 1891 census. In 1881 they had lived on Bath Street.

Alfred Ingham was born in Illingworth, Yorkshire, in 1849 and became a journalist. He set himself up as a local bookseller, stationer, publisher and historian in Altrincham and lived at 6 Norman's Place on the right beyond the Poplars. He published the *Altrincham Advertiser* and in 1879 wrote *A History of Altrincham and Bowdon.*

As a contemporary spectator of the 1879 Baptist building project, Ingham wrote of the original Downs church and the new building project: 'In 1872, this old chapel was taken in hand by another religious denomination (Baptist), which was introduced by the Manchester & Salford Baptist Union. The First Pastor was the Rev.H.J.Betts, and 26 persons formed the church Spiritual. Its constitution is "Baptist, with open Communion", and the seats are free. Its present minister is the Rev. W.S. Llewellyn, who is distinguished by great earnestness and practical piety. In 1878, the number of members having increased to nearly one hundred, the foundation stones of a new chapel and school, to be erected in Hale Road from the designs of Mr. William Owen, a rising young architect, were laid. The building will be Italian in character, and will afford accommodation for nearly 500 persons.'

On your left look out for number 23, a house called Fairhaven. This was where Cowell and Alice Lloyd lived by 1901. In 1904 Lloyd wrote an article in the church newsletter inviting all those who wanted to know more about Jesus Christ to visit him personally at Fairhaven. Living so close to George Mitchell at number 5, the two no doubt discussed tactics over the Passive Resistance protests. Also at Fairhaven was domestic servant Eliza Whitelegg, aged 27, who was a Baptist church member. She was born in Sale.

At the end of Norman's Place, continue straight on into The Narrows, a very ancient path running between Altrincham and Bowdon Parish Church. At the end of The Narrows, look at the house on the corner. It is called 'Calabar Cottage', although this was not its original name. Lloyd later in life endowed a scholarship at Calabar College in Jamaica which was founded in 1912. Sadly the house name is probably a coincidence and not connected with Lloyd as it is believed to have been named in more recent times after the former slave port of Calabar in Nigeria which in turn gave its name to the Jamaican Calabar.

As you stand at the corner of The Narrows, it is difficult to think of this whole area as once being pastureland called The Downs. Later it became developed and you can perhaps sense the difference in class and culture between Bowdon and Dunham Massey on the one hand, and Altrincham on the other in the late 1800s. The residents of Bowdon and Dunham Massey quite literally looked down on the poorer areas of Altrincham. Try also to imagine the Baptists nervously knocking on the doors of the rich and famous of Bowdon and asking for money for their beleaguered chapel.

View from the top of The Downs showing Bowdon 'looking down' on Altrincham.

The Downs, circa 1884.

Postcard of The Downs, circa 1905.

415

Woodville Road to Higher Downs

Opposite you now is a large white brick building, once a hospital called St Anne's Home which was previously a very large house called The Beeches. If you have left your car near here so that you can do the second half of the walk by car, now is the time to collect the car, pick up any passengers, and drive the rest of the way.

Turn left with The Beeches on your right and head along Woodville Road down the hill to the junction with Higher Downs, which is the first turning on the right. At the corner of Woodville Road and Higher Downs you can see the entrance to The Beeches. The gateposts visible at the time of writing are not the original ones and were added in the 1930s. The original house had a grand entrance sweeping through extensive grounds. For a brief history of this building and its connection with Bowdon Downs and the Crossleys, please see Box F at the end of this Appendix.

St Anne's Home in the early 1900s. Patients are wrapped up against the cold in the partially covered areas which were open to the elements. Note in the second photograph the open upper windows, all to help in the treatment of tuberculosis sufferers.

Just before you turn into Higher Downs, note that Frank Spence and his wife Fanny lived in 72 The Downs when they moved into the area. You can read their biography in Appendix 1. Sadly the house has been demolished. Hugh Wallis, a painter and art metalworker, lived there from 1911.

416

The top of the Downs in 1915

Higher Downs and Beechfield

Now walk up the hill along Higher Downs.

The grandfather of T.A. Coward, the Cheshire naturalist, lived at number 7. His son Thomas lived at number 8 until at least 1896 and was a calico printer and office manager. The Cowards attended Bowdon Downs Congregational Church. Thomas Alfred Coward married Mary Constance Milne, a domestic economy teacher, in 1904. Her father William Milne was a cotton yarn agent and supporter (but not member) of the Baptist church and also a trustee of St Anne's Home. The Milnes lived on Albert Square and attended Bowdon Downs Congregational Church.

Dr Arthur Ransome was the driving force behind St Anne's Home. He lived at 32 The Downs before moving to 12 Higher Downs in 1862. Later he moved to Devisdale House. His grandfather John Atkinson Ransome was one of the doctors who attended Huskisson when he was fatally injured by Stephenson's 'Rocket' in 1830, and may have been the same doctor who treated the wounded after the Peterloo Massacre in Manchester, famously turning one away from the hospital at Piccadilly when he refused to renounce his views. Ransome was born in 1834 and was the half-cousin once removed of Arthur Ransome, the author of *Swallows and Amazons*.

Ransome married Lucy Fullarton in 1862 and they had three sons and four daughters. Ransome was a graduate and Honorary Fellow of Gonville and Caius College Cambridge. He died in 1922. He was one of the pioneers in the research and treatment of tuberculosis, one of the biggest killers in Victorian England.

On your right part way up Higher Downs and opposite number 12 you will see a road which looks like a private driveway to the right. Walk up this towards Bowdon Downs Congregational chapel. Numbers 1-4 Beechfield on your left were built by Joseph Smith Grafton, a member of the church who lived at Richmond Hill and then at number 4 Beechfield. Isaac Watts lived at number 1 between 1871 and 1880. The Watts family were stalwarts of Bowdon Downs Congregational.

Ahead of you, you will see the chapel itself. This was one of the richest churches in the area and possibly in the country. As you will have seen in reading this book, this has been partly a tale of two churches, the poorer Baptist church and the comparatively rich Congregational church. Theologically however, the two were close cousins.

The chapel was completed by 1848 and then extended in 1868. The Congregationalists moved here from the chapel at the foot of The Downs which you have already passed, although for a while they continued to use the old Downs chapel as a Sunday school. Griffiths and MacKennal were pastors here. Many of the people of Bowdon and Dunham Massey worshipped at this chapel, and their servants may well have been some of the Baptists.

An old photograph of the front of the Congregational chapel, date unknown.

Walk up to the chapel. The iron railings were a 1984 addition. Frank Crossley worked in the Sunday school here. It was in this chapel that he told the congregation they should sell everything and move to the inner city. He and Emily duly sold their house, Fairlie, to live (and in Frank's case to die) in Ancoats.

The war memorial porch at the front was installed by George Faulkner Armitage in 1921.

It is well worth the effort to see if you can go into this gem of a building. Inside you will see the pulpit Queen Victoria rejected. The original communion table was made of wood from the Mount of Olives and the inlaid designs in the cup and paten were from cedar wood from Lebanon.

There is a memorial inside to Thomas Thompson, who lent the Baptists the money to build their chapel. There is also a memorial to Mary, mother of George Faulkner Armitage, whose biography is in Appendix 1.

Inside the chapel you can see the original building and also the substantial rear and side extensions, built later as the church grew and prospered. The chapel could seat around 1,000.

Part of the frieze inside the chapel donated by Frank Crossley. The frieze is of Lucca della Robbia's Singing Boys.

Memorial to John Mills in Bowdon Downs Congregational Chapel. He was a founder of the Lancashire and Yorkshire Banking Company. He was the organist and choirmaster and in 1868 he played the grand new Jardine organ when the chapel extension was opened. He composed music and sang as a baritone. He was also a poet and member of the local Roundabout Literary Club. His wife Isabel was a prominent Liberal and Passive Resister with Lloyd.

Marble statue of Mary and Martha. This is a memorial to Jesse Haworth. You can read more about him and his Egyptian connection in Appendix 1.

The inside of Bowdon Downs Congregational chapel after a morning service in 2007. At the time of writing the chapel is home to The Upper Room Christian Fellowship.

If you can, it might be worth looking over the wall at the old St Anne's Home to see the wing funded by William Crossley in 1886. This is still visible at the time of writing. Then you should go back down Beechfield and turn right onto Higher Downs.

You might be interested to note that Alison Uttley, famous for her Little Grey Rabbit stories, lived at Downs House (number 13) from 1924 to 1938.

Julia Ewing, the well-known Victorian writer of children's stories, lived at 14 Higher Downs in 1878. You can see a commemorative plaque on the house. She was much admired by people like Lewis Carroll and Rudyard Kipling. She invented the word 'Brownies', which was later used by the Baden-Powells as their name for the junior Girl Guides. She attended St John's Church.

Continue up Higher Downs. On your right near the top in 1878 was Bowdon Lodge, built in 1837 and demolished in 1939 to form the main part of Altrincham Grammar School for Girls.

Cavendish Road

At the end of Higher Downs, turn right onto Cavendish Road. This is believed to have been named after Lady Henrietta Cavendish Bentinck. Cross over Cavendish Road at the pedestrian crossing. This links the two parts of Altrincham Grammar School for Girls. On your left as you continue up Cavendish Road, look out for a small entrance marked 'Fairlie'. Fairlie was where Frank Crossley lived, multi-millionaire of his time, philanthropist and friend of MacKennal, McLaren and Mowbray. Crossley chaired the reconciliation service of the two Baptist churches.

Continue up Cavendish Road and turn left onto Catherine Road. A few yards down on your left you can see the original entrance to Fairlie and the outline of the house to the left, now part of the school. It was here that Emily poured all their wines down the drain when the Crossleys signed the pledge. It was here also that McLaren came to see his good friends; the Booths, founders of the Salvation Army, also visited. One of the Booth family, Booth-Tucker, was in charge of the Indian branch of the Salvation Army and startled a maid at Fairlie when she discovered he slept on the floor in Indian clothes.

Now go back to the junction of Cavendish Road and Catherine Road.

The junction of Cavendish Road and St Margaret's Road as it used to look.

St Margaret's Road

St Margaret's Road is straight ahead of you across the junction. Walk along St Margaret's Road. Before St Margaret's Church was built, this was called Turf Lane. On the left used to be Devisdale House where Arthur Ransome lived after he moved from Higher Downs. The house is now demolished, although the gatepost still remains. It was designed by Waterhouse, a schoolfriend of Ransome's. Waterhouse designed the Free Trade Hall and also the Knott Mill Congregational Chapel on which the Hale Road Baptist chapel's design may have been partly based. You can see Ransome's upward mobility over time.

If you walk just a couple of hundred yards up St Margaret's Road, you can look at Haigh Lawn on the left, MacKennal's home for a while. From the point of view of the Victorian Baptists, this was very much how the 'other half' at Bowdon Downs Congregational lived. The original house is best viewed from the second entrance you pass. In the First World War it was a hospital run by Margaret Johnson, wife of the radical vicar (and later Communist sympathiser) of St Margaret's, Hewlett Johnson.

In 1878 you would have seen the impressive spire of St Margaret's Church from a long distance away, but it has since been demolished. The church was financed by the Earl of Stamford, with its tenor bell inscribed to Victoria 'and may her subjects loyal be....'

You can now either re-trace your steps down St Margaret's Road or, if you wish to extend your walk, why not look at St Margaret's and the war memorial near it? The war memorial was designed by George Faulkner Armitage and carved by Charles Frederick Southwell of the Baptist church. The memorial was originally placed just off the main road near its junction with St Margaret's Road and was later moved to its current location.

When you get back to the junction of St Margaret's Road and Cavendish Road, turn back down Cavendish Road the way you first came. Look down Enville Road as you pass. At one time you would have seen in the distance the enormous dome of a Wesleyan chapel, which the Crossleys helped to fund.

Just past the junction of Cavendish Road and Enville Road is Beechwood, to where Alexander MacKennal moved from Haigh Lawn by 1891. In 1901 he lived there with his wife Fanny and his children Euphemia, Alexander and William. He had three servants, Lucy Lewis, aged 22, Margaret Moors the cook who was aged 26, and Annie Moors, aged 16.

Continue straight on down Cavendish Road and then follow Delamer Road by continuing on the road which curves to the left.

The Dome Chapel on Enville Road in 1928.

Delamer Road

Delamer Road is named after George Booth, 1st Lord Delamer. For both Nonconformists and supporters of the restored monarchy, his is an important name. You can read about him in Box G at the end of this Appendix.

In 1878 you would have seen the spire of the new Trinity Presbyterian Chapel on the right from quite a distance. The top part of the spire has long since been demolished. The chapel was opened on 22 September 1872. When the Presbyterians moved out of The Downs Chapel, they were the catalyst for the Baptists to form their own church.

At the junction of Delamer Road and St John's Road, turn right onto St John's Road, noting on your way Thornfield on the corner, where John Mills and his wife Isabel lived in the 1860s before moving to Dunham.

Delamer Road as it was in 1905.

St John's Road

As you go down St John's Road, on your left in 1878 were the vicarage and church school, followed by the church itself, built as a plant of Bowdon Parish Church for the poor people of the locality. The church was consecrated in December 1866. Canon Wainwright was the famous and ecumenically-minded evangelical vicar here. Mowbray became a Christian through his ministry. The Milne family, supporters of the Baptists but members of Bowdon Downs Congregational Church, lived in Albert Square, to the right off St John's Road.

At the end of St John's Road, turn right onto Ashley Road.

Ashley Road

At the mini-roundabout, do not turn left onto Hale Road but instead take a slight detour to Culcheth Hall School by continuing on Ashley Road. Culcheth Hall had little direct connection with the Baptists, but it was very much connected with Bowdon Downs Congregational Church. For a brief early history of Culcheth Hall, see Box H at the end of this Appendix.

The view from Culcheth Hall in 1878 was over fields. The road at the side of the school did not exist.

Now go back to the junction of Hale Road and Ashley Road.

Hale Road from Ashley Road junction to its junction with Willowtree Road

The memorial area at the junction of Hale Road and Ashley Road on the right used to be bigger than it is now, but was reduced in size to allow for the creation of the mini-roundabout. The land was donated to the public in June 1933 by Albert Edward Wilson and John Hilton Wilson in memory of their father, John Beech Wilson. In 1878, however the junction of Hale Road and Ashley Road was a simple T-junction.

As you begin to walk down Hale Road, note the house on the left side at the junction with Ashley Road. This is Brunswick Cottage and in 1851 a Mrs Bernard Roarke had a boarding and day school and music academy here. She was succeeded by John Bradford, Deputy Constable of Bowdon and a local developer. A Mr Delves then lived there until 1876. He was a member of the Local Board and a guardian of the local workhouse. He was also a building contractor and constructed both the new St Mary's Church, Bowdon, and the Altrincham and Bowdon Literary Institute.

Armstrong Cowsill then lived at Brunswick Cottage until he died in 1898, leaving his estate to his widow Jane. He was a draper and it was from his work premises in Altrincham that peas were poured over the Salvation Army.

As you walk down Hale Road, note that the houses on your right were built after 1896, so did not exist in 1878. This part of Hale Road was once tree-lined, but the trees were taken down when the road was widened.

The houses on your left were built on land belonging to the Earl of Stamford and did exist in 1878. Brunswick Cottage and numbers 3 and 5 were sold by the Earl of Stamford in 1839 to Samuel Delves in return for a ground rent of £35 a year. Delves sold numbers 3 and 5 to Robert Routledge in 1868 who in turn sold to Isaac Watts in 1874 for £11. You have already come across the Watts family when they lived close to Bowdon Downs Congregational Church where they were members. It is worth looking briefly at this local Nonconformist family.

Isaac Watts Snr was born in 1812 at Market Bosworth in Leicestershire and was at one time minister of a church in Boston in Lincolnshire. He was Secretary of the Cotton Supply Association and, when the cotton supply was cut off by the American Civil War, he was instrumental in opening up India as a new source of cotton. Isaac's son was, confusingly, also called Isaac and was described in the census as a 'Maker-up and Packing Master' and was later secretary to a cotton supply agent. He became Secretary of the Reform Club in Altrincham in 1887 and was a local councillor. He was also on the committee of the Bowdon Scientific and Literary Society. He and his wife joined Bowdon Downs Congregational in 1865. He was an enlightened man for his time: he settled the house and everything in it on his wife for her life to protect her interest. Isaac Watts Jnr died in 1909 and his widow died in 1924.

A Wesleyan minister, Revd Caleb Forster, lived at No. 7 (Thorncliffe) at one time.

On the right hand side of Hale Road, in 1898 Charles Gaddum lived at Hale Carr (number 2a), John Richardson at Hale Croft (number 4), James Currie at Newcroft (now Woodleigh and number 6), Henry Thritt at Thorneycroft (number 10) and Miss Reddy at the house at the corner of Hale Road and Willowtree Road. There is no number 8, due to house re-numbering when the current number 2 was built.

Two photographs of Hale Road looking from Ashley Road. The houses on the right in the photograph above were built around 1898.

When you get to the junction of Hale Road and Willowtree Road, turn right onto Willowtree Road.

Willowtree Road

Willowtree Road did not exist in 1878; this area was a field. The Ordnance Survey map of 1889 shows three buildings on the land on the left-hand side of Willowtree Road near the Hale Road junction. We do not know what they were; they certainly were not there in 1878.

On your left you will come to the Welsh Chapel. The Welsh Methodist Church met at the British School off Oxford Road until 1903 when their new chapel was opened. They paid £12-12s-0d in 1882 for rental costs to the British School while they were located there. The chapel cost £716-10s-0d to build.

At one stage, Lloyd lived on Willowtree Road in a house called Vona. It is the first house on the left just past the bowling club.

Now return to the start of your walk at the Baptist chapel on Hale Road. The author hopes you have found the walk interesting and informative. What a place Altrincham once was, and still is. You may now wish to read some of the following information if you have not already read it during your walk.

Box A: A brief history of the ownership of the Hale Road chapel site and surrounding land

This section is a detail section for those who live locally and are interested in knowing more about the ownership of the Baptist chapel and surrounding land from old deeds and wills. (For anyone interested in pursuing this further, the author has more material than can be described here.) However, it is useful to know more about one of the more important local families, and it solves the mystery as to why the Baptists built their chapel on such a narrow strip of land. The history of this family is confusing, not least because children and their parents often had the same Christian names.[9]

The Leicester family are the family in question and were significant landowners who lived at a house called 'Hale Lowe', which was situated between what is now Hale Low Road and Moss Lane. They lived there from at least 1616 until the first decades of the nineteenth century. The family appear to have had a number of tragedies. Over several generations, through a series of childhood and early adult deaths, the main line of the family dwindled out, so that eventually in 1869 the estate, which by then included land in the area of the chapel, had to be divided up amongst more distant relations.

Peter Leicester was an attorney and by 1828 was living in a new house called Spring Bank on Ashley Road. Local builder John Berry, who was born in 1841, recalled how in his youth Peter used to go shooting in the wood where Byrom Street now runs. Peter inherited the Hale Lowe estate and in 1842 married Elizabeth Ann Ashton at Bowdon. The couple had no children and so when Leicester died in December 1857 he left his entire estate to Elizabeth.

Elizabeth died at Spring Bank shortly afterwards in 1858. As there was no direct main line of the Leicester family left, Spring Bank and the surrounding land passed to another part of the Leicester family, and the Hale Lowe estate went to her husband's cousin, Peter Leather of Stretton. The estate was quite a large area of land measuring 25,916 square yards. It had as one boundary Hale Road and stretched to land near to Ashley Road owned by the Earl of Stamford. On the east side, the estate stretched to the railway and on its west side it was bounded by land belonging to Annie Moss.

On 8 August 1868 Peter Leather sold the whole Hale Low estate for £2,500 to John Tickle, who at the time described himself as a 'gentleman'. That land of course included the site of the Baptist chapel.

Spring Bank, home of the Leicester family, in 1989 before it was demolished.

[9] Particular thanks are due to Sue Nichols for her research into the Leicester family. The author's title deed information has been obtained from the chapel title deeds and deeds of nearby houses.

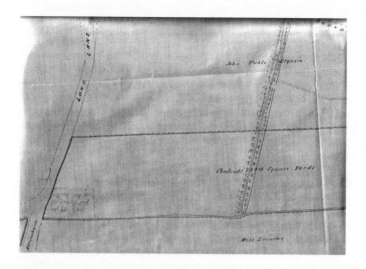

Part of Hale Low estate, which was sold in 1868. Note the stream running through part of the land and cutting across what are now Byrom, Bold and Brown Streets. This probably explains why some houses on Byrom Street have cellar pumps.

Tickle died on 29 September 1872. The lease to the Baptists was signed on 10 December 1878 by Tickle's executors, and shortly afterwards the foundation stones of the chapel were laid.

This accounts for the land ownership of the chapel site itself, but not the land immediately to its right when viewed from Hale Road, and it was a particular issue with this land that caused the Baptists a problem in the design of their chapel. We now therefore go back to Elizabeth Anne Leicester. When she died and the Leicester estate was split up, she left parts of the estate to four sisters who were distant relatives. The fields to the right of the chapel including Spring Bank itself were left by Elizabeth to the fourth sister, Annie Leicester. All of the sisters were born in Woolton in Lancashire where their father, another Robert Leicester, was the vicar. Annie was the granddaughter on her mother's side of Oswald Leicester, the celebrated vicar of St George's Church, who we have come across before.

Having inherited Spring Bank and the land to the right of the chapel, Annie married another Church of England clergyman, Revd Richard Moss, who was vicar of Blackburn in 1871. It appears she never lived at Spring Bank, but instead obtained income by renting it out.

There was, however, an interesting and unusual condition in Elizabeth's will. Annie was not allowed to sell any of the land she inherited for twenty-one years after the death of Elizabeth. Whether this was to prevent premature development or was for some other reason, we do not know. It is likely that the Baptists would have wanted to acquire the land adjoining the site of the proposed chapel to make a more sensible site. However, the condition in the will meant that, even if she had wanted to, Annie could not have sold any land to the Baptists until December 1879, which was a year too late for them. Thus the will of Elizabeth Leicester all those years earlier forced the Baptists to build their chapel on the narrow Tickle site and so to have a

428

schoolroom dug low into the ground with a narrow chapel frontage to Hale Road at an awkward angle. But for this land issue, the Baptists might have had a wider frontage to Hale Road and so a completely different design for their chapel. It might have been in the style of a Greek temple, which was also then much in vogue!

The title and proposed development arrangements have been traced for much of the land owned by Annie Moss to the present day, but as they are complex you will be spared them here. Suffice it to say that when the twenty-one years were up, the intention was to develop her land and to construct Willowtree Road. However, instead of the current Culcheth Road (which runs parallel to Hale Road), there was to have been a road running diagonally from the current junction of Culcheth Road and Willowtree Road to join Hale Road near its junction with Ashley Road at the current roundabout. That road was to have been called Leicester Road in honour of the family. When the road plan was abandoned and substituted by Culcheth Road, the original name for Culcheth Road was also going to be Leicester Road, but in the end the name was never used here. There is, however, a Leicester Road in Hale.

In 1902, Annie Moss allocated part of her land to be the current Welsh church on Willowtree Road.

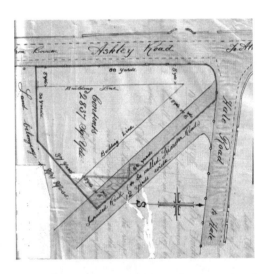

The original proposed layout of the roads at the junction of Hale Road and Ashley Road. Leicester Road was never built here.

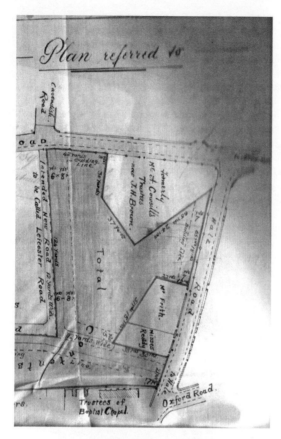

1899 deed plan showing the Baptist chapel and the revised road layout. The intention was that what is now Culcheth Road was to be called Leicester Road.

The gardens at the junction of Hale Road and Ashley Road in 1920. In the period covered by this book, this was a T-junction. Later the gardens were substantially reduced to make way for the mini-roundabout.

Spring Bank on Ashley Road as it used to look. You can still make out the old entrances today. The photograph is taken from the junction of Ashley Road and Culcheth Road. Culcheth Hall School entrance is to the right.

Looking at the title to 8 Byrom Street, one can get an idea as to how the street was developed. The overall abstract of title refers to J H Byrom and his mortgagees. On 10 August 1869 John Tickle, who we have already come across, sold a piece of land to John Wood, an Altrincham bricklayer. Even in 1869, there was a planned development of Byrom Street. Wood agreed with Tickle to build houses within one year and to pay a rentcharge of £7-10s-0d to him in perpetuity.

Wood sold the site five days later to Samuel Wright, a joiner. On 5 October 1870, Wright sold part of the land to Ann Acton, a widow, in return for his own rentcharge. It is likely he was the actual builder.

One can therefore see how Byrom Street was developed in small blocks (each having their own names such as Atherton Terrace, Beech Terrace and Eastbank) by smaller builders and tradesmen. This legacy is still visible as you walk down the street.

Box C: The Newtown Institute and the Peers family

The site of the Newtown Institute (or Free School) was donated by the Earl of Stamford on 11 May 1872 in return for a rentcharge of £1 a year. It was to be used solely for educational and missionary purposes. The site was 325 square yards and was bounded by Lloyd Street, Money Ash Lane and land belonging to a John Watson. Money Ash Lane originally crossed the land which now forms the railway as the railway came later. You can see this when you stand on the railway footbridge. The Institute was on the continuation of Money Ash Lane.

The Altrincham branch of Manchester City Mission may at one time have been based at the Institute. The Institute was principally sponsored by St John's Church, but was made available for others to use and for many years housed a mission hall on Sundays.

The Institute had a games room and coffee shop and provided free adult education for the poor of the area, mostly in the evenings. It promoted teetotal principles. Frederick Wainwright was a trustee. Individual Baptists helped out.

The Peers family lived for many years in the Newtown district near to the Institute. Thomas Peers, originally from Knutsford, was a gardener to an unspecified gentleman in the area. He was born in 1853 and married Margaret Smith. The family lived at 46 Islington Street, later moving to 71 Byrom Street. They had eight children. Ada was born in 1878 and was the seventh child. William was the eighth and was born in 1882.

William's daughter was also called Ada after her aunt and attended the mission church at the Newtown Institute as a young girl. Her son still lives in the Newtown area and at the time of writing is a member of the Baptist church.

Another branch of the family lived on the same streets. Jack Peers attended St Elizabeth's School before the Second World War, and St John's Church where he was in the choir. He recalls children from 'Calais' often had their heads shaved at the barber's shop on Tipping Street but left a crop of hair just at the front called a 'horse-tail' crop to make them look tough. Some children wore clogs. Jack used to deposit his pennies in the 'Penny bank' at the Newtown Institute and went to Sunday school at the British School. He also sang a solo in 1938 at the Trinity Presbyterian Chapel on Delamer Road in a Free church service.

His father, Thomas Peers, fought in the First World War and later became an Altrincham postman.

The Newtown Institute just before it was demolished as part of the reconstruction of the Newtown area of Altrincham. In the distance you can catch a rare glimpse of St Elizabeth's Church, now the site of the former Pownall Road Day Care Centre.

St Elizabeth School in 1963 not long before it was demolished.

Russell Street bordering Newtown taken in 1963 before demolition.

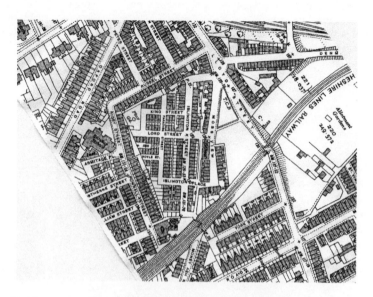

Map of the Newtown area from 1936, little changed since Victorian times. The Institute was at Moss View.

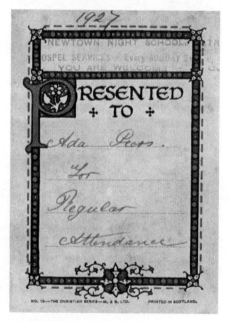

Certificate for good attendance dated 1927 given to Ada Peers at the mission based at the Newtown Institute.

Ada's uncle George, born in 1879. He lived at 12 Brown Street, where this photograph was taken. Like the Brewers nearby, he was a gardener

Ada outside the house of her aunt (also called Ada) at 13 Moss View in Newtown. The Institute was on the same road.

Ada's brother (also called George) and her cousins Bill and Eric outside 13 Moss View.

Ada aged 17 whilst working at Bannermans.

A rare photograph of children at St Elizabeth's School on Pownall Road. Ada is on the front row left. Note the child on the rocking horse.

Thomas Peers in the early 1900s made deliveries for a local baker behind the corner shop at the Hale Road end of Bold Street.

You may wonder why the original building appears to be further back from the street than the surrounding buildings. The reason is that the 1838 deeds stipulated that the chapel had to be built at least five yards back from the road. The subsequent shops have been extended forwards.

John Clarke owned at field called the 'Longcroft' at the foot of The Downs. It was there that he and John Broom, a local grocer, organised the building of a chapel for Revd William Essler, a follower of Robert Aitken.

The land at the time was described as being bounded on the northerly side by land belonging to William Burgess and on the southerly side by the highway 'leading from the lower town in Altrincham aforesaid to Bowdon Church'. On the easterly side it was described as being bounded by land belonging to William Royle and on the westerly side by other land belonging to John Clarke. The builders had to build in similar style to other property at Longcroft belonging to Thomas Raingill.

Bowdon Terminus

Inside Bowdon Terminus off Railway Street in 1878 were four tracks and two platforms. At the very end of the line was a large turntable, and inside the station were four smaller turntables which were used to move stock between the tracks. The illuminated station clock was installed in 1874, but was not very visible from the road as the station was so far below street level. When the clock was first erected but not yet operational, it caused some local amusement as it had a sign on it saying it was not yet 'opened'.

The station had an hotel and refreshment rooms. The Manchester Examiner & Times of 3 January 1852 contained an advertisement by Samuel Wright of the Stamford Arms Hotel and Bowling Green of Altrincham for his new refreshment rooms at the station.[10] Each establishment, he said, contained 'genteel sitting rooms for the accommodation of private parties, and well aired beds....Cabs and coaches will be in attendance on the arrival of every railway train, and visitors and others can, at all times, be accommodated with them, as well as with gigs and saddle horses...Soups, tea, and coffee, may be had at each bar in a few minutes.'

The new Altrincham Station

The old Altrincham Railway Station was near the modern pedestrian bridge to the north of the current station. In 1881 Bowdon Terminus was closed, together with the old Altrincham Station, and the two were amalgamated into the rail and tram station we see today.

Towards midnight on the final Sunday evening of the station in 1881, the discharge of fog signals alarmed local residents as the last train from Manchester arrived at Bowdon Terminus. Mr Walton took the opportunity to retire as stationmaster and

---

[10] The site of the Stamford Arms was where the Cresta Court Hotel now stands.

was replaced by a Mr Male who took over the new combined station. Of the new station, the Altrincham Guardian commented: 'We would certainly have preferred it had it been covered with a large semi-circular or span roof, so as to have more effectually protected passengers from the inroads of the elements, but this appears to have been rendered well nigh impossible by the construction of the platforms.'

The new station was, however, splendidly equipped, with separate waiting rooms for each of the three classes. The first class waiting room had English oaked seats with Utrecht velvet. The canopies were covered with glass and there was a total of 30,000 square feet of glass in the whole station.

There were buses to Bowdon via Langham Road and Dunham Road to ease the additional journey-time to Bowdon, although initial usage was disappointing.

Bowdon-Peel Causeway
Hale Station in 1878 was called Bowdon-Peel Causeway. The railway extension from Altrincham to Knutsford opened in 1862 and Peel Causeway, as Hale was then known, was very much a railway creation. The Cheshire Midland public house had been built by 1878, but there was little else beyond it along Ashley Road.

In 1876, in the early days of the Baptists, about 100 adults and children left from the station on a Sunday school outing to a Knutsford farm, followed by games and a splendid tea.

In 1862 there were six trains each way into Manchester from the station. The level crossing gates were opened by hand and the attendant sat in a little box at street level. At one time you could get into a railway carriage at the station and travel all the way to London without changing.

Ibotson Walker, merchant and manufacturer of fustian and fancy drill, came from Doncaster. He first lived in Norman's Place prior to building the house in 1837 that was to become The Beeches. He lived there for twenty years. In the 1841 census, he was noted as living at the house with his wife, four children and ten servants. Walker was a founder of Bowdon Downs Congregational Church in 1839. When the chapel at the foot of The Downs became inadequate for the Congregationalists, he was on the building committee and donated substantial funds to enable the site of the new chapel to be acquired in 1847 from the estate of John Clarke, the man who helped to build the original Aitkenite chapel at the foot of The Downs. At the same time, Walker took the opportunity to extend the boundary of his own land to meet that of the new chapel. The land on the other side of the chapel was bought by Joseph Grafton Smith, who built number 4 Beechfield in the early 1850s.

The house was called Beech Grove but by 1871 had been renamed The Beeches. Between 1864 and 1866, Joseph Thompson, cotton manufacturer and deacon of Bowdon Downs Congregational, rented The Beeches. He was a promoter of Owen's College in Manchester, which is now Manchester University.

By 1867, Joseph Sidebotham had moved into The Beeches, first renting it and then buying it from the estate of Ibotson Walker. He extended the house using white brick in an Italianate style. Sidebotham was born in 1824 in Hyde and married Anne Coward. Anne was the aunt of the well-known ornithologist Thomas A. Coward. Sidebotham himself was a bit of a renaissance man. He was a calico printer and colliery proprietor, a talented photographer, astronomer and botanist. The map surveyed in 1876 and published in 1878 shows that he had an amateur brick observatory in the grounds of The Beeches, which can now be found at Joseph's subsequent home, Erlesdene on Green Walk.

St Anne's Home

Higher Downs looking down towards The Downs from near the entrance to the hospital.

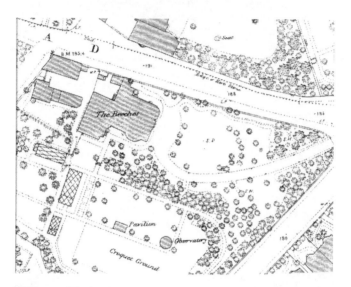

1876 map of The Beeches, then home of the wealthy Joseph Sidebotham. Note the observatory in the grounds.

Box G: Lord Delamer

It may seems strange to mention George Booth (1st Lord Delamer), but he was important to both Royalists and Nonconformists in the area. He was the second son of William Booth and his wife Vere of Dunham Massey. He played a key role in the English Civil War, being a moderate Parliamentarian.

His second marriage was to Elizabeth Grey, daughter of the Earl of Stamford.

He opposed the local Parliamentary commander, Sir William Brereton. After fighting on the side of Parliament at the siege of Chester in 1645, he resigned his commission to stand for Parliament. He was elected despite the opposition of Brereton, but was then ousted in Pride's Purge in 1648 by soldiers ironically under the command of his brother-in-law Lord Grey, son of the Earl of Stamford. The Purge cleared the way for the trial of King Charles.

Booth was subsequently elected to Cromwell's first protectorate Parliament and then to the subsequent two Parliaments, but he became a critic of the major-generals.

When Cromwell resigned, the 'Purged Parliament' was recalled. Booth demanded the re-admittance of Presbyterian MPs who had been ejected in Pride's Purge. All this eventually led the Roundhead Booth to conspire with King Charles II and he led an uprising in Cheshire and managed to take Chester itself. However, he was defeated at Winnington Bridge near Northwich. He tried to escape from the battlefield disguised as a woman but was arrested and put in the Tower of London.

In 1660 Booth was elected to the Convention Parliament which called for the return of the king. A grateful King Charles made him Lord Delamer but, true to his moderate Parliamentarian roots, Booth appealed for clemency for a number of Parliamentarians. During the Restoration he was active in support of Presbyterianism. It is interesting therefore to note that Trinity Presbyterian Church was built on Delamer Road on land donated by the Earl of Stamford.

Box H: Culcheth Hall

Edward Williamson bought the land on which the school now stands in 1858 from the Seventh Earl of Stamford. The new building was completed by 1863. His wife, Eliza May Williamson, had been running a school in another location for some twenty-two years, and this new school was built to replace it. It was called Culcheth New Hall simply because its founders came from Culcheth near Warrington. The school was very selective, and the pupils had to curtsy to the teachers.

By 1871, the total number of inhabitants at Culcheth New Hall was fifty, consisting of eleven staff including Mrs. Williamson and some servants, and thirty-nine pupils. Only five of the pupils were born in Cheshire. Mrs Williamson was a member of Bowdon Downs Congregational Church. It is not quite certain when Culcheth New Hall closed as records differ, but in 1879 MacKennal expressed sadness at the closure, no doubt because of the involvement of some of his congregation.

After the school closed, the building was bought in April 1880 by Ellis Lever who had been living at Spring Bank after the Leicesters had departed. Spring Bank was further down Ashley Road, and its entrance can still be seen by the park. Lever also bought adjoining land at Greenbank from a Mrs Gillibrand. His intention was initially to turn Culcheth Hall into an hotel, but he decided instead to use it as his offices and home and moved in with his wife and six children. He was a wealthy coal merchant and became something of a local hero when he helped bring gas to Altrincham. He was certainly a colourful character. In 1883 he offered £200 to the first person to design a portable and safe lamp for mines, and in 1887 he offered a £500 prize to anyone who could find a safe alternative to using gunpowder in mines. He was however later implicated in a bribery scandal and left the area to live in Colwyn Bay.

In 1881 we find a Miss Cowans at Culcheth Hall. She was a member of Bowdon Downs Congregational.

However, part of the Hall was to re-open as a school. Mrs Lever divided it into two houses and let the one nearest Ashley Road to the Lang sisters from Broughton near

Preston. They opened the building as a school with ten pupils in 1891, buying the freehold of the whole in 1905. The first prospectus of the Langs described the school as 'pleasantly situated in a neighbourhood of varied country walks...the school is intended for the daughters of professional men, merchants, and other gentlemen.' In 1899 the Culcheth Hall Ladies' School sports day was reported in the local newspaper, with unusual competitions and a needle-threading race.

The Langs were members of McLaren's Union Baptist Church, but transferred in 1893 to Bowdon Downs Congregational Church, renting pew number 62. They did not join the Altrincham Baptists, probably because the social class of the Baptists may not have suited their image as owners of the school. Mary Lang died in 1922.

Culcheth Hall as it used to look.

APPENDIX 3

WHAT THE NEW BAPTIST CHAPEL LOOKED LIKE IN 1879

If you are familiar with the chapel, some of the differences between the chapel when built in 1879 and at the time of writing may surprise you.[1]

The tower was visible from a considerable distance and was quite a local landmark. Now, without its tower, the building looks oddly lop-sided, but then the tower was a bold architectural statement, almost unique in its design in Altrincham.[2]

The visitor approaching the front entrance would find slightly different railings from those that now exist. The original railings were melted down in the Second World War to aid the war effort. The original entrance through the railings was at the bottom right of the stairs (when viewed from the road) rather than in the middle.

Round the outside of the church was a lower-level walkway. This was partly to keep damp from the church foundations and partly to provide ease of access for maintenance. Damp has been a perennial problem for the church. You can still see the remains of the walkway on the Byrom Street side, although it has been partly sealed up. The walkway went under the paving at the foot of the front stairs and round to the front right of the building.

At the top of the stairs were three arches and one could enter through any of them. There was no glass in them and the portico was open to the elements. The entrance was a reproduction of an Italian colonnade. The foundation stones were originally in the portico. There were small windows at the back of the portico and these let light into the rear of the chapel.

To enter the chapel itself, you turned left or right from the covered portico area. Let us turn right. This area was part of the entrance. You had to double back and enter the chapel on one side. The entrance doors to the chapel were quite narrow.[3]

If you turned left instead from the portico, you would find the stairs leading up to the balcony. The balcony had smaller railings at the front through which an adventurous child could easily slip. The Victorians were not quite as conscious of health and safety as we are now. Later on, the memorial to Alice Lloyd, Lloyd's first wife, was moved from the hall of the chapel to the front left entrance, but it was not in the chapel at all of course in 1879.

To get to the top of the tower from the balcony level, there was a trap door and ladders. The tower itself at top level was exposed to the elements. This was a reproduction of an Italian campanile tower, but without the bells.

On entering the main hall, look at the Italian-style barrel ceiling. A more conventional roof covers the barrel ceiling, so that the outside of the chapel gives no hint as to what is inside. Look up and you can still at the time of writing see the old capped-off gas pipes under the domed ceiling, but in 1879 these did not exist as

---

[1] The building may well of course change after the date of this book, so you will need to be alert to those changes when reading this Appendix.
[2] Before the tower was finally pulled down, several tons of pigeon droppings were dug out and netting was installed to cover the apertures. William Owen had not taken pigeons into account in his design.
[3] Brian Waterson, a deacon for many years, recalls coffins sometimes having to be partially upended to get through the doors.

there was no gas. This was despite the fact that one of the early trustees was a member of the local Gas Board.

The chapel also had no electricity. Candles and paraffin or oil lamps illuminated services in wintertime. This explains why so much of the chapel design focused on bringing in as much natural light as possible. There were nearly full-length windows. The windows from the entrance colonnade also let in light. The windows at the front of the main hall extended much lower than they do at the time of writing.[4]

The pews went nearly to the back of the hall. There were pews in two outer sections and there was one large central section of pews, which in turn was divided into two. The outer left-and right-hand pews were curtained off in the early days of the chapel, as the congregation was not sufficient to fill them until the days of Lloyd. An unusual feature was that the choir stalls faced inwards towards each other at the front of the chapel below the platform.

The floors were wooden and uncarpeted. The walls and the ceiling were probably bare plaster as the Baptists could not afford at first to pay a decorator. A large pulpit was in the centre of the platform. The baptistry was under the centre of the platform, ready to be uncovered for any baptismal service.[5] There was a communion table, and probably chairs behind it. There was no organ, as the church could not afford one.

We do not know how the building was heated. There are references in the church minutes from time to time to the poor state of the boiler. The original one was replaced in 1886. However, the heating was probably by means of a solid fuel pot boiler.[6]

Ventilation was a problem in the early building, and some of the first improvements made after 1879 were to deal with this. The schoolrooms downstairs were a particular problem. It is just possible that the ventilation cowls on the top of the building were not in the 1879 building. These took fumes up through the vents in the ceiling and to the outside through the cowls. There must have been quite a smell from the lamps.

There were two doors leading from the front of the main church hall, but they were nearer to the centre than they are now. They were moved further apart to make way for the organ. There was probably a staircase leading down, certainly from the left-hand door, but that staircase was not the one that exists at the time of writing.

The extension that can be seen at the back of the chapel today is not the original one. This was a smaller lean-to that can be seen on the architect's model. What was in the lean-to is a mystery, but there was an open area at its back. It may or may not have contained toilets, but it was more likely to have been a fuel store, or even to have contained the original boiler. Owen's design was for a larger extension at the back, so it is likely that a decision was taken early on to economise on cost by building a smaller extension. We know this because the *Freeman* magazine article about the chapel design reproduces Owen's drawing of the church building and shows the later extension as if fully built.

---

[4] The outline can be seen from the old organ loft.
[5] John Campbell, a former fabric steward, recalls how he had to move the pulpit for baptismal services.
[6] John Campbell and Brian Waterson recall Dr James Perkin, a former minister, arriving early at church each Sunday to light a later boiler and shovel fuel into it.

The building may also have had no toilets. When in 1904 the local Education Committee rented the schoolrooms, they installed seven toilets in the rear yard.

We do not know if there were stairs leading all the way to the downstairs schoolrooms via the small lean-to. The tower staircase down to the basement was, however, in place.

We know there were two classrooms downstairs and there is reference to a library, but we have little more information than that. If there was a kitchen, it is not where it is now. The kitchen as it existed in 2009 was originally a vestry.

Fortunately for future generations, the Victorians built durable buildings. However, the Baptists were forced to economise as much as they could. A comparison with other contemporary Baptist building projects at the time shows this was probably reasonable value for a building of this size. The only ostentation was the tower and the ornamental front, but the Baptists clearly wanted to create a striking impression. For just about everything else, they cut costs as much as they could. The rear extension was small, the ventilation was poor, the finish was to plaster only, there was no organ and there was no electricity or gas.

> Later, the church acquired a chair and communion table from Moss Side Baptist Church. The chair was called Dr McLaren's chair, as McLaren used to sit in it when at that church. The chair was kept on the platform at the Hale Road chapel in honour of the great preacher.

> The memorial stones installed at the rear extension contained time capsules behind them.

Original architect's model showing the rear elevation. This was the original extension to the chapel which was replaced in 1908. Little is known about what it contained.

THE MONA BOILER.

The much superior Mona boiler installed in 1903.

A railway delivery note from 1912 in the church archives. The early church boilers used coke, which was probably why Tinkers Coke Merchants advertised in the church magazine.

Wedding in 1965 of John Campbell's daughter, showing the chapel before the later alterations.

The front of the chapel in 1973 before the portico was enclosed. This is much as it would have been in 1879.

The front portico in 2009 showing it enclosed. In the original chapel, the entrance was through the door at the end where toilets were installed much later.

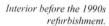

Interior before the 1990s refurbishment.

A view of the front of the main hall at the same time.

View from the balcony after the refurbishment which removed the pews.

The hall viewed from the platform in 2009. The large desk at the back housed a sophisticated sound amplification and lighting system.

The chapel in 2009 before the then planned alterations.

Ventilation was a constant problem for the church, particularly with the use of paraffin or oil lamps. This is a Ventilation louvre in the side wall.

An example of the sort of lamp that might have been used in the chapel. This example is taken from Lonan Old Church in the Isle of Man.

APPENDIX 4

LLOYD PREACHES IN JAMAICA

We are fortunate to have the text of two extraordinary sermons preached by Cowell Lloyd in Jamaica.

First, we need to remember the context. Lloyd's family, Baptist missionaries, had resisted the plantation owners. Racist attitudes, however still continued amongst the white population after the end of slavery. Even the Liberal Anthony Trollope, when he visited the West Indies in 1858, wrote that the liberated slaves were innately lazy and would 'recede from civilization' and become 'again savage'. Now Lloyd, son of two generations of Jamaican missionaries, was pastor of a predominantly black church.

Some of the phrases in his first sermon jar today in their directness, but the sermon is bold and striking and well ahead of its time. It is called 'Life's Compensations' and the text was one a modern preacher would hardly dare to use. The text was from the Song of Solomon: 'I am black, but comely, O ye daughters of Jerusalem, as the tents of Kedar, as the curtains of Solomon' (1:5).

Lloyd preached on the equality of all before God, whatever their race, class or colour. The king in the Song of Solomon, he recounted, fell in love with a village maiden. He tried to woo her, but she preferred the handsome shepherd. The king wanted her as his concubine; the shepherd wanted her as his wife.

Jesus was not white, Lloyd pointed out. This was at a time when pictures of Jesus almost always showed him as white. 'Race antagonism', he said, 'founded on colour is both tragical and farcical, unreasonable and unwarranted. Those who foment that flame are the enemies of mankind.' Not exactly softening his tone, this very English gentleman reminded his congregation that 'the white skin may cover...a despicable mind or a cowardly spirit'.

However, he went on to tell his congregation that if indeed they were disadvantaged (as many were), they would have compensation from God. Perhaps thinking of his wife who was no doubt lip-reading his sermon, he said if he were deaf, his intuitions might be unusually keen, or if he were poor he might have a cottage, but 'in love a palace'.

Perhaps remembering his Passive Resistance days, he said, 'When things are not what you would like them to be, if you can change them without violence to conscience and principle, go and change them. If you can't, accept them as from God's hands and learn, as in His wisdom you can, to convert them into fresh advantage.'

He said there were five attitudes of mind to apparent disadvantages.

The first was one of rebellion. We have to remember at this point that Lloyd's father and William Knibb helped bring an end to slavery in Jamaica, but not by violent rebellion. There was a violent rebellion, but it failed. Lloyd thought it understandable for a black man to say, 'That I am black is a great disadvantage. It shuts me off from desirable avenues of employment...I am angry with God about it.' This attitude though was counter-productive, for thinking hard thoughts of God 'is fatal to your peace of mind'.

Segregation into separate communities was not a good option either.

Submission was not ideal. That was the attitude of saying 'you are sorry you are black, but are making the best of it'. The best answer was to put their trust in the goodness of God. God's compensation was what they needed to recognise. In adversity, God would still bless.

Transformation was also required. 'It is not enough for a Christian to say: "I am contented to be black if this is God's will". We must say: "I am glad to be black...I have a Divine Lover, and He loves me all the more because I am black".'

It is no wonder Lloyd was one of the most respected Jamaicans of his time.

The second sermon was also preached in Jamaica and was called 'A wonderful Chain'. Here his Bible verses were 2 Peter 1:5-7: 'And beside this, giving all diligence, add to your faith virtue; and to virtue knowledge; and to knowledge temperance; and to temperance patience; and to patience godliness; and to godliness brotherly kindness; and to brotherly kindness charity'. The first thing that strikes one about the sermon is the use of imagery. This was a very visual sermon. Lloyd referred to seven links in a chain, the links being the key points in the text after faith. For each of these he painted a picture for his listeners. One of his reasons for doing this was because this was an 'all age sermon'. His listeners ranged from the very young to the very old.

Virtue he translated as manliness, with a picture of a soldier at attention: strong, brave, loyal and eager.

Temperance he translated as self-control. The picture was of a coach with four horses. The Christian's duty is to keep the 'horses' of 'intemperate behaviour' under control as the coach drives along the road of life.

Patience he called Christian heroism, with a picture of a Christian suffering with an incurable disease, and yet still smiling at God's goodness.

For godliness, he used the translation of piety. The picture was of the place of worship 'where we can learn how to render to God the homage which is his due'.

Brotherly love he translated as kindness, based on the idea of 'kin-nedness', a feeling one has for one's next of kin. For the Christian, these are his or her spiritual brothers and sisters. The picture was of believers gathered together at the communion table.[1]

Charity he felt had lost its meaning and was now a cold word. The picture he used was of Jesus' crucifixion. After the sermon, some of the younger people went home and drew a picture of the seven-fold chain and put Cowell Lloyd's pictures in it. It would be nice to think that, years later, they remembered the text through the imagery used.

---

[1] Perhaps Lloyd's reference to kindness reflected back to the 'Band of Kindness', the ecumenical movement for children, started in 1883 in Altrincham. The idea was to encourage children to be kind to animals and to other people. Wainwright and MacKennal both supported this. The children's theme song was 'Scatter seeds of kindness'.

APPENDIX 5

CHRONOLOGY

This table lists some significant dates in this book, linking local, national and international events. The selection of significant events is, by its very nature, subjective. You may care to note that before the chronology starts in 1836, Aitken was born in 1800, McLaren in 1826 and Spurgeon in 1834.

1836	Henry Leonard, future Hale Road Baptist Minister, is born.
1837	Frederick Wainwright, future vicar of St John's, is born. Victoria becomes Queen, aged 18. Lord Melbourne re-elected as Prime Minister and Victoria becomes his protégée.
1838	Aitkenite chapel built in Altrincham at foot of The Downs. Slavery abolished in British colonies. Poor Law workhouses extended to Ireland, having been introduced elsewhere in Britain in 1834.
1839	Aitkenite chapel closes and building sold to new Bowdon Downs Congregational church. Frank Crossley born. Great Chartist petition, signed by 1.2 million people, presented to Parliament and rejected. Chartists call for all men over 21 to be allowed the vote, secret ballots, men without property to be allowed to become MPs, equal constituency sizes (thus removing unfair representation), annual elections and the payment of MPs. Twenty Chartist demonstrators killed by soldiers in Newport, Wales. Melbourne resigns over Jamaican Constitution. Peel should be Prime Minister as leader of Conservative Party but Victoria refuses to give him public endorsement. Peel therefore refuses office. Crisis over the Dardanelles. Chinese refuse to accept British opium and Britain declares war under Foreign Secretary Palmerston.
1840	First Anglo-Indian invasion of Afghanistan. Victoria marries her first cousin Prince Albert. Nine months later Princess Victoria born. Her son is the future Kaiser Wilhelm of Germany.
1841	MacKennal born. Pusey preaches sermon 'The Holy Eucharist: a Comfort to the Penitent' and is suspended from preaching for two years due to his views which clashed with many of those in the Church of England. In election campaign Peel promises to protect the Church of England and by implication to discriminate against Nonconformists and Roman Catholics. Peel becomes Prime Minister and Gladstone is his President of the Board of Trade. Prince Albert is born. He will have to wait sixty years until he becomes King.
1842	Treaty of Nanking. Britain gains Hong Kong and China opens up six ports to British imports. Peel is persuaded by Manchester industrialists to bring in free trade, although does not do so for corn. These 'Corn Laws' restrict cheap imports and keep food prices high to protect British farming. Peel brings back income tax at 7% for those earning over £150p.a. For the first time this is not used simply as a war tax. It is never abolished. Edwin Chadwick publishes *The Sanitary Conditions of the Labouring Population of Great Britain* which is to open up a debate on the need for better sanitation. Women and children under 10 banned from working in mines. Chartists involved in many strikes but ultimately those on strike forced back to work.

1843	William Perkins, future Hale Road Baptist minister, is born. Daniel O'Connell forms the Repeal Movement to abolish the Union with Ireland.
1844	Factory Act improves some work conditions, for example stating that children between 8 and 12 can only work 6.5 hours a day. Engels publishes *Condition of the Working Class in England in 1844* based on his life and researches in Manchester.
1845	Newman becomes a Roman Catholic. Peel subsidises Maynooth and other Irish Roman Catholic institutions. Uproar, especially as this is seen as undermining Anglican church and against Conservative policy. Gladstone resigns from Peel's Government. Beginning of Irish famine. More than 1m will die and over 1.5m will emigrate. Peel tries to repeal Corn Laws to help Irish but fails.
1846	Corn Laws finally repealed, largely thanks to campaign of Richard Cobden and John Bright from Manchester. Disraeli attacks Peel and Peel is forced to resign. Russell forms replacement Government.
1847	Bowdon Downs Congregational relocates to new chapel on Higher Downs. Chapel at foot of Downs used as Sunday school. First recorded meeting of Roman Catholic church in Altrincham. Henry Mowbray born, who will be future minister of Bowdon Baptist Church. William Knibb, campaigner against slavery, dies. After election Russell forms minority Whig Government supported by Liberals and Peel Conservatives. Bentinck leads the Conservative Party. Palmerston as Foreign Secretary will lead Britain into increasing imperial disputes and adventures.
1848	William Llewellyn born. He will eventually lead the Altrincham Baptists through their new building project. Public Health Act. Local Boards of Health can be set up in areas where 10% of ratepayers so request or where high death rates, but Boards can only advise. Don Pacifo affair: Palmerston blockades Greece. Year of revolutions in Europe. Fear of Chartist attack on London. Third Chartist petition rejected by Parliament and Chartism begins to decline as a political force.
1849	Railway arrives in Altrincham. George Faulkner Armitage born.
1850	Spurgeon baptised by Revd W. W. Cantlow. Ruskin publishes *The Stones of Venice.*
1851	Construction of St Margaret's Church, Dunham Massey, begins. Manning ordained as Roman Catholic priest. Owen's College founded in Quay Street, Manchester. College is principally funded by Nonconformists and does not require religious tests for students to enter. Later becomes Victoria University and now the combined Manchester University. Crystal Palace erected in Hyde Park for Great Exhibition. Many visit, including Victoria who visits forty times. After Exhibition, Palace moved to south London. Palmerston recognises Louis Napoleon as French Head of State without consulting Cabinet and is forced to resign.
1852	William Owen, future architect of Baptist chapel, born. Whig Government collapses with Palmerston leading rebellion. Conservatives are largest party in ensuing elections. Disraeli's budget attacked by Gladstone and budget rejected. Fresh elections and Aberdeen becomes Prime Minister with Whig and Peelite coalition. Gladstone is Chancellor.

1853	Knott Mill Congregational Chapel built. Manchester and Salford City Mission founded. National Temperance Movement founded.
1854	Start of Crimean War.
1855	St Margaret's Church, Dunham Massey, opens. Samuel Francis Collier born. Aberdeen forced to resign over handling of war and Palmerston takes over.
1856	Alexander McLaren marries. End of Crimean War. Chinese seize the *Arrow*, a British-registered ship used by pirates. Consul threatens military intervention and Chinese back down. Palmerston uses incident to declare war on China. New Free Trade Hall opened.
1857	Despite being censured over *Arrow* affair, Palmerston wins election. Indian Mutiny over resentment at British rule, particularly through East India Company. Matters comes to a head over rumours that bullets used by Indian soldiers in British army use both pig and cow fat, which makes them taboo to both Muslims and Hindus. Government abolishes East India Company.
1858	Small Roman Catholic church built on New Street. Alexander McLaren becomes pastor of Union Baptist Church, Manchester. Hallé Orchestra founded. Darwin and Wallace have essays on evolution read out at Linnaean Society. Matrimonial Causes Act allows limited divorce. Assassins try to kill Napoleon III. Bomb made in Britain, although not by British subjects. To avoid upsetting French, Palmerston brings in Bill to make it an offence for people to plot against foreign governments while in UK. Bill defeated and he resigns. Derby and Conservatives form minority Government with Disraeli as Chancellor. Irish Republican Brotherhood and Fenians founded. Both dedicated to violent overthrow of British rule in Ireland.
1859	Derby and Conservatives elected as minority Government. Russell calls together coalition of diverse groups, namely Whigs, Radicals and Peelites to form the Liberal Party. This new party now forms a majority and Derby resigns. The Peelite Gladstone joins new party and becomes Chancellor. Darwin publishes *On the Origin of Species by Means of Natural Selection*. Beginning of Italian unification, supported by British.
1860	New St Mary's Church, Bowdon, opens. Roman Catholic church at New Street. Rodney Smith born. Nonconformists allowed to attend grammar schools. British army marches to Peking and burns down Emperor's summer palace. Chinese sign treaty opening up trade to Britain. Richard Cobden negotiates treaty with France to reduce import tariffs.
1861	British School opens on Oxford Road. Bowdon Downs Congregational Sunday School relocates to British School. Cotton manufacturers and workers assemble at Free Trade Hall to support north in American Civil War. Prince Albert dies of typhoid, aged 42. Victoria goes into permanent mourning and withdraws from public life. She becomes increasingly unpopular.
1862	Probable year of formation of Independent Altrincham Congregational Church. Railway opened from Altrincham to Knutsford. Opening of Peel Causeway Station leading to the eventual development of Hale. Alabama incident in American Civil War: British built Confederacy ships sink Yankee vessels. Britain refuses to apologise, showing differing British attitudes as to which side to support.

1865	Liberals win general election and Palmerston at age of 80 is Prime Minister. Dies soon after and Russell takes over.
1866	St John's Church, Altrincham, opens. F. Cowell Lloyd born. Methodists relocate from Regent Road to Bank Street. Russell and Gladstone defeated over legislation to broaden electorate. Government resigns and Derby becomes Prime Minister with Disraeli as Chancellor. Gladstone becomes leader of Liberal Party. Fenians attack Chester Castle. Attack on police van in Manchester to free the captured Fenians. Bomb at Clerkenwell Prison kills twelve.
1867	Independent Congregational Church relocates to Regent Road. Presbyterian Church starts at chapel at foot of Downs. MacKennal marries. Disraeli brings in his own legislation to widen electorate. In towns, all men whose accommodation costs over £10 a year can now vote. There are higher qualifications for the countryside. Mill's amendment to allow women to vote is defeated.
1868	Bowdon Downs Congregational extends chapel. Peter Leather sells Hale Low estate to John Tickle, thus allowing future development of the area. Church rates abolished so Nonconformists no longer have to subsidise Church of England. First women's suffrage meeting, held at Free Trade Hall. Manchester is also venue for first Trades Union Congress. Disraeli's gamble that the new electorate will elect him by way of 'thank you' for the 1867 extension of the electorate fails and Gladstone becomes Prime Minister.
1869	New Union Chapel opens in Fallowfield. Anglican Church in Ireland disestablished. It abolishes compulsory payment of tithes to the church by a population that is mostly Roman Catholic and Nonconformist and confiscates its property, paying some compensation and giving the rest to help the poor. Huge resistance from the Conservatives and Irish Anglicans who see this could eventually affect the Church of England everywhere. Victoria personally intervenes to ensure the Act is passed. Maynooth grant abolished. Suez Canal opens.
1870	Welsh church starts in Altrincham. Crossleys start production in Hulme. First Vatican Council- declaration of papal infallibility in certain circumstances. The Protestant lawyer Isaac Butt founds the Irish Home Rule Party. First Irish Land Act gives limited assistance to Irish tenant farmers. First Married Women's Property Act. Legislation between now and 1882 will give limited rights to women in marriage so that, for example, all their property does not automatically belong to their husband on marriage. First Education Act. Until now education has been principally in Anglican or Nonconformist schools or charitable Ragged Schools. The Act fills in some of the gaps by creating Board Schools and District Schools which are funded by a small fee, Government funding and from the rates. Religious education is strictly from the Bible with no denominational bias. Engels leaves Manchester for London.
1871	McLaren President of Baptist Union. Darwin publishes *Descent of Man*. Prince of Wales narrowly escapes dying of typhoid and Victoria begins to regain some public support. University posts at Oxford, Cambridge and Durham can now be held by non-Anglicans under the University Test Act. Trades Unions recognised by law but cannot carry out intimidation during a strike. This was interpreted against the strikers.

1872	Presbyterian church moves from chapel at foot of Downs to Delamer Road. Griffiths preaches on Hospital Sunday to independent Congregational church. Bowdon Baptist Church formed on 29 January. Location of initial meetings unknown. John Betts is pastor. Newtown Institute built. Education Act opposed by Nonconformists. Ballot Act introduces secret voting. Nonconformist and temperance backed Licensing Bill becomes law. Alcohol sellers must now apply for licences from magistrates who can also decide on opening hours and act as inspectors, checking that the beer has not been adulterated. C.P. Scott becomes editor of *Manchester Guardian* and stays until 1929. He espouses Liberal causes and will oppose Boer War. Britain seizes Gold Coast (now Ghana) from Dutch.
1873	Baptists rent chapel at bottom of Downs. Aitken dies on 28 February. McLaren preaches at inaugural meeting of Bowdon Baptist Church. Great Depression. The effects last until the mid-1890s. Competition from foreign goods undermines exports and forces down prices of industrial products. Between 1873 and 1879, wages fall by 5% in real terms. Unemployment rises from 1% to 11% in six years. Britain defends Fanti people of Gold Coast from Ashanti people moving in. Ashanti wars begin.
1874	Betts leaves and replaced by Llewellyn. Marriage of Henry and Jessie Mowbray. Moody and Sankey begin tour of Britain. Huge impact. Frank and Emily Crossley move to Fairlie in Bowdon. Griffiths leaves Bowdon Downs Congregational. Public Worship Regulation Act against Ritualism in the Church of England backed by Disraeli. Liberals lose national elections and Disraeli becomes Prime Minister. Fifty-seven Irish Home Rule MPs elected. Factory Act limits working hours to 10 a day with half a day's holiday allowed on Saturdays.
1875	Primitive Methodist church opens on Oxford Road. Altrincham United Mission. Alexander MacKennal becomes minister of Bowdon Downs Congregational. British Workman teetotal pub opens on Oxford Road. Spin-off Moody and Sankey events in Altrincham. Keswick Convention founded. Disraeli buys controlling interest in Suez Canal. Trades Unions allowed to picket peacefully. Bad weather makes harvests fail. Public Health Act brings in compulsory health measures. Medical officers and sanitary inspectors appointed for each area. Local councils can now build drains, sewers and reservoirs. They must ensure pure water and disinfect houses where people have contagious diseases. This legislation sparks the huge Victorian construction of proper drainage, water and sewage systems. Artisans' Dwellings Act also allows compulsory purchase of slum areas, although many councils slow to do this.
1876	Llewellyn claims he has baptised sixty in Altrincham since his arrival. Turkish crisis. Disraeli sends fleet to Dardanelles to stop Russia intervening. Turkish troops massacre Bulgarians. Gladstone publishes *The Bulgarian Horrors and the Question of the East*, criticising Disraeli for apparently siding with Turkey. Parnell and others supporting Irish Home Rule begin practice of 'filibustering', which is talking at length and using technical procedures to prevent legislation being passed.
1877	Baptists begin search for new building. Llewellyn marries Annie Barlow. Smallpox outbreak in Altrincham. Victoria refuses to attend opening of new Manchester Town Hall as she objects to the council having erected a statue of Cromwell.

1878	Baptists sign Hale Road lease. Launch of building fund. McLaren and Houghton lay foundation stones. Islington Arms teetotal pub formed. Liberal Party Reform Club founded in Altrincham. Economic depression worsens. William and Catherine Booth found the Salvation Army. Treaty of Berlin settles Turkish dispute and forms Bulgarian state. Britain invades Afghanistan again as concerned over alliances with Russia. Khyber Pass and some other parts ceded to Britain. Boers ask Britain to help in their fight against Zulus.
1879	Baptists take out mortgage with Thomas Thompson. Hale Road Baptist Chapel opens. Irish 'Land War' begins. Irish 'boycott' landlords and new tenants, causing harvests to fail. Charles Parnell of the Home Rule Party active in this. Gladstone launches Midlothian campaign against Disraeli and his imperial ambitions. Major victory for British in Zulu War.
1880	Llewellyn leaves Altrincham for Ogden. Methodist 'Dome' chapel opens. St Luke's, Bowdon Vale, opens. Gladstone wins election. Joseph Chamberlain, the radical Liberal from Birmingham, becomes President of Board of Trade. Charles Bradlaugh elected as MP for Northampton. He is an atheist and refuses to take the House of Commons' oath. Gladstone and some Nonconformists support his right to enter Parliament but he is opposed by Anglicans and Conservatives. Parnell becomes leader of Home Rule Party.
1881	Frank Spence moves out of the area and so leaves Bowdon Baptist Church. Henry Mowbray becomes pastor. Independent Congregational church moves to Market Street. Frank Crossley becomes deacon of Bowdon Downs Congregational until 1888. Bowdon Terminus and Altrincham Railway Stations close to be replaced by new combined station. More radical Irish Land Act passed. Education up to age of ten becomes compulsory. First Boer War. Boers win and gain autonomy but Britain claims right to control their international relations. Disraeli (now Lord Beaconsfield) dies. Salisbury eventually takes over.
1882	Crossley founds refuge home in Hale. Phoenix Park murders in Dublin. Britain invades Egypt to restore order and remains there for forty years.
1883	Crossley children baptised as believers. Frank Crossley pays for second refuge home in Hale.
1884	Marion McLaren dies. Richie Crossley dies. Electorate widened to about 5m people. About 60% of males now have the vote. Transvaal Gold Rush brings many to South Africa. Boers tax these people but refuse them voting rights. Chamberlain and Cecil Rhodes try to use as an excuse to go against the Boers and their German allies. General Gordon killed at Khartoum by the Mahdi's army. Government is slow to send help. West Africa Conference in Berlin. European powers carve up Africa, although Britain is overstretched and loses out in some areas.

1885	Independent Altrincham Congregational Church closes and members join British School Mission of Bowdon Downs. Armitage becomes deacon at Bowdon Downs Congregational. Cheap loans given to Irish tenants to buy land, but Land War still continues. Trial by jury suspended in Ireland. Chamberlain publishes radical reform programme for Liberal Party. General election. Parnell supports Conservatives. Liberals have largest vote, but Conservatives and Home Rule Party coalition form Government. Salisbury is Prime Minister. However, Conservatives back-track on Home Rule and Parnell ceases to support them. Salisbury resigns and Gladstone wins fresh elections.
1886	Charles Williams becomes President of Baptist Union. William Crossley finances major extension to St Anne's Home, Bowdon. Baptists and Congregationalists hold joint national meeting. Collier appointed at Central Methodist Hall, Manchester. Gladstone's first Home Rule Bill defeated. Chamberlain opposes Bill and forms Liberal Unionists. Randolph Churchill visits Belfast, supporting the continued Union. New election which Salisbury wins, supported by the Unionists. Churchill is Chancellor. Bradlaugh allowed to enter Parliament.
1887	23 March Baptist Church Meeting. Mowbray resigns. March and April first 'Downgrade' articles published. 19 April Altrincham Baptist Church formed. 29 October Spurgeon resigns from Baptist Union. Salvation Army 'peas incident' on George Street, Altrincham. Secret pact between great powers to counter Russia's increasing influence in the region of Turkey. Irish Crimes Act brings coercive measures to Ireland. Victoria's golden jubilee.
1888	Leonard appointed pastor at Hale Road Baptist. Altrincham Baptist Tabernacle opens on Railway Street. Frank Crossley chairs a meeting. Crossley holds first holiness convention at Fairlie and also holds conference at Bowdon Downs Congregational on duties of rich to the poor. Bradlaugh speaks in Altrincham and Leonard speaks at same meeting. Altrincham Baptists meanwhile engage Bradlaugh's Christian brother to lead a mission. Home Rule debate at British School. British open Suez Canal to all nations. All of Zululand annexed. Local Government Act. Magistrates no longer govern areas. County councils and county borough councils created. Directly elected. Single women can vote for them.
1889	Crossleys move to Ancoats. MacKennal approaches McLaren to form National Free Church Council. Great London Dock Strike.
1890	St Alban's Church in Broadheath opens. St Elizabeth's Church built in Newtown. Haworths present Egyptian collection to Manchester Museum. State education becomes free. Scandal over Parnell's affair with Kitty O'Shea. Parnell's career never recovers.
1891	Leonard leaves Hale Road Baptist. Perkins Hale Road pastor for three months. Nankivell assistant pastor and then co-pastor at Tabernacle. The two main Baptist denominations merge.

1892	Lloyd marries Alice Green. Hale Road Baptist Church ceases. Baptist reunification service at Hale Road presided over by Frank Crossley. Nankivell leaves. St Peter's Church, Hale, consecrated. Spurgeon dies. Free church Congress in Manchester and then Grindelwald Conference. General election. Gladstone wins with support of Home Rule Party. First three independent Labour MPs elected. Keir Hardie wears cloth cap on arrival at Commons.
1893	Lloyd appointed joint Baptist pastor with Mowbray. W. K. Hall speaks in Altrincham for Independent Labour Party in year of its foundation. New Home Rule Bill passes through Commons but defeated in Lords.
1894	Mowbray leaves Altrincham. Gladstone, aged 84, leaves politics and retires to Hawarden where he starts a public library based on his own book collection. Rosebery succeeds him.
1895	Lloyd appointed as sole pastor of Baptists. 'Pleasant Evenings' started. Liberal Government falls. Conservatives have overwhelming victory under Salisbury. Chamberlain Colonial Secretary and works to preserve empire and colonies. Harcourt becomes leader of Liberals.
1896	Union Chapel Mission led by Smith. Lloyd pays off most of Hale Road chapel debt.
1897	Hale Road Methodist Chapel opens. Frank Crossley dies. Smith appointed as national Free church evangelist. Victoria's diamond jubilee. Workers given limited compensation rights against employers for accidents at work.
1898	Betts dies. Hale Road Baptist Chapel renovated. MacKennal President of National Free Church Council conference. Altrincham and District Free Church Council formed. Lloyd appointed Secretary.
1899	Boxer Rebellion begins in China. Ebenezer Brewer flees in haycart. Second Boer War begins. Boers refuse to allow votes to those who are newcomers. President Kruger orders British troops to withdraw from the Transvaal border and then invades British Natal and Cape Colony. Huge loss of life. After armed clash, Britain and France agree Britain will control the Nile area and land west of watershed between Nile and Congo rivers will be French.
1900	McLaren President of Baptist Union for second time. Lizzie Burton killed on banks of Yellow River in Boxer Rebellion. British win Boer War and annexe Transvaal, but introduce concentration camps in face of Boer guerrilla resistance. Liberals lose national elections. Salisbury Prime Minister. Freud publishes *The Interpretation of Dreams*. Planck lays down foundations of quantum physics.
1901	Bowdon Downs Congregational plants new church on Ashley Road in Hale. British School Mission closes and merges with Bowdon Downs. Free Church simultaneous missions throughout country. New Salvation Army citadel on George Street. Victoria dies aged 82 after sixty-three years as Queen. Succeeded by Edward VII.
1902	Trelfa dies in accident in Altrincham nursery. Education Act passed despite Nonconformist opposition. Isabel Mills advocates passive resistance to Education Act in Altrincham. Treaty formally ends Boer War. Boers become British subjects but can keep language and culture. Balfour succeeds Salisbury.

1903	Altrincham Baptists finally become self-supporting. MacKennal's wife dies. Welsh Chapel opens. McLaren retires from Union Chapel. 140,000 demonstrate at Hyde Park against Education Act. Lloyd and others refuse to pay rates. First powered aircraft. Lenin founds Bolsheviks after London conference. Pankhursts form Women's Social and Political Union, the 'suffragettes'.
1904	MacKennal dies. Proposal to liberalise alcohol laws with substantial deregulation. Altrincham and District Temperance Federation formed. Demonstration in Altrincham against Bill. Welsh Revival begins. Lewis and Holt sent to prison in Knutsford for refusing to pay rates over education protests. Lloyd still refuses to pay rates. Hale Road schoolrooms used as temporary measure until Stamford Park School finished. Altrincham churches protest against Chinese labour in South Africa. Start of Russo-Japanese war. Lloyd fears major international war. Russian Revolution begins. Britain and France sign the 'Entente Cordiale' to settle some of their colonial differences.
1905	Lloyd nearly leaves Altrincham. Altrincham United Mission and midnight rally. Baptisms in the Bollin. McLaren President of Baptist World Congress. New St Vincent's Roman Catholic Church opens. Thompson and Games elected for Labour in Altrincham, but Thompson victory annulled. Suffragettes expelled from Liberal Party meeting at Free Trade Hall. Japanese sink Russian fleet. Einstein publishes *Special Theory of Relativity*. Balfour resigns after defeats in Commons and in by-elections. Campbell-Bannerman forms temporary Liberal Government. Manchester City Football Club forced to sell off squad after making illegal payments. Many of squad bought by rivals Manchester United.
1906	William Crossley becomes MP as part of significant Liberal national election victory. Stamford Park School opens. Twenty-six Labour Representation Committee members become MPs and found new Labour Party.

You may also be interested to note the following dates of death:

- McLaren in 1910,
- William Crossley in 1911,
- Collier in 1921,
- Mowbray in 1927,
- Smith in 1947,
- Lloyd in 1966.

ACKNOWLEDGEMENTS

Various people have helped me in the writing of this book. I am indebted to them all, but the work is my sole responsibility and all errors and omissions are mine alone. If you are not mentioned and should have been, that is my mistake. You know who you are and my thanks go to you.

I have used the resources of a number of libraries and archives. I am particularly grateful for the use of the library and archive material and for the assistance I received from the staff at the following:

John Hodgson, Keeper of Manuscripts and Archives, and the staff of The John Rylands University Library of Manchester; the staff of Manchester Archives and Local Studies, Central Library, Manchester; Susan Mills, former Librarian of Regent's Park College, Oxford, who went above and beyond the call of duty, and in particular for her help with access to the Angus Library; Patsy Williams, Librarian of St Deiniol's Library, Hawarden; the staff of the Records Office and County Archives, Chester; the Local Studies Librarians at Trafford Borough Council who have been most helpful; Judy Powles, Librarian of Spurgeon's College, London; the Librarian of Luther King House, Brighton Grove, Manchester; the Local Studies Librarians, Warrington.

I am especially grateful for permission to reproduce a number of photographs in this book from the Trafford Borough Council collection.

Special mention must go to Sue Nichols for very useful information and research about St Anne's Home, comments on manuscripts and permission to use photographs.

I must mention Jean Morgan for her helpful and professional editing. David Morgan, her husband and former Church Secretary of Altrincham Baptist Church, unwittingly spurred me into writing this book by letting me see the Minute Books from the church's early years, and so my very special thanks to both of them.

John Churchman and his colleagues Verna Platt and Samantha Reid have been very helpful in the preparation and formatting of the book for publication.

Dr Paul Beasley-Murray, former Senior Pastor of Altrincham Baptist Church, contributed recollections to and commented on this book.

Dr Roger Hayden of the Baptist Historical Society added helpful comments.

Ali Hutchison has been helpful in giving advice on publicity.

Special mention also goes to the following:

David Brewer and Sarah Brewer for photographs and information about their family;

Barbara Crowther (formerly Barbara Downes and grand-daughter of Charles Frederick Southwell Jnr) for information and photographs about the Southwell and Downes families; Shirley Godden (great-granddaughter of Frank Spence) and Paul Spence (great-grandson of Frank Spence) for information about the Spence and Duerr families and photographs; David Miller of Altrincham History Society for checking and advising on manuscripts; Basil D. Morrison for permission to use photographs of the Newtown Institute, St. Elizabeth's School, Russell Street and the Chapel on George Street; Joan Southwell (whose late husband Desmond was the grandson of Charles Frederick Southwell Jnr) for information about and photographs of the Southwell and Downes families, and also for her own reminiscences of growing up in Altrincham; Brian Waterson for his great knowledge about Altrincham Baptist Church, the use of photographs and his review of manuscripts.

The following people and organisations (in alphabetical order) have also helped me and I am very grateful to them:

Richard Abbott for his help in researching some Baptist church members through census records; Mary Armstrong for advice about the first chapters; Revd Christopher Bamforth-Damp and Revd Michael Heaney of the Congregational Federation; Emma Birchall for managing to read part of an early draft and telling me she quite enjoyed it, and then doing paid research for me at Trafford Local Studies; Jonathan Birchall, who said he would rather put his head in an oven than read this book, but who has actually been a source of inspiration, unbeknown to him; Judy Birchall for forthright comments on various manuscripts and for helping with the editing; Laura Birchall, for being herself; Bowdon Baptist Church, Georgia, USA; Alex Brodie for permission to use photographs; Catherine Brooke for her unpublished thesis on the history of Sale Baptist Church; Jim and Monica Brooke for photographs; Roger Brooke for information about the more recent mission history of Altrincham Baptist Church; John and Carol Brown for information about Brunswick Cottage; Mervyn Busteed for locating Ulundi Villa for me and providing background information and information about the Irish question; John Campbell, former fabric steward, for his insights into the chapel and for the use of photographs; Edna Cheetham for the loan of a book and for information about her family and the Crossleys; Francis Coackley for information about Robert Aitken; Bethsan Cocker for information about Culcheth Hall School; David and Anne Cook for the loan of title deeds; Murray Creed for the loan of books; Trevor Foster (son of Ada Peers) for information about the Newtown area of Altrincham and permission to reproduce photographs; Andrew Funnell and the North Western Baptist Association for the loan of documents; Claire Garvey for loan of a booklet and for assistance with some of the chapters from a contemporary Roman Catholic point of view; Jennifer George for assistance with research into Manchester City Mission; Colin Graham for information about the Southwell family; Rosemary Goulbourne for useful original research; Denise Laver and Hale Civic Society for helpful information and permission to reproduce photographs; Sally Hall of the Ministry Department at the Baptist Union; Andrew Hardcastle, minister of Altrincham Baptist Church, for providing references; Andrew Hawksworth for his insights about the fabric of the chapel; David Hill for information about the Independent Methodists; Stephen Ibbotson, minister of Altrincham Baptist Church, for his critique of some of the chapters on Victorian theology; Barbara James for collation of material and help with typing in editorial corrections; William Jones of the Eglwys Bresbyteraidd Cymru, Altrincham; David King of City Light Trust and his father Bob King for the loan of original texts, encouragement and thoughts on the Victorian revival history of Manchester and Salford; Mark Kenny and Helen King for the loan of title deeds and information about Isaac Watts; Glen Marshall of Northern Baptist College and formerly an assistant minister of Altrincham Baptist Church for academic references; Iain and Judy May for the loan of the *Gospel Herald*; David Mowbray for assistance in putting together the Mowbray family tree; Ogden Baptist Church for information about William Llewellyn; Bert Overton, Life Deacon of Denmark Place Baptist Church, London; Miles Rowland for information about railways and the loan of a document; Wendy Seddon for information about Brown Street ground rents; Norman Spilsbury for information about Bowdon Railway Station and other matters; Roger Sutton for his input into the chapter on the Welsh Revival and other chapters; Union Baptist Church, Fallowfield; the Upper Room Christian Fellowship for permission to photograph the old Bowdon Downs Congregational Chapel; Revd Andrew Wade for information about Revd Aitken and Revd Haslam; Nigel Wright, Principal of Spurgeon's College and former Senior Pastor of Altrincham Baptist Church, for help in the early stages of the book.

I have made every effort to trace and contact copyright holders of illustrations and photographs reproduced in this book. If I have inadvertently failed to obtain any permission for anything in this book, I apologise and hope that the relevant persons will excuse me. Any subsequent editions will contain an appropriate correction. I can be contacted via the publishers.

I have tried (unsuccessfully) to contact the estate of Frank Crossley for permission to use one photograph of Fairlie in 1877. I hope they will forgive me for using it on the basis of the friendship between Henry Mowbray and Frank Crossley and in the light of the paragraph below.

Finally, I am not intending to make any profit from this edition of this book. Any net profits will be donated to Altrincham Baptist Church or to another charity. It is on that basis that a number of the photographs in this book have been reproduced at favourable rates and I am grateful to those who have given me permission to do so, especially Trafford Local Studies.

TECHNICAL NOTES

I should perhaps explain some of the terminology I have used in the book.

Altrincham itself consists of more than one township. Unless it is otherwise apparent from the context, for ease I generally refer to all the townships that make up the wider area of Altrincham when I refer to 'Altrincham'.

The Baptists in Altrincham have changed their names several times.[1] When I use the term the 'Altrincham Baptists', I mean all those Baptists in Altrincham at the relevant time, whatever name they may have then been using. I have also, for convenience, sometimes shortened Bowdon Downs Congregational Church to 'Bowdon Downs' or similar.

Sometimes I have put forward a hypothesis. I have tried to make this clear by use of words such as 'probably' and 'it is likely'. Usually the hypothesis is likely from what circumstantial evidence I have found. For example, I cannot prove that the Downgrade Controversy involving Spurgeon influenced events in Altrincham, but I believe it is likely.

Prices are difficult to equate to modern values, and any book that does so will soon go out of date. Perhaps one standard to follow is that a Baptist pastor of a decent-sized church, who would equate in pay to the middle classes, might hope to have achieved an annual income of £150 by 1900. Where I have translated 'old money' into its modern equivalent in a footnote, I have not attempted to give a modern decimal equivalent in terms of purchasing power.

Newspapers of the time often quoted speakers in the passive voice, rather than using direct quotations. I have taken the liberty of changing their quotations into what it is obvious the speaker actually said. The local newspaper quoted is the *Altrincham and Bowdon Guardian* unless otherwise stated.

In Appendix 2, I have included a walk around Altrincham which could have been taken with the Baptists in 1878 when they were no doubt walking around the area and looking for their new site. Fortunately, the Ordnance Survey map was published in 1878, but the survey was carried out in 1876. As parts of Altrincham were very much under construction at the time, I have sometimes not been able to know for certain whether a particular piece of construction had been completed by 1878, so I may be out by a year or so.

To avoid clutter in Appendix 2, I have not referred to sources. These can be found in the footnotes in the main part of the book and in the bibliography.

Road names have changed over the years. Generally, I have referred to them by their modern name such as Hale Road, but in Appendix 2 I have attempted to show the earlier name such as (in the case of Hale Road) Long Lane.

House numbers and names also present a problem. I have tried where possible to equate to modern numbering, but sometimes this is difficult as roads and streets were often re-numbered. A similar consideration applies to people. Their names

---

[1] Names the church has used include Bowdon Baptist Church, the Tabernacle Bowdon, the Altrincham Tabernacle, the Hale Road Baptist Tabernacle Altrincham, Hale Road Baptist Church and Altrincham Baptist Church.

sometimes change in records, and sometimes church records use different spellings from those used in local newspapers. For example, is it Pierrepoint, Pierrepont or Pierrpont? Is it Hawkesworth or Hawksworth, Simmonds, Simmons or Symmonds? I have attempted to state what I think is correct in each case, usually based on census records, but spellings of names did change.

Astute readers may wonder why this book finishes in 1905 and not in 1901 (the death of Victoria) or 1906 (the Liberal Party victory). The answer is that 1905 forms a convenient pause in the history of the Baptist church. Church histories do not always sit happily with national ones. A future book may continue the history through the two world wars.

MISSING DOCUMENTS AND BOOKS

It is a great tragedy that many original manuscripts and photographs are missing. In the hope that someone somewhere may have them, here are some which I have been unable to locate or obtain.

The handwritten notes of Charles Frederick Southwell about the church's history are quoted in Comber's biography of Cowell Lloyd. 'Mr Southwell's beautifully handwritten notes are before the author now,' he writes. He recorded that he 'left Altrincham with a feeling of great respect for the church and a profound admiration for the almost pioneer work that Mr Cowell Lloyd had undertaken there'. Sadly, attempts to track down Comber's descendants have failed.

I have not found any personal papers belonging to Henry Mowbray. Sadly, his descendants have not provided me with any material.

When the Altrincham Baptists left the Iron Tabernacle to move back to Hale Road, they were encouraged by Mowbray to take photographs of the Tabernacle. In someone's loft somewhere, I hope there is a dusty photograph of an Altrincham Gospel Hall.

I find it extraordinary that there is not one surviving photograph of Bowdon Railway Station as a working station. Such photographs might also give more clues about the Iron Tabernacle.

I believe there are photographs of the inside of The Downs Chapel showing the baptistry and Bible verses. Although I believe I know where they are, I have not been able to obtain them from the owner in time for publication. I hope a future edition of the book may contain them.

I have been unable to locate *Souvenir of the Ministry of the Rev F Cowell Lloyd*, a book published in Jamaica, and some of Lloyd's books, although I have located most.

The Free Church Council Minute Books for its early period in Altrincham appear to be missing, as are some of the archives of the Altrincham Liberal Party.

The church has lost its copy of *How I paid the debt* by Cowell Lloyd, which Cynthia Walker used to write her book, but fortunately I have been able to obtain some of the information by other means. There appears to be no copy in any library and the North Western Baptist Association has no copy. This booklet was probably lost by the church when it was being refurbished and most of its records were thrown out at the same time. Fortunately Mildred Waterson climbed into the skip to retrieve the majority of the records, just in time. Without her doing that, this book would have been very different and Altrincham would have lost a part of its history. However, not even a copyright library appears to have *How I paid the debt*.

Finally, the church has lost the original handwritten notes of William J. Brewer which Cynthia Walker also had before her when she wrote her brief history of the church covering the period 1872-1972. It is fortunate that she quoted from them, and I have also been able to use other sources to fill in the gaps and (sometimes) respectfully to correct Mr Brewer's recollections.

BIBLIOGRAPHY

Records in the Cheshire Record Office are reproduced with the permission of Cheshire County Council and the owner/depositor to whom copyright is reserved.

Records of The John Rylands Library are reproduced by courtesy of the Director and University Librarian, The John Rylands University Library, The University of Manchester.

Where applicable, other records are reproduced with the permission of the relevant archive or library.

Scripture quotations are generally from the Authorised (King James) Version of the Bible as that is the version the Victorian Baptists probably used. Any other Scripture is taken from the Holy Bible, New International Version ®. Copyright © 1973, 1984 International Bible Society. Used by permission of Zondervan. All rights reserved.

The 'NIV' and 'New International Version' are registered in the United States Patent and Trademark Office by International Bible Society. Use of either trademark requires the permission of the International Bible Society.

Most items not noted with a relevant source are in the author's own collection.

The following abbreviations are used:

ABC:	Altrincham Baptist Church
CRL:	Central Reference Library, Manchester
CRO:	Cheshire Record Office
JRL:	John Rylands Library, University of Manchester
MLS:	Manchester Archives and Local Studies
RPC:	Regent's Park College, Oxford, and the Angus Library
SDL:	St Deiniol's Library, Hawarden
TLS:	Trafford Local Studies
WLS:	Warrington Local Studies.

Records and Archives

Altrincham and Bowdon Guardian 1874-1903 (TLS).
Altrincham Bowdon and Hale Guardian 1904-05 (TLS).
Altrincham Division Chronicle and *Cheshire County News* 1887-90 (TLS).
Altrincham and District Free Church Council: Participation of Visitation for the
1901 Mission-Suggested Scheme C18/2/4/2/3 (MLS).
Altrincham Baptist Church:
- Church Meeting Minute Books
- Deacons' Meetings' Minutes 1903-05
- Various photographs.
Altrincham Baptist Church Sunday School books (courtesy of the Southwell
family).
Altrincham Division Liberal Association: Hale Polling Station Minute Books
1903-05 DDX 387/1 (CRO).

Bank Street Wesleyan Chapel Altrincham District Synod 1898 (MLS).
Baptist Building Fund papers (RPC).
Baptist Union Handbooks (various years) (RPC).
Bowdon Downs Congregational Church (MLS unless otherwise stated):
- Baptisms Book
- Handwritten early history (authorship unknown)
- Minute Books 1840-1905
- New Chapel proceedings 1846 onwards
- Register of Marriages 1916 onwards
- Register of Members attending at the Communion of the Lord's Supper
1893 onwards
- Title deeds (CRO)
- Year Books (TLS).
British Architect and Northern Engineer 1878 (CRL).
British School Altrincham Title Deeds (CRO).

Chester Chronicle 5 December 1868 (courtesy of Angela Jenkinson and David
Miller).
Congregational Year Books (TLS and SDL).

Freeman (various years) (RPC).

HM Land Registry various deeds.

Lancashire and Cheshire Association of Baptist Churches Minute Books (JRL).

Manchester City Mission Archives (MLS unless otherwise stated):
- Altrincham yearly reviews (bound up in another book) (TLS)
- Handwritten notes on Mathew Swuz, Isabella Burns and William Easdon
- Minute Books
- Miscellaneous records
- Yearly reviews.
Manchester Evening News 31.1.2006

Primitive Methodist Church, Oxford Road, Altrincham: Minutes of Trustees' and
Leaders' Meetings 1896-1905 C18/16 (MLS).
Primitive Methodist Church *Leader* Magazine 23 March 1916 C18/16 (MLS).

Regent's Park College reports 1882 –99 (RPC).

The Spurgeon Jubilee Album (SDL).

Union Baptist Church, Manchester, Minute Books (MLS).

Books, pamphlets and other publications

Altrincham and Bowdon Guardian: review of book by Alexander MacKennal, 2nd edition.
Christ's Healing Touch, 4 March 1885 (TLS).
American Review and Expositer, 1911 (SDL).
Angus, Joseph: *Regeneration: The Sonship that saves men*, 1897 (copy annotated by Gladstone) (SDL).
Anon: *The story of St George's Church and Parish 1799-1899* (TLS).
Armitage, Thomas: *A History of the Baptists; Traced by their vital principles and practices from the time of our Lord and Saviour Jesus Christ to the year 1886*, Bryan Taylor & Co, 1888 (SDL).
Armstrong, John (ed): *Understanding Four Views on Baptism (Counterpoints: Church Life)*, Zondervan, 2007.

Bamford, Frank: *Mansions and Men of Dunham Massey: From Errant Earl to Red Dean*, 1991.
Bamford, Frank: *The Making of Altrincham 1850-1991– From Market to Megastore*, Northern Writers, 1991 (TLS).
Bayliss, Don (ed): *Altrincham: A History*, Willow Publishing, 1992.
Bayliss, Don: *A Town in Crisis – Altrincham in the Mid-Nineteenth Century*, 2006.
Bayliss, Hilda: *Altrincham: A Pictorial History*, Phillimore, 1996.
Beasley-Murray, George: *Baptists today and tomorrow*, Macmillan, 1966 (SDL).
Beasley-Murray, Paul: *Radical Believers: the Baptist Way of Being the Church*, Baptist Union, 1992 (SDL).
Bebbington, David: *Evangelicalism in Modern Britain*, Unwin Hayman, 1989.
Betjeman, John: *Archie and the Strict Baptists*, John Murray, 1977.
Breton Brian: *Story of St. Georges, Altrincham: A Bicentennial History of St George's Parish Church, Altrincham, 1799-1999*, 1999 (TLS).
Briggs, John: The English Baptist of the Nineteenth Century, Baptist Historical Society, 1994.
Broomhall, Marshall (ed): Last Letters and Further Records of Martyred Missionaries of the China Inland Mission With Portraits and Illustrations, 1901.
Busteed, Mervyn: Patterns of Irishness in Nineteenth Century Manchester, 2002.
Busteed, Mervyn: *The Manchester Martyrs* in *History Ireland*, November/December 2008.

Campbell, Christy: *Fenian Fire: the British Government Plot to Assassinate Queen Victoria*, Harper Collins, 2002.
China Inland Mission: *Journal of the late Miss Elizabeth Burton of the China Inland Mission*, 1900 (courtesy of the Brewer family).
Clifford, John: *The English Baptists: Who They Are And What They Have Become*, E. Marlborough & Co, 1881 (SDL).
Comber, Leslie Thomas: *Colour Blind: The Life of the Rev F Cowell-Lloyd, ATS, of Jamaica*, The Carey Kinsgate Press Limited, 1959.
Cooke, J. Hunt: *A Concise Manual of Baptism Baptist*, Tract and Book Society 1896 (SDL).
Corfield, Jack: *A Brief History of the Ogden Baptist Church*, 1983.
Cox, Francis Augustus: *History of the Baptist Missionary Society from 1792-1842*,

1842 (SDL).

Crosby, Thomas: *The History of the English Baptists, vol 1, Containing Their History to the Restoration of King Charles II*, 1738.

Crossley, E.K: *He heard from God – The Story of Frank Crossley*, Salvation Army, 1959.

Culcheth Hall Old Girls' Union Committee: *Culcheth Hall 1891-1991*, 1991.

Culross, James: *Founders and Pioneers of Modern Missions*, 1899 (SDL).

Darling, J. Millar: *Home Rule for Ireland: Speech at Altrincham*, 1888 (SDL).

Dayton, Donald W: *Theological Roots of Pentecostalism*, Scarecrow Press, 1987.

Denmark Place Baptist Church: *The Church under the Hill: the Centenary of Denmark Place Baptist Church*, 1923.

Disraeli, Benjamin: *Lothair*, Longmans, Green & Co., 1870.

Dolan, John: *The Independent Methodists – A History*, James Clarke and Co., 2005.

Edwards, B.B: *The Missionary Gazeteer; Comprising a Geographical and Statistical Account of the Various Stations of the American Foreign and Protestant Missionary Societies of all Denominations, with their progress in Evangelization and Civilization 1832*. (Note: this borrows extensively from Charles Williams' 1828 British Version.)

Eyre, Michael, Heps, Chris and Townsin, Alan: *Crossley Motors*, OPC Railprint, 2002.

Fitzpatrick, Gillian: *Altrincham Past and Present*, Willow Publishing, 1990.

Flanders, Judith: *The Victorian House, Domestic Life from Childbirth to Deathbed*, W.W. Norton and Company Ltd., 2003.

Flint, Richard: *A Brief History of the Openshaw Lads' Club*, 1948 (courtesy of Edna Cheetham).

Gardner, James: *The Faiths of the World, a Dictionary of all Religions and Religious Sects, Their Doctrines, Rites, Ceremonies and Customs*, Fullarton, 1880.

Glinert, (ed): *The Manchester Compendium – A Street-by-Street History of England's Greatest Industrial City*, Penguin Books Ltd., 2008.

Goadby, J Jackson: *Bye-paths in Baptist History, A collection of interesting, instructive, and curious information, not generally known, concerning the Baptist denomination*, 1871 (SDL).

Gospel Herald (various years).

Graham, Colin: 'George Faulkner Armitage (1849-1937)' in *Altrincham History Society Journal*, No. 27 September 2007.

Green, Michael: *Baptism Its Purpose Practice and Power*, Hodder and Stoughton, 1985.

Greenall, R.L.: *The Making of Victorian Salford*, Carnegie Publishing, 2000 (courtesy of David King).

Griffith, Henry: *Notes of a Sermon at the Bowdon Independent Church, on Hospital, Sunday, February 11 1872*, 1872 (WLS).

Groves, Jill: *The Fight Over Ringway Chapel 1640-1721: Religion and politics in a Cheshire township* – in Open History Special Conference Edition Religion 2007.

Guardian Year Book (various years) (TLS).

Hall, Catherine: *Civilising Subjects: Metropole and Colony in the English Imagination 1830-1867*, Polity Press, 2002.

Hall, Alan F: *Ritualistic Slum Priests, religious orders, the Oxford Movement and their involvement in social issues*- in Open History Special Conference Edition Religion 2007.

Hardy, Thomas: *Under the Greenwood Tree*, 1872.

Harris, J. Rendel (ed): *The life of Francis William Crossley*, James Nisbet & Co., 1899.

Haslam, William: *From Death Into Life: Twenty Years of my Ministry*, 1894 (courtesy of Revd Andrew Wade).

Hart, Richard: *Towards Decolonization – Political, labour and economic development in Jamaica 1938-1945*, Canoe Press, 1999.

Hattersley, Roy: *The Edwardians*, Little, Brown, 2004.

Helm, Elijah: *The Joint Standard: a Plain Exposition of Monetary Principles and of the Monetary Controversy*, Macmillan and Co, 1894.

Henry, Robert T: *The Golden age of Preaching – Men Who Moved the Masses – A British Case Study For preachers Of All Nations*, iUniverse.com, 2005.

Hopkins, Mark: Nonconformity's Romantic Generation: Evangelical and Liberal Theologies in Victorian England, Wipf and Stock, 2007.

Hoyle, William: Hymns and Songs for Temperance Societies and Bands of Hope, c.1890.

Industrial Celebrities: *Peter Spence* (reprinted from *The Chemical Trade Journal*), date unknown.

Jackson, George: *Collier of Manchester: A Friend's Tribute*, Hodder and Stoughton, 1923.

James, Lawrence: *The Middle Class: A History*, Little, Brown, 2006.

Jordan, E.K.H.: *Free Church Unity: History of the Free Church Council Movement 1896-1941*, Lutterworth, 1956 (SDL).

Kelly's Directory (various years) (TLS).

Kemp, Peter: *Higher Downs, Altrincham (A Short History)*, 1985 (courtesy of Claire Garvey).

Kendrick, Myra: *Schools in Victorian Bowdon*, Bowdon History Society, 1996 (TLS).

Koss, Stephen: *Nonconformity in Modern British Politics*, Shoe String Press, 1975.

Landels, William: *Baptist worthies: A series of sketches of distinguished men who have held and advocated the principles of the Baptist denomination*, Baptist Tract and Book Society, 1883 (SDL).

Laver, Denise and Rendell, Douglas: *Hale and Ashley the Past 100 Years*, Hale Civic Society, 1987.

Leadam, I.S: Parnellism and Conservatism or the Accusers in the Dock, *Altrincham Division Chronicles*, 1887 (SDL).

Lee, J: 'The growth of the Baptist Denomination in Mid-Victorian Lancashire and Cheshire' in *Transactions of the Historical Society of Lancashire and Cheshire*, vol. 124, 1973 (CRO).

Lee, Robert: *Mission Miniatures, Being a short history of the origin and development of Mission Hall activities in connection with the Manchester City Mission*, 1936 (MLS).

Lee, Robert: *Tales from Two Cities being descriptive phases of Gospel adventure amidst the industrial masses of Manchester – England's Northern Capital – its sister City, Salford, and adjacent districts in Lancashire, Cheshire and Derbyshire; an effort to enable others to visualise the varied and beneficent work of the Manchester City Mission*, 1927 (MLS).

Leech, H.J: *Tales and sketches of old Altrincham and Bowdon*, 1880 (TLS).

Leech, H.J: *Incorporation for Altrincham*, 1897 (TLS).

Lloyd, F. Cowell: *18 Axioms Concerning New Testament Baptism* (publ. Jamaica, undated) (RPC).

Lloyd, F. Cowell: *God's Way With Man*, (RPC).

Lloyd, F. Cowell: *Key-Words for the Sixty-Six Books of the Bible*, c. 1961 (from the author's personal collection; originally in the library of Princess Margaret and personally inscribed to her and Anthony Armstrong-Jones by Lloyd).

Lloyd, F. Cowell: *Titles for the Psalms* (with a brief exegesis of each Psalm), James Clarke & Co, 1954.

MacFadyen, Dugald: *Alexander MacKennal, B.A., D.D., Life and Letters*, J. Clarke, 1905.

McGuire, George: *1896-1996 100 years of the Club Theatre – The best kept secret in Altrincham*, 1996 (TLS).

MacKay, Ruddock Finlay: *Balfour, Intellectual Statesman*, Oxford University Press, 1985.

MacKennal, Alexander: *Political and Social Ungodliness: a sermon on some present questions (preached at Bowdon Downs Congregational Church 3 November 1878)* (in bound volume of tracts) (CRL).

MacKennal, Alexander: *Sketches of the Evolution of Congregationalism*, 1901 (CRL).

MacKennal, Alexander: *The Seven Churches in Asia Considered as Types of the Religious Life To-Day*, 1895.

MacLaren, Alexander: *The Pattern of Service* (in bound volume of theological tracts), 1871 (Note: this is an older spelling of the name of Alexander McLaren.) (CRL).

MacLaren, Alexander: *The Secret of Power and other Sermons*, 1882.

McKendrick, Neil: 'Home Demand and Economic Growth: A New View of the Role of Women and Children in the Industrial Revolution' in N. McKendrick (ed) *Historical Perspectives in English Thought and Society in Honour of J.H. Plumb*, 1974.

McLaren, Alexander: Expositions of Holy Scripture – Genesis.

McLaren, Alexander: *Last Sheaves*, 1903.

McLaren, Alexander: Sermons preached in Manchester by Alexander McLaren, First series, 1883.

McLaren, Alexander: Various sermons published in the *Freeman*, (RPC).

McLaren, Alex ('Alick' McLaren): *The Unchanging Christ* (SDL).

McLaren, Elizabeth T.: *Dr McLaren of Manchester: a Sketch*, Hodder and Stoughton, 1911 (SDL).

Mills, Isabel Petrie: *From tinder-box to the "larger light": threads from the life of John Mills, banker (author of "Vox Humana"): Interwoven with some early century recollections*, Sherratt & Hughes, 1899.

Mills, Mrs John: *The Education Bill: an appeal to women householders' by the President of the Altrincham and Bowdon Womens' Liberal Association*, 1902 (SDL).

Minister, A (anon): *Nonconformity and Politics*, 1909 (SDL).

Murray, Iain H.: *D. Martyn Lloyd-Jones: The First Forty Years, 1899-1939*, The Banner of Truth Trust, 1982.

Mynott, Edward: 'Frank Crossley: Saint or Sinner'? *Manchester Region History Review Vol 11*, 1997.

Newhill, John: 'Interesting Graves in Brooklands Cemetery in Ashton and Sale' *Historical Society Newsletter*, No 23, June 2006.

Nicholls, Mike: *C.H. Spurgeon: The Pastor Evangelist*, Baptist Historical Society, 1992.

Nichols, Sue: 'St Anne's Home', article in *Altrincham History Society Journal*, No. 25, October 2005.

Nichols, Sue: *St Anne's Home – An Architectural, Social and Medical History of the Bowdon Branch of The Manchester Hospital for Consumption and Diseases of the Throat and Chest* (unpublished manuscript), 2007.

Nickson, Charles: *Bygone Altrincham: Traditions and History*, Mackie and Co, 1935.

Nixon, Margaret M: *A History of the Baptist Church Milton Rough, Acton Bridge from September 1899 to September 1972 and Other Early Notes Preceding*, 1998.

Page, Nick: *And now let's move into a time of nonsense...why worship songs are failing the Church*, Authentic Media, 2004.

Payne, Ernest A: *Freedom in Jamaica – Some chapters in the story of the Baptist Missionary Society*, The Carey Press, 1933.

Pollock, William: *Foundations; being a series of essays, argumentative and didactic, on fundamental truths*, 1856 (JRL).

Pusey, Edward B: *On Baptists and Cathedrals*, (copy personally inscribed by the author to Gladstone) (SDL).

Pusey, Edward B: *Scriptural Views on Holy Baptism*, 1836 (SDL).

Radcliffe, C.J: 'A Textile Workers' Chapel: A Study of a General Baptist Church 1837-1852', *The Journal of Regional and Local Studies*, No. 9, 1989.

Rendell, Douglas: *Photographers in the Altrincham Area*, 2006.

Ridgway, Maurice H: *A Short Guide to The Parish Church of St Mary the Virgin Bowdon*, undated (courtesy of Murray Creed).

Ridgway, Maurice H: *The Story of Bowdon Vale – St Luke's Church 1880-1980*, (courtesy of Murray Creed).

Robertson, Douglas S: Unpublished theses on '*Conversion of Martin Luther*' and '*The Historical Roots of Classical Pentecostalism*', 2006 (courtesy of the author).

Robinson, H. Wheeler: *The Life and Faith of the Baptists*, Kinsgate Press, 1927, (SDL).

Robinson, W. Gordon: *A History of the Lancashire Congregational Union 1806-1956*, Lancashire Congregational Union, 1955 (TLS).

Sankey, Ira D. (compiled under direction of): *Sacred Songs and Solos Revised and Enlarged with Standard Hymns.*

Searle, John: *Freedom and Neurobiology: Reflections on Free Will, Language, and Political Power*, Columbia University Press, 2007.

Sellers, Ian (ed): *Our Heritage: the Baptists of Yorkshire Lancashire and Cheshire 1647-1987*, Yorkshire, Lancashire & Cheshire Baptist Associations, 1987.

Shakespeare, John H: *Baptist and Congregational Pioneers: Eras of Nonconformity*, National Council of Evangelical Free Churches, 1905 (SDL).

Shaw, Henry: *The story of the Church of the Congregational Order Meeting at Bowdon Downs 1839-1900*, (TLS).

Sim, Robert Samuel: Memories of Crosby Isle of Man 1868-1916, *Isle of Man Weekly Times.*

Slater's Directory (various years), (TLS).

Smith, Gipsy: *Gipsy Smith His Life and Work, by himself*, The National Council of The Evangelical Free Churches, 1902.

Stockwell, Arthur H. (ed): *The Baptists of Lancashire*, 1910 (RPC).

Stott, John: *Evangelical Truth: A Personal Plea for Unity, Integrity and Faithfulness*, InterVarsity Press, 1999.

Tarbolton, Alfred: Typed and handwritten draft submissions and notes to *Altrincham Guardian*, 1907 (TLS).

Teagle, Frances and Midgley, John (eds): *The Unitarian Congregation in Altrincham 1814-1997– Essays in Celebration*, 1997 (TLS).

The New Selection of Baptist Hymns for the Use of Baptist Congregations Enlarged by the addition of such of Dr. Watts's Psalms and Hymns as are most highly esteemed and generally used in Public Worship.

Tomlinson, David: *The Post-Evangelical*, SPCK, 1995.

Walker, Cynthia M: *Century of Witness: A Short History of the Baptist Cause in Altrincham 1872 to 1972*, 1972.

Walker, Michael J: Baptists at the Table: The Theology of the Lord's Supper amongst English Baptists in the Nineteenth Century, Baptist Historical Society, 1992.

Warner, Robert: Reinventing English Evangelicalism, 1966-2001, Paternoster, 2008.

Waugh, Evelyn: Brideshead Revisited: The Sacred and Profane Memories of Captain *Charles Ryder*, Penguin Books Ltd, 2000.

Weeden, Len: 'Dr Richard Marsden Pankhurst, LLD' in *Ashton and Sale Historical Society Newsletter No. 23*, June 2006.

Weyland, John Mathias: *Those Fifty Years* (Jubilee Volume of the London City Mission) (MLS).

Wheeler, Geoffrey: *St Peter's Centenary 1892-1992*, St Peter's Centenary Committee, 1991 (TLS).

White, B.R: *The English Baptists of the Seventeenth Century*, The Baptist Historical Society, 1986.

Whitley, William T: *Baptists of North West England 1649-1913*, Kingsgate Press, 1913 (SDL).

Williams, Charles: *The Principles and Practices of the Baptists – a Book for Inquirers*, 1879.

Wilson, A.N: *The Victorians*, W. W. Norton & Co.Ltd, 2002.

Wilson, A.N: *After the Victorians – The World Our Parents Knew*, Arrow Books Ltd, 2006.

Wilson, C. Anne ed: *Eating with the Victorians*, NPI Media Group, 2004.

Wright, Mavis: *Rebecca, My Father's Dream – a Memoir*, iUniverse, 2003

Wright, Nigel G: *Disavowing Constantine: Mission, Church and the Social Order in the Theologies of John Howard Yoder and Jurgen Moltmann*, Paternoster, 2000.

Wright, Nigel G: *Free Church, Free State – The Positive Baptist Vision*, Paternoster, 2005.

Wright, Nigel G: *The Radical Evangelical: Finding a Place to Stand*, SPCK, 1996.

Wyke, Terry: *The Hall of Fame – A History of the Free Trade Hall*, Radisson Edwardian, 2004.

A

Abbott, James, 108, 142
Accrington, 100, 167, 173, 182, 183, 200, 221
Adamson, Mr, 117, 146, 260, 303, 399
Addy, Mark, 103
Afghanistan, 103, 297, 303
Aitken, Robert Wesley, 17-19, 21, 404, 453, 457
Aitkenites, 18, 22, 23, 27, 32, 453
Albert Hall, Peter Street, Manchester, 327
Albert Road East, Altrincham, 356
Albert Road, Altrincham, 289
Albert Square, Altrincham, 417,424
Albert Square, Manchester, 88
Albert Terrace, Altrincham, 357
Alcock, Edith, 217
Alcock, Father, 15
Alcohol, 17, 41, 258, 261-262, 267, 269, 271, 300, 305, 333, 354, 382, 397, 461
All Saints' Church, Altrincham, 8
Altrincham
  brief history, 40
  Church of England in, 7-11
  mayors of, 261, 276, 326, 348, 353, 391-392
  population, 7
Altrincham Amateur Orchestra, 106
Altrincham and Bowdon Provident Society, 242
Altrincham and Bowdon Total Abstinence Society, 265, 267, 307, 371, 384, 387
Altrincham and Bowdon Women's Liberal Club, 297
Altrincham and District Temperance Federation, 263, 279
Altrincham Baptist Church, 28, 35, 49, 64, 76, 86, 108, 109, 134-143, 147-159, 163-187, 190-199, 203-205, 213, 218, 219, 222, 226, 231-233, 236, 238, 246, 268, 272-273, 286, 293, 296, 303, 321, 356-358, 369, 371-372, 382, 387, 394, 401, 408, 413, 465
  Communion table and Second World War, 228
  Reasons for growth, 198, 345
Altrincham Grammar School For Boys, 393
Altrincham Educational League, 319
Altrincham Football Club, 38, 39, 361, 412

Altrincham Funeral Society, 241
Altrincham Grammar School for Girls. See Fairlie
Altrincham Literary Institute, 53, 54, 74, 122, 263, 319, 322, 340, 424
Altrincham Parade Ground, 41, 413
Altrincham Patriotic Fund, 298
Altrincham Railway Station, 40, 437
Altrincham Wakes, 77
Altrincham Workingmen's Liberal Club, 310, 365, 368
Alum, manufacture of. See Spence, Peter
Ambleside, 46
America, United States of, 38, 45, 48, 49, 52, 125, 173, 178, 198, 212, 227, 236, 252, 272, 300, 315, 330, 349, 358, 361, 425
Ampleforth College, 377
Anabaptists, 29, 210
Anarchists, Altrincham, 307, 406
Ancoats, 52, 67, 69, 70, 171, 188, 189, 328, 363, 369, 418, 459
Anglican. See Church of England
Angus, Joseph, 173, 181, 182, 214, 216
Appleton Road, Hale, 88
Ardwick, 103, 382
Armenia, 67
Arminianism, 208, 211, 212, 251
Armitage Place, Altrincham, 197
Armitage, Annie (neé Rigby), 353
Armitage, Elkanah, 294
Armitage, George Faulkner, 71, 191, 263, 264, 276, 278, 294, 303, 319, 322, 323, 326, 353-356, 374, 377-378, 385, 418-419, 422, 454
Armitage, William, 219, 353, 402
Army, 41, 298, 440
Arrowsmith, Mr, 283
Arthog Road, Hale, 323, 382
Ashfield Road, Altrincham, 27, 289, 398, 399
Ashley Mill, 344
Ashley Road Congregational Church, 14, 23, 289, 303, 340, 356, 383, 460
Ashley Road, Altrincham and Hale, 14, 55, 71, 83, 87, 88, 159, 262, 265, 289, 322, 342, 356-357, 362, 371, 390, 399, 403-404, 414, 424, 427, 429-431, 438, 441
Ashton–on Mersey Baptist Church. See Sale Baptist Church
Ashton–on–Mersey Congregational Church, 109
Astley, Rick, 93
Aston Villa Football Club, 38
Atonement, theology of, 130, 225

Cobden, William, 304
Cocks, Kitty, 9
Cole, Lewis, 152
Collier, Samuel Francis, 1, 252, 262, 287, 329, 330, 459
Collins, J, 403
Communion, 5, 7, 107, 141, 142, 168, 198, 202, 215, 224-228, 260, 268, 288, 313, 418, 444-445
Concerts, 38, 106, 109, 122, 126, 144-146, 192, 253, 276, 358
Congo, 171, 182, 305
Congregationalists, 4, 22, 23, 31, 35, 44, 48, 50, 55, 56, 80, 82, 99, 107, 108, 125-127, 130, 211, 214, 219-221, 229, 231, 247, 259, 279, 287, 290, 294, 301-302, 306, 345, 354, 404, 411, 418, 439, 459
Congregational Union, 5, 22, 31, 53, 109, 127, 130, 211, 259, 279, 287, 301, 353
Conservatives. See Tory Party
Constantine, 207
Conventicle Act 1664, 313
Cook, Captain James, 209
Cook, Thomas, 262
Cotton Famine, 104, 211
County Bank, King Street, Manchester, 53
Coward family, 417, 439
Cowie, Wilson, 183
Cowsill, Armstrong, 73, 75, 424
Cresta Court Hotel. See Stamford Arms Hotel
Crewe, John, 10
Crimean War, 242, 269
Cromwell, Oliver, 29, 175, 245, 289, 441, 457
Crosby, Fanny, 252
Crosby, Isle of Man, 17, 19
Crossley Engineering, 65, 66, 69
Crossley, Emily, 66, 67, 71, 73, 76, 189, 259, 384, 418, 421
Crossley, Emmeline, 65, 66
Crossley, Frank, 63-78, 90, 121, 124, 170, 171, 187, 189, 259, 279, 363, 365, 384, 416-419, 421, 453, 458-460
Funeral of, 188, 189
Crossley, William, 7, 72, 187, 188, 263-264, 282, 293, 303, 305-307, 322-323, 328, 353, 392, 416, 421, 461
Cryer, Edwin, grocer, 272
Cubitt, Thomas, 90
Culcheth Hall School, 107, 424, 431, 441, 442
Culcheth Road, Altrincham, 83, 429, 430

Culross, James, 141

D

Daily Telegraph, 38
Dale Square, Broadheath, Altrincham, 340
Dale, R W, 301
Darwin, Charles, 53, 161, 175, 208, 210, 455
Daughters of Charity, 15
David Rowell and Co, 154
Davies, H, 105
Davies, Revd, 55
Deaconess, 231
Deacons, 59, 66, 67, 120, 127, 134, 135, 138, 139, 141, 142, 150, 183, 186, 206, 226, 227, 231-234, 236, 283, 294, 321, 354, 356, 362, 369, 371-374, 381, 384, 392, 439, 443
Deansgate, Manchester, 87, 91, 93, 241
Death, Alice, 71
Debt, 82, 99, 109, 117, 120-122, 132, 134, 135, 137, 138, 140, 144, 146, 150, 161, 163-166, 170, 190-192, 194, 336, 372
Delamer Road, Bowdon, 27, 28, 35, 63, 64, 82, 167, 199, 245, 283, 286, 290, 404, 423, 441, 457
Delamer Sanatorium, 72
Democracy, 37, 229, 301, 313
Denmark Place Baptist Church, Camberwell, 345
Denmark Street, Altrincham, 197, 373
Dennison, Justin, 204
Depression, economic, 103, 104
Determinism, 208
Devisdale, 263, 422
Dewar, A, 31
Dickens, Charles, 38, 368
Disley, 403
Disraeli, Benjamin, 37, 201, 241, 296-297, 301, 454, 457
Disraeli, Conningsby, 263, 300, 319, 322-323
Dissenters, 4, 29, 220, 245, 301
Donegan, Lonnie, 402
Dore, R N, 83
Downes family, 344, 357, 380, 394
Downgrade Controversy, 129, 130, 140, 150, 151, 160, 161, 167, 204, 212, 459, 465
Downs Chapel, Altrincham, 27, 33, 35, 55, 56, 58, 59, 61, 80, 82, 83, 86, 98, 105, 108, 117, 120, 125, 247, 258, 267, 283, 403-404, 423, 437, 457, 467

Altrincham Provident and Dispensary
Hospital, 136, 242, 244, 296, 385,
398, 412-413
Ancoats, 52
Guy's Hospital, London, 312
Hospital Sunday, 239, 411, 457
Lloyd's Fever Hospital, Altrincham,
239, 242-244, 408, 412
Manchester Hospital for
Consumption and Diseases of the
Throat, 72
St Mary's Hospital, Manchester, 44,
238
Houghton, Mr, 98, 100, 105, 161, 182,
390, 403, 458
Houghton, Peter W, 193
Hoy, Edward, 164, 165
Hoyle, William, 253, 264
Huguenots, 4, 65
Hume, David, 208
Hunter, Joan, 271, 374, 394
Hymns, 141, 230, 253, 256, 278, 327-
329
Hyperinflation, 86

I

Immigration, 7, 15, 80, 201
Independent Congregational Church,
Altrincham, 31-33, 35, 125-128, 237,
239, 260, 392, 404, 411, 455, 457,
459
Independents. See Congregationalists
India, 39, 180, 181, 191, 272, 297, 324,
425
Infants Custody Act 1839, 293
Ingham, Alfred, 7, 29, 414
International Bible Reading Association,
205, 283
Ireland, 15, 38, 65, 160, 201, 260, 275,
307, 309, 315, 317
Iron Tabernacle, Altrincham. See
Tabernacle
Isaacs, Mr, 196, 324
Isle of Man, 17-19, 21, 65, 247, 295,
359, 365, 450
Islington Arms Temperance Public
House, Altrincham, 263, 401
Islington Street, Altrincham, 7, 76, 263,
401
Italy, 37, 55, 89-97, 113, 115, 182, 200,
246, 443
Ivy Cottage Church, Didsbury, 76

J

Jamaica, 175-181, 351, 451, 452
James Dilworth and Sons, 366
James, A, 321
James, Alfred, 23
Jeffreys, George, 212
Jenkins, D R, 100, 105
Jenkins, Sam, 333
Jenner, Edward, 243
Jewish Museum, 87
Jinja Christian Centre, Uganda, 180
John Rylands Library, Manchester, 46
John Street, Altrincham, 403
Johnson, Hewlett, 422
Johnson, J, 113
Johnson, Thomas L, 178
Johnson, William, 108, 414
Johnston, W T, 27, 105
Joshua, Seth, 333-334
Jowett, J M, 288
Jumpers. See Aitken, Robert

K

Kant, Immanuel, 208
Kay, Robert, 219
Kay, Ronald, 219
Keach, Benjamin, 253
Kean, Frederick, 165, 303
Keats, John, 160
Keble, John, 5
Keene, Frederick, 403
Kenworthy, Mr and Mrs, 55, 59, 232
Kesselmeyer, William, 320
Keswick Convention, 196, 212, 213, 333
King Edward VII, 45
King George V, 411
King George V Pool, Altrincham, 407
King Street, Manchester, 53, 87
King, Martin Luther, 29, 324
Kipling, Rudyard, 297, 421
Kirby, Edmund, 15
Kitchener, General Horatio, 297
Knibb, Mary, 177
Knibb, William, 176-179, 181, 451, 454
Knott Mill Congregational Chapel,
Deansgate, Manchester, 91, 92, 422,
455
Knott Mill Station, Manchester, 91
Knutsford, 15, 22, 40, 73, 87, 103, 285,
323, 438
Koch, Robert, 242

L

M

Manchester City Mission, 63, 66, 67, 71, 76-78, 121, 151, 155, 259, 262, 279, 307, 340, 384, 406

Manchester Guardian, 38, 45, 67, 88, 103, 188

Manchester Museum, 366

Manchester Road, Altrincham, 320

Manchester Royal Infirmary, 384

Manchester School of Art, 87

Manchester Ship Canal, 72, 275, 381

Manchester University, 45, 241, 366, 439, 454

Manchester, Bishop of, 5

Manning, Cardinal, 200 201, 260

Manor Road, Altrincham, 197

Mansfield College, Oxford, 353

Marburg Colloquy, 227

Margaret Heald Mission Hall, 155

Market Hall, Altrincham, 74

Market Square, Altrincham, 321, 354

Market Street, Altrincham, 41, 126, 127, 134, 136, 324, 340, 356, 413

Marriage of clergy, 206

Marriott, William, 88

Marshall, Glen, 219

Marshall, Professor, 168

Martindale, Adam, 4

Matrimonial Causes Act, 1858, 292

McCappin, Mr, 321, 324

McKendrick, Neil, 292

McLaren, Alexander, 1, 45-47, 49, 50, 53, 57, 62, 63, 65–67, 77, 79, 90, 96, 102, 114, 117, 127, 129, 130, 138-146, 151, 152, 161, 162, 166, 167, 169, 171-174, 182, 183, 185, 187, 188, 190-194, 197, 200, 202, 204, 209, 211, 215, 220-222, 224, 225, 229, 231–233, 235, 236, 238, 239, 252, 259, 268-269, 291, 300-301, 305, 327,-331, 336-337, 342, 380-382, 384, 390, 403-404, 408, 421, 445, 455-461

McLaren, Alick, 66, 331

McLaren, Marion, 46, 47, 458

Meldrum, Thomas, 322

Methodists, 4, 5, 7, 12-14, 17-19, 32, 33, 48, 50, 66, 74, 80, 125, 126, 162, 165, 167, 183, 202, 204, 211, 246, 252, 262, 265, 267, 279, 287, 289-290, 302, 322-323, 327-328, 330, 340, 368, 374, 398, 410, 413, 426, 456-460

Independent, 29

Primitive, 13, 48, 82, 98, 100, 102, 144, 165, 167, 273, 289, 303, 319, 322-323, 330, 340, 368, 403, 413

Wesleyan, 12, 13, 38, 126, 191, 239, 273, 289-290, 302, 315, 340, 357, 412, 422, 425

Methodists, Welsh. *See* Welsh Church

Metropolitan Tabernacle, 48-51, 129, 150, 151, 168, 331

Micklem family, 125

Midland Terrace, Ashley Road, Hale, 357, 360

Midnight Rally, 1905, 341

Mill, John Stuart, 208, 293

Millais, John Everett, 90

Millbank, Margaret Henrietta Maria, 9

Millington, Booth Bank Farm, 12

Mills, Isabel, 310, 317, 323, 419, 423, 460

Mills, John, 384, 419, 423

Milne, Francis, 259

Milne, William, 121, 183, 278, 417, 424

Milton Baptist Church, 225

Ministers, pay, 86, 107, 137, 142, 147, 164, 174, 185, 186, 193, 328

Mission Praise, 62

Mitchell, Elizabeth, 121

Mitchell, George, 322, 413-414

Mitchell, Sarah Anne, 142

Mobberley Congregational Church, 23

Montagu, Lady Mary Wortley, 243

Monyash Road, Altrincham, 197

Moody, Dwight, 62-64, 79, 80, 82, 330, 457

Moriah Chapel, Llanelli, 333

Morris, William, 353

Mortgage, 85, 109-111, 137, 163-166, 458

Morton and Sheldon, 113

Moss Lane, Altrincham, 310, 362, 412

Moss Side Baptist Church, Manchester, 183, 324, 445

Moss, Annie, 83, 428-429

Mowbray, Henry, 77, 119-124, 129, 130, 132-150, 159, 160, 161, 163-174, 178, 180, 183, 185-188, 190, 198-200, 213, 222, 226, 229-231, 233, 236, 247, 253, 267-268, 273, 278, 284, 294, 297, 305, 356-357, 367, 369, 371-373, 384-385, 387, 394, 396, 399, 408, 413, 424, 458-460, 467

Mowbray, Jessie, 119, 123

Mowbray, Robert, 121, 123, 187

Mursell, Arthur, 329

Museum of Science and Industry, Manchester, 69

Music, 191, 253, 256, 279, 365, 419, 424

Rothschilds, 309
Royal Lancastrian Institute for
    Promoting the Education of the Poor,
    278
Rugby Union, 38
Rusholme, 45, 109, 371, 382
Ruskin, John, 90, 113, 160, 292, 353,
    454
Russell Street, Altrincham, 197, 433
Russia, 49, 297
Ryland John, 210
Rylands, John and Enriquetta, 46

S

Sacramentalism, 202, 220
Sale Baptist Church, 82, 108, 141, 185,
    252, 284, 357, 363, 384
Sale Congregational Church, 321
Sale Presbyterian Church, 107
Salford, 16, 17, 34, 35, 76, 100, 307,
    309-310, 336, 369, 381-382
Salisbury, Lord Robert Cecil, 310
Salomons, Edward, 87, 88
Salvation Army, 66, 73-76, 189, 252,
    275, 330, 340, 421, 424, 460
Salvation Army Housing Association,
    189
Sandiway, Altrincham, 136, 353, 374
Sanitation, 241-242
Sankey, Ira, 62-64, 79, 80, 82, 252-253,
    330, 457
Scott, George Gilbert, 8
Scott, Walter, 160
Second Lateran Council, 206
Second World War, 89, 228, 293, 248,
    361, 379, 395, 400, 402, 443
Sermons, 44, 45, 130, 135, 144, 146,
    173, 183, 185, 195, 215, 224, 225,
    235-238, 239-240, 252-253, 256, 263-
    264, 269, 297, 303, 319-320, 325,
    411, 451-452
Servants, 9, 14, 42, 87, 107-109, 119,
    145, 187, 243, 292, 366, 371, 374,
    382, 391, 414, 418, 422, 439, 441
Sewers, 40, 84, 242, 389
Shaw's Lane, Altrincham, 74
Shiner, George and Julia, 371, 373
Shrewsbury, Bishop of, 15
Siddeley, John, 261, 397
Sidebotham, Joseph, 439
Simmons, Mary E, 247, 253, 321-323,
    372, 395, 399
Simmons, William, 55, 82, 108, 111,
    117, 120, 122, 139, 140, 146, 232,
    267, 289, 372, 395, 466

Skippers, 273
Slavery, 1, 175-181, 301, 305, 324, 345,
    347-349, 451
Smallpox, 239, 243-244, 332, 457
Smith, Rodney, 288-289, 291, 328-330,
    332, 455, 460
Smyth, John, 194, 230
Snape, Arthur, 394
Social Purity Campaign, 66
Sons of Temperance, 263, 270
Southwell, Charles Frederick Jnr, 183,
    271, 299, 306, 308, 353, 370, 380,
    394, 414, 422, 467
Southwell, Charles Snr, 108, 134, 136,
    139, 183, 191, 232, 234, 344, 358,
    373-380, 394, 399
Southwell, Ernest, 344
Southwell, Joan, 271, 400, 402
Southwell, Michael ('Chunk'), 299, 373,
    380
Spence, Fanny, 382, 416
Spence, Frank, 59, 60, 62, 98, 105, 106,
    109, 117, 191, 222, 321-323, 380-
    383, 416
Spence, Peter, 60, 98-101, 121, 380-382
Spencer, William, 108
Spring Bank, 83, 427, 431, 441
Spurgeon, Charles Haddon, 1, 48-51, 56,
    59, 62, 79, 117, 129, 130, 140, 141,
    143, 147, 150-152, 160, 161, 167,
    168, 173, 181, 183, 204, 207, 209,
    212, 213, 221, 222, 225, 235, 236,
    251, 269, 342, 434, 459-460, 465
Spurgeon's College, 49, 59, 60, 147, 152,
    204, 225
St Adamnan's Church, Lonan, Isle of
    Man, 247
St Alban's Church, Broadheath, 7, 459
St Anne's Home, Bowdon, 22, 72, 241,
    416-417, 421, 439, 459
St Elizabeth's Church, Altrincham, 7, 11,
    386, 401, 459
St Francis Basilica, Assisi, 92
St Francis of Assisi, 66
St George's Church, Altrincham, 7, 246,
    317, 379, 398, 414
St John's Church, Altrincham, 6-8, 10,
    14, 27, 62, 66, 119, 123, 260, 280,
    357, 385, 396, 398, 401, 421, 423-
    424, 432, 456
St John's Infant School, 7, 11
St John's Road, Altrincham, 82, 424
St Luke's Church, Bowdon Vale, 7, 458
St Margaret's Chapel, 219

St Margaret's Church, Dunham Massey,
8, 9, 66, 128, 219, 245, 263-264, 398,
422-423, 454, 455
St Margaret's Road, Dunham Massey,
112, 377, 422
St Margaret's Church Tea and Coffee
House, Chapel Street, Altrincham,
263
St Mary's Church, Bowdon. *See* Bowdon
Parish Church
St Paul's Cathedral, 13, 39
St Peter's Church, Hale, 11, 460
St Vincent de Paul, 15
St Vincent's Church, Altrincham, 15,
279, 407
St Vincent's School, 15, 407
Stamford Arms Hotel, 437
Stamford New Road, Altrincham, 157,
273, 409
Stamford Park Road, Altrincham, 197,
407
Stamford Park School, Altrincham, 282,
368, 371, 374, 461
Stamford Road, Bowdon, 65
Stamford Street, Altrincham, 27, 272,
303, 340, 365, 384, 391
Stamford, Earl of, 7, 9, 15, 82, 278, 401,
422, 424, 432, 440-441
Star Hall, Ancoats, 70, 171, 188, 189,
363
Star Life Assurance Society, 111
Stephenson, Robert, 65
Stevenson, Hugh H, 108
Stewart Thompson and Co, 384
Stokoe, John, 242
Stott, John, 204
Stretford, 105, 293, 381
Streuli, A, 183, 284
Strict Baptists, 225, 227, 237, 245-246
Students Temperance Society, 260
Suffragettes, 293, 308
Sugar, 175, 176, 276
Sunday Closing Association, 161, 305
Sunday School, 13, 23, 31, 39, 66, 82,
110, 117, 121, 146, 180, 191, 196,
197, 243, 253, 260, 273, 275, 279,
294, 337, 345, 357, 361, 367, 369-
375, 385, 392, 398, 403, 414, 418,
438
Sunday School Union, 141, 283
Sutton, Roger, 329
Sword and Trowel, 49, 62, 129

T

Tabernacle, 141, 149-160, 163, 166-173,
187, 190, 198, 199, 229, 247, 253,
408-410, 413, 459, 465, 467
Tatton Park, 273, 371-373
Taxicabs, 41, 60, 77, 156, 243, 406, 408,
437
Taylor, Hudson, 363
Tea and tea parties, 14, 58, 59, 76, 82,
100, 108, 120, 125, 174, 195, 262,
272-273, 279, 285, 289, 307, 328,
337, 365, 367, 372-373, 438
Telephone, 117
Temperance, 103, 162, 253, 271-272,
279, 285, 305-306, 356-358, 384,
397, 403
Tennis, 38
Tennyson, Alfred, 52, 235
Test Act 1672, 313
The Beeches. *See* St Anne's Home,
Bowdon
The Downs, Altrincham, 18, 22, 23, 27,
31, 32, 35, 36, 40, 57, 58, 60, 61, 79,
80, 82, 98, 100, 107, 114, 125, 127,
159, 221, 247, 267, 273, 278, 307,
362, 382, 404-408, 410, 414, 415,
418, 437, 439-440
Thomas Street, Altrincham, 197
Thomas, W D, 322-323, 336
Thompson, Jabez, 113
Thompson, John, 74, 76, 77, 183, 262,
303, 384
Thompson, Joseph, 278, 439
Thompson, Labour Party candidate, 307
Thompson, Leila (neé Kerr), 384
Thompson, Mr and Mrs S, 276, 392
Thompson, Thomas, 109, 110, 310, 419,
458
Thorley Moor Lane. *See* Ashley Road,
Altrincham and Hale
Tickle, John, 83, 84, 89, 427-428, 432
Timperley, 7, 40, 242, 358
Tipping Street, Altrincham, 197, 279,
340, 396, 400, 433
Tithing, 107
Tobacco, 269-270, 382
Toleration Act 1689, 313, 322-323
Tory Party, 103, 175, 241, 300, 310-311,
319, 322, 368
Toxteth Tabernacle, Liverpool, 119, 151
Trades Unions, 37, 114, 350, 456-457
Trams, 57, 156, 406, 437
Transubstantiation, doctrine of, 224
Transvaal, 297, 303, 306, 324

Wordsworth, William, 52, 53, 208, 235, 275
Workhouses, 103, 373, 424
Wright, Nigel, 49, 204, 207, 312-313

Y

Yangzhou, China, 363
Yarwood Street, Altrincham, 400
Yeng–Cheo College, China, 363
YMCA, 63, 279, 384, 402
York Street, Altrincham, 197

Z

Zulu wars, 297
Zwingli, Ulrich, 227

Lightning Source UK Ltd.
Milton Keynes UK
26 February 2010

150699UK00002B/2/P